VERSIONS OF ZIMBABWE:
new approaches to literature and culture

Edited by
Robert Muponde and Ranka Primorac

WEAVER
W
—PRESS—

© Robert Muponde and Ranka Primorac 2005

Published by Weaver Press, Box A1922, Avondale, Harare. 2005 Distributed in the UK and US by the African Book Collective, Oxford.
www.africanbookscollective.com

The publishers would like to express their gratitude to Hivos for the support they have given to Weaver Press in the development of their fiction programme.

Typeset by Fontline Electronic Publishing Pvt Ltd.
Cover design: Myrtle Mallis
Cover picture: Liliana Vlacic
Printed by: Ligntning Source.

ISBN: 1 77922 036 7

*For Chipo Mary Mandivavarira, Tatenda Wayne Muponde
and Tino Muponde*

and

*to the memory of Tichafa Maswinge and
Nesbert Kambani*

Contents

Acknowledgements

This book drew its impetus from a stream of interdisciplinary and inter-continental conversations on Zimbabwe, its culture, and its present crisis. We owe a debt of gratitude to many individuals and institutions.

First, to Irene Staunton and Murray McCartney of Weaver Press in Harare for being, yet again, encouraging and courageous. Special thanks are due to Stephen Chan, Elleke Boehmer and Sarah Nuttall for practical help, kind advice and constant interest in 'the book'. The Wits Institute for Social and Economic Research in Johannesburg created a stimulating intellectual environment and provided institutional support. Mai Palmberg invited us to participate in Looking to the Future: Social, Political and Cultural Space in Zimbabwe, an international conference held at The Nordic Africa Institute, Uppsala, on 24 and 26 May, 2004; Terence Ranger extended a similar invitation for the 2004 Zimbabwe Research Days, entitled What History for Which Zimbabwe?, and held on 12 and 13 June 2004 at St Anthony's College, Oxford. Participating in these events enabled us to share our thoughts and sharpen our understanding of how literature functions in times of social crises.

Our warm thanks to all the contributors to this volume for their commitment to alternative understandings of the role of Zimbabwean literature in relation to history and politics – and especially to those academic colleagues who are based in Zimbabwe itself (the coal-face of the struggle), and who continue teaching and writing despite the difficulties and obstacles they face. Finally, to our families: our gratitude for your love and support extends far beyond books, and words.

About the contributors

Jane Bryce lectures in African and post-colonial literature and cinema at the University of the West Indies, Cave Hill, Barbados. She has contributed numerous chapters to collections on women's writing, popular fiction, and contemporary African and Caribbean writing and film. She is now working on popular narratives and urban culture in Africa, and a personal memoir.

Anthony Chennells retired in 2002 as Associate Professor of English at the University of Zimbabwe. He has since taught at the University of California at Santa Cruz and Arrupe College, Jesuit School of Philosophy and Humanities in Harare, and the University of Pretoria where he is Extraordinary Professor in the Department of English. His current research interests include reading Zimbabwean literature in different literary and theoretical contexts.

Lene Bull Christiansen has recently completed her M.A. in International Development Studies and Cultural Encounters at Roskilde University in Denmark. Her work is concerned with the interaction between culture and politics, a subject that has led her to focus on the political implications of the novels of Yvonne Vera. Lene is currently associated with the Cultural Encounters programme at Roskilde University.

Annie Gagiano is Professor of English Studies at the University of Stellenbosch in South Africa. She has published a number of articles on African English Fiction and South African Poetry by a range of authors, as well as the book *Achebe, Head, Marechera: On Power and Change in Africa* (Lynne Rienner: 2000). Her current research is on gender issues both in post-colonial fiction (in contemporary novels such as Unity Dow's) and in southern African folktales of various cultures. She has also written on dimensions of racial portrayal in J.M. Coetzee's writing, and on reconceived nationalism in Nuruddin Farah's more recent fiction.

Ashleigh Harris was born in Bulawayo, Zimbabwe in 1976. She is a lecturer in the Discipline of English at the University of the Witwatersrand where she completed a Ph.D. on the fiction of Toni Morrison in 2002. Her current research focuses on the role of metaphor in articulating traumatic narratives in Zimbabwean, South African and African American fiction.

Preben Kaarsholm has a background in comparative literature and teaches international development studies at Roskilde University in Denmark. In 1991, he edited *Cultural Struggle and Development in Southern Africa*, which was published by Baobab Books in Zimbabwe, and in 2000 – with Deborah James – a special issue of the *Journal of Southern African Studies* on 'Popular Culture and Democracy'.

He has published articles on literature, theatre, and democratic aspirations in Zimbabwe and South Africa, and has taken a special interest in the history of Bulawayo's townships. He is currently writing on slum areas around Durban and the dynamics of violence and political culture in KwaZulu-Natal from the 1980s to the present.

Tommy Matshakayile-Ndlovu is a senior lecturer in the Department of African Languages & Literature at the University of Zimbabwe. He teaches Ndebele literature and culture and has published in the same areas. His current research is on the Ndebele war novel and minority cultures of Zimbabwe.

Kizito Zhiradzago Muchemwa is a lecturer in English, Literature and Media Studies at the Zimbabwe Open University. He did his BA (Hons.) and MA in English at the University of Rhodesia, and Graduate Certificate in Education at the University of Zimbabwe. His research and teaching interests are African, African-American and Caribbean literature. He has edited the poetry journal *Two Tone* (June 1976) and *Zimbabwean Poetry in English* (Gweru: Mambo Press, 1978). His poems have appeared in *New Writing from Rhodesia* (ed. by T. McLoughlin), *When My Brother Comes Home: Poems from Central and Southern Africa* (ed. by F. Chipasula; Middleton, Conn.: Wesleyan University, 1985) and *And Now the Poets Speak* (ed. by M. Kadhani and M. Zimunya; Gweru: Mambo Press, 1981).

Robert Muponde is a Researcher at the Wits Institute for Social and Economic Research, University of the Witwatersrand, South Africa. His research explores concepts of childhood/children, politics of nationhood, and history in Zimbabwean literature. His publications include *Children's Literature* (Zimbabwe Open University, 2000); *No More Plastic Balls: New Voices in the Zimbabwean Short Story* (College Press, 2000), co-edited with C. Chihota; and *Sign and Taboo: Perspectives on the Poetic Fiction of Yvonne Vera* (Weaver Press; James Currey, 2002), co-edited with M. Taruvinga.

Mickias Musiyiwa is a lecturer in Shona literature, oral literature and literary theory in the Department of African Languages & Literature at the University of Zimbabwe and music and culture at the Zimbabwe College of Music. He has written articles on children's literature and Shona poetry. His current research is on Shona oral literature and modern poetry and music.

Sarah Nuttall is a Senior Researcher at the Wits Institute for Social and Economic Research (WISER) at the University of the Witwatersrand in Johannesburg, South Africa. She is co-editor of *Text, Theory, Space: Land, Literature and History in South Africa and Australia* (Routledge, 1996), *Negotiating the Past: The Making of Memory in South Africa* (OUP, 1998), *Senses of Culture: South African Culture Studies* (OUP, 2000), and *Johannesburg: The Elusive Metropolis* (forthcoming with Duke Unviersity Press) and editor of *Beautiful-Ugly: African and Diaspora Aesthetics* (Kwela Books and the Prince Claus Fund Library).

Ranka Primorac has degrees from the universities of Zagreb, Zimbabwe and Nottingham Trent. She has taught Africa-related courses at several institutions of higher learning in Britain, including the University of Cambridge and New York University in London. She is interested in theoretical approaches to the novel and the narrative production of space-time; her monograph *The Place of Tears: The Novel and Politics in Zimbabwe* is forthcoming with I. B. Tauris.

Terence Ranger is Emeritus Professor at St Antony's College, Oxford. He has written on Zimbabwe's political, social and religious history. He is currently writing a social history of Bulawayo between 1893 and 1960.

Caroline Rooney is a senior lecturer in the Centre for Colonial and Postcolonial Research at the University of Kent. She has written on African literature and philosophy and on creativity and politics, and her recent publications include: *African Literature, Animism and Politics* (Routledge, 2000); 'Monstrosity, Race and Technology / The Unentitled of the Earth' in *The Oxford Literary Review*, special issue on 'Monstrism', Vol. 23 (2001); and 'From the Universal to the Cosmic' in *The Journal of European Studies*, special issue on *Beau Travail*, Vol. 34, no. 1 (2004). She is currently working on a theory of postcolonial complementarity.

Maurice Taonezvi Vambe holds a PhD in Zimbabwean Literature from the University of Zimbabwe. He has edited *Orality and Cultural Identities in Zimbabwe* (2001) and written numerous essays on Zimbabwean literature. He works at the Institute for Curriculum and Learning Development, University of South Africa (Unisa) as a Learning Developer. His critical work, *African Oral Story Telling Tradition and the Zimbabwean Novel in English* will be published by Unisa Press in December 2004.

Dan Wylie was born in Bulawayo and raised on nature sanctuaries in Zimbabwe's Eastern Highlands. He has written articles on various Zimbabwean writers, including Dambudzo Marechera, N H Brettell and John Eppel. He has also published *Savage Delight: White Myths of Shaka* (2000), a memoir entitled *Dead Leaves: Two years in the Rhodesian war* (2002), and two volumes of poetry. From his current base at Rhodes University, Grahamstown, South Africa, he is concentrating on ecologically-orientated literary studies.

Introduction: writing against blindness

Ranka Primorac and Robert Muponde

> *blind moon,*
> *doomed to see*
> *all these corpses.*
>
> Chenjerai Hove[1]

1.

Since the beginning of the twenty-first century, political events in Zimbabwe have given rise to multiple re-evaluations of the country's previous history. Some have been officially sanctioned: when, in 2000, Zimbabwe's ruling party first experienced a serious challenge to its hegemony, mounted by a number of agents and alliances (on this, see Alexander, 2003 and Chan, 2003: 129-216), it instigated a violent take-over of much of the country's privately-owned farmland. Although this process, known as 'the fast-track redistribution of land', led to the collapse of the nation's economy, and was accompanied by a breakdown of the rule of law and an increase in political repression, it was officially represented as the glorious final act of decolonization. The narrative of 'the Third Chimurenga' – the third and last instalment of the liberation struggle first mounted in the 1890s – entails a reinscription of both the nation's past and the officially-sanctioned national identities. This narrative is the backbone of what, in the final chapter of this volume, Terence Ranger calls Zimbabwe's 'patriotic history'.

Patriotic history both builds on and departs from previous nationalist narratives through a series of omissions, additions and simplifications (see Sylvester, 2003).

It attempts to fix socially produced meanings by designating the possession of 'land' as the sole source of African communal well-being, lost with the arrival of white settlers, and now irrevocably reinstated. Furthermore, patriotic history mimics nationalist narratives generated by Rhodesian (Zimbabwean colonialist) discourses (as described by Chennells, 1995) in that it assigns sole agency in initiating this historical movement and counter-movement to those associated with the political party in power on the one hand, and to externally-located enemies able to breathe

---

[1] From 'blind moon', in Hove, 2003: 32.

life into internal puppets, on the other. In the 'patriotic' narrative of the three successive Chimurengas, time is conceived of as linear (with the three phases of the liberation war dovetailing neatly), and space as sharply divided: rural space is seen as more 'authentic' than urban, and the same can be said of the space inside Zimbabwe as opposed to spaces outside it (so that a statement such as 'Zimbabwe is not England' begins to function as an act of sharp ideological evaluation). As a discursive construct, patriotic history is thus both neatly symmetrical and curiously familiar: present struggles echo past ones, and future goals magnify past victories. In Chapter 9 of the present volume, Anthony Chennells pinpoints an eerie sense of historical *deja vu* when he writes: 'In Zimbabwe, minor and major histories have swapped places and probably will swap places again'. However, Zimbabwe can also be said to be entering the future by re-enacting the past in ways which are far from being purely discursive. When it comes to the levels of violence it has incurred, the 'Third Chimurenga' indeed resembles a war; and rural Zimbabweans are currently cut off from both the cities and the outside world through means that are painfully material. All this makes it possible to refer to the present Zimbabwean historical moment as blind – in the sense of an unseeing, unprofitable position engendered by a wrong turning, but also in the more specific sense, brimming with moral outrage, powerfully conferred on this word by Chenjerai Hove in the lines of poetry quoted at the outset.

In another recent poem, Hove refers to the future by announcing: 'from now on/ we tread the road/ the footpath of illegitimacy' (Hove, 2003: 57). The second group of recent re-evaluations of Zimbabwe's past comes from counter-discursive voices wishing to challenge the officially sanctioned blindness and illegitimacy, but also asking questions about how these could have been avoided. In Zimbabwe, the opposition, civil society activists and (what remains of) the independent media are courageously challenging the official version of Zimbabwe's past, and of what it is to be 'Zimbabwean' (see Meldrum, 2004). World wide, scholars in a broad range of academic disciplines are re-assessing both recent history and earlier accounts of Zimbabwean experiences, and asking questions about why these accounts failed to give sufficient warning of the violence that was to come. Broadly speaking, it is among such attempts at re-assessment that *Versions of Zimbabwe: new approaches to literature and culture* may be situated. However, to the extent that much academic work to date has echoed the Zimbabwean government's agenda in focusing directly on questions to do with nationhood and the land (see, for example, Bond and Manyanya, 2003; Campbell, 2003; and Hammar et al., 2003), the present volume carves out a direction of its own. *Versions of Zimbabwe: new approaches to literature and culture* is about creative literature, and how it may be related to Zimbabwean history and politics. A key aim of this volume is to showcase new and untried approaches to Zimbabwean writing, and to start addressing Zimbabwean literature and culture from angles (and with the aid of methodologies) that have hitherto remained overshadowed. But literature and culture cannot, of course, be understood separately from larger social trends –

and so it is through foregrounding literary and cultural issues that *Versions of Zimbabwe: new approaches to literature and culture* seeks to make a statement about the Zimbabwean crisis of today.

The chapters that follow will show that Zimbabwean culture texts relate complexly to the narrative of the Third Chimurenga. It will be seen that some literary works (such as some xenophobic novels in indigenous languages, monologic popular texts and nationalist narratives of patriotic childhoods) helped to pave the way for it, or even to rehearse it. Others (for example, the plurivocal texts of Yvonne Vera and Dambudzo Marechera and films such as Ingrid Sinclair's *Flame*) continue to function as models of opposition to it; yet others resemble the poetry of Chenjerai Hove in poignantly condemning it. Some of this is summarized at the book's beginning: *Versions of Zimbabwe: new approaches to literature and culture* opens with Preben Kaarsholm's overview of post-independence Zimbabwean literary trends. This initial chapter argues that literature has made an irrevocable contribution to the development of a Zimbabwean public sphere, and that the memory of the process of public contestation and discussion to which it has contributed will be difficult to erase despite the current repression. There are therefore still grounds for optimism in Zimbabwe, and grounds for hope. There is even – ironically – reason to think that it was the present crisis that brought about the beginnings of questioning what was previously kept 'under the tongue' (Vera, 1996) – a struggle against spiritual blindness and inertia, and an opportunity to question past habits of thought. Together, Kaarsholm's literary-historical overview and Terence Ranger's survey of struggles in Zimbabwean historiography form a framework for the debates and views contained in the rest of this volume. Yet to say this is not to suggest that the ideological or narrative *neatness* of Zimbabwean 'patriotic' discourses will be replicated here. Literary texts, we would maintain, imagine multiple *versions* of Zimbabwe, and it is only a multiplicity of approaches and opinions that can do this variety true justice.

2.

The contemporary official demands for 'patriotic' behaviour and writing are not a sudden eruption – nor are they an overnight advance of 'primitivism', or a reversal to the 'bush tactics' of governance. In Zimbabwean literary studies, calls for patriotism could be heard since the first decade of independence. After 1980, as previously banned texts by authors such as Stanlake Samkange, Wilson Katiyo, Stanley Nyamfukudza, Charles Mungoshi and Dambudzo Marechera were finally able to be re-published inside Zimbabwe, critics occupied themselves with systematising, reviewing and evaluating the nation's literary achievements. Although Zimbabwean writing (both before and after independence) comes in three languages – Shona, Ndebele and English – it was generally agreed that the English-language tradition represented the mainstay of Zimbabwe's literary heritage (see Kahari, 1980 and Zimunya, 1982). And while it seemed important to examine 'the birth' of this tradition, some critics were baffled by what seemed to them to be an inexplicable gloominess of outlook that characterized many of the English-language texts. This apparently unwarranted pessimism seemed all the more grating at the time when the nation was celebrating the arrival of majority rule.

In a volume designed to function as an introductory overview (*Those Years of Drought and Hunger: The Birth of African Fiction in English in Zimbabwe*, 1982), Musaemura Zimunya found himself caught between the need to assert the value and importance of pre-independence Zimbabwean writing in English, and, at the same time, voice ideological objections. After praising Dambudzo Marechera's deft use of language (in the novella *The House of Hunger*), Zimunya concludes by saying: 'Unfortunately, [Marechera's] vision is preponderately private and indulgent. The social and moral undertaking is cynically dismissed. The artist curries favours and succumbs to the European temptation in a most slatternly exhibition' (Zimunya, 1982: 126). (Zimunya's essentialising use of 'European' as a denigrating descriptor is to be enhanced and magnified in the decades to come). In a similar vein, Zimunya blamed Charles Mungoshi's novel *Waiting for the Rain* for presenting an insufficiently 'socially and historically fulfilling vision of the educated elite of Zimbabwe' (Zimunya, 1982: 93). At a time when national 'fulfilment' appeared to have been triumphantly achieved, Zimunya – a member himself of Zimbabwe's educated elite – could not help but dislike the wry worldliness of Mungoshi's and Marechera's texts.

Some years later, Zimunya's University of Zimbabwe colleague, Rino Zhuwarara, agreed with Zimunya – and extended a condemning judgement to other pre-independence writing in English. In an essay review entitled 'Zimbabwean Fiction in English', he writes, frowningly, of the 'cultural malaise which gripped Black Zimbabweans during the 1960s and 1970s' (Zhuwarara, 1987: 134). Such well-meaning but ultimately repressive literary-critical evaluation can be linked to the socialist realism-inspired brand of Marxist aesthetics officially adopted and taught by the University of Zimbabwe's Department of English at the time (for an example of its theoretical articulation, see Ngara, 1985). The most sweeping statement encapsulating this aesthetics came in the early 1990s when, in the introduction to her influential social history of Zimbabwean literature, Flora Veit-Wild referred to the '"anomaly" of Zimbabwean literature which on the very eve of independence gave birth to highly unpatriotic writings' (Veit-Wild 1993: 7). Veit-Wild's volume thus echoed Zimunya's in combining a palpable admiration for its subject matter with an equally palpable unease about its political correctness in 'socialist' Zimbabwe (for a discussion, see Chennells, 1993). At the same time – although the 1980s were also meant to be a decade of 'reconciliation' (see De Waal, 1990), and although the Veit-Wild volume took into account black writing in the three main Zimbabwean languages – literature produced by white authors and literary works in Shona and Ndebele were critically assessed separately from the black Anglophone mainstream, and this remained true in the decades to come (*cf* Chennells, 1982; Kahari, 1986 and Chiwome, 1996).

With the benefit of hindsight, it is possible to see the prescience of the ill-received literary works by Mungoshi, Nyamfukudza and Marechera: Zimbabwean literature challenged the discourses of Zimbabwean nationalism long before its historiography did so, and it called for a broader and more complex definition of 'patriotism' than either the critics or the politicians could summon. (In a memorable recent speech, Stanley Nyamfukudza used the Shona expression *kuvhiya kadembo* – 'to skin a skunk' – to describe a sense of distaste and disapproval with which 1980s critics described Zimbabwean literary 'indiscretions'. See Nyamfukudza, 2004.) In the 1990s and onwards, as the government abandoned the 'socialist' ideological stand, the disappointments of independence became more obvious, and a new generation of writers (such as Tsitsi Dangarembga and Yvonne Vera) emerged into international prominence, some Marxist critics modified their views to an extent (See Zhuwarara, 2001; for volume-length discussions of Zimbabwe's literary 'stars', see Veit-Wild and Chennells, 1999; Willey and Treiber, 2002; and Muponde and Taruvinga, 2002). Others, however, retained and sharpened the demands for a narrowly understood 'patriotic' stance, while abandoning Marxist vocabularies. A 1998 volume centrally concerned with development stresses Africa's need for 'people who are patriotic, reliable, committed and disciplined' (Chivaura and Mararike, 1998: ix) – precisely the values later extolled as necessary for those 'inside the Third Chimurenga' (Mugabe, 2001). One of the chapters of *The Human Factor Approach to Development in Africa* is devoted to literature and culture. In it, the critic Vimbai Chivaura chastises European Marxist critics for 'listen[ing] to the rhythm and heartbeat of Africa with a Leninist stethoscope, rather than African first-hand experience' (Chivaura and Mararike, 1998:102) and condemns 'imaginative works in which Zimbabwean characters appear, also sound[,] vapid, with mangled visions celebrating defeat and acquiescence to European enslavement and cultural hypnotism' (ibid: 108). In a related article, Chivaura extends this category to include the entire corpus of Zimbabwean writing in English: 'the literature that the Zimbabwean writers in English produced and still produce, are [sic] modelled along the same lines as European novels, plays, short stories and poems. Characters in their novels, for example, are imitations of those in European fiction in their anti-social behaviour and oppositional stances to national struggles' (Chivaura, 1998: 62). Here, echoes of Zimunya's earlier understanding of the dangers of outside, 'European' influences on African writing merge a literary-critical debate involving Nigerian literature (see Chinweizu et al., 1985) and pave the way for a Zimbabwean historical moment that is still to come. The critical and theoretical merits of such views have been discussed elsewhere (see Chennells, 1993). In the context of the political situation in Zimbabwe today, it is possible to see Chivaura's statements as preparing the ground, in the area of cultural production, for the denunciation of all things 'non-African', on which the Zimbabwean 'patriotic' narrative is predicated. In the same article, Chivaura mounts a personal attack on a white colleague at the University of Zimbabwe's Faculty of English.

In a context such as this, and at a time when both literature and criticism are well placed to question their own traditions and canons, *Versions of Zimbabwe:*

new approaches to literature and culture places a deliberate emphasis on plurality, inclusiveness and the breaking of boundaries. The result of a collaboration of scholars situated both in southern Africa (including, of course, Zimbabwe itself) and overseas, the chapters that follow address a wide range of questions and problems, employing a variety of critical methodologies. We have sought contributions dealing with Zimbabwean cultural products (in each of the three main languages) and chapters on internationally celebrated authors such as Yvonne Vera and Dambudzo Marechera appear alongside discussions of writers not widely known outside Zimbabwe: it is hoped that these juxtapositions will add depth and nuance to current perceptions of the Zimbabwean literary landscape. Furthermore, critical examinations of literary works (prose fiction, poetry and drama) are complemented by chapters on related cultural forms such as film and autobiography/memoir, making it easier to discern some of the shared, underlying cultural trends and tendencies currently underpinning Zimbabwean cultural life. Even more importantly, several chapters discuss white Zimbabwean authors in comparison to black ones, in an attempt to work towards putting an end to the needless segregation of Zimbabwean literary traditions demarcated by 'race'. In all of these ways, *Versions of Zimbabwe: new approaches to literature and culture* makes a stand against proscriptive evaluation and is in favour of a plurality of textual attitudes and approaches. It is our hope that this volume will help contribute towards the envisaging of a new, more broadly inclusive history of Zimbabwean literature and culture, as well as the Zimbabwean nation – and 'patriotism' itself.

3.

In the chapters that follow, several key themes emerge and interweave. One of them is the struggle between language and what Caroline Rooney calls 'the over-determined cessations of dialogue' – between meaningful debate and monologue that leads into silence. This struggle underpins many of the contrastings and comparisons made on the following pages: the juxtaposition, for example, of opposing ways of understanding certain formal devices in African films, the widely differing attitudes towards ethnicity in Shona and Ndebele novels, or the two ideologically opposed kinds of Zimbabwean thrillers. What is at stake in Zimbabwean culture at the moment is whether it is possible for political discourses to freeze and fix *all* socially produced meanings. Despite the ferocity of the ruling elite's attempts to do so, this, ultimately, seems unlikely – but the struggle against these attempts is a bloody one, and one that affects all writing in and about Zimbabwe. This points to the second theme threaded through the present volume – the relationship between writing and violence. Violent acts are often thematized in Zimbabwean texts – for example, in the novels of war, or stories of violent childhoods. However, the chapters that follow record also the textual outrage at violence that has taken place *outside* texts and is too great to be contained by them, and the violence done *to* texts through what is perceived as constraining or constricting interpretations or readings. And finally, there runs through this volume the recurring theme of the relationship between writing and identity – expressed either as memory or a sense of belonging, and articulated through genres as diverse as poetry, autobiography, fiction and historiography. Each of the five sections that follow highlights these key thematic undercurrents in several ways and from a different set of angles.

In Section One, entitled *Text and Violence*, Preben Kaarsholm surveys Zimbabwean literary texts' engagement with the violence that took place during the liberation war as well as the less publicized violence of the post-independence era. In debating and representing violence, Kaarsholm states, Zimbabwean literature has fulfilled the function of social conscience (and has, as stated above, contributed to the emergence of civil society); Zimbabwean writers have shown a passion for commitment unparalleled in neighbouring national literatures. The same commitment may be seen in director Ingrid Sinclair's film *Flame*, analysed in depth by Jane Bryce in her contribution to this section. Bryce enters into a polemic with the Tanzanian film critic Martin Mhando, arguing that quasi-documentary voice-over techniques used by Sinclair in the film should not be assigned meanings independently of Zimbabwean social contexts. Bryce maintains that the analysis of artistic form is inseparable from struggles 'over representation, over definitions of heroism, nationalism and history itself.' In her chapter on Dambudzo Marechera as a writer of war, Annie Gagiano provides further examples of this struggle. In the early 1980s, Marechera had been accused of an unpatriotic attitude towards the liberation war. In an essay on *The House of Hunger*, a critic charged that 'Marechera's disillusionment is so complete that he fails to discriminate between self-seeking opportunists and selfless dedicated revolutionaries in the struggle for independence' (Mzamane, 1983: 208). Gagiano shows that precisely the opposite is true. In his prose, poetry and plays, Marechera demonstrated a passionate, *complex* loyalty to his nation, speaking out – like Yvonne Vera after him – against torture and the desecration of vulnerability.

Section Two – entitled *Questions of Lack and Language* – centres on issues related to language as both a means of communication and a conceptual system, and it is comprised of chapters pointing out various kinds of absence, insufficiency and lack. Caroline Rooney's moving essay on the poetry of Chenjerai Hove articulates the poet's reaction to the abuses of language that precede and accompany the abuses of power. This chapter speaks of poetic texts which, in their minimalism, inhabit the edges of language, and refers to the many occasions on which words fail in the context of modern Zimbabwe. Both Hove and Rooney voice a paradoxical demand for both more and less language in such a situation: more truth-speaking and genuine dialogue, fewer corrupt words to which the only answer is silence. In their discussion of representations of ethnicity in the Zimbabwean literature in African languages, Mickias Musiyiwa and Tommy Matshakayile-Ndlovu also refer to a lack. They outline a number of attitudes towards ethnic difference that belies George Kahari's thematic division of Zimbabwean non-Anglophone fiction into 'Old World' and 'New World' narratives (see Kahari, 1990). The chapter – which stands apart from most discussions of Zimbabwean writing in African languages by taking into account both Shona and Ndebele texts – designates and condemns some of the works it discusses as 'xenophobic'. Such attitudes towards ethnic difference may be linked to both the present-day official stance on 'people without totems' (e.g. the farm workers of non-Zimbabwean origin seen as 'alien' to the Zimbabwean soil) and the colonial-era ethnic stereotypes (pitching, for example, the 'warlike' Ndebele against the 'docile' Shona ethnic groups). In his contribution to this section, Maurice Vambe, too, questions Kahari's categorization of Shona and Ndebele texts. He, however, concentrates on the lack he perceives in the language of *theory* used in the sociologies of Zimbabwean literature authored by Flora Veit-Wild and Emmanuel Chiwome. While previous critics attached the connotations of 'drought and hunger' to literary works themselves, Vambe maintains that such images are more properly suited to the conceptual 'poverty' of the theoretical lenses through which literature has been viewed, and which sometimes fail to discern in it traces of agency and resistance.

In the third section of this volume, *Childhood, Memory, Identity*, three chapters inter-relate contrapuntally. This section deals with the nostalgia pervading memories of white Zimbabwean childhoods, the hardships adhering to the appropriation of black childhoods into the African nationalist cause, and the ways in which white Zimbabweans relate, in retrospect, to the notions of land and home. Ashleigh Harris looks at how two recent, internationally-acclaimed accounts of white Zimbabwean upbringing – Peter Godwin's *Mukiwa* and Alexandra Fuller's *Don't Let's Go to the Dogs Tonight* – narrativise white Zimbabwean identities and work with discourses of victimhood and belonging. Although they address different historical moments, Godwin and Fuller each situate themselves in relation to land and landscape, while also confronting personal and historical trauma. In the end, Harris argues, both texts gloss over some of the complexities of Zimbabwe's racial history in order to be able to construct a sense of belonging. In contrast, Robert Muponde's chapter looks at how, in novels by Wilson Katiyo and Ben Chirasha, the space of war converts the symbolism of a black childhood into a social structure that rehearses imaginatively the foundational moments of the Zimbabwean nation. Within that structure, moments of colonial violence and dispossession are emphasized, and the violence inherent in 'traditional' rural childhoods is erased or ignored. Thus the ideas of 'sons of the soil' and 'children of resistance' become foundational moments in the history of decolonization from which a new, liberated nation is seen to descend. Finally, in the chapter authored by Anthony Chennells, the autobiographical texts by Ian Smith, Peter Godwin and Doris Lessing are made to interrogate aspects of contemporary theoretical thought on autobiography and each other's constructions of self and the nation. Chennells' textual analysis progresses from Ian Smith's unshakeable certainty that justice and pure rationality were inherent in Rhodesian nationalist ideology, to Doris Lessing's recognition that it was the stupidity of precisely such notions of white 'authority' that created a militant black nationalism. The Rhodesia that Lessing remembers is more diverse than either Smith's homogenous white 'nation-family' or Peter Godwin's violent place from which whites are excluded; she also realizes that both individual and group histories rest largely on contingencies, and does not attempt to fix hers within the convention of reliable narration.

This volume's fourth section, which deals with *Imagining the Spaces of Belonging*, focuses on three very different generic frameworks for imaginative (re)constructions of the physical and social spaces in which texts embed concepts of the self. In an invigorating contribution to the field of ecologically-oriented criticism, Dan Wylie compares the attitudes towards language and landscape in the lyrical poetry of two poets who lived not far from each other in Zimbabwe's Eastern Highlands: the Shona poet Musaemura Zimunya, and the English-born immigrant poet N. H. Brettell. Strikingly, Wylie finds that both poets struggled to locate their 'true roots' in the landscape about which they write, and to find an 'authentic' language with which to capture it. In the chapter that follows, Ranka Primorac performs a reading of the interface between ideology and genre in a Zimbabwean thriller published in the mid-1990s. Rodwell Machingauta's *Detective Ridgemore Riva* situates its hero in a Zimbabwean space that is imagined as utterly transparent – at least to the eyes of a select elite. Detective Ridgemore Riva conducts his investigation mostly by simply looking around him; and once he catches his criminals, they are subjected both to torture and to sardonic remarks about the general uselessness of the process of law. A decade after its publication, this thriller reads as a rehearsal of a whole range of practices associated with state-sponsored violence in independent Zimbabwe. In an essay that is in several ways antithetical to Wylie's, Sarah Nuttall turns her attention to a hitherto unexamined aspect of the novelistic work of Yvonne Vera. She examines the urban spaces and assemblages that underlie the re-assemblings of gendered selves in Vera's two Bulawayo novels, *Butterfly Burning* and *The Stone Virgins*. Vera's work illuminates how the township practices of assembling 'city things' may be seen as shaping – often in circumscribed ways, and by way of protest – the essence of the colonial and post-colonial African city.

The fifth section, *Writing, History, Nation*, traces the inter-linkages between writing, memory and national history and opens with Kizito Muchemwa's meditation on Zimbabwean literature as an alternative form of remembering and imagining the nation. In a sequence of intellectual vignettes structured around some key texts in both the 'black' and the 'white' Zimbabwean literary traditions, Muchemwa touches on themes of political and gender repression, the silencing of dissenting voices and historical distortion. He sees literary representations of spirit possession as a 'strategy of recovery of the tongue' and concludes by bringing the two seemingly separate Zimbabwean traditions to bear upon each other: although differing in style, texts by black and white writers 'address the same historical experience'. Enlarging on some of the topics touched on by Muchemwa, Lene Bull Christiansen's contribution is also in direct dialogue with Terence Ranger's chapter that follows it. Building on the notions of 'patriotic history' and 'ugly history' referred to by Ranger, Christiansen considers the historical span of narrated time separating Yvonne Vera's first novel, *Nehanda*, and her most recent one, *The Stone Virgins*. Although *Nehanda* diverges from official Zimbabwean nationalist narratives by presenting a woman-centred version of the Second Chimurenga, Christiansen argues that the notion of spiritual temporality it employs in order to imply a continuity of the liberation process renders this novel vulnerable to being appropriated by the discourses of 'patriotic history'. *The Stone Virgins*, on the other hand, rewrites both the temporal underpinning and the 'feminist nationalism' of the earlier text, and – Christiansen argues – can thus be read as a significant departure in Vera's thinking about the nation.

As it has been stated at the outset, Terence Ranger's detailed survey of the struggles over the past in contemporary Zimbabwe may be seen as a frame and a background to all the chapters preceding it. Covering the period between 1997 and 2003, it outlines a key discursive dimension of the violent and tragic Zimbabwean turn of the century. The chapter ends by stressing the need to provide an alternative to 'patriotic history'. In the sphere of literary studies, this volume is intended as a contribution towards such an alternative. Above all, it is hoped that *Versions of Zimbabwe: new approaches to literature and culture* might counter-act what Christiansen describes as the 'desiccation of kindness', and add to what Caroline Rooney calls 'safekeep[ing] the capacity to love', so threatened in present-day Zimbabwe.

Part I.

Text and violence

Chapter 1

Coming to terms with violence: literature and the development of a public sphere in Zimbabwe

Preben Kaarsholm

Introduction: writing, reading and the notion of civil society

In this chapter, I discuss the role played by writers and by literature in Zimbabwean society, and the contributions made by literary expression to political transformation. I shall focus specifically on the ways in which writers have attempted to come to terms with the liberation war and the experiences of post-colonial political development that have dominated the post-1980 period. In this recent history and literature, violence in various forms seems to provide a pervading theme – the violence of the liberation war, the violence of post-war Matabeleland (the Gukurahundi), the violence of relations at various levels of everyday life, and – most recently – the violence of land invasions, the expulsion of white farmers and 'non-national' farm labourers, and the government mobilization against the challenges of democratic opposition to overthrow it.

It has been argued that Third World literature is distinguished from other types of writing by its special 'moral' and 'national allegorical' quality, and that Third World societies do not possess the 'private spheres' that in European history provided the hothouses for the development of literary genres and aesthetics (Jameson, 1986: 70ff. and Habermas, 1962: II, §§ 5, 6 and 7). While I do not agree with this in general terms, it is certainly true that it would be difficult in contemporary Zimbabwe to meaningfully understand personal lives in abstraction from their social and historical contexts.

On the other hand, I would argue, one of the contributions of literary writing to social development is to help establish a sphere of personal life, and of relationships that are not directly bound up with interests of state or political ambition. Literary production and consumption, debates over literature and the institutionalization of writers as a special profession in society may help to create or strengthen the foundations of what in an ambivalent and sometimes romanticized term has been called 'civil society', but for which the German

3

Öffentlichkeit, 'public sphere' or literally 'openliness' is more precise (Habermas, 1962; *cf.* also Kaarsholm and James, 2000).

While there is no doubt that literature and writers may work to transmit ideology and help keep people's minds in bounds, they are also important in building democratic potentials from below, and in destabilizing powerfully established structures of mental authoritarianism – be they racist, colonial, patriarchal, traditional, the result of wartime intimidation, or imposed by an authoritarian post-colonial state. I shall try to demonstrate this by looking at the treatment of issues of violence in different types of writing, and examine the role of literature in providing a privileged space for polyphony and the 'intermingling of disagreeing voices' (Fuentes, 1989).

Writing in Zimbabwe from independence to 'Unity'

Compared with the productivity of the last years of Rhodesia, the quiet which dominated the first years of post-independence Zimbabwe on the literary front is striking. It could have been expected that the experience of a national liberation war which went on for fifteen years, killed 40,000 people, and turned social structures and everyday relationships upside down, would have sought expression in a mass of new writing and publication, freed from the shackles of colonial control and manipulation. This did not happen straightaway.

There could be three major reasons for the relative quiet of the early 1980s: a) the backlog in publication due to the war, sanctions and censorship, which meant that there was a large amount of exiles' and other writing to catch up with for publishers; b) continued formal censorship, which was not often used, but whose presence helped to keep in place a well-established tradition of caution and self-censorship among black intellectuals; and c) the government's insistence that it had a 'socialist' cultural policy, but without ever being clear about its aims and contents. Therefore writing from all sorts of perspectives – be they platforms of politically correct Leninism, African traditionalism or Western-oriented liberalism – could in principle be interpreted as being critical of the government, which had wide-ranging emergency legislation to protect itself as well as a huge and intact Central Intelligence Organization taken over from the Rhodesians. If direct censorship was rarely used, there was enough in the post-war atmosphere to encourage active self-restriction.

The situation was, of course, particularly tense in Bulawayo and Matabeleland, where from 1982 it escalated into a semblance of civil war and full-scale repression of ZAPU (Zimbabwe African People's Union, led by Joshua Nkomo) and anything to do with that organization's history of contributing to the nationalist struggle and the liberation war. As has since become clear, there were also campaigns of undiscriminating terror against people in the countryside by 'the small, plucking rains' (Shona *gukurahundi*), alias the Korean-trained Fifth Brigade, to unseat any sign of support of 'dissidents' (Werbner, 1991; Godwin, 1996; Catholic Commission of Justice and Peace, 1997; Alexander et al., 2000).

A major reason, however, behind the sometimes bland and celebrationist character of some of the immediate post-independence-period writing may also have been a genuine euphoria about the 'revolution' being accomplished. This certainly seems to be the case in a lot of the poetry published in Mudereri Kadhani and Musa Zimunya's *And Now the Poets Speak* (1981) or Chenjerai Hove's *Up in Arms* (1982).[1] Another publication of poetry, of Shona propaganda and mobilization songs from the war years was in fact more interesting and innovative – Alec Pongweni's *Songs that Won the Liberation War* (1982), which contained examples of both ZANLA choir songs and of the dense and cryptic texts of popular singers and township performers like Oliver Mutukudzi and Thomas Mapfumo.

If early post-independence war novels tended to be 'celebrationist', this did not prevent them from also containing elements of criticism and articulated frustration. A main concern in all of them was to provide models for the understanding or legitimation of wartime violence.

Edmund Chipamaunga's *A Fighter for Freedom* (1983) is a good example. The three parts of the story describe a family and society in crisis, the struggle to overcome the crisis, and the re-establishment after the struggle of a natural structure of harmony. Mr Gari, a missionary school headmaster, has his personal integrity undermined by the contradictions and humiliation of colonial society and falls to drink. His son Tinashe becomes the rescuing force of the family as he joins the ZANLA guerrillas and helps to defeat colonialism. At the end of the novel Mr Gari is healed, the family's dignity and self-respect restored, and the parents remarried in a traditional African ceremony.

Imagery in the novel consistently contrasts the 'natural' with the 'unnatural' – urban life and life under colonialism is unnatural, life in accordance with tradition is natural. The Rhodesian forces are like machines, breaking their way through the landscape, while the guerrillas are at one with it, allied to the wild animals and inspired by the spirits which inhabit the rock formations. Similarly, violence has a dual nature – the violence of the security forces is ruthless and against nature, while the violence of guerrillas is sanctioned by spirits and natural forces, and by their efforts to re-establish an 'authentic' African life of dignity. Also – in almost Fanonian terms – guerrilla violence is justified as a healing force needed to break the shackles of mental colonization.

A similar representation of the war as a struggle to re-establish 'authenticity' can be found in Garikai Mutasa's *The Contact* (1985) that contrasts the urban world of colonial civilization characterized by general prostitution, with the 'eco-system of equilibrium' which dominates nature and traditional African life. Nature has violence in it, but it is a violence of reproduction and regeneration. Similarly,

---

[1]   For an extended discussion of Chenjerai Hove's poetry, see Chapter 4 of this volume.

the guerrillas are like natural forces, when they purge the ground to prepare for new life – they are like the rain, which is described as a 'revolt' and 'rebellion' against the earth, needed to bring forth a flowering of 'animals, blossoms and insects' (Mutasa, 1985: 66). The war violence is a cleansing which will free the land of 'foreign ideology' (Mutasa, 1985: 106). So at the end of the novel there is victory and triumph:

> *Spirits spoke in multiple languages. Gods excitedly released rain. The cloud taps were forgotten. Happiness filled the day. And there was hope. Hope for the future. Giant hopes and happinesses.*
>
> *In the Assembly Points guerrillas and mujibhas were singing. They eulogised their leader and sang of the dead, and sang of victory... The gun had done it. The AK. The gun and the vote were the liberators (Mutasa, 1985: 123).*

The celebrationism of *The Contact*, however, is tempered in a one-page 'Postscript', in which the ex-combatant Hondoinopisa reflects on the post-war careers of the characters of the novel. While one ex-guerrilla has become a brigadier in the Army with a big Mercedes Benz, another a 'personnel officer with one of the large multinational firms in Harare', Hondoinopisa himself has been less lucky: he has ended up committing unsuccessful robberies in town. 'Such were the facts of life. Not everyone was lucky' (Mutasa, 1985: 125).

Alexander Kanengoni was himself a guerrilla from 1974 to 1980 and has written three novels about the war: *Vicious Circle* (1983), *When the Rainbird Cries* (1987), and *Echoing Silences* (1997). *Vicious Circle* is inspired by Stanley Nyamfukudza's *The Non-Believer's Journey* (1980) and concentrates on the effects of the war on people who are only indirectly involved, like the family members of Tendai who has gone off to join the guerrillas. Kanengoni describes violence in the form of the torture of civilians by Rhodesian authorities, but also – like Nyamfukudza – the oppression that exists within the 'traditional' African family, under which Tendai's independent-minded sister suffers. Attention is focused, however – again in the style of Nyamfukudza – on the indecisiveness of the protagonist, Noel, who only manages to take a political stand at the point of dying in the last scene of the novel, as he has a vision of redeeming violence:

> *He would join his brother Tendai. That was the solution. He took off his dark glasses and tossed them away. Then he began hearing voices in his head. The voices became clearer. They chanted slogans of a new tomorrow, a new identity. His mind relaxed, edging closer and closer to the voices.*
>
> *He distinctly heard the screeching tyres above the voices and the air painfully exploded with a fusion of smells – medicine, asphalt, burning rubber, and cowdung. He saw yellowness, and out of it a vase of wilting flowers. But his eyes were now fixed on something else, the AK47 lying in front of him. He picked it up and brandished it, smiling. And in long,*

swift and unearthly strides panted towards a shimmering range of mountains on the edges of his mind ...(Kanengoni, 1983: 110).

So tragedy here is something very different from what befalls Nyamfukudza's existentialist hero: Kanengoni's 'man-in-the-middle' dies just as he has decided heroically to lose himself in the struggle and its necessary violence.

A similar situation of indecision provides the central theme in a war novel by N. S. Sigogo – *Ngenziwa Ngumumo Welizwe* ('I was influenced by the political situation' – Sigogo, 1986).[2]

The protagonist of the novel, Lisho Thobela, is a teacher at a country school near Gwanda in Matabeleland South, also a confused 'man-in-the-middle'. He attempts to keep his life outside the polarizations of the war, believes what he reads in the papers and hears on the radio about the invincibility of the Rhodesian forces and the superiority of colonial society, and wishes to focus his existence on personal matters like his engagement to Phikeselwe Khumalo and his job. The upheavals of the larger society, however, catch up with him: his fiancée is an activist for the African nationalist cause in the townships of Bulawayo, and while Lisho insists on speaking in derogatory terms about the prospects of the freedom fighters, Phikeselwe leaves town to join them.

As the war zone spreads to the area around Lisho's school, which is invaded alternately by security forces and guerillas, and violence escalates, the school is forced to close down. Lisho gets a 'white' job in a Bulawayo bank, and this entails his eventual enlistment as a soldier in the Rhodesian Army. Exasperated by the brutality of the security forces, of which he is now a member, and troubled by the information that Phikeselwe has disappeared to join the guerrilla forces, he decides to desert and make his way to the other side. During a nerve-racking journey – in the course of which his bus is stopped at a series of roadblocks manned by alternately Rhodesians and guerrillas – he is pointed out to the guerrillas by his fellow passengers as a sell-out, and punished so violently that he regains consciousness only after independence. He goes searching for Phikeselwe again, only to find that she is lost to him forever, living happily in Mpopoma with a new husband and a baby. Had he listened to her in the first place, she tells him, things might have developed differently.

Sigogo's story differs from those of Nyamfukudza and Kanengoni by letting the protagonist survive into post-war Zimbabwe. An important moral is that while the war may have settled issues of power at the macro-level of society, it has simultaneously opened a multitude of wounds in people's local and personal lives which remain to be healed.

---

[2]   My understanding of Sigogo's novel is based on a summary prepared by Luke Mhlaba, an interview I did with Mr Sigogo in Bulawayo in July 1992, and on subsequent correspondence with the author.

Discussion of the nature and different types of 'good' and 'bad', legitimate and illegitimate, forms of violence is a central theme in a novel by another ex-guerrilla – I. V. Mazorodze's *Silent Journey from the East* (1989), which also deals with violence committed by guerrillas against civilians. The narrative follows three schoolboys as they set off from Zimbabwe to join the ZANLA forces in Mozambique. Illegitimate violence – i.e. undisciplined terror against civilians or violence based on private motivations – is personified in Donald, alias 'Dinkaka'. It is exorcised in the novel as a general problem by being identified with an individual psychological disposition – through the portrayal of Donald as an emotionally violent psychopath. Otherwise, the story is constructed around the classical pattern of Rhodesian massacres followed by guerrilla counter-massacres, and the story culminates in an apocalyptic air attack on guerrillas and villagers seeking refuge near a 'forest of the ancestral spirits':

> *The great day of judgment had come at last it seemed. Women clutched their young babies like baboons dispersing from danger and confusedly rushing to nowhere in particular. The men, caught between the natural instinct to protect their families and the unfathomable, danced around their homesteads like children afraid of their mothers' sticks but with nowhere to run to... Yes, the Rhodesians had the advantage of firepower but alas for the Rhodesians, they had not the blessing of 'Truth'. They had no blessing from the God of revolutionary wars. Thus, after the initial upsetting moments of attack, the comrades quickly recovered. The truth in them, the God in them reminded them that they were fighting a holy war and that those under the soil would protect them (Mazorodze, 1989: 170-1).*

The Rhodesians are forced to retire, and in the heat of apocalyptic battle, the problem of Donald's illegitimate violence is finally solved in a way which serves the cause: he acts as a suicide bomber and the novel is able to uphold its celebrationist message of the war as the victory of 'good' over 'bad' violence.

A less celebrationist type of war novel emerges in more experimental formats of writing in Zimbabwe in the late 1980s and early 1990s – e.g. in Tim McLoughlin's *Karima* (1985), Chenjerai Hove's *Bones* (1988), Shimmer Chinodya's *Harvest of Thorns* (1989), Hove's *Shadows* (1991) and Charles Samupindi's *Pawns* (1992).

Karima is the first Zimbabwean war novel to focus centrally on problems of point of view. The objectivity of the narration is carefully underlined as a construction – a debatable, but necessary attempt at distance from the multitude of subjectively limited and ideologically embellished versions of the story that would be forthcoming from its individual actors and victims. This is a prominent theme in the novel – the war experience is characterized by extreme murkiness, the flow of information is regulated by censorship and propaganda, misinformation and rumours abound, and the most immediate experience of civilians caught up in the war is one of confusion and meaninglessness.

The plot concerns a historical episode: the massacre of villagers at Karima (to the north-east of Mount Darwin) in June 1975. This was an incident of extreme violence, which in one version was said to have resulted from people being caught in cross-fire during a 'contact' between ZANLA guerrillas and security forces, and in another was alleged to have been staged by Selous Scouts pseudo-guerrillas holding a *pungwe* (a night-time meeting with civilians) at the village which was then subsequently attacked. This is a war 'in which each individual has a story to tell,' and where 'facts are less important than what people want to believe' (McLoughlin, 1985: 12, 14), and though the accounts and descriptions rendered by the novel make the second story more probable than the first,[3] this is less important than the very opaqueness, doubt and confusion that surrounds events, and the problem of violence as such.

Although *Karima* shows members of the village going off to join the guerrillas and – after the central massacre – describes sympathy for the African nationalist side to be growing, this point is made without celebrationist heroics: people become politicized against their will, or because they come to see a nationalist victory as the only possibility of bringing an end to violence, of 'taming this hostile world, torn with bestial killing' (McLoughlin, 1985: 158).

A polyphonic approach – which is not unlike that employed by McLoughlin in *Karima* – is used in Chenjerai Hove's novel *Bones* (1988). Hove's text is more experimental – the story is told through different voices and without a central narrator, and the ultra-poetic, English rendering of the voices is an attempt to reproduce Shona idiomatic characteristics. The novel is also unusual for this period in placing female characters at the centre of its plot – Janifa and Marita are the lover and mother respectively of a young man who has disappeared from the village to join the guerrillas, and the central thread of action that runs through the novel is the quest for this absent hero by his relatives as well as the Rhodesian security forces.

An important point in Hove's text is to bring together violence at different levels and to show their interrelatedness. The 'bones' of the title have a variety of meanings, one of which refers to the violent nature of basic living conditions in colonial Rhodesia – the poverty, sickness, hunger, drought and repression which are represented as having resulted from colonial conquest. 'Poverty is worse than war,' says the novel, and reminders of the history of deprivation are provided by the bleached animal and human bones which lie scattered around the arid countryside (Hove, 1988: 85). But the bones also point to a history of resistance, which is represented by the ancestral voices of the spirits in Chapter 7, calling for 'the bones of the land' to rise and 'clean the sky if it cannot give us rains' (Hove, 1988: 57).

---

[3]   Late in the novel, old Chief Karima stubbornly insists to the Rhodesian officers torturing him that 'the ones who came to the village were not terrorists. He knew them. He had seen one of them before at the police camp' (McLoughlin, 1985: 206).

The structural violence of colonization provides the background for the more specific instances of brutality, which escalate during the period in the 1970s on which a major part of the novel focuses, where the mother and martyr figure, Marita, is captured by the Rhodesians, tortured and sexually molested. A counterpoint is represented by the revolutionary violence of the nationalist guerrillas who are fighting to make sure 'that our people cannot continue to be buried in this ant-hill of poverty' (Hove, 1988: 86). The violence of the war is gruesome, but also a necessary and heroic sacrifice, and the descriptions are mostly given through the voices of the freedom fighters themselves, as they address villagers at *pungwe* meetings. Represented in this way, the problem of guerrilla violence is minimized, and the text makes a point of asserting a basic sympathy and agreement between the point of view of guerrillas and that of the villagers:

> How can people fear death when they are dying slowly in poverty, disease and ignorance? A people that fears death will never enjoy freedom from the heavy chains of being called boys by people of the same age, men and women. To refuse to die for the motherland is to refuse to wear the medal of birth which gave us this land ... so the fighters would speak long into the night so that those who are friendly with sleep would be struggling to hear a little of those things the fighters were saying ... (Hove, 1988: 87ff.).

Other forms of violence are taken more seriously and shown to transgress the boundaries between colonial Rhodesia and post-independence Zimbabwean society. One is the violence of men against women, where the text draws an explicit parallel between the rape of Marita by Rhodesian soldiers during torture, and the rape of Janifa at the hands of Chisaga – the lecherous African cook of the rich white farmer Manyepo – i.e. 'falsehood' (Hove, 1988: 111). Chisaga's violence against Janifa is sanctioned by her mother as a prelude to marriage and continues later in the advances of a herbalist to whom she is sent for treatment of the mental disturbance occasioned by the rape (Hove, 1988: 114). Like colonial violence, the violence of traditional society is dismissed, as Janifa rejects her mother – 'she crawls away like an injured cockroach, to go to her place of death' (Hove, 1988: 134).

Even after independence, women continue to be kept at the bottom of the hierarchy, and in the countryside the domination and wealth of Manyepo continue to increase:

> The air here belongs to Manyepo. Nothing belongs to the farm workers who are so full of fear for Manyepo that if he tells them not to eat for many days, they will stop. Old people the age of Manyepo's father kneel in front of Manyepo. "There is nothing the government in the city can do. I rule here," says Manyepo. "If your government wants to run this farm, let them bloody take over. Then we will see if they can run a farm," Manyepo says in his way of speaking badly about things he does not like. (Hove, 1988: 120ff.).

At the end of the story, Janifa finally comes together with Marita's prodigal son who is now a crippled ex-combatant and together they face a new battle which 'is bigger than the fight of guns and aeroplanes' (Hove, 1988: 130). The continued struggle is for a society which is less brutal and exploitative, but also one for mental healing and a change in human and social relations. But while in *Karima* the healing force was sought in religion, *Bones* looks to the power of words and song: 'I will sing to the ears of those who have died so that the bird which once had broken wings can fly for all to see' (Hove, 1988: 133).

Shimmer Chinodya's *Harvest of Thorns* (1989) is less experimental in form, and in both style and theme echoes Charles Mungoshi's existentialist realism.[4] It is in many ways the closest Zimbabwean literature has come to the kind of large-canvas and complex epic representation of the history of the liberation war one would have expected to come out of the 1980s. Within a frame of everyday scenes from a disillusioned post-independence Zimbabwe, the novel is divided into parts, which treat the 1950s, 60s, and 70s separately. Violence is a focal point – the novel contains some of the most brutal scenes in Zimbabwean literature. It is violence committed by Rhodesian forces, but the novel also, and prominently, represents scenes of *pungwe* violence perpetrated against civilians by guerrillas, including by the protagonist Benjamin Tichafa (alias Pasi NemaSellout – 'down with' or 'death to' sell-outs):

Pasi NemaSellout clutched his stick. His hands were damp. His eyes swam round the crowd. The chants rang in his ears. The woman sprawled motionless in front of him. She did not move. There was a dark stain at the end of his stick where the green bark had shredded off, where the exposed wood shone white. The woman's calves were fat and shiny. Her canvas shoes were still on her feet. He did not want to look at her legs. He did not want to look at her head. The hair stretched out in wild wings over her face.

The crowd was chanting. Women were ululating. Men were clapping hands (Chinodya, 1989: 208).

An important point in the novel is to bring out images of the war as tragedy and trauma, which had been suppressed in the propaganda-style writing of the first years of independence. In this sense – in being published as late as 1989 – Chinodya's novel becomes a verdict, not only on the war, but indirectly also on developments in post-1980 Zimbabwe. The liberation war is broadened out to become also a symbolical battlefield within which both social confrontations in the aftermath of the war and more general existential conflicts are fought out:

---

4   Ranka Primorac has suggested that two "traditions" complement each other in post-independence Zimbabwean literature – a "Mungoshi-Chinodya line of tradition" and a "Marechera-Hove stylistic tradition" (Primorac, 2002: 104).

When you are trying to piece together the broken fragments of your life it hurts to think back. The worst thing is to come back and find nothing has changed. I look at my father and mother and brother and sister, at the house in which I was born, at the township in which I grew up – people prefer to call it a suburb now – and I see the same old faces struggling to survive. We won the war, yes, but it's foolish to start talking about victory... The real battle will take a long time; it may never even begin (Chinodya, 1989: 272).

At the end of the novel, hope is vested, not in visions of social revolution, but in biological reproduction – in a new-born baby, a 'little bundle of humanity', which may grow up and develop a new kind of life without the scars of its parents and ancestors. The subdued nature of the novel's hopefulness is characteristic of the late 1980s in Zimbabwe at the end of 'the period of silence', which had surrounded anti-dissident campaigns and government violence in Matabeleland between 1982 and 1987. Healing, dialogue and humanity were now hoped for as outcomes of the 1987-8 'Unity' agreement between ZANU(PF) and PF-ZAPU, providing new prospects for a Zimbabwe of the 1990s that would be able to move beyond the trauma and violence of the war and early independence.

Literature and the new struggles: after 1990

Post-liberation war violence, dissident terror, and the *pungwes* of the Fifth Brigade in Matabeleland – all important themes to come to terms with, but silenced during the 1980s – were addressed for the first time in a published novel in Chenjerai Hove's *Shadows* (1991). Following his national (multiple printings) and international (prestigious Picador edition) success with *Bones*, Hove again employed experimental, modernist techniques, breaks of chronology, and a dense poetical style to represent an array of mental states emerging from an extended period of violence which stretches from colonialism far into independence.

But the novel also attempted – as an antidote – to represent a traditional Shona political culture that was both peaceful and inherently democratic. In a historical section of the novel, the people of Gotami defeat the warlike Ndebele through the power of their groundnuts which are so good that the *impis* eat themselves to death. A similar idea of a traditional political culture is mobilized in a critique of contemporary leaders towards the end of the novel:

... the old men and women were sad with the new rulers. They could not understand how it was that people who had fought the same enemy could become greedy when the enemy ran away. They must learn that chieftaincy is taken in turns, others whispered. Others asked what chieftaincy is if it is not shared. What is a chief without good followers?... We do not like guns, they talked inside their hearts. Guns are not food, they continued, afraid all the time that there were so many things which they did not understand any more... They wanted the big people to talk,

to sit down with gentle words in their mouths, not guns. No one eats guns, they said. These guns must be locked away so that people can talk properly... the land was now theirs, but they could not farm it. Guns stared at them all the time... The pain told them that the white man was happier than before, on the lands which he had stolen from their ancestors (Hove, 1991: 97ff.).

Like in *Bones*, the panacea for healing is dialogue – 'Talking is the medicine for troubles' (Hove, 1991: 48).

Another important early 1990s novel focusing on violence is Charles Samupindi's *Pawns* (1992), which takes us back again to the liberation war. Samupindi is obviously inspired by Hove and Chinodya, presents his narrative in fragments, interspersed with songs and newspaper quotations, and employs a contemporary frame to place his war story in perspective. In this frame, his protagonist Fangs is a vagabond in late 1980s Harare, who with his comrades of tramps and street vendors is persecuted by the police, as they attempt to clean the city in preparation for a summit meeting of the Non-Aligned Movement. In the main story, Fangs is a young 'ghetto boy' who becomes acquainted with Mugabe and accompanies him and Edgar Tekere on an epic journey to join the ZANLA forces in Mozambique in 1975, after the killing of Herbert Chitepo. This part of the story has biblical overtones – of the sufferings of the Saviour, or of Moses wandering in the wilderness before being able to take his people home.

But Samupindi's story abruptly turns away from hagiography. Having at long last reached their goal in Mozambique, the leaders disappear from the scene, and the narrative develops into a highly critical account – both of the violence and sufferings of the war, but also of the internal struggles within the nationalist camp, and of the ways in which its leadership and politics develop. The novel describes the ZIPA divisions and the brutal suppression of the Leftist *vashandi* movement in 1976, it depicts a growing presence of tribalist sub-politics within ZANU, an opportunist attitude towards ideology that wavers between Maoism and Africanist populism, and a growing personality cult developing around the figure of Robert Mugabe.

In this representation, the war violence and its after-effects are difficult to come to terms with – not because 'the revolution' was betrayed after independence, but because the sufferers, both guerrillas and civilians, were 'pawns' all along in a game played by the leaders who are now coming together in 'Unity'.

Pre-independence divisions within ZANU, and the harsh ways they were dealt with, were also brought to the fore in Alexander Kanengoni's *Echoing Silences* (1997). The liberation war scenario is presented in more gloomy terms than ever, and guerrilla life – rather than foreshadowing liberation – is a nightmare of authoritarianism in which a paranoid 'Security' exposes sell-outs like witches, and where loyalty can only be proven by extreme acts of violence. In this presentation, the war provides the scene for a story of unfulfilled ideals. At the end of the novel, Kanengoni's war-crippled protagonist, Munashe – before finding peace in death – has a vision of Chairman Chitepo, surrounded by other early nationalist leaders, talking 'angrily of a series of monumental historical betrayals' and reviving the original slogans of a battle to fight nepotism, tribalism, regionalism and corruption:

> It's shocking to see the reluctance that we have to tell even the smallest truth. Ours shall soon be a nation of liars. We lie to our wives. We lie to our husbands. We lie at work. We lie in parliament. We lie in cabinet. We lie to each other. And what is worst is that we have begun to believe our lies. What I fear most is that we will not leave anything to our children except lies and silence ...
>
> It all began with silence. We deliberately kept silent about some truths, no matter how small, because none of us felt that we would compromise our power. This was how the lies began because when we came to tell the history of the country and the history of the struggle, our silences distorted the story and made it defective. Then the silence spilled into the everyday lives of our people and translated itself into fear ... (Kanengoni, 1997: 87).

Like a truth commission – or the spirit medium seeking to explain the reasons for the drought and 'the strange new incurable disease, and the dark shadows stealing across the land' (Kanengoni, 1997: 85) – literature in *Echoing Silences* is given the function of de-silencing, and thereby helping to remove the fears and mental distortions that continue to make people un-free, many years after the war of liberation ended.

It has taken time for literature and writers, though, to catch up. Apart from Hove, authors did not immediately address the violence of the 1980s. They took as long to come to terms with it, as they had taken to address the contradictions of the liberation war.

Peter Godwin's *Mukiwa: A White Boy in Africa* has remarkable and detailed insights into Fifth Brigade intimidation and violence in Matabeleland – along the Bulawayo-Kezi road, and at Antelope Mine in particular. It came out in 1996 – one year before the Catholic Commission for Justice and Peace and the Legal Resources Foundation published their report entitled *Breaking the Silence* (Godwin, 1996; Catholic Commission, 1997). It created a stir internationally and in the British press, but in Zimbabwe fell into a genre of 'white memoir' whose belongings within the literature of the new nation could be questioned, and whose local impact was therefore limited (see the discussion of white memoirs in Chapter 9 of this volume).

The first attempt to deal with the violence of the 1980s in literary form from a Zimbabwean nationalist perspective was Yvonne Vera's *The Stone Virgins*, which only came out in 2002, fifteen years after 'Unity'. *The Stone Virgins* is different in its more recent focus from Vera's earlier historical fiction, e.g. *Nehanda* (1993), dealing with the 1890s, or *Butterfly Burning* (1998), on Bulawayo in the late 1940s. Like the earlier novels, it is a historical fantasy, but – being closer to living memory – it is more economical and to the point in its poetics, with more clearly drafted borderlines between the streams of consciousness of the authorial narrator and of the novel's characters. It seems to have been written more deliberately, in a sense, than the earlier texts, where Vera found it 'better to write ... almost intuitively, out of my consciousness of being African, as though I were myself a spirit medium' (Bryce, 2002: 220). At the same time, *The Stone Virgins* remains a fantasy in accordance with Vera's almost Nietzschean ideals of being the master, rather than the servant of history – 'as Africans, our history is there to serve us, not us to serve it. In Nigeria, they can create new gods, isn't it? That's how we were as well. The legend, the history, is created in the mouth, and therefore survival is in the mouth' (Bryce, 2002: 221).

Vera's novel is about dissident violence in the 1980s and the government's response in the form of *Gukurahundi* intimidation, violence and repression. Like the last part of Godwin's *Mukiwa*, it plays in Matabeleland South along the Bulawayo-Kezi road – in the Matopos, which Vera calls the hills of Gulati, and in the landscape of shrines which Terence Ranger has depicted in *Voices from the Rocks* (Ranger, 1999). The novel poses two kinds of violence against each other. On the one hand, there is the cruelty of the ex-ZIPRA dissident, Sibaso, who senselessly decapitates Thenjiwe, cuts off the lips of her sister Nonceba, and pollutes the holy caves of the hills with his violence. This is matched by the inhuman behaviour of the Fifth Brigade which wipes out the Thandabantu Store in Kezi and the social cohesion it represents, and tortures and murders its owner, Mahlatini. Healing and reconciliation are brought by the historian Cephas Dube, who has travelled from the Eastern Highlands to Matabeleland, and after the violence comes to nurse Nonceba and to rebuild the royal beehive huts at Old Bulawayo, achieving unity also at ethnic or provincial level.

With the violence in *The Stone Virgins* being presented so symmetrically, the action of the novel has a tendency to coagulate into myth or allegorical tableau, and its symbolism remains opaque. The novel's title refers to a cave wall painting in the Gulatis, and to rock formations resembling petrified young women. The painting is interpreted as representing a sacrificial theme, but this is an instance where it is unclear whether the interpretation is that of the authorial narrator, or of the violent dissident, Sibaso, who is hiding in the cave with the rock painting, as the narrative slides from one to the other:

Disembodied beings. Their legs branch from their bodies like roots. The women float, moving away from the stone. Their thighs are empty, too fragile, too thin to have already carried a child. They are the virgins who walk into their own graves before the burial of a king. They die untouched. Their ecstasy is in the afterlife. Is this a suicide or a sacrifice, or both?

15

Suicide, a willing, but surely a private matter? Sacrifice means the loss of life, of lives, so that one life may be saved. The life of rulers is served, not saved. This, suicide. The female figures painted on this rock, the virgins, form a circle near the burial site, waiting for the ceremonies of their own burial (Vera, 2002: 103ff.).

The motive of royalty here somehow matches the reconstruction of Lobengula's beehive huts at the end of the story, but it is not clear where this is supposed to lead readers, and what they are to make of the relationship between the ancient painting of sacrificial virgins, and Sibaso's beheading of Thenjiwe and disfiguring of Nonceba. The novel's conclusion becomes a spiritual one of sacrifice, restoration, reconciliation and unity – of getting beyond the tragedy of a violence whose political dimensions are downplayed.

Conclusion: Democracy vs. 'the Third Chimurenga'

If violence is represented as meaningless yet symmetrical in *The Stone Virgins* – and the restoration of unity posed as its solution – this can be said to be in accordance with hopes and aspirations that surrounded the agreements between ZANU(PF) and PF-ZAPU in the late 1980s. It appears somewhat anachronistic, however, in the face of the forms of terror and intimidation that characterized the period leading up to its publication in 2002. In these later confrontations, violence has been used rather in the name of unity – and to prevent opposition and pluralism – and the political and cultural agenda for disagreements in the early 21st century is in many ways a very different one from what it was in the late 1980s and 1990s.

In a recent article, Christine Sylvester has argued that political development in Zimbabwe after independence can be divided into three phases – 1980 to 1990, 1990 to 1997, and 1997 onwards (Sylvester, 2003). 'Unity' in 1987-8, the establishment of the Executive Presidency, and the 1990 elections mark the divide between the first two periods, while the challenges for compensation presented to the ZANU(PF) government in 1997 and the concessions made to war veterans – and the break with structural adjustment – signal the transition into a third period. A second wave of challenges came with the establishment of the National Constitutional Assembly, and – in September 1999 – with the formation of the Movement for Democratic Change, leading up to the defeat of Mugabe and ZANU(PF) in the constitutional referendum of February 2000. This was followed by the parliamentary elections of June 2000, which the Movement for Democratic Change nearly won, and which established a pluralism and balance of forces between two parliamentary parties that had never been political realities in Zimbabwe before (Helen Suzman Foundation, 2000).

Coinciding with – and accelerating in response to – this development, was the government's encouragement of land invasions and of campaigns against white farmers and their farm-workers of 'alien' origin, followed by new land laws and the confiscations of large numbers of commercial farms. Many of these farms were appropriated by ZANU(PF) dignitaries and allies, though land reform was clearly also being re-launched as a populist political resource which had been kept on reserve to bolster challenges to the one-party regime. It was an attempt to set the rural masses against an urban population, which was voting against and being increasingly critical of ZANU(PF) governance, and protesting against unemployment, sky-rocketing inflation, and declining living standards. Also – both during election campaigns and in the wake of the MDC's strong performance – there were increasing attempts to discourage opposition through violence and intimidation, with war veterans, ZANU(PF) village committees, and youth militias like the 'Green Bombers' tracking down and punishing initiatives in dispute of the ruling party, thus reintroducing high levels of violence to the politics of both township and countryside in Zimbabwe (Amani Trust/IRCT, 2003).

In this way, the 'Third Chimurenga' was unleashed – following those of the 1890s and 1970s – to keep the ruling party in power and undermine the new forces of opposition, but this campaign and its violence represented – in Christine Sylvester's terms – a return to 'the first "will be" ' , i.e. a re-hashing of a political promise and agenda from two decades ago, which had not been fulfilled then. This was now being reintroduced mainly to repress a powerfully new 'now', which was that of a new quality of opposition, and of a new political culture showing itself as a real possibility (Sylvester, 2003: 46). If both the violent intimidation of opposition during the June 2000 election campaigns and the repression after were depressing experiences, then the election performance of the MDC, and the fact that more than 47 per cent of voters – including rural voters in most of Matabeleland and in widespread other constituencies – had supported a political programme which tried to reconcile simultaneous priorities of redistribution and of rights, were definitely indicators of a sea-change in the political development of Zimbabwe (*cf*. Raftopoulos, 2001).

The very fact that the MDC had not won a massive victory and 'ousted' the former government, but had instead entered parliament as a powerful opposition party – and had thus been given time to develop its programme and policies in critical dialogue with ZANU(PF) – could be interpreted as a step forward, even if this dialogue became in the first instance overwhelmed by a violent reverse. Democracy had been placed on the political agenda as a matter of everyday and immediate urgency, and had been so, not as an outcome of 'political conditionality' imposed from outside, but as the result of recent historical experience and political developments inside Zimbabwe.

The recent history of Zimbabwean literature should be seen in the context of this political development, and of the emergence of new forms of democratic opposition. The debates undertaken in literature – and within other cultural genres and institutions in Zimbabwe – have helped to develop elements of a Zimbabwean public sphere – or, perhaps more accurately, of interacting local public spheres in different parts of the country.[5] And these have helped to move political differentiations and disagreements from centering on issues of nationalism, identity politics and post-colonial rivalry or unity to matters of accountability, democracy, and the problems involved in reconciling priorities of redistribution and of rights.

Prominent in the literary history of post-independence Zimbabwe have been authors struggling to understand and articulate the contradictions of a violent past and present – of confronting the lies and silences surrounding violence, and interpreting its meaning. At the same time, this literary history has been in itself structured by dialogue. In tracing the theme of violence in novels from independence onwards, patterns of inter-textual relationships come out prominently, with texts quoting, echoing and debating each other – and in the process reformulating and challenging earlier tales of the impact of violence. This is obvious, for example, in the many 'responses' to Stanley Nyamfukudza's *The Non-Believer's Journey* which come out in war novels of the 1980s, and also in the very direct way in which Yvonne Vera's *The Stone Virgins* takes on Solomon Mutswairo's *Feso* (1974), as the nationalist text which makes the dissident-to-be, Sibaso, leave his home for the guerrilla camps in the 1970s (Vera, 2002:120). In this sense, the 'coming to terms' with violence, which the literature represents, is a process of ongoing discussion and contestation – and has helped to create expanded spaces for debate and meeting places for disagreement. Compared to other African national contexts, the dynamism of the post-1980 literary history of Zimbabwe is exceptional in this respect.

A growth in outspokenness and critical confidence – which is parallel to that displayed in treatments of the violence theme – can be found in other types of literary expression in Zimbabwe from the mid-1980s onward. In poetry, examples can be found in the bitter expressions of post-war disillusion by ex-guerrilla writers like Ducas Fambai or Freedom Nyamubaya (Nyamubaya, 1986).[6] The poetry aims itself at the continuation of inequality and injustices after independence (as in

---

5   For a discussion of public spheres in the plural, see Negt and Kluge (1976). I am drawing here also on the ongoing research work of Isabel Hofmeyr, Karin Barber and others to map out the interactions of 'complexly layered' local public spheres, and study 'popular literature and its publics' (Hofmeyr, 2002; Barber, 2002; Barber and Farias, 2002).

6   Ducas Fambai's poetry was published in the 1980s in the trade union periodical *Vanguard*, as well as in the anthology *Another Battle Begun* (Zimbabwe Project, 1985). He trained as a guerrilla in Zambia and Mozambique from 1973, had first-hand experience of the Nhari rebellion and the left-wing ZIPA and *vashandi* reform movements, and spent the years between 1976 and 1979 imprisoned in Beira as a 'dissident'. At independence, he re-joined the army, and later trained as a teacher. Freedom Nyamubaya later co-authored a collection of poetry and short stories in Shona with Irene Mahamba – also a former guerrilla (Nyamubaya and Mahamba, 1993). She continues to read poems publicly, and in the late 1990s took up a career as commercial farmer.

Nyamubaya's Mount Pleasant poem, 'They Live Up There'), or criticizes the betrayal of the 'real' revolution that politicians have been guilty of, and their giving up of any pretence at more fundamental social transformation. Like other writings by former guerrillas, this poetry is critical of the post-independence state, but can also be seen as foreshadowing resentments that could be mobilized at the end of the 1990s, when war veterans were called upon by Robert Mugabe and a ZANU(PF) government under pressure to help invade and expropriate white-owned farms.

Critical confidence is powerfully present in the post-independence publications of Dambudzo Marechera, first and foremost in his *Mindblast, or The Definitive Buddy* from 1984 – an energetic and irreverent mixture of poetry, prose and drama fragments, which became a cult book among young readers in Zimbabwe, was withdrawn from circulation, but kept re-surfacing. After his death in 1987, there were further publications of Marechera poetry (*Cemetery of Mind,* 1992) and of his early novel *The Black Insider* (1990) – books, however, which lacked the Allen Ginsberg-like freshness and audacity of *Mindblast,* and never had anything like its provocative appeal within Zimbabwe.

Even more directly than in print literature, the development of freedom and confidence of expression has been found in some of the abundant township theatre which came into being also from the mid-1980s, and which represented a much more direct way of interacting with audiences than written literature. At the same time, theatre practitioners performed to much broader publics – both in township community halls and in the rural areas, often using schools as venues for plays and discussions and liaising with school teachers as influential, 'organic' local intellectuals, and go-betweens between town and country.

Some of this theatre – like the productions of Cont Mhlanga and the Amakhosi group, or of Andrew Whaley and Meridian Theatre Company – was of a very high quality and belongs to the most exciting specimens of popular culture in post-independence Zimbabwe (*cf.* Kaarsholm, 1994). Such writers and dramatists represented new and different types of intellectuals – relating to society, to the state and to readers in new ways which were a far cry from both the moralizing and the existentialist focus on alienation of some of the colonial-era writers. The repercussions of radical theatre have been felt also in the production of television and radio serials – thus in mid-2003, a very popular radio soap series, *Mopani Junction,* was closed down by the Ministry of Information. The series had had American funding to disseminate information about the background and consequences of the HIV/AIDS epidemic, but had also taken on the epidemic's political and social context in a sophisticated and critical way. Both Amakhosi Studios and former Meridian theatre activists were involved in the production of the series, which was broadcast in Shona, Ndebele and English (Chimhete and Makiwa, 2003).

The removal of *Mopani Junction* from the airwaves coincided with the banning of the independent newspaper *The Daily News,* which since 1999 had been the most critical public media outlet in Zimbabwe. Under new media laws – introduced by a Minister of Information, Jonathan Moyo, who had posed as a major spokesman for democracy in Zimbabwe in the early 1990s (*cf.* Moyo, 1992) – this was not the first attempt at the life of *The Daily News*. Neither was it the first Government strike-out at critical cultural voices. Since 1999, for example, the band which more than anybody in the 1970s and 1980s seemed to culturally embody Zimbabwe's revolution – Thomas Mapfumo and the Blacks Unlimited – have had three albums banned: *Chimurenga Explosion*, *Chimurenga Rebel*, and *Toyi-Toyi*. All contain songs critical of government corruption and the increasing misery of living conditions. In this way, Mapfumo's career as a performer was brought full circle – in 1977, he was imprisoned by the Rhodesian authorities for ninety days because of his song 'Hokoyo' (Watch out!) (Johwa, 2003).

Critical media have played a leading part in the battle for 'openliness' in Zimbabwe. The 'Willowgate' corruption scandal in 1988 coincided with the arrival of national 'Unity' and was bravely exposed by the Bulawayo *Chronicle* and its editor, Geoff Nyarota, in the face of violent threats from the government and, in particular, the Minister of Home Affairs, Enos Nkala. After studies in journalism at Columbia University, Nyarota went on to become editor of *The Daily News*. Even earlier than newspapers, monthly magazines – from the Catholic Church's old *Moto* to the more outspoken *Parade* and *Horizon* of the late 1980s – were at the forefront of debating society's woes and holding politicians to account. For the first twenty years of independence, this was made, if not easy, then not impossible either, by legislation. Theatre group magazines would also contribute to critical debate. In the late 1990s, Amakhosi's *Nomdlalo Township Theatre News* criticized the suppression of radio plays mentioning the Matabeleland atrocities of the 1980s (*Nomdlalo*, 1998).

Literature and media have also interacted: novels in English, Shona and Ndebele have been reviewed at length, and the monthlies have carried short stories and poems. Literary writers have also crossed over into journalism and political commentary – as in Stanley Nyamfukudza's powerful article on 'Zimbabwe's Political Culture Today', published in *Moto* in 1988, which heralded the democratic challenges and changes in opposition under way (Nyamfukudza, 1988). More recently, satire and critical analysis have been brought together in Chenjerai Hove's weekly columns in *The Standard*; they were collected as *Palaver Finish* in 2002 (Hove, 2002).

Palaver Finish provides insights into the ways in which local public spheres are unfolding in rural buses and around school teachers traveling between town and countryside – carrying loads of old newspapers with them to satisfy the reading hunger of villagers. Which, again, is why

Teacher is the first target of violence by ZANU(PF). The ruling party wishes it could post a few youths at every growth point, with tins of paint so that they repaint all those buses with horrible slogans deriding the new

political parties. But they cannot afford it. They send youths with boxes of matches to burn the buses that bring such wrong ideas to the villagers. They also wish roads had not been constructed to some parts of the country so that everyone would stay where they have always been, without having Teacher travelling to and from the city, conveying dangerous new ideas (Hove, 2002: 50).

Hove also writes of what is happening to reading in Zimbabwe in the political and economic crisis of the new millennium – how Zimbabweans are 'a nation of talkers' who 'prefer to borrow the book rather than buy it,' and therefore the libraries – now, like schools, without money to buy books – have much greater significance than they do in e.g. Europe:

The European book is meant for the shelf. The African book is meant for circulation. When I sell ten thousand copies of one of my titles in Europe, I know it means about five thousand readers. If I sell the same number of books in Africa, I know it means at least fifty thousand readers: the book circulates until it falls apart. In Europe, the book is arrested on the bookshelf (Hove, 2002: 84ff).

Since this was written, Chenjerai Hove has gone into exile, joining Thomas Mapfumo and a growing diaspora of intellectuals and other Zimbabweans for whom life inside the country has become difficult or intolerable. Following the new media laws, the closure of *The Daily News*, and the charges being laid against its editorial staff, fears were expressed that this would now be followed by a more general clamp-down on civil society organizations (Shaw, 2003). In many ways the prospects for democracy and human rights in Zimbabwe – as well as for redistributive growth – look gloomy, and it might seem that the political development process, which was gaining momentum internally in Zimbabwe in the late 1990s, has now been reversed.

Such a reversal has been stimulated by the stand that the South African government – together with a number of other African governments – has taken on Zimbabwe, and the ways in which South African 'quiet diplomacy' has assumed that a new 'unity' – an amalgamation between ZANU(PF) and the MDC – would be the only sustainable 'African' solution to aim for, rather than the pluralism and right to oppositional alternatives which people have fought for in Zimbabwe. On the other hand, South African trade unions and other civil society groupings have acknowledged the importance of the constitutional and human rights issues at stake in Zimbabwe – not only for Zimbabwe, but for the region as a whole.

In this sense, from a struggle for power between political parties, the Zimbabwean contestation has become a broader battle between different political cultures, and for or against a new democratic agenda which has grown out of the nation's post-independence history and a process of learning from experiences of violence and abuses of power. From this point of view, the political development of Zimbabwe has been a progressive one, in which the quality of opposition has increased, as the nationalist agenda coming to power at independence has become outdated. There are reasons to believe that this learning process will be difficult to reverse: the memory of struggles for democracy from the late 1990s onwards will prove to be as difficult to erase as those of the violence of 1980s, or of the liberation war.

In this process of development and remembering, Zimbabwean literature and authors have had a prominent part to play: they have contributed to the critical dialogues which laid the foundations for the emergence of locally based democratic demands. In spite of external pressures, intimidation, and circumstances conducive to self-censorship, writers have taken on the understandings of history and the myths of the birth of the nation, sanctioned by the powers that be in order to keep themselves in place. Authors have questioned and analysed the contradictions of the liberation war, whose brutality outlived it and influenced politics and social interaction in the 1980s and 1990s. Similarly, at a certain remove and with delays, literature has tried to come to terms with the unfolding of post-independence violence, with dissident threats and violent government reprisals, and has been part of the debates which carried forward the movement for democracy and a revised constitution from the late 1990s. This movement for pluralism involved not only the Movement for Democratic Change but also an array of other parties and mobilizations for political and cultural recognition.

At the same time, as was pointed out above, there are also elements in the critical discourse of post-independence literature – and in the writings of ex-guerrillas in particular – which emphasize the incompleteness of the Zimbabwean revolution after 1980, and can be seen as pointing forward to the 'Third Chimurenga' at the turn of the millennium, when Robert Mugabe and the ZANU(PF) government were able very skillfully to deflect social resentment from anti-government criticism and re-direct it into mobilization for 'accelerated' populist land reform. It will be interesting to study the songs and writings forthcoming in support and criticism of this belated resumption of the liberation war.

In their debating of violence, Zimbabwean literary writers have fulfilled a function of social conscience, and have shown a passion of commitment unparalleled in neighbouring national literatures. There is nothing like it in South Africa yet, and in Kenya, for example, debates over Mau-Mau and the ambiguities of the struggle for decolonization seem to have had a quite a different function in post-independence society – they can perhaps be said to have prolonged the lifespan of nationalist discourse, rather than helped to get beyond it (cf. Maughan-Brown, 1985, and the entry on 'War literature' in Killam and Rowe, 2000: 295-8). At the same time, literary writing as aesthetic enterprise has also helped to establish and preserve the boundaries of a particularly 'cultural', privileged sphere of debate, where critical thinking, thought experiments, satire, dreams and utopias have been more possible than elsewhere – although these boundaries have often been infringed.

The passion for writing that has been persistent in Zimbabwe, and that has shown itself in the numbers of manuscripts submitted to publishers, may indicate something about what Isabel Hofmeyr calls 'the constitution of publics' (*cf.* Hofmeyr, 2002). No matter whether a writer is published or not, he or she puts into the writing ideas of an implied readership, of a public reception, which help to decide the genre of the writing as well as its narrative dynamics and style. Through writing, the writer also establishes him- or herself as such, as an individual voice that enters into dialogue with other voices, whose individuality becomes recognized in the process, and also contributes to a community of communication by entering into it. Writing may involve the adoption of a 'cultural style' of modernity in the sense of James Ferguson (see Ferguson, 1999) – a 'longing for modernity' as transparency and freedom from impeding boundaries. In this sense, the very idea of writing is closely related to the ways in which the interaction between private and public spheres takes form.

Together with other cultural forms – magazines, theatre groups, churches, newspaper-carrying teachers, country buses, musicians, story-tellers, *n'angas* – literature in post-independence Zimbabwe is part of a landscape of voices, genres and institutions that make out the contours of a public sphere. This has been a landscape full of breaks and ruptures, but one also entailing much movement towards overcoming these breaks; and much intellectual noise and music, made in order to be heard and understood, not silenced. The dynamics of this landscape (a small section of which has been examined in this chapter) would make it difficult to maintain that a notion of civil society as organized public life, providing a counterpoint to that of the state, has no serious meaning in a country like Zimbabwe – or that democracy is not an African or locally rooted project.

Chapter 2

Incendiary interpretations and the patriotic imperative: the case of *Flame*

Jane Bryce

The First International African Film and History conference, which took place in July 2002 at the University of Cape Town, signalled a recognition of the place of film in African historiography. This might seem like nothing new, considering the extent to which Africa has been the subject of image-making since the birth of photography, as manifest in the whole project of ethnography. Recently, the relationship between empire and image-making has been the subject of academic studies (Landau and Kaspin, 2002; *Kronos*, 2001; Ryan, 1997; Tomaselli, 1996) which examine the symbiosis of the appropriation and visualization of space and people. Within film studies, the politics of image-making – the inherent power relations between the looker and the looked upon, the authority of the Gaze over its object – has long been acknowledged. Roland Barthes pinpoints a key aspect of the power of film, its mimetic seductiveness, when he says:

> *Film can no longer be seen as animated photographs: the* having-been-there *gives way before a* being-there *of the thing; ...[this] would explain how there can be a history of the cinema, without any real break with the previous arts of fiction, whereas the photograph can in some sense elude history...and represent a 'flat' anthropological fact (Barthes, 1977: 45).*

The apparent *'being-there* of the thing' – the capacity of film to convince the viewers that they are present as events unfold, as history is made, has been challenged by the proponents of Third Cinema, for whom seamless illusion is the trademark of Hollywood, and therefore of capitalist, imperialist image-making. The only possible response for oppositional film-makers, it is suggested, is the deliberate disruption of the realist codes by which cinematic illusion is naturalized, drawing attention to the constructedness of the image and therefore of its unreliability. This necessitates a different way of arriving at the meaning of a film, one which is not content with the first level of interpretation – the 'iconic' representation of objects on screen – but goes further, to examine the conditions of production, the intentionality of the film-maker, the relationship between the audience and the object in view, the means of dissemination of the image and the possible outcomes; in other words, the politics of interpretation. As the South African cultural studies scholar, Keyan Tomaselli, puts it:

> *Film criticism, then, needs to move beyond mere analysis of the produced text, and integrate questions of form, content, and con-text (sic). Films, or even criticism of them, should never be taken for granted … few books and articles deal with con-text/historical context, and the cycle of relationships that develop between the conceived and public texts. As important, is the need to examine the above intertexts in relation to con-texts and, indeed,* concealed *texts, those discourses and information suppressed by preferred readings. (Tomaselli, 1999: 55)[1]*

The Film and History conference of 2002 responded to this challenge in its examination of the way film has been a tool of competing ideological interests in Africa, particularly over the way stories are told and who has control over the meaning of the past. I want to respond to a challenge thrown out to me personally at the conference by one of the presenters, and to do so through the method recommended by Tomaselli – of 'situating both producer subjectivities and intentions (if these can be determined) and reception within their respective contexts' (Tomaselli, 1991: 34).

At the conference, the Tanzanian film-maker and critic Martin Mhando presented a paper entitled 'Documentary and history: a discourse on authority'. The thrust of Mhando's argument was that documentary as a generic form is permanently and irredeemably condemned for its complicity in colonial mis-representations of Africa; that any space for interpretation, difference of perspective or counter-discursive meaning has always-already been contaminated by its 'inherent thinking condition, at the level of epistemes' (Mhando, 2002: 3), so that 'the African subject … was wrest from the hands of a historical interpretation into a semiology' (Mhando 2002: 4). With this breathtaking generalization, Mhando explicitly opposes himself to that school of African film criticism, represented in his discourse by the Malian critic Manthia Diawara, which acknowledges and analyses the interrelationship of European and African cinematic and cultural codes as not only inevitable, but productive of powerful

---

[1]   Tomaselli explains the distinction between 'context' and 'con-text' as follows. 'Con-text' refers to 'the historical environment within which (a film) is both produced and perceived…the web of conflicting historical, social, economic, political, and psychological discourses out of which all kinds of texts arise…Context (without the hyphen) refers to historical material processes into which individuals are born and of which they may be unaware' (34-35). This distinction is one which I shall observe in this paper.

new modes of signification, capable of carrying anti- and post-colonial meanings.[2]

But what shocked me the most, and precipitated this chapter, was that, after citing *The Gods Must Be Crazy* in illustration of his proposition that documentary techniques somehow encode an authoritarian point of view, Mhando went on to place the Zimbabwean film, *Flame*, in the same category. 'Likewise Ingrid Sinclair uses the documentary style in her film *Flame* ... but it conceals a number of intentions and expectations of readings.' (Mhando, 2002: 5)

Furthermore, and in apparent contradiction of his earlier assertion, he subsequently *commends* selected African documentaries for 'experimenting with documentary forms in order to communicate the complex reality of modern life in the continent' (Mhando, 2002: 6), thereby acknowledging that documentary is not, after all, necessarily an intrinsically 'colonial' genre. In placing such documentaries in opposition to *Gods* and *Flame*, however, he overlooks both generic specificity – i.e. the important fact that these two films are *not* 'documentaries', but fiction features that use some documentary techniques for effect – and the (to me at any rate) glaring *differences* between the two films, subsuming both into a homogenous ideological category.

Mhando's conference paper, as posted on the UCT web-site, is frustratingly elliptical, making it difficult to take on his points in depth. Seeking further elaboration, I have turned to an earlier paper, in which he reiterates the often cited criticism of Zimbabwean-made films as donor-funded and therefore shaped by the ideological priorities of development agencies, rather than the desires and preferences of the audience or the aesthetic judgement of the film-maker. Foremost among these priorities, he suggested, are 'the pedagogic imperatives of narratives' which are important to his analysis:

> ... since (they) show how relations between cinema politics and cinematic narration are maintained. The didactic imagination employed in the film positions the viewer in a receptive mood and corresponds to the type of films produced during the colonial era. This situation prevails even today in films about the region produced both by Hollywood and local filmmakers. A good example is when we compare the aesthetics of production of supposedly diametrically opposed films such as Gods Must Be Crazy and the recent controversial feminist perspective of the war of liberation - Flame. (Mhando, 2000: 8).

---

2   At the narrative level, one thinks, for example, of Djibril Diop Mambety's appropriation of the Swiss playwright Frederich Durrenmatt's play *The Visit*, for his film *Hyenas*, or Cheikh Oumar Cissoko's use of the biblical story of Jacob and Esau for his revisionary anti-genocide and fratricide film, *La Genese*; at the level of cinematographic style, of Mambety's embrace of montage and French New Wave, Sembene's debt to Russian realism, or Akin Omotoso's playful MTV-style cutting in *God is African*. To dismiss these films as 'un-African' or epistemologically flawed on the basis of such intertextuality of form and content, is to see the whole of African cinema condemned.

The evidence he offered at the conference for this pedagogic/didactic/colonial tendency in *Flame*, specifically, was the use of the voice-over and the documentary-like style of parts of the movie.

In the ensuing discussion, I asked Mhando if he wouldn't exempt *Flame* from his category of crypto-colonial didactic film-making on account of its con-text within Zimbabwe, especially in view of other attempts by Zimbabwean women to bring women's war stories to light by means of recorded interviews, in particular in the two collections of interviews entitled *Mothers of the Revolution* (1990) and *Women of Resilience* (2000). I suggested that the project of these books was similar to that of *Flame*, (released in 1996, mid-way between their two publication dates and after five years of preparation), and that all three were driven by a common political concern arising out of post-independence marginalization of certain voices. Taken together, they therefore constituted a counter-discursive movement towards the writing of an alternative history, which otherwise would have remained invisible and unarticulated.

I probably didn't say anything of the sort. It's much easier to be articulate in retrospect, and I was temporarily destabilized by what I perceived as the complete lack of sympathetic identification with the project of the people who produced and those whose stories were dramatized by *Flame* and the two collections of interviews. Probably, too, I myself was guilty of over-identification, since the project of empowering marginalized women to speak, giving their stories the authority of textualization, is dear to my heart as someone who works with – writes about and teaches – African women's writing. I don't mean to revision the discussion to make myself look cleverer than I was capable of being at the time, so I had better confess that my emotional investment probably detracted from my objectivity. However, in answer to whatever I did say, Mhando responded by pointing out that he wasn't concerned with the correctness or otherwise of the film-maker's intentions or even with the content of the narrative itself, so much as with foregrounding the techniques of presentation and giving them a political interpretation. The long and short of it was, the use of the voice-over was patronizing to the audience and assumed authority over the images by mediating them, while the documentary style created an illusion of actuality which was not only deceitful in a fiction film, but bought into a history of colonial film-making practice.

This can be better illustrated from Mhando's earlier (2000) paper, from which I have already quoted:

> *This process is used to its full advantage in the film* The Gods Must Be Crazy. *In the film the documentary style helps in indicating a context. Even the name "Bushman" locates the relationship that the intended audiences will have with the film. There are two discourses at play here. First there is the discourse of the civilised in which the civilised speak: they are able to communicate amongst themselves as well as being able to translate between the various contending groups. The discourse of the "Bushman", on the other hand, is that of those that don't speak but*

*are spoken about. In this there is a perverted sense of authority ...
Therefore there is a methodological purpose to the use of the
'documentary' style. The director uses the form and techniques of
documentary to induce responses from audiences. So too does Ingrid
Sinclair use the documentary style in* Flame *to position us within the
receiving mode in order to ascertain conventional interpretations and
expectations about the subject. (8-9)*

Post-discussion interactions with a number of women audience-members
suggested to me that one way of reading the difference in perspective between
myself and Mhando was through gender. In this reading, the politics of
interpretation predispose me, as a feminist viewer, to accept the didactic overtone
of the voice-over because I am already constructed within its frame of reference.
I therefore readily suspend judgement on such issues as the illusion of actuality,
willingly submitting myself to the narrative flow without questioning its factual
basis. While there may be some truth in this, I believe the issue is more complicated.

Since I'm positioning myself within the argument as exemplar of a particular
perspective, I might as well go on and admit that not only am I invested in it as a
woman and a feminist, but also as a self-defined white African (from the same
country, indeed, as Martin Mhando). Ingrid Sinclair, the director of *Flame*, is a
white immigrant who arrived in Zimbabwe five years after independence and
married a white Zimbabwean. Irene Staunton, co-editor and publisher of *Mothers
of the Revolution* and *Women of Resilience,* is also a white Zimbabwean. At
stake here, I believe, is a question of nationalism: not only who is allowed to tell
stories or make films about Zimbabwe, but who *is* a Zimbabwean, and ultimately
what it means to be 'African'. This question, which gained considerable urgency
in the decade in which the two books were published and the film released, has
become even more pressing since. When *Mothers* came out, with its expressed
intention of providing 'a new perspective on the war, as it is remembered by
women ten years after independence' (Staunton, 1990: xi), a second war-campaign
had just concluded: the Gukurahundi. The peace accord or amnesty, which ended
that campaign to wipe out dissent in Matabeleland and destroy the support base
of ZAPU, was signed in 1987. The full measure of what transpired during the
Gukurahundi is still emerging, with the recent discovery of bones and graves,
and the writing of reports.[3] The prolonged silence on the part of its victims
replicates that of the women interviewees, and suggests that a whole new potential
area of counter-discursive historical record-making has now presented itself.

---

[3] See *Breaking the silence, building true peace: a report into the disturbances in
Matabeleland and the Midlands, 1980-1988.* The introduction to the Summary of this
document states: '...most people from other parts of Zimbabwe have no idea what it was
like for those who were suffering. They have no idea how people still suffer as a result of
the violence which took place. People who were affected also do not have ways of talking
to people in other parts of the country about what happened. Ordinary people all over
Zimbabwe, need to know what happened during those years in their own country' (1).

The continuity between the experiences of those whose voices were suppressed or silenced in the decade following the liberation war, and post-1987, is strongly foregrounded in a film on the aftermath of Gukurahundi by an ex-combatant, Prudence Uriri: *Soul in Torment* (1999). This film, one of a series of four dealing with violence and reconciliation in Southern Africa, was co-produced by SACOD and SABC3 with funding from several sources, including Denmark. (Is its message therefore already subverted by its being a 'donor film'?) Although it is explicitly a documentary, not a fictional treatment, the style and method have points of correspondence with the two collections of interviews and *Flame*. They are all engaged in a project of memorialising the past through the words of some of its participants and actors. They all speak from a position of personal involvement in the political processes they examine. And they all, explicitly or by implication, call the post-independence government to account for what it has caused or allowed to happen. It may be fortuitous that the film-maker is, in this case, also a woman; but the fact that she is a black Zimbabwean and an ex-combatant – one of those whose story appears in *Women of Resilience* – is surely germane to the meaning and interpretational politics of the film.

The epigraph by Nelson Mandela which begins the twenty-six minute documentary reveals its political intention: 'By remembering we can ensure that never again will such inhumanity tear us apart.' In the first scene, we see a lake in the distance and a rock; a woman walks across and sits on the rock with her back to the camera. By entering the film in person, Prudence Uriri signals her own investment in the story she is about to tell, her sense of agency and responsibility. By this, she deliberately subverts the assumed objectivity of the documentary genre, by her demeanour and the tone of her voice creating a space for feeling, for guilt and sadness. The conventional celebration of liberation is undercut by the mournfulness of the voice-over, the turned back of the speaker, as though she cannot face the camera with what she has to say.

In the following sequence, drums and the singing of the *Chimurenga* anthem, 'Zimbabwe', are heard over a sequence of still photographs of the liberation war. Then Uriri's voice is heard: 'In a determined and anguished spirit, I took up arms and went to war; shoulder to shoulder with my brothers and sisters we pushed on.' A male voice-over now takes over: 'We sacrificed our spirits, our souls, our flesh, for this soil, our motherland.' Uriri again: 'We destroyed the enemy. We won, sweet freedom.' Cut to pictures of election queues in 1980, the announcement of the ZANU(PF) victory, the inauguration and oath of Mugabe as the new Prime Minister, promising to 'well and truly serve Zimbabwe', dissolving to Mugabe in an interview stating in measured tones: 'There is no intention on our part to use the advantage of the majority we have secured. We will ensure that there is a place for everybody in this country.' Cut to Uriri on her rock, asking: 'But why after independence did we turn against each other? We who fought for freedom together, we're now enemies in our country. So much killing and mutilation after we had found peace. Who was responsible for this war amongst ourselves? Did the apartheid government of South Africa or the former Rhodesian security forces play a role in the Matabeleland conflict? Or was it power games and tribalism? These questions have tormented me ever since, and made me ask what I have achieved as a former freedom fighter after nineteen years of independence.' During this speech, she has been looking at a journal with the headline 'More Bones', its inside pages showing pictures of victims of violence accompanied by text detailing their experiences. The voice-over gives us fragments of these testimonies spoken by Uriri, recorded in such a way as to sound like an echo in the mind.

The rest of the film follows Uriri as she visits first an ex-member of the Fifth Brigade, which carried out the Gukurahundi atrocities, and then an ex-ZIPRA fighter who went into hiding. Their evidence, especially that of the Fifth Brigade soldier, gives the lie to the idea of tribalism as an underlying cause of Gukurahundi. This man is haunted by what he saw and desires only to make restitution and be released from guilt. In seeking to find an answer to the question of who is responsible, Uriri does not absolve herself, but rather makes a claim for the personal implication of all Zimbabweans in what happened, and the necessity of disclosure to enable reconciliation to happen.

In a similar way, *Flame, Mothers of the Revolution* and *Women of Resilience* insist on speaking out about women's experiences during the war, not in the spirit of vilification or revenge, but of a historicising partnership with the women concerned. The necessity for this is made quite clear in an interview published in the Zimbabwean journal, *Social Change and Development* (No 40, July 1996): 'Sexual Violence and War: When will we tell our own story?' with 'A woman called "Sarah"'. In describing her two rapes, first by a comrade and then by a Rhodesian soldier, and the resulting pregnancies, she is less concerned with bewailing the events, than with dealing with the subsequent shame and silence. As she tells us:

> *What happened to me was painful and unforgivable...It pains me more that many years after independence nothing much has been said about the experiences that some of us, women and girls, had – from both sides in the war. I am not saying all the comrades were like this, but let us talk about what happened in certain cases. We often talk about reconciliation and forgiveness. I will never forgive or forget.' (26)*

The testimonies in *Women of Resilience* echo Sarah's dignified acceptance of the reality of her situation, and reiterate the importance – the essential historicising process – of bringing what happened into the public arena. At the launch of the book in Harare in July 2000, another woman ex-combatant, the poet Freedom Nyamubaya, provided a powerful witness to this cause when she said: 'It is high time someone from Zimbabwe started to collect women's words. We are living history. We can write the history because we *are* the history. We don't need an outside researcher to document our words ... but what we lack is courage. Fear is an act of withdrawal from all community involvement. Fear thrives on ignorance.'[4] As the introduction to the book puts it:

> *As people come to terms with this suffered part of our heritage as a country, a larger, more complex history of the armed struggle is gradually emerging: the tensions within and between the two armies, the ethics of leadership, the command structure, the alliances that were forged, as well as the suffering and deprivation in the camps and in the rural areas. No-one was unaffected. The recollection and the analysis all provide us with insights that will help us to understand our development, our setbacks and our future as Zimbabweans. (xiii)*

While I suspect that this process is not what Martin Mhando was specifically objecting to in Cape Town, what I am trying to do is to demonstrate that *Flame* does not occur in a vacuum. His critique of its filmic practice – its language – by isolating one element of an essentially collective project, ignores the larger context of a dialogue that was already in progress, a dialogue moreover in which no one voice predominates.[5] However, so as to respond concretely to Mhando's objections, I will now describe the opening sequence in some detail.

The film begins with a voice-over over a blank screen: 'This story, the story of two friends, is only one of many. It all began a long time ago.' The voice is that of Nyasha/Liberty, who will narrate the story, frequently focalising Florence/Flame, but with Nyasha's perspective as the controlling narrative device. By this means, the film sets up a dual perspective – Florence/Nyasha – decentering the identificatory process for the viewer. Instead of a central protagonist, we have two centres of consciousness, which play off against each other, signifying to the audience that this is not one person's story, or even the story of two friends, but a collective story – 'one of many'. Underlining this and providing the context – the material historical background – there follows a photographic montage of sepia-tinted images of key moments in Zimbabwean history. The voice-over explains the events that led up to the war, situating the personal and individual stories in a collective historical frame. While it provides a broad, necessarily schematic sweep from 1890 to 1980, the montage serves to anchor the action within the parameters of nation-building and its symbolic superstructure: settlers carried in a litter, farming the land and hunting, a bullock cart fording a river, scenes of captive Africans from the First Chimurenga, soldiers in uniform from the second, victory. The voice-over tells us: 'The new country was called Zimbabwe', and the opening credits roll with the *Chimurenga* anthem, 'Zimbabwe', on the soundtrack. As in *Soul in Torment*, the stirring sound of this anthem not only signifies that this is a film

---

4   Freedom Nyamubaya speaking at the launch of *Women of Resilience* at the Book Café, Harare, July 2000.

5   Ingrid Sinclair told me in an interview in Harare, in July 2000, that the fact that *Mothers* had 'got away without being banned' encouraged her to go ahead with her film.

about the liberation war, but also functions as a patriotic statement and a reminder of the ideals of the war – the peace, freedom and inclusivity promised by Mugabe in 1980. Furthermore, this rendition is not a pre-recording, but sung by the *Flame* choir – the singers assembled for the film, led by choirmaster Comrade Chinx, playing the role he played in the war itself. From the outset, then, we may remark that a considerable effort has been made to reproduce as nearly as possible the sound and emotional colouring of the all-important *Chimurenga* songs. As in the war, music is not just decoration, but an intrinsic part of the way meaning is created. The voice of Thomas Mapfumo, also on the soundtrack, is indivisible from the *Chimurenga* musical style for which he is known, and represents a history of participation through expression which needs no explanation to a local audience. Like the photographic montage, it constitutes a semiotic shorthand easily decoded by Zimbabweans.

The first diegetic scene also begins with photographs, linking the story to the contextual framing device. Flame is standing with her mother and daughter, showing them photographs of herself during the war, including a press photo of herself and Liberty in combat fatigues, holding guns, on a hospital porch, with the message on the back: 'Forgive and forget', and Liberty's address in Harare. Like snapshots in a family album, these pictures function as personal memory, while being linked semiotically to the previous set of pictures, denoting national history. The personal/private is thus placed in a metonymic relationship with the public/political. The story begins at the point, fifteen years after the war, when Flame is leaving her home in a rural area to look for work in the city. Over a scene of urban activity, Liberty's voice tells us: 'Florence was my hero. Well, I should say heroine. My days were safe and quiet and grey. Florence was full of life. We had left home together to try and liberate our country, but life did not measure up to our dreams. And Flame, driven by poverty but still fighting, came to town to find me.' Flame stands in front of a shop window looking at a pair of red shoes, a talismanic symbol of her femininity and her dreams of a better life. Cut to office block, and then to interior of office, Liberty on the phone. Flame enters, the friends greet each other, a man comes out from the inner office and asks: 'What does she want?'

Liberty asks Flame to wait for her at home, and then delays her return until almost too late. Flame pins the photograph of herself and Liberty to the front door and is already leaving when Liberty arrives and calls her back. The main action of the film takes place in flashback from the moment when Liberty takes down the photograph. The picture, therefore, acts as a mnemonic device, a trigger which releases the memories of the past which are the film's main subject.[6] Apart from the 'iconic' or denotative meaning of the picture – two women fighters

---

6   This use of the photograph recalls Yvonne Vera's description of her own storytelling method: 'I start with a moment – visual, mental – that I can see, and I place it on my table, as though it were a photograph...Everything ripples around that, the story grows out of the image...For me, an entire history is contained in such a moment.'(Bryce, 2000, 219.)

during the war – it also signifies friendship, shared experience and the possibility of reconciliation. The words 'Forgive and forget' on the back invite a wider reading than the purely personal, and recall 'Sarah's' confession that, as long as her experience remains hidden, she cannot do either of these things. Although the words refer to the quarrel which drives the two women apart, taken together with the picture, they function as a sign within the film. The picture shows two women (Liberty and Flame), one of whom (Flame) had been raped by a man who had subsequently been killed in a bombing raid, along with the son born as a result of the rape. The injunction to 'Forgive and forget', therefore, suggests the need to overcome the legacy of the war in order to move forward in the new Zimbabwe. But the picture exists: the past must be acknowledged before reconciliation can take place.

Since criticism of the film is founded on its pedagogic/didactic/colonial situating of the viewer as recipient of information provided by the voice-over, we should try to establish what this sequence actually does. Does the voice-over function as in the colonial propagandist films, to fix and categorize the image beyond any contestation? Or, as in *The Gods Must Be Crazy*, to revision an African reality (that of the 'Bushmen'), against all material evidence, to accord with the mystificatory project of the film? If in *Gods,* the Bushman is made to serve the myth of an untouched, edenic world populated only by primitives, a displacement of the Afrikaner's sense of his own unmediated title to the land, what ideological sub-text can be detected in *Flame?* Certainly its documentary style is not in dispute – Sinclair herself draws attention to the way she tried to balance the personal and the historical narratives: 'The style reflects these two qualities: partly using a 'documentary' style to give a feeling of realism, and partly a more composed view to bring us close and steady to the humanity and softness of the characters in the film.'[7]

However, as in Uriri's film, the fact that the voice-over is that of a woman unsettles the usual paradigm of confident male authority which characterizes both colonial films and *Gods*. Furthermore, the voice is that of a black woman and an ex-combatant, neither of which, as categories, signifies authority. On the contrary, as we have seen, bringing them into view requires an ongoing struggle against the dominant nationalist narrative of male heroism and patriarchal political leadership. While the sepia-toned photographs function, at one level, as a guarantee of historical truth and accuracy, this is undercut from the outset by the voice-over's insistence on the plurality of stories. Furthermore, I think it is disengenuous to imagine that the story could proceed *without* some form of historical contextualization. The film-maker's challenge is how to present this in a palatable way, without appearing to lecture the audience. The film, *The Blue Eyes of Yonta* (1991) by Flora Gomes confronts a similar problem in respect of Guinea Bissau. There, the opening sequence of a group of young boys bowling along

---

[7]   'Director's Intentions' from the Flame web-site, http://www.zimmedia.com/flame/

tyres each marked with a significant date in the country's history may appear to circumvent the problem of explicit didacticism. But it is followed soon after by a classroom scene, in which a teacher explicates the very same dates for a group of students, thus ensuring that key historical facts are known by the audience. Incidentally, this film also prefigures *Flame* in its presentation of the ex-liberation war hero, now assimilated into the post-independence elite, who receives a visit from his old war comrade from a rural area. In *Yonta*, this precipitates an existential crisis and mental breakdown on the part of the neo-bourgeois ex-combatant, placing an inevitable question mark over issues of leadership and ideological direction; in *Flame*, Liberty, though similarly destabilized by Flame's reappearance, struggles with herself and comes to terms with it, making a deliberate choice to accept the past and her old comrade: 'When Flame walked in, all those years I spent alone seemed like death. She was all I had, and yet I was terrified. I wanted to forget the past. Why did she want me now?'

The struggle for Liberty arises from the way women ex-combatants were regarded after the war – as 'loose', if not prostitutes, or as uncontrollable and masculine, with the result that they are 'the most jobless and unmarried group of women in society'.[8] It is clear from the scene in her office, where she is subservient to a male boss, that she has had to undergo a process of reconstruction since the war in order to conform to expectations of appropriate feminine post-war behaviour. The meaning generated by Liberty's decision to accept Flame is that acknowledgement of the past, mutual support and collective action can be the solution to problems of alienation, disillusion and marginalization, and that inequality and prejudice must be fought.

A question that might be asked of *Flame* is 'whose voices do we actually hear?' Since it is palpably *not* a documentary but a fiction feature, they cannot be the voices of 'real' women ex-combatants. Their credibility therefore must rest on the degree to which the women's stories are based on 'real' experience. Since there is no hard evidence, this is extremely difficult to assess, and we are thrown back on a con-textual discursive reading of things like audience reception, research method and the film-maker's intention. How 'realistic' is the narrative from the perspective of a Zimbabwean audience? On what did the film-maker base her narrative and what outcome did she hope for? To begin with the last, Sinclair declared her aim as being: '[t]o realize and remember what a fighting woman does, what that fight does to her and how people look at her afterwards ... Fighting women are my heroes – I admire their strength, their knowledge, their

---

8   From the *Flame* web-site, a quotation from Neka Kazingizi, 'ex-combatant mother of three'. See also the interview with Carine Nyamandwe in *Women of Resilience*: '...my in-laws didn't want a daughter who was a comrade... They wanted him to marry a proper wife. What is a proper wife? People do not understand...They think that because ex-combatants were taught to be harsh and tough, maybe that will always be their way of life.' (12)

physical abilities, and yet they hide their past. I want to remember it.'[9] Sinclair researched the film through interviews with a dozen women over a period of five years, using her skills as a documentary maker to achieve verisimiltude.[10] There were also ex-combatants in the crew and the cast – for example Comrade Chinx. Freedom Nyamubaya's statement in support of the film could also be seen as an endorsement of its historical relevance and accuracy: 'I, Freedom Nyamubaya, was raped and that is the truth. A society which denies the truth cannot move forward.'[11] Though not referring directly to the film, Prudence Uriri's testimony in *Women of Resilience* bears a striking resemblance to the events in *Flame* (74-77). In the absence of any systematic audience research, then, we can still conclude that, for women ex-combatants at least, the film achieves a level of historical accuracy which accords with their own experience of the war.

Another reading is afforded, however, by the angry responses to *Flame* from some male war veterans and press commentators around the time of the film's release. The story of how the print was seized from the editing room by the police and taken away to be scrutinized for subversive or pornographic content, returned and taken hurriedly to South Africa for final editing, ensured that its release would be marked by controversy. Although the script had been seen by the war veterans association before shooting began, it evidently did not represent them or the war in the way they would have wished. According to Comrade Bornwell Chakaodza, Director of Information for the Government of Zimbabwe: 'The film's failure to balance the negative scenes of the freedom fighters with their resilience and values suggests an insidious attempt to make sure future generations will have no sense of their gallantry'.[12] According to Sinclair, the war veterans 'wanted a script that would glorify the war', while she wanted a film from the women's point of view. They therefore mounted a campaign of vilification in the media against her, claiming she was denigrating the war and possibly traitorous. After cutting was finished, she showed the completed film to the war veterans, whose then leader, Chenjerai Hunzvi, threatened to burn down any cinema that tried to show it. Sinclair emphasizes, however, that this was not a unanimous response, and that some of the military men to whom they showed it approved of the film. Moreover, the government and the army gave her support in the making of the film, and the censorship board approved its release. Even so, she herself was personally hounded, with representatives of the Central Intelligence Organization parked outside her house, and a visit from a delegation which tried to implicate her in an anti-government plot. Pressure was also applied to members of the cast, 'but no-one dropped out'.[13]

---

9   From 'Director's Intention' on the *Flame* web-site.

10   Interview with Jane Bryce, Harare 2000.

11   California Newsreel website information on *Flame*, at http://www.newsreel.org.films/flame.htm

12   From the California Newsreel web-site.

13   All details on the seizure of the film and the treatment of Sinclair are from her interview with Jane Bryce, July 2000.

Clearly, this was a struggle over representation, over definitions of heroism, nationalism and history itself. The war veterans' preferred version was articulated in a Zimbabwe newspaper as follows: 'The bare facts regarding the liberation struggle ... are that all the pillaging and raping was done by the colonial regimes' security forces and their agents.' According to the author, Sinclair had completely overlooked 'the big story ... about how the poor peasants were able to stand up to the might and terrorism of the racist minority regime', producing instead 'a work of sabotage ... meant to justify the racist belief that the freedom fighters were terrorists.'[14] A second article a few months later neatly pinpointed what was at stake: 'At the root of this conflict is the question: Who is the guardian of our standards and values?' The author identified 'a lot of white liberals' as self-appointed custodians, and accused the film of reducing the war to 'a pointless exercise in which (the war veterans) are portrayed as villains and not heroes.'[15] Tafataona Mahoso, formerly a lecturer, since elevated to chairman of the Media and Information Commission, in a more measured, but no less oppositional response entitled 'Unwinding the African Dream on African Ground', takes as the basis of his argument the proposition that: 'There is an African cinema, an African identity and an African reconstruction project. Therefore, we cannot afford to be lulled to sleep by pseudo-universalist claims by Euro-Americans and their Third World supporters ...' (Mahoso, 2000: 197).

Like Mhando, Mahoso takes the film to task on the basis of form, specifically, 'the attempt to mix two incompatible approaches: a Hollywood approach based on strict linear perspective; and an African approach based on the circle of mutuality and reciprocity leading to a work of solidarity' (Mahoso, 206). The opposition Hollywood/African should alert us to the latent ideological message in Mahoso's treatise: the idea that there is an irreconcilable difference between Euro-American ('Hollywood') and 'African' narratological approaches, expressive of essential, fixed and unalterable philosophical differences. This bears some looking at, since what it seeks to do is exclude any possibility of dialogue or plurality of perspective, drawing strict boundaries around who may speak and what may be said. Within this formulation, no white person can claim to speak for, or as, an African, since 'the "gaze" on African life which they bring is not African ... It merely uses African bodies in African space ...' (Mahoso, 207). This may look sophisticated, but is in fact no more than a repackaging of the essentialism and Manicheanism that typify dictatorial regimes everywhere. Mahoso's rationalization takes the form of a prescriptive account of the way 'symbolization' – the creation of meaning through language and images – ought to work in Zimbabwe.

At the centre of the controversy is a contestation of the nature of heroism, and how it is to be symbolized. Early in the film, Liberty's words: 'Florence was my hero. Well, I should say my heroine,' implicitly acknowledge the gendered definition of

---

14   From *The Sunday Mail*, February 4, 1996.

15   From *The Sunday Mail*, June 2, 1996.

'hero'. Similarly, towards the end, when Flame asks if the Heroes' Day celebrations aren't for them, she responds: 'No Flame, we're just women.' Mahoso anticipates a gendered critique of his argument by putting forward archetypal female models of heroism: Nehanda, Queen Nzinga and the Queen of Sheba – as part of an 'African' signifying system. Such figures (think of Boadicea, Cleopatra, the Statue of Liberty), safely dehistoricized and distanced from material struggle, are available to be appropriated for nationalist causes the world over (Mahoso, 208). In a recent study of what he calls 'the exhaustion of the patriarchal model of liberation' in Zimbabwe, Horace Campbell points out: 'As in the case of Queen Nzinga of Angola, the history of Mbuya Nehanda, the spirit medium, was mobilized to give authenticity to the dominant party, ZANU (Campbell, 2003: 282)'.[16]

The symbol which, however, signifies the party's true sense of itself and its place in the world, is the cockerel: 'The pre-eminent symbol of maleness ... transformed into a trademark of male valour and fighting capability', used both by Savimbi and Mobutu, before being taken over as the ZANU symbol (ibid.). In *Flame*, on the contrary, the symbol which signifies the aspirations of the women ex-combatants is the red shoes which Florence names as her major ambition in an early scene before she and Nyasha leave for the front. Easy to dismiss as the trivial adornments of a superficial femininity or a consumer driven desire for the benefits of capitalism, the red shoes are in fact a symbol of Flame's fighting spirit. Seen in context, as a rural woman, she is doubly removed from the rewards of liberation so conspicuously enjoyed by the uniformed male leaders in the Heroes' Day parade which closes the film. Campbell informs us that: 'Women constitute the majority of farm workers, 80% of which work the land in the communal areas', and contrasts this with the 'fast track land policies of the Zimbabwean government', which have overwhelmingly benefited male members of the powerful elite (83). We see Flame working the land with a baby on her back before she leaves for the city; once there, she gazes at the red shoes in a shop window, separated not only by glass but by lack of opportunity, recognition and material power. When she finally gets to wear a pair of red shoes – borrowed from Liberty on Heroes' Day – a man misrecognizes her at the bus-stop as an available woman. Flame and Liberty's amused reaction, the complicity of their laughter, signifies their understanding of femininity as masquerade with a potential multiplicity of costumes: from the traditional wrappers they wear in the village, to battle fatigues to smart urban suits. The red shoes, metonymically linked to her liberation name by their colour, symbolize Flame's refusal to accept conventional limitations on what she can accomplish as a woman. In Freedom Nyamubaya's words: 'I'm a freedom fighter, not an ex. Freedom fighting is a culture, and you can't take leave from your culture.'[17]

---

[16] Terence Ranger gives as a further example - the burial of Joshua Nkomo in Heroes' Acre, where his widow was lauded as 'the dear Mother of the Nation'. See Chapter Fifteen of this volume.

[17] At the launch of *Women of Resilience*, Harare, July 2000.

Nyamubaya's words give the lie to Mahoso's further objection to the film for its inauthenticity in the representation of 'true' feminine behaviour. He contends:

> An African woman combatant standing on African ground and accusing her male comrades of raping and abusing her will not fail to make those males recognize her, identify with her, accept her motivation and even thank her for pointing out the abuse within the context of fighting for the liberation of the whole nation, the whole culture, the whole paradigm, even from its own worst weaknesses' (Mahoso, 207).

By now it should be clear that the ideological struggle being waged on the battleground of language and image is between a prescriptive patriarchal power elite and 'ordinary' people – women, workers, anyone not defined as a 'hero'. The according of a burial in Heroes' Acre to selected individuals is palpably a weapon in this war, as evidenced by a recent report on one such burial, in which Michael Hartnack characterizes Mugabe as 'the man with the jam-ladle'. He describes how, delivering a graveside eulogy, the President attacked leaders 'who fear to be complete Africans, hesitate to be in complete solidarity with us', explicitly aligning 'heroism' and 'Africanness' with conformity to ruling party ideology.[18] In such a climate of linguistic and conceptual hegemony, the interpretational politics surrounding *Flame* inevitably become part of a larger contestation over how independence, the liberation war and 'African' identity are to be represented. Terence Ranger addresses this issue in Chapter 15 of the present volume, in which he surveys the wholesale appropriation of history by ZANU(PF) for the purposes of 'patriotism': the way the party's current policies are being dubbed the Third Chimurenga, the equation of history with the liberation war, the synonymy of 'selling-out' with dialogue with whites, the claim to a purity of 'African' culture possessed only by those approved by the party, with the President himself as chief historian. It becomes increasingly clear that Mahoso's attack on *Flame* is simply one more manifestation of his allegiance to a patriarchal revisionist political culture.

Why *Flame* was so peculiarly the subject of attack speaks to the power of film to mobilize consciousness through its multi-layered possibilities of interpretation. As Ranger points out, Zimbabwe is a country in which books have much less effect than radio, TV or the press. Indeed, *Flame* simply continues a dialogue started by, for example, Chenjerai Hove's *Bones* (1988), Shimmer Chinodya's *Harvest of Thorns* (1989) or Yvonne Vera's *Nehanda* (1993) or *Under the Tongue* (1996), as well as the two books of interviews to which this essay refers. The fact that it caused such a furore testifies to the capacity of film to exceed the parameters of a monologic interpretation, and the threat to ruling party ideology of its dissenting voices.

---

18 ZW News Online, 4 December 2003: 'Succession lottery roll-over', by Michael Hartnack.

Chapter 3

Marechera's wordhorde and the scrapiron of war

Annie Gagiano

> 'What if I told you and you wrote it for me?' ... 'I mean my experiences in the Struggle – the fighting, you know.'
>
> ... 'I've never seen a gun in my life, man!'
>
> ... 'Oh, I'll explain it all to you. Tell you everything. All you'll have to do is just write it literature-like.'
>
> ... 'I'm scared', I said simply. (Marechera 1994: 23)

The epigraph above, taken from *Scrapiron Blues* (posthumously published in 1994), expresses something of both the compulsion Marechera seems to have felt to write about the Zimbabwean war of liberation, and the fear he had of possible exploitation of, ventriloquism or condescension (should he do so) towards the actual participants – a complex, ambivalent response. Fully aware that only superb writing can 'short-circuit' the 'slow brain death' of apathy and complacence (Veit-Wild, 1992a: 40-41), he understood also that there had to be a vital connection between experience and expression, such as he perceived in the Robben Island prison poems of Dennis Brutus, published in 1968 as *Letters to Martha* (Marechera, 1992: 210). Marechera knew the need to 'use certain techniques' so as to achieve a 'visionary apprehension of suffering in order to convince the reader that the suffering is unique and meaningful and, at the same time, a universal expression of life' (Marechera, 1992: 211), and yet he was plagued by the sense that 'a developing country doesn't really need a writer like me' (Veit-Wild, 1992a: 34). The deeply wry, parenthetical self-accusation '(Steve Biko died while I was blind drunk in London. Soweto burned while I was sunk in deep thought about an editor's rejection slip.)' (Marechera,1980: 114) by the narrator in *Black Sunlight* seems a deliberate reflection of Marechera's own notoriously 'decadent' lifestyle in Britain (concerned, in his own words, 'only [with] drink and writing' – Veit-Wild and Chennells, 1999: 242). This can be contrasted with the description of his youthful yearning 'to become *part of* the national struggle' in Rhodesia and with his full '*involve*[ment] in the politics at the university [of Rhodesia]' up to his expulsion from it in 1973 (Veit-Wild, 1992a: 19, emphases added).

The persistent, plaguing criticisms (by others) of Marechera as supposedly 'un-African' in his writing, as a self-indulgently effete artist or as lacking in patriotism, are often most searingly expressed by the writer himself – 'He spoke of himself collecting prizes in London while his people were being killed in Zimbabwe' (Veit-Wild, 1992a: 189). A parallel may be traced in this respect between Marechera and another Southern African 'Oxford exile', the poet Arthur Nortje. What Marechera refers to as 'the terrible anxieties of exile' (Marechera, 1984a: 65) – a combination of 'survivor's guilt', a sense of dereliction of political duty, nostalgia for home, and alienation from the immediate 'Western' social context – are probably what Nortje attempted to resolve in the well known concluding lines of his poignant 'Native's Letter': 'for some of us must storm the castles / some define the happening' (Nortje, 2000: 361).[1]

What complicated Marechera's position (in a different way than Nortje's) was his inability to see liberation, and the possible achievements of a war of liberation, simplistically. It is this quality of complex vision that Marechera so memorably expressed in the exhortation demanding that 'black fire' must come, neither Eurocentrically 'from the rhyme & reason of England', nor in a doctrinaire Africanist manner 'from the negritude that negroed us', but should arise 'from what within you / Fused goals with guns & created citizens instead of slaves' (Marechera, 1992: 195). While he felt the pressure from his 'detractors … [who] associated him with an intellectual conservatism in spite of his revolutionary … subjects' (Marechera, 1980: 111),[2] he was perhaps always 'more preoccupied by individual liberty than by national liberation, the defence of those who cannot defend themselves' (quoted in Caute, 1991: 97). Nhamo Mhiripiri refers to Marechera's 'sensitiv[ity] to all forms of violence' (Veit-Wild and Chennells, 1999: 152), yet Marechera was clearly also aware of the inevitability of the liberation war, and could write about it with a combination of pride and a sense of poignancy. In what follows, Marechera's responses to the Chimurenga, as manifested in different texts, are exemplified and analysed by shifting from text to text, in turn.

---

[1] Shortly before his death (probably by suicide) in Oxford, Nortje wrote a poem titled 'Dead Roots', in which he implicitly contrasts youthful stone-throwing protest with the sense of a receding, perhaps defeated political cause by indicating how exile has detached him from the leaders of the South African liberation struggle: 'There were the stones wherewith / sparks were struck against the asphalt: / memory of my youth, / how they seem almost ancestral / totems that inhabit dreams / carved faces now uncarvable. // They are dead igneous / breaking rock / on Robben Eiland, / and I myself have lost / sight of the long night fire.' (Nortje, 2000: 391-92) – see also my chapter, 'Concepts of Exile in the Poetry of Arthur Nortje' in the collection *Arthur Nortje: Poet and South African* (eds, McLuckie and Tyler, Unisa Press, forthcoming).

[2] These lines evoke the experience of the poet Nick, a minor character in *Black Sunlight*, but it is difficult to overlook that this description closely resembles an aspect of Marechera's own experience, particularly after his return to Zimbabwe. Compare 'We do not even have to interrogate you. We just know you're not one of us' from Part Two (Prologue) of *Mindblast*, as well as the reference to 'my ideal reader, the real drunk, with no... chip on his shoulder about "The Struggle" ...giving all... to the black electricity of his inner nerves' in the Journal Section of the same text (Marechera, 1984: 54; 121).

I want to suggest that one of the earliest (published) manifestations of this complex response to the liberation war occurs in the novella 'House of Hunger' (Marechera, 1978), on pp. 60-69 of the eponymous collection. Here the narrator gives us, in the figures of the schoolboys Stephen and Edmund, a clear distinction between a loud-mouthed Africanism (embodied in Stephen) on the one hand, and true courage and loyalty (embodied in Edmund), on the other. It is Stephen who 'had appropriated ... Nkrumah, Kaunda, Che, Castro, Stalin, Mao, Kennedy, Nyerere' (63) – a ridiculous hotch-potch that reveals both his stupidity and his dishonesty – whereas Edmund 'refused to have anything to do with our student armchair politics' (60). Whilst Stephen 'was an avid reader of the Heinemann African Writers Series' (63), Edmund 'could not read enough of Gogol' (61). When Stephen pulps Edmund in a schoolyard fight after insulting his mother, the bully reappears with a big bloodstain on his shirt, resembling 'a map of Rhodesia' (65). Yet it is the pathetic Edmund who (later) is shown on a photograph, 'erect' (albeit 'morosely' so), as 'sole survivor' among 'twenty-two dead guerrillas laid out for display' – and for purposes of political intimidation – by the Smith regime. The contrast between the two youths is carefully contrived to indicate Edmund's understated and self-sacrificial patriotism and to allow it in its irony to show up the shallow and suspect claims of the braggart 'strong-man', Stephen. (Edmund in his puny physique and in his literary tastes is also evidently linked with the Marechera-type narrator, who is constantly getting beaten up.)

Interestingly, Marechera in this text also includes a brief but sympathetic portrayal of a white conscript ('then the military got hold of him' – Marechera, 1978: 69), Richter. This youth is something of an artist (his 'word-drawings' are referred to), but his wartime experience – of 'atrocities he had either witnessed or taken part in, in the operational area' – destroys him psychologically; he is afterwards 'cold, white, as though already dead' and dies physically, either by suicide or through a despairing carelessness, 'crunched to a stain by a train' (Marechera, 1978: 69). Marechera's portrayal of these three youths presents something of a social spectrum of Zimbabwe in the early stages of the war.

The poetry collected in *Cemetery of Mind* (Marechera, 1992) is the next text to be considered. It is worth noting that in this form Marechera gives clearer utterance to his Zimbabwean loyalty (as distinct from narrowly understood nationalism, or patriotism) than in most of his prose works. In an early poem in this collection, tellingly titled 'Pledging My Soul' (Marechera, 1992: 6), the speaker expresses a lover-like commitment to his country, conveyed in the sexualised evocation of the Zimbabwean landscape (in the first stanza). The second (final) stanza in somewhat stilted diction refers to the speaker's later 'exile[d]' and distanced condition, a position from which he offers, or yearns (the expression 'shall I not ... Shall I not' is ambiguous on this point) to return in order to liberate the beloved land by 'rout[ing]' his 'enemies' and 'bind[ing] the wicked husbandmen' (both the latter expressions being recognizable expressions of detestation against colonial rule and settler occupation in Rhodesia). A much later poem that links interestingly with this rather juvenile composition is called 'My skin is the map' (Marechera, 1992: 161). In this poem, there is again an alignment, even a physical identity between the speaker and his country, but that country is (still) no more than a merely *imagined* community – the opening lines read: 'My skin is the map / Of a country beyond thought.' As in many other places scattered through his writings, Marechera here expresses his troubled, 'scar[red]' commitment to Zimbabwe through an allusion to the landscape of his childhood – 'the rivers / The valleys, the mountains of Lesapi' are, to the speaker, the 'blood and muscle' of his 'broken heart.' Expressing simultaneously his visceral identification with the country (or at least the region) of his birth, and a yearning – though perhaps somewhat baffled – love for it, this late poem has a distinct poignancy: it may well double as a love poem to a human beloved.

Reflections of the war's beginnings, when 'The settler's placid houseboy / Turned into deadly guerrilla', occur in 'Throne of Bayonets' (actually a post-independence text), with its sneering reference to the UDI Prime Minister as 'a certain blacksmith' (Marechera, 1992: 55). Another poem which looks back to the outbreak of the war tells of 'Ninety years of pure white blood / Turning black at the smouldering / Edge of reconciliation, revenge, / And reprisal' (Marechera, 1992: 79). Even Marechera's earliest verses resist glorification of war or an ideological anti-white triumphalism when he makes references to this conflict. In the first of the collected poems, ironically titled 'Liberty', the speaker focuses in fascinated horror on the mutual bestialisation of opposing parties engaging in deadly conflict – there is no trace of a simplistic binary heroisation of the resistance fighters versus a vilification of the settler forces in the final four lines, which refer to 'Two men now two killers / settling the difference of their separate / ideologies, but each now alone / bent on his prey'. Yet the initial image in the poem, portraying the destructive effects of storms (in nature), fearfully acknowledges the dreadful inevitability of violence.[3] Not only the actual atrocities such as the brutal extermination of communities, but the bleak no-man's land of the war years, are caught in the image of 'that unmarked tomb Zimbabwe' (in the poem 'Without' – Marechera, 1992: 28).

As Dirk Klopper suggests in his essay on 'Throne of Bayonets' (Veit-Wild and Chennells, 1999: 121-35), Marechera in this later, lengthy poem shows a particular concern with Zimbabwe's war veterans (see Marechera, 1992: 35-56). He senses their 'battered souls' and their 'wrecked hopes', the harvest of thorns that many of those who made heroic sacrifices during the war came home to. The speaker (whose voice resembles Marechera's own in its indignation and unrestrained fierceness) mourns the 'Long lost friends whom the struggle buried'. In this poem Marechera explicitly castigates the profiteers of the post-colonial state – 'Finger-fat delusions wash themselves / in the dish of dollars / And proceed to eat liberation's sadza and stew' – while the *povo* starve (Marechera, 1992: 35; 40; 44). Indeed, the 'Oracle of

---

3   Nhamo Mhiripiri's reading of the poem accords largely with my own (see Veit-Wild and Chennells, 1999: 152-53). Mhiripiri stresses correctly that 'there are no *direct* allusions to the historic context' of the eruption of settler-native conflict in this poem (emphasis added).

the Povo' (finely analysed by Flora Veit-Wild – see Veit-Wild and Chennells, 1999: 96-8) both sadly and fiercely describes the 'out-of-work heroes / Who yesterday a country won / And today poverty tasted' (Marechera, 1992: 67). More explicitly angry (indeed, expressive of a profound moral and political wrath) are Marechera's lines from the poem 'Raid!' (Marechera, 1992: 89):

> Yes it is independence
> But your homelessness is a great crime
> ...
> Yes we have Uhuru
> Your poverty does not make prostitution legal

The poems cited and linked above make it clear that Marechera's engagement with the liberation war – though mainly from abroad (for the duration) and from his recognition of its after-effects (after his return) – is the sign of a writer intensely concerned with the well-being of his own society. It is this loyalty, necessarily critical of the forms of failure and oppression that he saw in Zimbabwe, which emanates undeniably from (any careful reading of) his work. *Complex* loyalty of this kind of course often gets mistaken for an uninvolved, anarchistic position by those (like the bully Stephen in 'House of Hunger') who desire sloganeering proclamations of patriotism from fellow-Africans.[4] Marechera himself best sums up the profoundly felt commitment that drove him to write of the war (and of Rhodesia and Zimbabwe) in the well known lines stating 'I am against everything / Against war and those against / War. Against whatever diminishes / Th'individual's blind impulse' (Marechera, 1992: 59).

The poems, as discussed, bear many traces of Marechera's engagement with various aspects and stages of the war. Both *The Black Insider* (Marechera, 1990) and *Black Sunlight* (1980) are futuristic evocations of war, the latter mostly in the form of urban terrorism (in which the members of an anarchistic group wage war on society, mainly through bombings and assassinations), whereas *The Black Insider* is set within the context of a collapsing society beset not only by the plague and street terrorism but by full-scale war. Even though the group of refugees ensconced in the ruined Faculty of Arts is mainly or initially pacifist, they are shown at the end of the novel preparing to defend themselves against an army of invaders. One interesting point is that the invading soldiers are 'face-blackened paratroopers' (Marechera, 1990: 115) – a detail that unmistakably recalls the practice of Smith's soldiers during the liberation war.

In the prose pieces and plays written by Marechera after his return to Zimbabwe, collected and published posthumously as *Scrapiron Blues* (Marechera, 1994), the author wanted to reflect on what it is to be Zimbabwean today. A majority of these

---

4   Cf. the Nigerian critic Juliet Okonkwo's declaration that the continent 'cannot afford the luxury of such distorted and self-destructive "sophistication" from her writers' (Okwonkwo, 1981: 91).

pieces is set in a post-independence Zimbabwe (or in some indeterminable time), but even so they seem somehow shadowed by the war period, or carry explicit references to it. Marechera felt that there was something both evasive and repressive about the official discouragement, or direct repression of war experiences – particularly those of ex-combatants (Veit-Wild, 1992a: 45; 336). This may very well have been the lever that brought him to address and (in a minority of the pieces in the *Scrapiron* collection) evoke experiences of the war itself. Anything officially 'not to be spoken of', or ignored by the public voice of the post-war society, was precisely what needed to be articulated and challenged – if psychological and communal health were to be seriously aspired to. 'It is a superhuman task, trying to wash away all that blood. But it is only the insurmountable that brings out of us our monumental origin. ... [The ex-combatant Tony's 'quest' is] To *exorcise out of* his ... body the rippling incredible Power ...' (Marechera, 1994: 10, emphasis added). The pun on 'exercise' in this excerpt indicates Marechera's notion that, to become 'fit' and healthy, individuals and society need to achieve a detachment from war's terrible power preoccupations. The term 'exorcise' itself again emphasizes the contaminating, desecrating influence of war.

Tony, of course, is one of Marechera's examples of a war-traumatized individual. He is shown compulsively, regularly, intermittently scrubbing the walls of his apartment, which he (nightmarishly) sees as 'gory'. His relatives and friends 'try and convince Tony that, because he had been part of the thing called the Struggle, he was under a curse.' Their intended method of healing is 'to take him "home" and engineer him with the spirits' – a treatment Tony forcefully resists as both he and Jane (his partner) see it as suspect, merely concocted by these 'sulky, yet sharp-eyed' people to 'get something out of' them. Tony scares them off by 'suggest[ing] that they [need] a wash like the walls' do – not only a discouragement to would-be parasitical relatives, but an insistence (I believe) that *everyone* in a war-ravaged society is bloodied and soiled, in need of cleansing (Marechera, 1994: 14).

For her part, Jane 'hunger[s] for the time when the spill of blood and the crump of bombs would have been wiped off the face of the countryside and the streets' (Marechera, 1994: 14-15). Although Jane has only 'seen the pictures ... [of] massacres ... dying sons and slogans ... [and] vivid hatreds' – these 'nightmares of blood and mutilation' – they are, to her, a 'terrible *and tangible* ... past .. [lying] in ambush ... [and] bar[ing] its teeth', like a soldier unable to accept demobilization, bestialised beyond redemption (Marechera,1994: 14, emphasis added).

The intense feelings of these two sensitive individuals are contrasted with what the narrator perceives as the general Hararean 'elaborate hollowness ... [which] paralyse[s]' even the writers (Marechera, 1994: 26). He intersperses the pieces depicting Tony and Jane's life with a number of others, in which he depicts the narrator's and his associates' aimless lives. The narrator of the 'Tony Fights Tonight – Pub Stories' sequence, himself a Marechera-type writer in his sardonic attitude and frequently surreal perspective, is connected with Tony in that they are both plagued by red ants that seem to symbolise a nagging sense of guilt.

The narrator, however, has a neurotic habit of '*idly* scratching off the back of [his] hand the dead skin that had appeared [the previous] night' and this flaking, 'dead skin [has] … an *Ian Smith* in it' (Marechera, 1994: 3, emphasis added) – an association that (again) sets him off from those like Tony and Jane who are deeply suffering the consequences of the war. Passivity and idle chatter (illustrated in the series of funny pub stories) make no contribution to the restitution or regeneration of the damaged society.

Marechera's play 'The Alley' (1994: 33-47) is a darkly surreal work. Like several other pieces in this collection, it illustrates the author's refusal to 'let bygones be bygones', to smooth over the hellish ugliness of wartime deeds. As in the previous story, he uses the symbol of a wall to indicate the repression of those shameful and anguishing memories (compare the presence under the floor of the hut where Hannes and Bolt, in Part Three of 'The Concentration Camp', are holed up). In the alley the two tramps Rhodes (who is black) and Robin (who is white) have an encounter amidst the city's rubbish. In their dialogue, Rhodes's voice is always the more probing, pushing Robin eventually into facing and acknowledging 'what's behind the wall' (1994: 39) – a family history of incest forced by Robin on his young daughter, paralleled (in the second part of the play) with the memory of his war role – as rapist and sadist and racist, insane with power and fear. A former military commander in Smith's army, his mode of speech at that time – 'We'll screw the ancestors out of you … and your God will be the Big White Cock!' (1994: 41) indicates the particular and terrible combination of sexism and racism underpinned by a power-anxiety that Marechera frequently imputes to those who resisted black liberation. The multiple ironies of making 'Rhodes' black *and* the owner of the more probing voice *as well as* the carrier of the link with Marechera himself would not escape most readers.

When Robin surfaces from his (possibly drunken) nightmare, he attempts to re-repress the memory – 'It wasn't like that. We weren't such barbarians' (1994: 43), he claims. But this, the typical censoring of the historical record afterwards, in a 'saner' time, is resisted by Rhodes. Sarcastically and ruthlessly, he lists what is considered 'indecent to remind ourselves of … Bayoneting children, ramming primed grenades into vaginas, bombing cattle and herdboys, shooting schoolboys in so-called crossfire, murdering missionaries and blaming it on the boys.' Rhodes sneers at the repression of unpalatable, 'indecent' yet undeniable memories: 'Nobody talks about the war', no one wants to be reminded of 'genocide at Chimoio … massacres at Nyadzonya … mass executions at Rusape'[5] (1994: 43). Robin is consistently (merely) self-preoccupied, a squirming and contemptible (rather than pitiable) character, whose pettiness is constantly overwhelmed by Rhodes's 'voice of honest indignation'.[6] While Robin asserts that 'the war is over,

---

5   Marechera links himself with the Rhodes figure by mentioning that, like himself, Rhodes grew up in Vengere Township, Rusape (Marechera, 1994: 43).

6   I am here echoing a saying of William Blake's, that 'the voice of honest indignation is the voice of God.'

dead and forgotten', Rhodes persists in reminding him of the 'thousands [who] died like animals ... during the war' (1994: 45). He forces Robin to listen to the *'prolonged thin mournful wail, like a fierce wind ... from a tomb'* that represents the (vainly) silenced voices of the war dead, 'restlessly ... searching for you and me so that again and again we can retell their story, which is not our story' (1994: 46). Dreadfully, but necessarily, 'all those shrieks and cries of mercy' (1994:46) need to be heard.

'The Alley' is a powerful and (in the full sense of the word) *conscientious* piece of work. It deserves recognition for being a kind of cameo Truth and Reconciliation Commission for Zimbabwe, but perhaps, in its surreal and sardonic aspects, it resembles more closely a South African play like Jane Taylor's *Ubu and the Truth Commission* (1998).

Amongst the four 'City Stories' grouped together in *Scrapiron Blues* as such, two show signs of Marechera's awareness of the incursion of war (or its after-effects) into the post-war lives of people. 'The Skin of Loneliness' is an unusually idealistic and somewhat romantic tale, whereas 'Black Damascus Road' is brief and bleak. In the narrative of 'The Skin of Loneliness' one cannot help detecting a form of symbolic wish fulfilment that probably expresses an unassuaged yearning on the author's part – a longing for acceptance. The narrator-figure, who at the end of the tale begins to compose poems under the title '"The Cemetery of Mind"' (1994: 122), is evidently a Marecheran persona, since this title refers intertextually to the author's own poetry. Through a chance encounter between the bookish narrator and a female ex-combatant called Grace, a promising relationship begins. They meet Grace's former commander in the Causerie at Meikles Hotel:

> Mike ... was in his early forties. He laid his arm round my shoulders. 'I've heard of you, young man. I've just returned from Bucharest – one of those aid conferences ...' ... I suddenly remembered him – one of our finest commanders. It made my mouth dry, just to be sitting with him. (1994: 119)

Once the narrator has been 'cleared' (which he furiously resents, but then accepts), the relationship seems set to bloom; Grace uses her demobilization pay to buy the narrator a bookshop, and a life of fairly stable domestic companionship seems to lie ahead for these two.

As an evocation of the aftermath of the war, the suggestion of (personal) peace, prosperity and happiness, even if qualified by various minor ironies, is quite exceptional (within the context of the generally far harsher accounts of the after-workings of war in the *Scrapiron* collection). It must be noted, though, that Marechera does balance the narrative of recovery and achieved harmony with, in particular, Grace's harrowing memories of her wartime experiences and her (invisibly but permanently) damaged body. She was so badly raped when captured by soldiers of the regime during the war that she can never have children (Marechera, 1994: 122). Her dreadful and violence-inducing nightmares (during the earlier part of her cohabitation with the narrator – 1994: 116-17) testify to the psychological violation she has had to endure. A 1984 report citing Marechera's views, is relevant here:

> He notes an eerie silence on biographies of the struggle which don't have 'permission from a higher authority'. Female ex-combatants are the 'worst off', he says. Conspicuous by their absence from anthologies on the struggle or its literature, most have reverted to 'working as secretaries or unofficially as prostitutes. I wonder why there is just total dead silence. Is our own tradition acting as a censorship device as far as women expressing themselves is concerned?' ... (Veit-Wild,1992a: 336)

This is confirmed by what Marechera said in a 1986 interview: 'anyone who has direct experience of the struggle is finding it hard to write about it; it's not permitted' (Veit-Wild, 1992a: 45). The story entitled 'The Skin of Loneliness' may then have been intended to go some way towards recording women soldiers' courage and suffering – and their yearning for a more accommodating post-war society in Zimbabwe.

There is a direct reference to the liberation war in the first paragraph of 'Black Damascus Road', a brief tale of a librarian, a man seemingly 'without regrets, without questions', who returns from the war and resumes his old profession, but kills himself on the day he gets married (1994: 123). The only clear clue to his reasons for this shocking deed is supplied in the opening sentence itself, which refers to the mind of the protagonist (Paul) as that of 'a man who has seen too much too soon' (1994: 123). The story is a sketch, barely two pages long, presented in surreal mode as the narrator imagines himself an invisible presence in Paul (the suicide's) 'ugly', 'mean' and small bachelor room, on his last day of life. His 'despair' is noted by the narrator, a state of mind emblematically represented by the 'barren thorn tree' on a poster on the wall (1994: 124; 123).

The narrator registers: 'I remember many like him' (1994: 124); Paul, then, is representative of the many ex-combatants to whom the war's clinging tentacles and searing memories do *not* permit the entry into the (relative) domestic peace and prosperity that Grace (in the previous story) achieves. It is also worth noting that this very brief story, without employing the 'realistic' style of 'The Skin of Loneliness', is far more convincing (and contains far better writing?) than its more 'hopeful' counterpart.

The lengthy compilation 'The Concentration Camp' (1994: 157-209) consists of eight short pieces in different genres. In an interview quoted by Flora Veit-Wild in her Introduction to *Scrapiron Blues*, Marechera said that his use (in this particular collection of stories) of 'expressionist' as well as 'surrealist techniques' in combination with 'straight narrative' was the result of his desire that these accounts should *not* 'come out as a documentary' (recalling the bit of dialogue I use as this chapter's epigraph, and again confirming Marechera's scrupulous anxiety about speaking 'for' those who had – unlike himself – been 'in' the war). Later in this (quoted) interview Marechera also says: 'So I am not just exploring the concentration camps, I am trying to bring out the psyche, the psychological personality of that particular period, especially from 1978 to the end of 1979, to independence'. He refers to this as 'the most dangerous time' for those in the camps,[7] as at that time paranoia about the war increased among Smith's soldiers (1994: xiv).

Marechera conducted a number of interviews to be able to write these accounts. And yet these pieces are unmistakably 'Marecheran' in their style – brilliantly, harrowingly visceral accounts of bodies in pain and of mental anguish, offset by limpid moments of beauty and peace. In them, Marechera penetrates to the most rotten core of war – its abuse of children. He succeeds unforgettably, here, in communicating his unique combination of 'humane considerations' (Marechera,1980: 68), unsparing exposure of social evil, and hyper-real intensity in the rendition of feelings and experiences.

Two of the eight pieces in 'The Concentration Camp' section of *Scrapiron Blues* (Parts 4 and 5) will not feature in the discussion that follows as they have little overt connection with the theme of this chapter; I shall also deal only briefly with Part 3 which, even though it is confusingly called 'The Camp' like two other pieces, engages a very different setting and cast from the concentration camp stories. It is a surrealist playlet with only two characters, Hannes and Bolt, who are identified as *'deserters from the Bishop's paramilitary Pfumo Revanhu'* (1994: 168).[8] The jitteriness of these two uneasy comrades is not, one soon realizes, the sign merely of anxiety about being punished for desertion, but a far deeper, eery, obscure fear and guilt – its signs are their paranoia: firstly about a monstrously super-human power figure ('the Bishop') by whom they feel hunted and yet (still) bound to, by duty, secondly, about a mocking voice emanating from one man's boots, and thirdly about a presence supposedly under the floor of their claustrophobic shelter. The latter phobia suggests unbearable, repressed memories and conscience challenges which are obscurely associated with a female victim, either betrayed or tortured (or both). Like 'The Alley' (a play with which I have earlier in this chapter linked it), this play ends with a 'melody' that suggests a haunting by unspeakable deeds and silenced voices, refusing to remain repressed.

The two dominant narrative threads in 'The Concentration Camp' are parallel but mostly unlinked accounts of, on the one hand, the victimized families kept captive in a specific concentration camp and, on the other, a group of urban terrorists who (from various motives) conspire and act against those who maintain

---

[7]   The 'protected villages' or 'keeps', in which many black Rhodesians were confined during the later war years, were brutally administered by white and black personnel and were intended to prevent the rural population from aiding those who fought in the liberation war against Prime Minister Ian Smith's forces.

[8]   'Pfumo Revanhu', meaning 'Spear of the People', was the military organization led by Bishop Abel Muzorewa, referred to here as 'The Bishop'. Widely reviled as a pawn of the Smith regime and scorned by the nationalist leaders, he was considered (by the majority) a traitor and a threat to his own people.

settler power in Rhodesia. Only at the end of the last concentration camp piece, just before the second 'City of Anarchists' section (which then concludes the entire sequence of eight pieces) does Marechera explicitly – but surreally – link the children in the camp with the urban revolutionaries (1994: 202), thus emphasizing the common cause that binds them.

Aspects of 'The City of Anarchists' (Part 2) are distinctly comical – the association between Otto, the solemn, inhumanly dedicated but idealistic revolutionary and the two rogues 'Jimmy the Dwarf and thin Larry Long' (1994: 164) is highly amusing. Not because they are not all three ruthless, efficient and deadly men, but because the two scoundrels are clearly profiteers who see in the revolutionary conspiracy just another opportunity to make money and to satisfy their callous taste in entertainment. They posture as committed comrades, raising toasts 'To the revolution!' (1994: 164) while their educated associate Otto continues to believe that these cynical social parasites can be taught his non-racial, non-sexist and class-free principles by means (simply) of lucid explanation. 'Altruism did not exist in Jimmy's vocabulary', the narrator dryly remarks (1994: 166).

In the final piece of the sequence of stories, also titled 'The City of Anarchists' (Part 8), Marechera rounds off the collection by depicting the grotesque 'Mister Win-Some-Lose-Some', a military commander in Smith's army (apparently British; perhaps a mercenary). His impenetrable, brutal arrogance makes him an easy target for cajolery by his intermittent sex partner, whom he desires and despises. She is, unbeknownst to him, setting him up for assassination by the revolutionaries – along with a number of other unidentified soldiers frequenting the same pub. Win-Some-Lose-Some sees himself (self-glorifyingly and highly absurdly) as 'defender of civilisation, ... a lean and swarthy Knight of the Frontier ... strafing the heathen hordes', though his overheated aggression ('hurling grenade after grenade') is an accurate self-description (1994: 206). Marechera's poetic justice depicts this man dying (at the end of the story) 'when the whole world erupt[s] inside out of itself' as the anarchists' bomb detonates (1994: 209).[9]

The best writing in *Scrapiron Blues* as a whole, and (to my mind) the finest things Marechera wrote about the war are the three sections evoking the lives of the families who endure the brutal concentration camp conditions (Parts 1, 6 and 7 of this section of the text). Because of Marechera's profound empathy with children's utter helplessness in the face of violent adult power, these pieces (with their concentration on a boy protagonist, Tonderai, and his friend Rudo) achieve a haunting resonance.[10] Utter exposure to danger and complete injustice have to be faced by an eight-year-old boy when he sees the traditional family protector withering under the cruel pressures of the war:

---

[9]   Hannes, the other war sadist who is depicted in the sequence called 'The Concentration Camp', dies similarly, at the end of Part 3, when '*he bursts himself inside out*' (1994: 176).

[10]   Compare Ben Okri's harrowing and remarkable story of children, love and war, 'Laughter Beneath the Bridge' (1986).

His father, Tonderai could see, had been beaten again. One eye was closed and seemed to throb through the fiercely swollen flesh; the other was half open. The right arm was in a rough sling; they had broken it for him the week before. Through the rends in the dirty khaki shirt, Tonderai could see his father's weakening ribcage. How thin, how terribly thin he is, Tonderai thought, watching his father's gaunt bulbous knees perched on the dry maize stalks of his feet. The heels and soles were split in many places. When he looked up at his father's bowed head, he realised in shock that his hair had turned completely white within the last twenty-four hours (1994: 159).

Although Marechera shows us (as in the above passage) 'the beginning of a terrible knowledge' (1994: 160) in the child, he simultaneously evokes Tonderai's innate purity of being, which has something (somehow, perhaps, miraculously) inviolable about it.

This is a child who has been subjected to interrogation methods that included having two of his teeth kicked out and seeing a bayonet held to his mother's throat with the warning that her death would be 'his fault because he was not telling them about his father's "friends"' (1994: 160) – unbearable pressure resulting in the boy's (first?) epileptic fit. On one of the mornings when Tonderai and the other boys from the camp are herding the few remaining cattle of the camp dwellers, they are wantonly strafed by a helicopter of the Rhodesian army, producing 'a panoramic scene of horror' that kills four out of the nine boys. Unforgettably brilliant is Marechera's evocation of the vision of the dazed and wounded boy (ordered to his feet by the same brutal sergeant, a black man who plays up to the dreadful white camp commandant):

His eyes were coming into focus, but it was as if he was seeing the whole world through a thin screen of fresh blood. ... He looked up into the sergeant's face. All the darkening twilight of the universe was streaming into the sky from a point at the back of the sergeant's head. Getting darker and darker, minute by minute, month after month, year after year. Century after century (1994: 161).

The writing in this emblematic confrontation between victimized innocence and brutal power is more than empathetic – it is visionary. It shows the true face of war to be, not the conflict between roughly equal and armed adult men, but the unequal encounter between ruthless brutalisers and the harmless, tender lives they attack and destroy.

Yet Marechera balances that terrible, *learning* look of the boy (at the sergeant's face) with the 'strange sweetness' which flows from face to face as the girl Rudo, Tonderai's five-year-old friend, comes to sit with him, holding his hand, after his return home. Somehow surviving the dreadful imminence of destruction, their childish love functions as a guarantor of hope and endurance ('the two of them would never die' – 163). Especially poignant in that context is the fact that the name 'Rudo' means 'love', and that 'tonderai' is the plural imperative of the word 'to remember' in Shona – together supporting one of Marechera's underlying themes, that remembering the personal, familial and national past is an act of love. This is the very opposite of a lyingly sentimental moralisation (of the 'love conquers all' variety) – for here in the camp, 'death was everywhere' and 'affection ... a double-edged sword' (1994: 163).[11]

Part 6 is a very brief section of not more than two-and-a-half pages. In it, Marechera describes a period much closer to the end of the Second Chimurenga – when even the awful bullies of the camp begin to seem 'like monstrous images in a slowly fading photograph' (1994: 194). Although they sense that the end of their ordeal is in sight, terrible danger remains – Tonderai earnestly warns Rudo to 'lie still ... very tight with the ground' in the event of an attack – which comes by the end of this piece as the adults' 'horrible game' of war goes into its final rounds (1994: 194, 195). The birth of hope is beautifully emblematised by Marechera in this piece through his description of an experience of the herdboys (Tonderai and his remaining four friends). This description, given in the first part of the story, prefigures the dawning of hope among the camp's inmates. It shows the boys first satisfying their hunger because their hunting skills have improved, and then succeeding in killing a snake without any adult assistance. The snake (subtly suggesting evil power, but very real to these boys) is 'overcome' by their combined assault. As they succeed in destroying the threat, the boys feel (in a wonderful image of resurgent life and hope) 'a merriment beginning to bubble in their bellies' as, 'through tears of laughter', they launch their joyous shout: 'WE DID IT!' (1994: 193).

Marechera is a delicate, symphonic orchestrator of mood. In the next piece (Part 7: 'Tonderai's Father Reflects') he resumes a more tragic perspective. It opens with a long poem invoking the speaker's 'ship, The Wordhorde', which is also his 'burial ship'(1994: 195). It is hard not to sense Marechera's own presence, or voice, within this poem, with its reference to a 'stuttering tongue' (like the author's own), and in the question he poses (resembling the alternatives articulated in the Arthur Nortje poem quoted at the beginning of this chapter): 'To fight the fight / Or from sideline / Sound its progress' is contrasted with a role of mere imperviousness and ensconced power: 'Or from the tower / Merely note its screaming / Fiery wake?' (1994: 196). It does seem as though the author may, here, be recording a poignantly subtle plea for recognition of the fact that he *participated* in the struggle – *through* the courageous and enduring act of writing. His effortful verbal art is likened to the shipwright's, who works the 'tough hardwood' material to bring the craft itself, 'The Wordhorde', into being – serving simultaneously as the author's 'burial ship' or testament, and as the ark-like container in which the life and sufferings of the present can be preserved to sail out of disaster into the future (1994: 195-8). Perhaps Marechera, too, should be

---

11 For a discussion of very different constructions of wartime childhood, see Chapter 8 of this volume.

seen as 'Tonderai's Father' – the progenitor of memory – along with Mr Murehwa: the writer, too, is dying, leaving a testament of commemoration, and becoming (thus) one of the Zimbabwean ancestral spirits.

But the piece shifts (after the main part of the poem) into what is unambiguously the boy's biological father's mind while he undergoes yet another bout of torture. Elaine Scarry has noted that 'War and torture have the same two targets, a people and its civilization' (Scarry, 1985: 61). The reductive effect of the deliberately inflicted pain leaves Mr Murehwa 'bawling like a tormented child', but deep inside himself holding on to a loyalty, to gain the 'comrades time to get away.' His heroism is thus implied, and a new stanza of the poem then confirms that one so 'purified by fire' is given a burial befitting his moral and political stature in the 'ship' that is called the Wordhorde (1994: 198).

Marechera's writing acknowledges the 'breaking' of the torture victim's body and the inevitable 'breaking down' of his spirit – representing and commemorating the many victims of such treatment during the Chimurenga period. Mr Murehwa suffers (different forms of) torture on several occasions. Remarkably, he learns from these experiences that pain itself can generate a resistant counter-energy (to the torturers' force) – 'It is one thing to hate only with the mind; when the body physically hates, that is something else' – and so he resolves, by means of this hatred, to become a historian and witness for his people: 'To remember every detail of this gross and evil time' (1994: 200).

The above quotation is my final example of Marechera's engagement with the liberation war. It succinctly expresses many of the points I have been making about the nature of this engagement. Presumably the act of remembering the war period can by now be seen to involve not only those who actually went through the experiences, but also those who (most memorably) recorded them. The vividly detailed quality of Marechera's 're-memory' (to adapt the expression from Toni Morrison's *Beloved*) is the sign of his listener's, historian's fidelity to what the voices of war survivors – and the echoes in those voices – must have told him, producing descriptions which, through his brilliant and truthful re-imagining, became the texts that have been touched on in this chapter.

Another writer of war said of another terrible time (World War One) that its poetry should 'not [speak] about heroes ... Nor ... about deeds, or lands, nor anything about glory, ... or power except War'; noting that 'the Poetry is in the pity'. Wilfred Owen's well-known injunction, that 'the true Poets must be truthful' (Owen, 1968: 31), was stunningly and honourably fulfilled – for another time, on another continent – by Dambudzo Marechera.

Part II.

Questions of lack and language

Chapter 4

Against the corruption of language: the poetry of Chenjerai Hove

Caroline Rooney

This chapter will begin with a consideration of the political essays of Chenjerai Hove, collected in *Palaver Finish* (2002), with regard to their concern with a pervasive corruption of language as instrumental in the undermining of democracy. It will then proceed to explore how a consciousness of this predicament may be reflected in the poetics of two volumes of Hove's poetry, *Red Hills of Home* (1985) and *Rainbows in the Dust* (1998). Here, an attempt will be made to trace a movement in Hove's poetry: from the satirical stagings of empty performativity (conceived of as a response to the failures of decolonisation), to the paradoxical statements and withheld speech - enacted as forms of resistance to the unspeakable dimensions of a socio-political crisis.

In the course of this reading, I will be drawing provisionally on theorizations of authoritarianism as developed by Theodor Adorno and Frantz Fanon, particularly with respect to the former's analysis of the erosion of democracy as dependent on a manipulation of language. An attempt to refine the critique-in-process will be offered in conclusion.

I.

Palaver Finish. The title itself says everything concerning the frustration with voluble yet meaningless deliberations, the failure of effective action in the midst of crisis, the lack of political and economic accountability, the over-determined cessations of dialogue, negotiation, and all verbal exchange, with physical violence as often the cause or effect. In the title piece, 'Palaver Finish', the phrase 'palaver finish' acts as a frequently repeated refrain that punctuates a dramatic monologue so as to mark the many ways in which, and occasions on which, words critically fail in the context of modern Zimbabwe. More specifically, the monologue dramatizes in a colloquial manner the various experiences and resultant perspectives of an ordinary worker in his encounters with the educated elite, and a biting and spirited facticity is shown to tricksterishly outwit the traders in words and blows, for example, as follows:

I go talk free free. De man want give me punch on my face [...]
'Me, I understand politics,' de man go say.
'Me live politics' I go say.
Palaver finish. (2002: 28)

The term 'palaver' comes from the Portuguese for 'word', *palavra*, where the word acts as a sign of both verbal and economic exchange, particularly in a colonial context, as the OED definition indicates:

> **palaver** *1. n. conference, (prolonged) discussion, esp. (Hist.) between African or other natives and traders etc.; profuse or idle talk; cajolery; (sl.) affair, business. 2. v.i. talk profusely. 3. v.t. flatter, wheedle. [f. Port. palavra word f. L (as PARABLE)]*

What is of interest in this definition for what is to come is the vague implication of a shift from a spiritual register, the religious word as sign of truth, to an economic one, implying a reification of language, where words are given as a wasting or waste of time or as merely a means of procuring a favourable predisposition to whatever the real deal might eventually turn out to be. It is ineffectual palaver or idle talk that is further the target of Hove's essay, 'Party Symbols', in which he writes: 'The problem that we face in Zimbabwe is one of small-talk. No one is ashamed of talking nonsense at a time when we need serious argument and debate.' (2002: 30) In the same essay, the 'Untruth upon untruth' of African politicians is denounced along with the censorships of the ruling party in Zimbabwe. Then, in 'Collapse of Law: Collapse of Conscience', written on the occasion of the Abuja agreement, Hove offers the following important testimony: 'I believe that corruption begins with the corruption of language. If a senior politician uses vulgar language in public, that is the beginning of corruption [...] Once language degenerates into a vehicle for untruth, people are engulfed in a form of corruption' (2002: 5).

I wish to juxtapose the above statement by Hove with some comments made by Frankfurt School critic, Theodor Adorno, in *The Jargon of Authenticity* (2003). Adorno, like Hove, considers socio-political corruption to derive from a wrong use of language. It should be noted that the terms in which Adorno sets out his argument can be misleading, for he addresses a cult and a jargon of 'authenticity'. For Adorno, the authenticity in question is actually thoroughly *inauthentic* and, in fact, amounts to what Hove would call a corruption of language. Adorno, speaking of 'the dark drives of the [German] intelligensia before 1933', states:

> *The theological addictions of these years have seeped into language [...] [T]he sacred quality of the authentics' talk belongs to the cult of authenticity [...] Prior to any consideration of particular content, this language molds thought. As a consequence, that thought accommodates itself to the goal of subordination even where it aspires to resist that goal. The authority of the absolute is overthrown by absolutised authority (2003: 2-3).*

What is of some use here is the general explanatory value of Adorno's ability to perceive a causal connection between the deployment of a deceitful language of truth (truth become only a jargon of truth) and the slide into authoritarianism. For both Adorno and Hove, a certain manipulation of language is what precedes abuses of power in that language comes to be used in such a way as to set up and sanction the malpractice of authority. Adorno maintains, with the severity of hindsight, that the corruption of language with which he is concerned can come to constitute a linguistic refuge within which: 'evil expresses itself as though it were salvation' (2003: 3).

Hove, reflecting on how an inflammatory use of language can lead to violence, appeals to a sense of shame, and comments: 'Most Zimbabwean politicians are thugs masquerading as our national saviours.' (2002: 40) Apart from the different circumstances being addressed to different ends, the mutual point that arises from this far-flung echo (evil expressing itself *as though* it were *salvation*'; 'thugs *masquerading as* our national *saviours*'), is that it is the reduction of the redemptive to the merely performative, the masquerade, that may allow for its shameless perversion.

There is obviously a considerable gulf between the historical and cultural contexts that Hove and Adorno respectively address: not least, the fact that Adorno is particularly interested in mass complicity with authoritarianism, whilst for Hove, given his historical cirmcumstances, the engagement is with a critically divided nation at odds with a debased – debased because unrealized – rhetoric or jargon of national unity, and its intimidations. Then too, there would be different stakes in the failure to grapple with economic realities, given the incommensurate national and international economic circumstances, where Zimbabwe's economic crisis cannot be divorced from the inequalities of globalization. As far as Adorno's scene of analysis is concerned, the hypocritically pious use of jargon constitutes a false and doomed attempt to re-authenticate a capitalist society that is alienated, reified and highly mechanized. In the dissimiliar case of Zimbabwe, it could be considered that claims to authenticity arise in the first place as a defensible negation of colonialism, which then later come to be singularized and hypostatized in a static and unconvincing manner. That said, there remain a few potentially useful intersections between the critiques of Hove and Adorno, as will be further indicated.[1]

Of evidently closer relevance to Hove's criticisms are Frantz Fanon's far-sighted analyses of the potential failures of post-independence African nations, as will here be noted for their tangential relevance concerning authoritarian propensities. In 'The Pitfalls of National Consciousness', Fanon looks to Latin American countries as exemplifying an emergent African trend in Africa's own period of independence, and observes:

---

[1]   The postcolonial significance of Adorno has been variously deployed elsewhere. See, e.g., Lazarus (1990); Varadharajan (1995); Noyes (2002).

In the same way that the national bourgeoisie conjures away its phase of construction in order to throw itself into the enjoyment of its wealth, in parallel fashion in the institutional sphere it jumps the parliamentary phase and chooses a dictatorship of the national-socialist type [...] In these poor, under-developed countries, where the rule is that the greatest wealth is surrounded by the greatest poverty, the army and the police constitute the pillars of the regime [...] The strength of the police force and the power of the army are proportionate to the stagnation in which the rest of the nation is sunk. (2001: 138)

Fanon claims that this situation arises in states which were semi-colonial during the period of independence, whereby a relatively educated elite betrays a broad-based nationalism, narrowing nationalism to what Fanon calls 'ultra-nationalism', which he sees as prey to chauvinism and forms of racism. He also speaks of the censorship of any dissent and states: 'This party which used to call itself servant of the people [...] hastens to send the people back to their caves.' (2001: 147)[2]

Adorno identifies as one feature of the cult of authenticity that he seeks to clarify, the equation of authenticity with fixity where this becomes a celebration of genuine rootedness. (2003: 39-48) Adorno's identification of this pitfall has been widely disseminated beyond its own context, including in post-colonial critiques, where sufficient attention has not always been paid to the historical contexts.[3]

In 'Rural Teachers, Rural Buses and Violent ZANU(PF)', Hove speaks of the importance of roads and transport for the dissemination of ideas. He writes: 'They [ZANU(PF)] also wish roads had not been constructed to some parts of the country so that everyone would *stay where they have always been*, without having Teacher travelling to and from the city, conveying dangerous new ideas'. (2002: 50, emphasis added) Here, the teacher is a moderniser and mobile purveyor of mobilizations that may lead to protest at the lack of economic amelioration. Hove also writes: 'The bridge does not have to be repaired for the time being so that teacher with his strange ideas, strange clothes and strange new drinks can be kept away from "innocent villagers".' (2002: 51) Insistence on fixity in rural innocence is thus given as a means of securing or attempting to secure subordination, whilst it also serves as a means of justifying economic stagnation. In addition, Hove writes critically of the maltreatment of those deemed to lack authentic rootedness or belonging: 'Corruption begins with the corruption of language. Recently people of foreign origin were called "people without totems" [...] They have no totems and so they will be victimized, or so Zimbabwean political thinking would have it.' (2002: 6-7)

---

2   Patrick Bond and Masimba Manyanya in a recent study, *Zimbabwe's Plunge* (2002), also engage with the prescience of Fanon as regards recent Zimbabwean history.

3   For example, rootedness may be claimed more easily on the part of those usurped or colonized than on the part of those attempting to limit ownership of the land in the name of ethnicity.

What could also be reflected upon regarding the above is the ways in which ruling elites assume an easy identification with the peasantry in their living immediacy. It is as if those elites imagined themselves to be automatically self-actualising, in denial of the psycho-social mediations of identity and power.

This is an attempt to broach the rendering of authority as singular or non-relational and immediate, an authority that has become both automatic and free of constraint. At any rate, Adorno writes of a self-absolutising form of superiority, that of 'people who elect themselves'. (2003: 61) In a more empirically grounded way, Hove addresses an elite arrogating power to itself regardless of appropriate training and experience, where this can involve a literal self-election. Hove writes: 'If a man has never been elected to public office, he should have never been given political power.' (2002: 60) And: 'Surprisingly, some of our ministers, ones who are only too happy to talk about and on behalf of "the people, the *povo*, the masses" don't even have a constituency. They have not even been elected. Such men are often dangerous.' (2002: 61) In this there is the identification of the elite with the immediacy of the masses, by-passing the mechanisms of mediation with the dangerous positing of an assumed collective singularity whereby accountability in relation to the other as indeed other is annulled.

Whereas, as Hove strongly argues, political leadership needs to be granted by the people, in the case of self-election, the people become, as Adorno maintains, the pre-text for 'leadership-in-itself'. A self-sufficient and unquestionable authority then arguably has to maintain itself through 'the vulgar jargon of authenticity' (Adorno, 2003: 71). That is, an inauthentic discourse of authenticity comes to compensate for a lack of democratic legitimation, the jargon courting and coercing commitment to its empty credo. However, it is also the case that this 'vulgar jargon' paves the way for self-aggrandizement in the first place as it facilitates self-election and a predisposition towards authoritarianism. Both Adorno and Hove speak of the use of 'vulgar' language, where the vulgarization in question might be specified and explained as a vulgarization of the sacred, the sacred not so much giving way to mere political sloganeering as being reduced to this, being used in its service. Coincidentally, Adorno speaks of would-be 'authentics' as 'constantly *palavering*' (2003: 26, emphasis added) and indulging in 'idle talk' (2003: 86). Of course, it could easily be maintained that the deployment of ineffectual and/or insincere jargon is widely symptomatic of the political: the focus here is on its usage in the setting in place of authoritarian mechanisms.

One aspect of Adorno's critique of jargon that is undeniably problematic, particularly in the context of an essay that is to address poetry, concerns the fact that it extends to poetic expression more generally. Indeed, he even goes so far as to speak of 'the evil of poetry', where he sees this as pertaining especially to the lyric and poetry in a Romantic vein. Adorno writes: 'The evil, in the neo-romantic lyric, consists in the fitting out of the words with a theological overtone, which is belied by the condition of the lonely and secular subject who is speaking there: theology as ornament.' (2003: 69) Adorno is surely being much too sweeping and extreme in this for you cannot legislate against experiences and expressions of the sacred *per se*, as if they were automatically invalid, and inspired or enthusiastic art is possible in all societies, including largely secular late capitalist ones (Adorno singles out Rilke for attack as well as Hölderlin). Moreover, the fact that some German intellectuals may falsely appropriate a quasi-poetic jargon of the sacred does not mean that lyrical poetry is to blame for its crass misuse or is itself retrospectively rendered necessarily inauthentic. Rather, what is at stake concerns both a capacity to distinguish between the poetic and its suspect and potentially harmful appropriations, and an acknowledgment of different versions and periodizations of cultural and political nationalisms, as will be touched on shortly. In contradistinction to Adorno's mistrust of the poetic, this essay will work towards distinguishing a politicized or politically aware poetry, as is widely to be found in a Southern African context, from a poeticising (sacralising, etc.) of the political, where the former can work against the latter, as I hope to show regarding the work of Hove.[4]

II.

Poetry and, even more so, musical lyrics have clearly played an important part in the forging of a nationalist-revolutionary consciousness in Zimbabwe.[5] An epoch-marking poetry collection in this respect is *And Now the Poets Speak*, published in 1981, which describes itself as: 'Poems inspired by the struggle for Zimbabwe'. I wish to approach Hove's poetry through this anthology both as a means of contextualising his work and as a means of speculating about the transition from this anthology's modes of consciousness into the ensuing state of the corruption of language, as posited by Hove's essays.

The work in *And Now the Poets Speak* is divided into sections so as to convey a sense of successive stages of the revolutionary struggle. The final section, 'And the People Celebrate', marks the coming of independence, and these poems are particularly marked by appeals to the sacred, movingly in some instances and slightly ominously in others, as the discussion of a few instances might convey.

Chris Magadza's 'The Return' evokes Ezra Pound's 'The Return', whether intentionally or not is hard to ascertain. In Pound's poem, heroic ancestors – quasi-Ancient Greek warriors – are mythically pictured as making a tentative return, where the return would seem to be of proudly untamed instinctive being for, presumably, mechanized late-capitalist man. (1977: 39) In contradistinction to this, Magadza's 'The Return' concerns no merely mythical return but the imagining of the re-emergence of actual guerillas from their hideouts with the coming of independence:

---

4   Hove distinguishes between a shamelessly pious hypocrisy on the part of political leaders and a true sense of reverence for 'the natural world, the heavens, humanity'. (2002: 81)

5   See, especially, Turino (2000) for the role of music.

And as the dying spirit
Faded from the glades
They came down from the mountain,
Bearing arms on their shoulders
And palm branches in their hands [...] (Kadhani and Zimunya, 1981, p. 154)

Whilst Pound's scene of return is just phantasmatic and nostalgically archaic, Magadza's poem is poised on intersections between actual historical event, living legend and a becoming mythical. Its natural imagery of mist is also figuratively spectral, where the dying spirit of colonialism is echoingly depicted in aptly slightly archaic English as having 'Faded from the glades'. The guerillas are accorded an aura by the historical moment – 'more than mortals/ They seemed' – whilst their fallen comrades are heroically redeemed: 'Yet not in death they lie/ But in immortal love of Nehanda'. The poem serves to offer a blending of heritages, not only the re-moulding of European modernist poetry through the event of an African contextualization but also the bringing together of different spiritual legacies in a laying down of arms, for not only are there references to Nehanda and Chaminuka ('primordial priest'), but the poem ends with a hymn-like chorus in Latin conferring a benediction of *'lux perpetua'*, eternal light. This poem conveys a sense of being true to the momentous occasion of its composition.

Prior to the poems marking independence in the anthology, there is a section of 'Tributes' in which Hove has a poem, 'Death of a Soldier'. Whilst a number of the tributes celebrate the heroism of sacrifice, Hove's poem strikes a dramatically different note as this stanza evidences:

He died in summer greens, and mud,
Emmeshed, bathed in sorrow
Of stinking unsheltered nature
Caged in open skies.
Nothing romantic: I saw him
Flooded with christened hate
And fouled with justice and dread
Sinking into piggish death
As at butcher's. (Kadhani and Zimunya, 1981: 135)

'Nothing romantic.' Indeed, this poem refuses to romanticize or redeem the sacrifice of life, the reality of a brutal loss which may not be ultimately hallowed: 'Which the living shall scorn.' The poem is clear in its ambivalences. Nature is given as fertile but indifferent to the deaths that 'manure' it (the term is the poem's), and given as stifling rather than liberating. Death is not here collectivized even as it is as anonymous as that of an animal. The 'christened hate' is suggestive of a spirituality turned destructive: 'fouled with justice'. And yet there is a certain tenderness in the poem's unflinchingness; its refusal to falsify and forsake the destitution of the soldier in the nature of his death and its refusal to pacify the consciences of the living with the expected platitudes of noble sacrifice.

Whilst writers in the anthology come from a range of backgrounds, one of the poet-politicians included in the anthology is Canaan Banana, and his poem 'Together' accompanies the ideology of reconciliation launched at independence. Placed alongside Hove's 'Death of a Soldier', it can sound too hastily generalized, as these lines may indicate:

The lives laid down in lonely spots
and the crimson blood shed on thirsty land
cry out loud against fragmentation (Kadhani and Zimunya, 1981: 166)

This poem calls for immediate unification ('beckoning Zimbabwe's offspring to solid Nationhood', 'National solidarity pours scorn on tribal mongers'). However, this 'solid solidarity' seems rather empty, as differences are not so much to co-exist but to be eradicated in a predisposition towards a collective singularity, which could only be phantasmatic as a political ideal. This absolutising gesture is continued in the final stanza where the ideal of singularity is sublimed as sacred:

The Obligation of independence challenges one and all
to the solemn duty and sacred vocation of Nationhood:
that sacramental state of being
that includes all and excludes none.

In terminology and tone, this sounds more like a mixture of political speech and religious sermon than a poem, arguably constituting the use of a posture that merely seems poetic for what is not truly poetry. It would certainly be unfair to discredit the sentiments expressed, concerning the hope for national unity, which could well have been genuine at the time of its writing, especially given the very urgent political necessity of combining rival factions. That said, the poem may be seen as possibly marking the beginnings of what later becomes a mere discourse of authenticity, a discourse emptying itself of content, on the way to becoming jargon. This could be accompanied by an ideological failure to distinguish between the tragic sacrifice of life to achieve liberation – 'the lives laid down' – and achieved liberation. That is to say that this poem calls for an attitude of self-surrender *in itself, beyond* the self-sacrifice that leads to the achieved goal of independence, and subordination-in-itself could serve to pave the way for leadership-in-itself. However, retrospective blame cannot be accorded to what is well-intentioned, as this poem does come across as well-intentioned.

Unfortunately, it is not possible to give a more representative account of the dynamic and plurivocal *And Now the Poets Speak*. Nor is it possible to examine here the non-monolithic history of how both missionary culture and African spiritual legacies have played diverse and constructive roles in the variegated emergence of a national consciousness. However, it may be worth making just one point in this context. Very briefly, Terence Ranger shows that Benedict Anderson's account of nationalism emerging through the demotion of sacred languages and the establishment of a vernacular print culture has limited relevance in the history of Rhodesia. Considering the promotion of literacy by missions, Ranger states: 'In the Southern Rhodesian case, the written or printed vernacular functioned in the first place as a sacred language in itself.' (1989: 142) Given that spiritual traditions, both European and African,[6] have been significant in helping to forge a national consciousness prior to independence, the question becomes one of adjustments required in the assumption of secular power, especially regarding the challenges posed by socio-economic inequalities to a discourse of sacred national unity. Mungoshi's moving 'Mwari Komorerai Zimbabwe' serves to point the way forward with lines such as these:

> *Take this day, people of Zimbabwe, take this earth*
> *Knead them and forge a new hopeful song that is all your own*
> *A song that will echo to generations to come*
> *But a song that also remembers the mistakes*
> *and the long bloody road [...]*
> *Only you who have been thirsty*
> *Can tell us what a drop of water is [...] (Kadhani and Zimunya, 19\81, p. 161-2)*

III.

We can now turn to Hove's *Red Hills of Home* (1985). In this volume, Hove's 'You Will Forget' resonates with Mungoshi's poem, as, 'If you stay in comfort too long',

> *You will forget*
> *the thirst, the cracked dusty lips*
> *of the woman in the valley*
> *on her way to the headman who isn't there [...] (1985: 3)*

This poem indicates that the spirit of humanity resides in awareness of the material conditions of existence as affect and afflict us, concerning the basic necessities of labour, life and death. This recognition is shown to motivate and be motivated by the attempts to both bridge and recognize economic and class divides. Along with this taking stock of reality, the poems in *Red Hills of Home* also serve to register the failure to realize the hopes of independence: 'Independence came, / but we still had the noose [...] and the people's bare feet maul the dry earth / till freedom come.' (1985: 35) What accompanies this sense of a loss of momentum is a persistent attention to an empty performativity on the part of members of elite groups, where some of the poems are especially pertinent to the arguments unfolding here.

In 'Professor', the occasion of an academic addressing an assembled crowd is recalled from the perspectives of his disappointed audience. This event is primarily determined by its formal structure rather than there being any content to

---

6   See, further, Gumbo (1995); Lan (1985).

communicate: 'A speech ceremony couldn't start / unless the empty crowd came.' (1985: 29) The 'empty crowd' signifies, firstly, the fact that a critical mass has failed to arrive of its own motivated accord, and also that the constituency and views of the crowd do not matter, as long as an audience or silent majority can be there as a passive performative pre-condition or pre-text, in a posture of subordinate reception. The term 'speech ceremony' is a subtly ironic tonal retort in being so casual and even bored. This scene set, a sombre-suited man pitches up: 'Heavily ploughed brows showing, / he was not a thing of fun / Thatched with a cap'. Although he is no thing of fun, the poet has fun with him offsetting his presumably Western formal attire with imagery relating him to a rural background. The delivered address amounts to nothing but a 'rumble' and 'the emptiness of paper and ink'. His failure is detailed as follows:

> Then simple matters
> of breath and flesh came
> But all the time he shrugged
> a lonely 'I don't know'
> Or another pompous 'I have to read about that.'

All the Professor can perform is an education of no use; learning becomes administration without content or practical purpose but sanctified by scraps of Poetry and Philosophy for effects of depth. (And this?) Hopefully, what emerges is at least satirical humour towards instituting a critique. Hove's poem offsets the pompous Professor with a comic satirical energy, in a manner generally comparable to Christian Schütze's parodic 'Speech for Festive Occasions' which Adorno cites appreciatively as an exposé of inauthentic authenticity: 'In a time like ours, in which the true human values have more than ever to be our innermost concern, a statement is expected from us. I do not wish to present you with a patented solution, but I would merely like to bring up for discussion a series of hot potatoes which do after all face us.' (2003: 72-3)

Hove's Professor, 'shrugging for survival' is similarly bereft of meaningful communication and: 'all were agreed: he was an ox.' In 'The Pitfalls of National Consciousness', Fanon maintains that the ineffectiveness of the newly independent bourgeoisie in the economic field is accompanied by: 'fine-sounding declarations which are devoid of meaning'. (2001: 131)

Hove stages or mimics the performance of the Professor; however, there is obviously a difference in the two kinds of performativity, that of the Professor and that of the poem. The academic performativity that is mocked is mechanically and pedantically ritualistic, whereas the mimicry of it is lively, intelligent, spirited. In this way, the Professor is revealed to be a mere puppet of a wider symbolic order whilst a certain theatrical agency is re-located on the level of the audience. Mockery becomes a means of dissent as a refusal to be complicit. Moreover, what makes for the difference between the two kinds of performativity is that for the Professor, the formality of words is accorded pre-determining abstract priority;

and in the poem, the theatrical or dramatic mediates between language and lived realities or live experiences so that words may have a thinking and/or feeling content.

A similar poem to 'Professor' in *Red Hills of Home* is 'Inaugural Thoughts' whose first line is, tantalisingly, '(Meditations of a State President)' (1985: 50). This poem boldly takes the form of an interior monologue, playing with our fantasies as to what really goes on in the minds of leaders. In this case, as the President is inaugurated he speculates on his eventual personal historical destiny: 'Maybe full military honours / Or a bullet-printed body / Or life abandoned to exile'. His narcissistic preoccupations concern his own survival and the manner in which he will be remembered. It is written:

> I am renewed
> in newly-made headloads of commitment.
> When my old load wears out,
> new legs grow like a lizard's tail.
> Then these treading feet
> continue the same old song
> heard from afar.

Whilst his justification is to be the thinking head of state, he can but maintain himself by a kind of treading on water or air, keeping going without going anywhere. In the striking metaphor of the lizard, he is given as an auto-generating power, but rather impotently where all he generates is 'the same old song'. What is implied is a sheer imperative of recycled endlessness, whereupon he is threatened by the thought of an 'over-due death'. Given that his Presidency consists only of a will to prolong a sovereign existence, thought of a perpetual inauguration, one of absolute selfhood, in death all he can be remembered as is finally dead. The poem ends with the line: 'Only the flies thank him.' Fanon's comments are also relevant to this poem: 'the bourgeoisie in miniature that thrusts itself into the forefront is condemned to mark time, accomplishing nothing.' (2001: 140) From this, we can move on to Hove's 'Child's Parliament'.

In 'Child's Parliament', 'child and fly' have to set up their own parliament, for mother is despairingly destitute, father has abandoned them and the politicians' parliament has nothing to do with them: 'Over the radio / we hear there is a crisis / members of Parliament demand higher salaries, / so there is no debate about us.' (1985: 43) The child's parliament that ensues powerfully satirizes the ineffectual non-democracy of the real parliament (as enacting nothing but the mere formalities of democratic debate), whilst underscoring the reduction of survival of the elective and the elected: 'a thousand million diseases / standing for the Grave constituency. / And figures of population increase / standing for Survival constituency.' (1985: 44) What the children are left to share amounts to only 'parliamentary jargon', on the one hand, and 'pocketfuls of blood', on the other. Words fail them, and us.

In the context of the failure of words and the corruption of language, the obligation of the poet, as poet, is especially to find ways of maintaining the truth-speaking potential of language. As has been touched on, Hove partly manages this through the satire of the jargon of professionals and leaders, and also through a persistent anti-ideological avowal of material conditions. His work also looks to the long tradition of English poetry to consult possible precursors, as his 'The Journey' affirms. (1985: 32-3) In this poem, Pope and Dryden are discarded in favour of Wordsworth whose 'God in nature' is rejected by audiences deeming pantheism 'mad'. A more rigorous Yeats is said to 'bleed', thus feel, his poetry, but this is in the service of patrons, and Frost disappoints with 'public relations poetry'. For the writer of 'The Journey', somewhat drawn to a Romantic tradition, it is Blake who finally emerges as the significant poet:

I read Blake for a poetry partner
his lines mauling my schooled heart.
Shaking the reverend's God by the collar.

In *And Now the Poets Speak*, the editors, Kadhani and Zimunya, compare Hove's talent and 'prophetic vision' to that of Blake. (1981: xv) Why Blake?[7] Regarding the lines cited from 'The Journey', Blake's poetry challenges the 'schooled' (in poetry?) with what is strongly felt, and also challenges the theological institution or those who claim to *own* God: 'reverend's God'. In 'All Religions Are One', Blake writes: 'The voice of one crying in the wilderness [...] No man can think, write or speak from his heart, but he must intend truth. Thus all sects of philosophy are from the Poetic Genius adapted to the weakness of every individual.' (Blake, 2001: 55) Here, poetry does concern a source of authenticity, but it emphatically cannot be conscripted in the service of any one sect, philosophical or religious. Some of Hove's poems are slightly expressive of the frustration of the Blakean voice 'crying in the wilderness' – 'Terms! Terms! Terms! / the terms of my engagement?' (1985: 11) – but the engagement is sustained beyond the commissioning bureaucratic demand for and of 'terms of engagement'. We will now turn to Hove's later collection, *Rainbows in the Dust* (1998).

IV.

This later volume of poetry has a markedly different style from *Red Hills of Home*, in particular, in the direction of a poetics of stark minimalism. Moreover, a number of the poems in the later volume paradoxically articulate a condition of withheld speech. This is partly reflective of writing under the constraints of censorship; beyond this, what is at stake is the defiant use of words in an exacting mediation between the silence of the unsayable and the obligation or desire to speak. This is particularly so in poems such as 'i will not speak', 'silence' and 'words'.

---

[7]   It is a question that Ngara (1990) also debates.

The opening lines of 'words' are: 'i will not waste you / like words in a poem'. (1998: 19) The promise would seem to be immediately broken, both in this utterance and as the poem continues, and yet we are to understand that the poem is not saying what it could say, thus the promise of words remains as such: the whole poem as a promise of the non-expenditure of words. Words are to be saved. The metaphoric scene of this is, in the first instance, apparently economic, where literary critics speak of 'poetic economy'. However, the economising on words points towards their value *beyond* abstract exchange value. On the one hand, the words in a (minimalist) poem are offered as the non-substitutable words, precisely unexchangeable. On the other hand, the words are offered as token signs of what is given as reserved from public circulation. The entire poem reads:

i will not waste you
like words in a poem;
i will not throw you away
like a frightening dream;
i will keep you,
like the feather of a magic bird
in the bank of memories
where treasured tales are kept.

The opening ambiguity of the poem is that the 'you' of the initial line is unspecified, so that it could refer to words or to the value of what cannot be named at all – the words' other. It may be that the linguistic power of conjuring is being referred to, hence the references to magic and memory as that which is in excess of words as signs of exchange. This evocative or demonstrative potential could not be located in any one particular word, or only fetishistically (magic 'feather'), the archival, folkloric bank signifying a collective deposit, the whole of what is most valued, transforming the economic metaphor. It may be our affective capacity that is to be crucially safeguarded, where literature and memory concern our abilities not just to remember but to do so with feeling. I think this poem and other similar poems in the collection are written to safekeep the capacity for love, especially in a context of hatred and brutality increasingly spreading hatred and brutality.

Other poems in the volume also take up an interplay between 'you' and 'words', where 'you' could be both healing love and the loved. In 'casting lots', it is written: 'let me wrestle with injured *words*. / i will come to those closest to *you*: the ones that create faces [...] and chase death from your face'. (1998: 20; emphasis added) A language that has been damaged has yet to reckon with the need to humanize and to heal (as both Adorno and Fanon knew). And here is the poem 'love' in its entirety:

i almost forgot
you lived
as i watched the police baton
printing hatred

on the back of a civilian
protesting food prices. (1998: 41)

So, succinctly: 'love' is 'you', and 'you', 'love'. Whilst hatred is destructively printed on the flesh, love is what lives and may be kept alive in words, whilst being in excess of them. The poem serves as a recollection of this. In 'love', words reach out to the nameless life, the stranger being beaten, and even the namelessness of what makes for life. Thus, the 'you' may be finally nameless, in relation to the words that name: 'i will not waste you / like words in a poem'.

The poems in *Rainbows in the Dust* avoid the use of capitals, of capitalizations. The poem 'tributes' is composed out of the titles of Zimbabwean novels, where the names of their authors are evoked in silence, as the parentheses in the following indicate: 'i have been waiting in the rain [Mungoshi]; / in this dry season: [Mungoshi] / a house of hunger. [Marechera] / no more country dawns / no more city lights: [Zimunya] / it is a non-believer's journey [Nyamfukudza] / where they harvest only thorns [Chinodya] / and nervous conditions. [Dangarembga] / i am on trial for my country, / i, the mourned one. [Samkange]' (1998: 29). Readers of Zimbabwean literature are bound together in these recognitions that take place in silence, where the brief allusive poem manages to conjure a whole literary history and a history in literature, especially of 'rainbows in the dust'.[8]

The poem 'silence' constitutes another articulation of what lies beyond articulation. The poem calls for: 'a minute's silence / for an ancestor who died / with an angry stick in her hand' (1995: 8). This poem, read in silence, could take about a minute to read and so it enacts itself as a minute's silence. But the poem is more than the performative social ritual of a minute's silence in that it has a transformative effect, if you give it its time. It is the stick that is called angry and this is gentle in that it absolves the woman from her anger so that, in a sense, she no longer dies in anger: it may be that the pen as stick takes on itself the anger too. At the same time, in transferring anger to the stick(s), we are able to understand how this anger can no longer be contained. Then a minute's silence is called for again which returns us to the start of the poem: the poem unwrites itself as it also pluralises the call for silent remembrances and accordingly we are asked to think of other ancestors 'whose illiterate hands drew maps / in the hearts of their children'.

The philosopher Jacques Derrida, in answering the question 'What is poetry?' says that a poem is that which makes an appeal to learning by heart: 'The poetic, let us say it, would be that which you desire to learn, but from and of the other, thanks to the other and under dictation, by heart'. (Derrida, 1991: 277) Thus, the poetic may be conceived of in terms of the other's capacity to inspire us, an inspiration that the poem seeks to convey in the encounter of a reader, inspiring him or her in turn. What is being suggested is that this understanding of the poetic is especially

---

[8]   For the double meaning of this title, see the poem 'rainbow (for south africa, 1995)'.

apt for Hove's poem 'silence', where in learning its lesson by heart (concerning the lessons of lifetimes, the anger at the betrayal of what the illiterate hands may yet have inscribed by heart), you would no longer need the words on the page. In silence you will remember 'silence'. Moreover, in learning by heart, the words are non-substitutable (non-exchangeable as in 'words'), even as they are translatable as transferable. This poem suggests a guarding of the poetic as such.

Having cited Blake earlier on the irreducibility of what is sacred to any sect, this may now be cross-referenced with Okara's *The Voice*, where the narrator reflects: 'There may be only one meaning in life and everybody is just groping along in their various ways to achieve it like religion – Christians, Moslems, Animists – all trying to reach God in their various ways. What is he himself trying to reach? For him it has no name. Names bring divisions and divisions, strife. So let it be without a name; let it be nameless'. (1983: 82) Many of the poems in *Rainbows in the Dust* reach towards, or may be written from, a sense of the nameless, the sacred and its barely speakable violations.

But if Hove is Blakean in his prophetic vision, this is not a clairvoyant matter of seeing into the future. Rather it is a case of being able to clearly see and respond to the realities or events of your time as they are happening, where others might be 'drugged', or too conditioned, by history (the phrase 'drugged history' is used in 'silence'). Hove is a truly important Zimbabwean poet, as Ngara (1990) has affirmed, in that his writing both bears witness to its historical moment and makes the precise use of language itself reflect its historical scene of composition. In the later poems it becomes necessary to create some kind of reserve for or of the sacred yet worldly (given a state of jargon coming to accommodate violence). In addition to this reservation in the later poems (which ought not to imply a quietism), there is also in them the move away from the representational and the minimizing of performative enactments,[9] which leads towards a more ostensive mode of address.[10] That is, the aim is to direct us to an object or scene of primary attention rather than to have words substitute for it. This is especially so in 'i will not speak' where the refusal to speak directs our attention to the *existence* of that which is being placed beyond representation.

The historical scene of writing of Hove's work is primarily that of Zimbabwe but it is also that of post-colonial Africa. In 'on the death of ken saro-wiwa (november 10, 1995)', the painful realization is that: 'they were wrong / the negritudes' (1998: 57). The negritudes, which celebrated the beauty and creativity of Africa, are wrong given the 'murderers for rulers' of post-colonial Africa, that is, this Africa not exempt from the dark drives of humanity.

---

[9] The former is both pervasive and explicit, e.g. 'I did not take a picture of you' (1998: 1). The latter may be observed in 'politician i' (45) and 'politician ii' (46).

[10] Gans (1993) proposes the ostensive as an addition to the Austinian categories of constative and performative speech acts, especially when language is used to single out a sacred object of attention for the group. However, Gans advances this in terms of his theory of society based on envy and renunciation in ways that I would take issue with.

V.

One of the underlying concerns of this essay has been the tentative consideration that the absolutising of creativity in terms of a sovereign principle of unity, or in terms of any singularising institution, can be destructive in that it sanctifies power and abolishes mediations. I will now conclude by attempting to briefly address the rather neglected question of historical contextualization, with reference primarily to two separate approaches.

Firstly, what would need far more rigorous examination and consideration is the extent to which a sacralising of the political has been deployed by or in the service of the ruling party in Zimbabwe. As but the merest move in this direction, Terence Ranger's 'The Zimbabwe Elections: A Personal Experience', written in 2002, proves a useful source. Ranger cites Chikowore writing in *The Herald*: 'The armed struggle should serve as the guiding spirit through the presidential elections and even beyond [...] It is the advancement of a historical mission of liberating Zimbabwe'. (2002: 2) Ranger speaks of the media's colonizing and commodifying of 'war-time tragedy for party purposes' as 'cheapening liberation history'. (2002: 3) This seems to me similar to Adorno's and Hove's protests against the vulgarization of language. Dumisani Nkomo satirically critiques ZANU(PF)'s style of nationalist history in these terms: 'Our nationalist leaders have lead us out of Egypt [...] but beyond that they do not have a clue of the location of the promised land.' (2002: 5) Ranger notes: 'The new Anglican Bishop of Harare, Kunonga, told Mugabe that he had put all Christians to shame distributing land: 'Actually you have been more merciful than God Himself!' Baba Nzira announced a prophesy that Mugabe was 'divinely appointed King of Zimbabwe and no man should dare challenge his office.' (2002: 8) And so on.[11]

Whereas Adorno considers the theologisation of the political to be symptomatic of a nostalgia for a lost authenticity, constituting an impossible attempt to re-authenticate a reified, say, 'over-developed' capitalist society, this is not so in Zimbabwe. Rather, the post-independence political appeal to the sacred concerns an attempt to distract from the failure to confront economic under-development, in terms of both internal and external inequalities, and the failure to move from nationalism into a more grounded, necessarily administrative politics. Fanon states that the leader, 'incapable of urging the people to a concrete task' is seen to be constantly 'reassessing the history of independence and recalling the sacred unity of the struggle for liberation. The leader [...] asks the people to fall back into the past and to become drunk on the remembrance of the epoch which lead up to independence.' (2001: 135) In 'hymn', Hove writes: 'a hymn wafts through the cold air / a groan, hungry-grown encounters this hymn [...] / battle of the hymn and the groan / may the lord be impressed.' (1998: 16) And, in 'creed': 'refuse to wear the creed of death' (1998: 7).

---

11   It should also be noted that Ranger gives examples of church opposition to the corruption and violence in Zimbabwe.

In *Absolutely Postcolonial*, Peter Hallward defines the post-colonial absolute in terms of a creative singularity: 'the postcolonial as subjective, singular and non-relational'. And of this singularity, he writes:

> The singular creates the medium of its own substantial existence or expression. The singularity of a Creator-god provides the concept with its exemplary form [...] A similar logic helps legitimate the expansion of the contemporary multinational market, the all-inclusive market of global capital [...] Once the confrontational class-relational approach is pushed aside [...] the market begins to look like a fundamentally singular institution – singular in the sense that it is neither specific to any particular place nor constrained by any logic outside the immanent criteria of its own operation. (2001: 2-3)

Whilst it is possible to be very sympathetic to Hallward's project of attending to the creativity of post-colonial writing, the above conflation seems incredible. Capitalism is here accorded a *self-generating* capacity considered *all-inclusive*, which is very much to bypass the whole import of Marx's analyses of capitalism as not auto-generative and constitutively not all-inclusive, and whilst, furthermore, the counter-Marxist move is to align the economic with the theological. Although this is too rushed, Hallward argues for an aesthetic and theoretical approach to the literary post-colonial, against the historical materialist approaches of post-colonial critics such as Benita Parry, opposing himself to Parry's objection that 'the analysis of the internal structures of texts, enunciations and signifying systems has become detached from a concurrent examination of social and experiential circumstances.' (2001: 334)

I would affirm that it is crucial to attend, concurrently rather than alternatively, to the societal and experiential contexts of creative expression, particularly as regards the quasi-mystical generativity that Hallward addresses, given the ways in which creativity and a sense of the sacred are sometimes mobilized in national struggles. Hallward's celebration of a creative singularity as a *post-colonial* phenomenon could be in danger of falling into the pitfalls of national consciousness, as periodized by Fanon. The significant moment for such movements seems to me to be especially in *anti-colonial* resistances, where the nation as a whole and as one is invoked against colonial exclusions, and where the transition to the *post-colonial* necessitates a secular reckoning with the mechanisms and stratifications of the economic and the administrative rather than the (lonely, at best, else inauthentic) pursuit of a post-colonial absolute. Fanon, much in the manner of Adorno, maintains that the independent nation 'ought not to speak a language destined to camouflage a bourgeois administration.' (2001: 145) He further maintains that whilst nationalism constitutes a 'magnificent song': 'Nationalism is not a political doctrine, nor a programme.' (2001: 163) The economy needs be accepted in its technological performativity without the human being reduced to this: *as, in fact, would be paradoxically effected by the sacralising of the political economy*. The political, as a form of theatrical performativity (i.e. it cannot authenticate itself), should but mediate between economic performativity, on the one hand, and values irreducible to the economic, on the other.

Finally, Neil Lazarus (whose work has significantly advanced and probably even initiated the critical deployment of Adorno in a reading of post-colonial African literature), maintains that the decolonising post-colonial period cannot be spoken of as a 'disillusionment' in that the moment of revolutionary liberation is 'fundamentally "illusioned"'. (1990: 23) I take Lazarus' point, but wish to make a slightly different one in relation to it. The 'magnificent song', of Fanon's phrase, can be said to be authentic, especially when faced with the hypocrisies and exploitations of colonialism, but authentic as such: hence its non-translatability (except as inauthentic jargon) into a practical politics. Varadharajan, another critic to turn Adorno towards post-colonial critique, emphasizes his negative dialectics to maintain that the subaltern may be re-configured in terms of a resistant object, or an instance of negation that cannot be assimilated by the dominant subject. (1995: *passim*) Hallward argues that Varadharajan's suggestion constitutes a 'thingification' of the subaltern (2001: 38), but I would say, with reference to the steadfastness of Hove's work, resolutely loyal to the subaltern, that it is really the reverse: precisely negation as a resistance to reification. Hove's writing, especially the later poems, may be said to constitute a space of reservation, of withholding, of sanctuary, and of *refusal*, so as to resist the corruption – commodification, vulgarization – of language. Hove:

> *my words have died a painful death*
> *murdered on the pavement*
> *slaughtered in the streets*
> *crushed along the path to the empty tap*
> *silenced by the roar of the factory machine.*
> *i will not speak (1998: 10)*

Chapter 5

Ethnicity in literature of Shona and Ndebele expression

Mickias Musiyiwa and Tommy Matshakayile-Ndlovu

Introduction

This chapter deals with the representation of ethnicity in Zimbabwean literature of Shona and Ndebele expression. We analyse the perspectives in Zimbabwean vernacular texts towards Shona, Ndebele, Malawian, and intra-Ndebele identities. Our focus is primarily fiction but we also consider selected plays published since the 1950s. Although ethnicity is a major theme in only a few Shona and Ndebele novels, it forms a thematic undercurrent in others. It is thus important to examine the contribution of indigenous literature towards understanding the interface of ethnic identities in the country. Zimbabwe is a multi-ethnic nation, and its social progress is affected by how its citizens of diverse cultural backgrounds interact discursively. While there are varied cultural, socio-historical, political and educational factors that shaped each Shona and Ndebele writer's construction of ethnicity, we argue that the writers' perceptions of the theme are polarized between a minority who project a more or less xenophobic outlook and the majority with a more pluralistic perception.

A brief background to Shona and Ndebele literature

Since the inception of literature in indigenous languages in the mid-1950s, the novel in Shona and Ndebele languages has been very popular (Veit-Wild, 1992: 19). It has been studied in schools and universities as well as being read on radio in programmes on literature in local languages. Although not as popular as the novel, drama has also been studied in educational institutions at all levels. Shona and Ndebele plays have also been aired on radio and enacted on television. The pioneers of Ndebele literature include Ndabaningi Sithole, Peter Mahlangu, Isaac Mpofu, David Ndoda, Elkhana Ndlovu and Ndabezihle Sigogo. Their Shona counterparts are Solomon Mutswairo, Herbert Chitepo, Bernard Chidzero and Patrick Chakaipa.

According to George Kahari (1990: 73) most of the Shona and Ndebele novels published in the 1950s were of the romance genre, and drew their material from an existing oral traditional culture in the form of legends, folktales, chronicles and mythology. These romance narratives largely aim to foreground the cultural life of the Shona and Ndebele people during the pre-colonial period, i.e. pre-1890. Most novels and plays published from the 1960s onwards indicate a shift from a pre-colonial to a colonial setting. From then on most Ndebele and Shona writers were more interested in portraying the profound social change engendered by colonialism: the impact of industrialization, urbanization, the cash economy and Christianity on Ndebele and Shona institutions (Chiwome, 2002). In 1980, Zimbabwean independence gave birth to the war novel in Shona and Ndebele.

The Shona novels discussed in this chapter are: Patrick Chakaipa's *Karikoga Gumiremiseve* [The-Lonely-One: Master-of-the Ten-Arrows] (1958); Claudius Matsikiti's *Shungu Dzomwoyo* [The Heart's Desire] (1980); Matthew Chikowo's *Shanje Ndimauraise* [Jealousy Kills] (1981); Genius Runyowa's *Akada Wokure* [She Loved a Foreigner] (1982); Regis Nhunduma's *Wazvaremhaka* [You Have Created Trouble] (1985) and Herbert Chimhundu's *Chakwesha* [The Stubborn One] (1991). We will also discuss Herbert Chakamba's Shona play *Nziramasanga* [True Path in Life is a Chance] (1991). Among the Ndebele texts, we focus on Ndabaningi Sithole's *Umvukela WamaNdebele* [The Ndebele Uprising] (1956); James P.Ndebele's *Akusimlandu Wami* [It is Not My Fault] (1974); Eggie Makhalima's *Ukhethwe Yimi* [I Chose Him] (1987); Joseph Sibanda's *Kusempilweni* [It Happens in Life] (1982); Barbra Makhalisa's *Qilidini* [What a Cheat!] (1974); Phelios Khumalo's *Umuzi Kawakhiwa Kanye* [A Home is Not Built Once] (1970) and David Ndoda's *UVusezindala* [The Reviver of Old Affairs] (1958). As for Ndebele drama Cont Mhlanga's radio and television plays, *Stitsha* [One-Who-Stitches-Things-Together] (1995) and *Sinjalo* [We Are Like That] (2003) will be analysed. The translations of Shona and Ndebele titles and extracts in this paper are ours.

Ethnicity in the novels of 1956 - 1979

Among novels published during this period, there are those whose stories are set before the advent of colonialism (i.e. pre-1890) and those set during the colonial period (1890 – 1980). Shona novels whose stories on ethnicity are set in the pre-colonial period are Patrick Chakaipa's Karikoga *Gumiremiseve* [The-Lonely-One: Master-of-the- Ten-Arrows] and Matthew Chokowo's *Shanje Ndimauraise* [Jealousy Kills]. Among Ndebele writers only Ndabaningi Sithole's *Umvukela WamaNdebele* [The Ndebele Uprising] concerns itself with ethnic identities in the pre-colonial times.

Patrick Chakaipa and Matthew Chikowo's romances portray the relationship between the Shona and Ndebele peoples as hostile. Both works draw their material largely from orature, particularly from the *ngano* (folktale) genre (Kahari, 1990: 118-24); both represent the Ndebele as ruthless and unsympathetic to their Shona neighbours. Patrick Chakaipa's novel tells of the life of Karikoga (literally, 'the lonely one'), an orphan who experiences a difficult upbringing. When he becomes a young man, his village is raided by Ndebele warriors and his wife Marunjeya is captured and taken to Matebeleland. Throughout, Chakaipa associates the Ndebele with cruelty and violence. A typical Ndebele raid of a Shona village is described as follows: 'Chembere dzakanga dzisingagoni kufamba dzaingogarwa nawo mapfumo. Twana tuchiroverwa misoro kumiti [.]' (p.33). [Old people who could not walk were mercilessly speared to death. Toddlers were seized and had their heads hit against tree trunks.] Chikowo's *Shanje Ndimauraise* is also awash with similar images. In the novel Chief Nyamunda (Owner of the land)'s army general says: 'Mati maDzviti vanhu vane mwoyo savamwe vanhu here? Vanhu vepi vanofarira kuuraya vamwe nokuvaonesa nhamo? (p. 60). [Do you think Ndebele warriors have the same (sympathetic) hearts as other people? What sort of people are they when they enjoy killing other people and making them suffer?].

While the Shona are depicted as peaceful, the Ndebele are portrayed as highly militarized and aggressive, forcing the Shona to hide in caves and mountains. Most of the time they have a *nharire* [alarm-caller] who stays on top of a high mountain or hill looking for any approaching Ndebele raiding armies and then blows his *hwamanda* [kudu horn] or beats a 'mutumba' [huge drum] to alert villagers to flee to the mountains. In *Chaminuka: Prophet of Zimbabwe*, a post-independence novel in English by Solomon Mutswairo, similar images of violence are employed to describe the strength and ruthlessness of Ndebele warriors. In this novel, Nehanda (a female spirit medium executed by the British in 1898 for leading anti-colonial resistance) says to another character: 'Even if our men banded themselves together into a warrior-like packed army, they could not be matched for the highly seasoned veterans of Lobengula's fighting forces, ... killing a muHole is like killing a fly to them' (Mutswairo, 1983: 152).

The hostility between the Shona and Ndebele is also evident in the language used by the texts. All the writers discussed so far use the derogatory term *madzviti* to refer to the Ndebele warriors. According to Solomon Mutswairo the term refers to 'the lazy, lousy, wandering, greasy, stinking locusts' (1983: 30). The analogy with locusts is meant to show the pervasive nature of Ndebele warriors during their raiding campaigns. As will be discussed later, Ndebele writers also have derogatory terms to refer to the Shona, such as *amasvina* (the dirty ones).

Chakaipa and Chikowo's perceptions of ethnicity were greatly influenced by their childhoods, during which orature – especially in the form of *ngano* – dominated juvenile entertainment (Fortune, 1973: i). Stories about Ndebele raids on Shona communities are part of the folklore tradition from which the two writers drew material for their romances. However, there is also the impact of colonial and missionary education – and the colonialist myth of Africa as a 'dark continent' filled with tribes engaged in perpetual warfare – to consider. This is perhaps especially important in the case of Chakaipa, who was educated at St Michael's Mission in Mhondoro and later trained to be a Catholic priest at Chishawasha Seminary (Kahari, 1990: 184). At the time of his death in 2003 he was the Archbishop of Harare.

In contrast to the Shona novelists Chakaipa and Chikowo, the Ndebele writer Sithole constructs his novel, *Umvukela WamaNdebele* [The Ndebele Uprising] stressing the positive values underlying the foundation of the Ndebele kingdom. This was a highly centralized state composed of people of various ethnic groups incorporated into the small Khumalo clan that Mzilikazi (the founder of the Ndebele kingdom) led from Zululand in the first half of the nineteenth century (Rasmussen, 1978). Sithole sets out to celebrate the idea of unity in diversity as one of the core values of the Ndebele state, by representing the Ndebele as a courageous people who were able to create a nation and defend it against all odds. While acknowledging the identity of each ethnic group, Sithole does not want ethnicity to be a source of division. He depicts the social structure of the Ndebele society as having three distinct groups namely, *AbeZansi*, (also referred to as *AbeNguni*) *AbeNhla* and *AmaHole* (also referred to as *AbakaMambo*). The first group forms the core of the Ndebele state in the form of the Khumalo clan. The second group is composed of people of Sotho and Tswana origin who were captured and incorporated into the Ndebele as the Khumalo were pushed northwards (see Bhebe, 1979). The *AmaHole* comprised the natives of western Zimbabwe, the former subjects of the Rozvi empire (see Cobbing, 1983). In his novel Sithole also refers to them as *AbakaMambo*, to mean 'subjects of the *Mambo*. '*Mambo*' was the title of the Shona rulers of the Rozvi state. Sithole persuades readers to the idea that unity among these cultural groups should continue and be further strengthened in the colonial era as they struggle against colonial exploitation.

In his reconstruction of the Ndebele past, Sithole emphasizes the bravery of the Ndebele as they fought the South African Boers. He says: 'Buphi ubuqhawe bezolo na obabamba ibhunu ngendevana labuyela emuva?' (p.26) [Where is yesteryear's bravery that grabbed the Boer by the beard and forced him to flee?]. However, Sithole the Zimbabwean nationalist does not pay much attention to how the Ndebele conquered other African ethnic groups that Mzilikazi incorporated into his following. He also glosses over the manner of conquest of the Shona by the Ndebele. He writes that both ethnic groups feared each other and that, because of the unique knowledge that each group possessed, the Shona did not resent assimilation into Ndebele society. He says:

> *Ngamazwi abufuphi umTshabi wesaba umZansi ngenxa yesibindi sakhe, umZansi wesaba umTshabi ngenxa yemithi yakhe. Lokhu kwenza lababantu bezwanane kakhulu babebantu banye ezintwni ezinengi ezaziphathelene lombuso wamaNdebele. Ukuthathana kwanda, ukuhloniphana lakho kwanda kwahlaliswana kuhle (p. 13). [In short, people of Shona origin feared those Ndebele who came from Zululand because of their courage; on the other hand those Ndebele who came from Zululand also feared the Ndebele of Shona origin because of their knowledge of traditional medicine. This made the two groups respect each other and they became one group in matters concerning the affairs of the Ndebele kingdom. Intermarriage became more prevalent and mutual respect between the two ethnic groups increased.]*

Sithole further stresses that when the Ndebele kingdom was destroyed by the British in 1893 and its second and last king, Lobengula, forced to flee, later dying in the wilderness, *all* the subjects of the kingdom suffered a great loss. He thus celebrates the Ndebele aristocratic philosophy and the all-embracing Ndebele identity, emphasizing that all subjects of the state were *abantu benkosi* [the king's people] (Bhebe, 1979: 8). He expresses this point in the following lines:'Yikho-ke ekunyamalaleni kukaLobengula akuhluphekanga abeZansi bodwa, kwahlupheka labeTshabi bonke. Kwahlupheka isizwe samaNdebele sonke' (p. 13). [That is why when Lobengula disappeared it is not only the Ndebele of Zulu origin who suffered but also the Ndebele of Shona origin. The entire Ndebele nation suffered.]

Sithole's attitude towards ethnicity was decisively influenced by the rise of African nationalism in Rhodesia in the 1950s. He felt that a second uprising against the colonial regime would not succeed if Africans in Rhodesia remained polarized along ethnic identities. Born in 1920, he became active in African nationalist politics after receiving a missionary education and training as a Methodist church minister (Veit-Wild, 1992). When ZANU (the Zimbabwe African National Union) was formed in 1963, he was its first president. Although in his subsequent political career, Sithole's path diverged sharply from that of the current ruling party, his stand on downplaying ethnic difference for the sake of a common goal was later echoed by the Unity Accord of 1987, which purportedly buried the political differences between the Ndebele and Shona so as to create a unity of 'common allegiance, common loyalty and a common struggle against both internal and external forces of destabilization' (Mutasa, 1989: 293). We return to this below.

Unlike Chakaipa, Chikowo and Sithole, writers of a younger generation in the pre-independence period do not remain anchored in ethnic shells. In *Shungu Dzomwoyo* [The Heart's Desire], *Wazvaremhaka* [You Have Created Trouble], *Akada Wokure* [She Loved a Foreigner], *Ukhethwe Yimi* [I Chose Him] and *Akusimlandu wami* [It's Not My Fault] the writers Claudius Matsikiti, Regis Nhunduma, Genius Runyowa, Eggie Makhalima and James P. Ndebele criticize members of older generations in both cultures for discouraging inter-ethnic marriages.

Set in colonial Bulawayo in the 1970s, the story of Claudius Matsikiti's *Shungu Dzomwoyo* [The Heart's Desire] is about a Shona young man, Taruvinga, and an Ndebele young woman, Sibongile, who fall in love and agree to marry. But when Taruvinga makes the marriage formality of paying *amalobolo* (the Ndebele word for 'bride wealth'), Mpofu, the would-be bride's father, refuses to formalize the marriage, arguing Ndebele ethnic superiority. He says: 'Ini neshamwari dzangu unonyatsoziva zvatinoitirana. Iwe unofunga kuti ungaite muchato unofadza here nomusvina uyu?' (p. 48). [I think you know what my friends and I do to each other. Do you think you can have a happy marriage with this socially inferior (non-Ndebele) person?]

The Shona term *musvina*, which Mpofu uses, is derived from the Shona noun, *svina*, which means 'dirt'. The Ndebele use the word *amaswina*, to refer to the

Shona they conquered. Even today the term still enjoys wide usage. The name of the Shona youth in the story – 'Taruvinga' – literally means 'we have come to confront it' (usually death). In the narrative, the name symbolizes the young man's boldness in confronting tribalism. His fiancé's name, 'Sibongile', means 'we are thankful' in Ndebele. The name signifies Taruvinga and Sibongile's gratitude to Mpofu for his eventual repentance in allowing them to marry. This novel's stance towards ethnicity is directly linked to Matsikiti's career as a clergyman. In the 1970s, when he wrote his novel, he was the vicar of the Bulawayo parish in charge of parishioners from diverse cultural backgrounds, and also a marriage counsellor (M. Musiyiwa, interview with the writer, 2002).

Similarly to the situation described in *Shungu Dzomwoyo*, the traditional Ndebele culture forbade intermarriage between the *AbeZansi*, *AbeNhla* and *AmaHole*. Authors James Ndebele, in *Akusimlandu Wami* [It's Not My Fault] and Eggie Makhalima in *Ukhethwe Yimi* [I Chose Him], argue that love should have no such boundaries. The story of Ndebele's novel centres on a young Nguni girl, Sizalobuhle, who wants to marry Kepesi, a young man from the *AmaHole* group. ('Nguni' refers to a cluster of ethnic groups, which include Xhosa, Zulu, Ndebele, Swazi and others originally from southern and south-eastern coast of South Africa. The *AbeZansi* (meaning 'those who came from downstream' or the South) section of Ndebele society in Zimbabwe are the only Ndebele group who are of Nguni origin). Like Sibongile's father in *Shungu Dzomwoyo*, Sizalobuhle's father, Thebe, cannot accept the idea of having a *Hole* for a son-in-law. In spite of this, Sizalobuhle elopes to Kepesi's home. Unable to prevent the marriage from taking place, Thebe is compelled to sanction it. Like Matsikiti, Ndebele constructs the names of his characters in order to communicate his attitude towards ethnicity. In the Ndebele language, 'Sizalobuhle' literally means 'we bring good things'. 'Kepesi' is a Shona name derived from the English noun 'cap'. A person who wears a cap partially hides his face and identity. In the context of the novel's theme, the name projects the point that there is no need to insist on Kepesi's ethnic identity but on his character as a suitor. The poetic ending of the story underlines the writer's moral perspective:

> *Akusimlandu wami ukuthi ngibe liTshabi.*
> *Akusimlandu wami ukuthi ngiliNguni.*
> *Phambi kukaSomandla siyafanana sonke, ngakho masihloniphane.*
> *Lasekuthatheni kakubuse uKhethomthandayo! (p. 104).*

> *[It is not my fault that I'm Shona.*
> *It is not my fault that I'm Nguni.*
> *In the eyes of The Almighty we are the same, therefore we must respect each other.*
> *Even when marrying let free choice be the guiding principle.]*

While the novelist castigates ethnic consciousness in Ndebele society, he also sees it as a universal problem. Human folly is seen as the source of all conflicts in this world. All people are creatures of *Somandla* (God Almighty) there is every reason to work together in mutual respect.

In Eggie Makhalima's Ndebele novel, *Ukhethwe Yimi* [I Chose Him], an educated Nguni young woman, Buhle, threatens to commit suicide if her father insists that she cannot marry Nkosana, a non-Nguni young man. Mafu is therefore forced to let her daughter marry the man of her dreams. ('Mafu' is an Ndebele name derived from the Ndebele noun *amafu* which means 'clouds'. The name alludes to the character's ethnocentric belief that the Ndebele were superior and above other ethnic groups. The Ndebele noun *buhle* means 'beauty'. *Nkosana* means 'prince'.) Unlike James Ndebele's novel, which gives a moralistic twist to the problems that arise from ethnic identities, the female novelist Makhalima's narrative attempts to give them a sociological basis. She associates them with political and economic power, referring to the increased physical mobility in the colonial period, which resulted in people from diverse cultural origins meeting and living together in urban areas, mines and commercial farms. Segregation in Ndebele society is represented as caused by the *AbeZansi* group by virtue of the fact that it wields more political and economic power than the other groups.

The only novel set in the colonial era that depicts peaceful interaction between the Ndebele and Shona people is Joseph Sibanda's *Kusempilweni* [It Happens in Life]. Two high-school boys, an Ndebele from Inyathi named Paul, and a Shona from Chihota, named Hakurotwi, meet in Bulawayo and become close friends. They learn each other's mother tongues and after graduating from college both teach in the Chihota area of Mashonaland where Paul socializes with Shona people without any difficulty. The Shona name 'Hakurotwi' literally means 'a place or thing not to be dreamt about' – this could be linked to the idea that there should be no place in Zimbabwe where one should ever dream to belong *only* to a particular group of people. Sibanda debunks the myth that Mashonaland is for the Shona and Matabeleland for the Ndebele people only.

While the novels analysed so far focus on Ndebele-Shona and intra-Ndebele social relations, there are yet other Shona and Ndebele novels whose concern is with Shona-Malawian and Ndebele-Malawian relations. Novels by Shona writers Genius Runyowa and Regis Nhunduma, *Akada Wokure* [She Loved a Foreigner] and *Wazvaremhaka* [You Have Created Trouble] represent the attitude of the Shona towards people of Malawian origin as xenophobic. The conflicts over intermarriage between Malawians and the Shona lead to intense human suffering and death. In *Akada Wokure*, Aleke Phiri, a young man of Malawian origin falls in love with his employer's daughter, Wadzanai, against the wishes of her parents and other Shona characters in the novel. Aleke's Shona workmates, who are also vying to win Wadzanai's love, connive to destroy the relationship. In the end, Wadzanai is poisoned, Aleke marries Wadzanai's younger sister and those who killed Wadzanai are punished by accidental death. In Nhunduma's *Wazvaremhaka*, a Malawian man, Chandafira, who comes to stay permanently in the Zvimba area is murdered and his wealth seized by his in-laws. He had married Magumo, the daughter of his Shona workmate and friend Takaendesa. Takaendesa's wife, Kasinyare, cannot accept this. She connives with her sons to have Chandafira murdered. One of her sons assures her that he had committed himself to murdering Chandafira by saying: 'Chandafira kuenda ari mupenyu ane mhanza, naiye ari kuzofa senguruve chaiyo' (p. 23) [If Chandafira leaves this place alive then he is very lucky, he has to die like a real pig.]

In both novels the Shona characters depict Malawians as socially inferior. Disparaging names are used to ridicule them. They are referred to as *mabhurandaya*. In *Wazvaremhaka*,Magumo criticizes her husband, saying, 'Vakomana vose vandaida ndakavarega pamusana pekamubhurandaya zvako'. (p. 20) [I made a serious mistake of jilting all the young (Shona) men for this Malawian.] In *Akada Wokure*, Wadzanai's father, also uses the same term to justify why he does not want his daughter to marry Aleke saying: 'Handifi ndakabvuma kuita mukwasha wechiBhurandaya ini' (p. 23) [I will never accept a Malawian as my son-in-law.]

The term *bhurandaya*, which is used here, is derived from 'Blantyre', the capital city of Nyasaland (now Malawi). The term was used to refer to Malawian migrant labourers who came to Rhodesia in search of employment. Any marriage between a local woman and a man of Malawian origin was considered illegitimate and denounced as *kuchaya mapoto* [co-habitation]. Chandafira and Magumo's marriage is castigated as such. Another derogatory term that is used to show the Shona's contempt of Malawians is *mubvakure*. The terms literally means 'one who comes from distant places' – a foreigner.

Runyowa and Nhunduma's characters' names also contain meanings that symbolize the novelists' moralistic stance against the negative effects of ethnocentrism. In Runyowa's *Akada Wokure*, the main character's name, Wadzanai, derives from the Shona verb *ku-wadzana*, which means 'to be at peace or in agreement with others'. Thus, as a name, 'Wadzanai' calls upon people to socialize and live in peace with one another. The character Wadzanai encapsulates Runyowa's moral teaching. Her death is a Christ-like sacrifice so that Shona society may be liberated from ethnic prejudice. Indeed, after her death normalcy is restored when everyone repents of the 'sin' of ethnic hatred. Aleke goes on to marry Wadzanai's young sister, Rungamirai, now with his father-in-law's unreserved approval. Rungamirai's name is derived from the Shona verb *ku-rungamira* which means 'be as straight or level as something ought to be'. The name persuades those who are imbued with xenophobic dispositions to shun such socially destructive tendencies. In the novel *Wazvaremhaka*, the mother-in-law's name, Kasinyare, comes from the Shona verb *ku-sanyara* which means 'to have no shame'. 'Magumo' denotes 'an end'. 'Chandafira' literally means 'what I have died for'. The name invites the reader to contemplate the cause of all the tragedies that take place in the story. Unlike what happens in *Akada Wokure*, Chandafira's death results in the disintegration of Takaendesa's family as a result of the intervention of Chandafira's *ngozi* (avenging spirit). In the Shona culture, leaving a wronging unresolved until the death of the wronged person results in that person's spirit returning to torment the wrongdoer seeking compensation (Bourdillon, 1987: 233). The anger of the *ngozi* is more devastating if it is of a foreigner, as is the case with Chandafira's, which kills children and destroys livestock in the extended Takaendesa family. The title of the novel, 'You Have Created Trouble', is thus both a moral and a warning.

In the Ndebele novel, *Qilindini* (What a Cheat!) Barbara Makhalisa represents the Ndebele as strongly antagonistic to people of Malawian origin. The novel narrates the story of a police detective of Malawian origin, James Phiri, who disguises himself as a herdboy while investigating criminals who are stealing and killing the sheep of the people of Filabusi to extract bile from them to be used in traditional healing. Among the offenders are a local Ndebele headman and a traditional healer. On realizing that James Phiri is a Malawian, the local Ndebeles begin to deride him as 'Mnyasa', a term derived from Malawi's colonial name, Nyasaland. The name 'Phiri' is a surname of the people from Malawi. In spite of the ridicule, James executes his work very professionally, apprehending all the sheep rustlers. While making his investigations, he falls in love with an Ndebele girl whom he later marries. At the end of the novel, similarly to Ndebele's *Akusimlandu Wami* [It's Not My Fault], Makhalisa's didacticism is humanistic in tone. She argues that it is a person's contribution to society rather than their ethnic origins that matters. As a result of this, James Phiri ceases to be 'Mnyasa' and is fully accepted and integrated into Ndebele society through marriage to an Ndebele girl.

The humanistic stance that reverberates in the novels analysed so far can perhaps be attributed to their authors' educational, professional and personal experiences. They acquired their secondary education at boarding schools and trained as teachers and priests at colleges and seminaries where students from different cultural backgrounds were able to meet and work together. Such experiences broke the shock of colonial cultural and tribal confrontation. In a different context, Victor de Waal (1990: 91) states that free interaction of Shona and Ndebele students in colleges and universities, as well as intermarriage between them, makes ethnic divisions less important.

In contrast, Phelios Khumalo's Ndebele novel *Umuzi Kawakhiwa Kanye* [A Home is not Built Once] also shows a negative attitude towards people of other ethnic groups. In this novel every non-Ndebele character commits all sorts of evil. The story is about an Ndebele couple, Nsimbi (an Ndebele word that literally means 'iron') and Ntombenhle (an Ndebele name for a beautiful woman) whose marriage breaks up resulting in Ntombenhle's falling in love with another man, whom the writer merely identifies as a non-Ndebele. Nsimbi feels insulted to be jilted by a woman of his own ethnic identity. The man is tried before an Ndebele chief and mocked for failing to speak the Ndebele language fluently. In another episode, Khumalo portrays a non-Ndebele man who works as a miner approaching Nsimbi in order to sell him some gold illegally. Nsimbi reports the man to the police and he is arrested. It is important to note that Khumalo does not identify non-Ndebele characters by their names or ethnic identities but merely refers to every one of them as *umuntu wezizweni*, meaning 'a foreign person' or 'alien'. This illustrates his ethnic bias. His prejudice is further reflected through his contrasting of Ndebele and non-Ndebele characters. Ndebele characters, especially Nsimbi, are paragons of virtue; they are endowed with positive attributes and are morally conscious. Non-Ndebeles lack any morals; they are portrayed as thieves; they steal gold and take other men's wives.

Similarly, in the Ndebele romance *UVusezindala* [The Reviver of Old Affairs], David Ndoda lampoons a Malawian as a buffoon. A young man from Malawi named Bhanda, who works as a cook for a local white police officer, is persuaded by an Ndebele woman to marry her niece. She hopes to benefit materially because Bhanda is employed. However, the Ndebele girl exploits Bhanda's ignorance of Ndebele social relationships and cheats on him. She introduces her former boyfriend into her matrimonial home and they pretend to be brother and sister. Ndoda portrays Bhanda as too naïve to realize that the Ndebele people, who pretend to like him, are only after his money.

Both Khumalo and Ndoda share in professional and educational terms a similar background to other writers discussed in this chapter such as Runyowa, Matsikiti and Makhalisa; they also claim to be linked to Ndebele aristocracy. Ndoda claims that his father was the herdboy of King Lobengula's cattle while Khumalo belongs to the descendents of Lobengula. Consequently their attitude towards people of other ethnic groups may have been influenced by their upbringing. Cattle symbolized Ndebele economic pride and superiority over other ethnic groups. Hence the two writers seem to revive pre-colonial Ndebele pride and prejudice against their neighbours and other distant groups such as Malawians (For more details on pre-colonial Shona-Ndebele relations see Cobbing, 1976; Bhebe, 1979 and Beach, 1994).

Ethnicity in Novels and Plays of 1980 – 2003

Although the coming of independence in 1980 saw the proliferation of Ndebele and Shona war novels depicting the liberation struggle, few focused on ethnicity. Despite the fact that Herbert Chimhundu's historical Shona novel, *Chakwesha* [The Stubborn One], largely focuses on colonial and neo-colonial issues, it shuns the tribally-induced divisions between ZANLA (Zimbabwe African National Liberation Army – ZANU(PF)'s military wing) and ZIPRA (Zimbabwe People's Revolutionary Army).[1] It only implies that they were suspicious of each other without giving more historical detail about the nature of the suspicion. At a

---

[1]   Throughout their armed struggle for independence ZANLA became synonymous with the Shona by virtue of the fact that it recruited mostly from the Shonas whilst ZIPRA generally assumed an Ndebele identity because most of its guerrillas were recruited from the Ndebele ethnic group.

London meeting, a ZANU representative, Zvenyika (a Shona name which means 'about or dedicated to country or nation') says: 'zvose zvavana ZIPA hazvina kumbenge zvanyatsoshanda nokuti vokuZAPU vakanga vasingadi kupinza varwi vakawana ... vaida kumborega ZANLA ichirwa ivo vozouya vokohovedza (p. 130). [in every respect ZIPA did not succeed from the start because ZAPU did not want to deploy many forces ... its strategy was to have ZANLA do most of the fighting and then only intervene at the end to assume victory.]

'ZIPA' stands for Zimbabwe People's Army – a united military force composed of ZANLA and ZIPRA guerrillas during the struggle for independence in Zimbabwe, formed in 1976. The writer represents ZIPRA forces as cowards because they ran away from the battlefield and returned to their homes. The novel does not refer to the political differences between ZAPU and ZANU during the struggle for independence. However, the didactic ending, in the form of a poem entitled '1990', attacks weaknesses among Zimbabwean citizens such as corruption, political hypocrisy, tribalism and regionalism. Zimbabweans are urged to renounce these evils as they approach the new decade of the 1990s, which the author visualizes as bringing profound positive change for the nation. One stanza of the long poem focuses on national unity and satirizes those who are bent on dividing the nation along racial, ethnic, tribal and regional identities. Some selected lines of the stanza of the poem are as follows:

Muchazovepi kana tsuri yorira:
Muchazovepi tabatana Zanu neZapu?
Muchazoti chii pasisina anoti pasi neZapu?'
Kana tose tangova maZimbabwe
Munyika musisina anonzi Mabhunu,
Munyika musisina anonzi Madzviti,
Musisina kana anonzi Masvina,
Musisinazve kana anonzi Mavhitori?
Kana Zimbabwe yose isisadi kunzwa nezvematunhu,
Kana maZimbabwe ose oti pasi nezvamarudzi? (pp. 196-7)

[Where will you be when the call is sounded?
Where will you be when we Zanu and Zapu are united?
What will you say when there is nobody saying 'down with Zapu'?
When all of us are only Zimabweans?
When there are no citizens called Mabhunu (Boers) in the nation
When there are no people called Madzviti (Ndebeles) in the nation
When there are no people called Masvina (Shonas)
When there are no citizens called Mavhitori (Karangas)
When the entire Zimbabwean nation doesn't want to listen to regionalism
When all Zimbabweans shout, 'Down with tribalism!']

Chimhundu chides those who continue to foment ethnic and racial tensions to divide the nation, and applauds ZANU and ZAPU for burying their differences by uniting to bring peace and tranquility in the nation. However, by glossing over some of the extent and historical detail of the differences between the two political parties during the liberation struggle and after independence, his celebration of a broader Zimbabwean identity is misleading. There was, and is, a need for readers to know more about these tribally-informed evils so as to justify the need for reconciliation and unity among Zimbabwe's ethnic groups, and make it meaningful.

Like some Shona novelists of the colonial period, Shona playwrights during the same period largely circumvented ethnic issues. It is only after independence that playwrights, clearly inspired by the policy of reconciliation and the Unity Accord, started to devote major themes of their plays to condemning regionalism and negative ethnic consciousness. One post-independence Shona playwright who has written specifically to condemn tribalism is Herbert Chakamba. One of his plays, 'Kuwadzana' [Mutual Interaction] in the collection of plays, *Nziramasanga* [True Path is a Chance] (Chakamba, 1991), reflects on the suffering experienced by ordinary people during the liberation struggle. Like Runyowa in *Akada Wokure*, Chakamba encourages Zimbabwean citizens from all backgrounds to co-operate in all spheres of life. The marriage between Prudence Sibanda (an Ndebele woman) and Comrade Pfutseke Mabhunu, a Shona freedom fighter, that forms the play's ending symbolizes the dramatist's call for ethnic interaction. The master of ceremonies at the couple's wedding is the playwright's mouthpiece. He moralizes by saying: 'Prudence naPfutseke Mabhunu ndivo vanyatsoratidza gwara rehurumende rekuregererana … nokuwadzana kwemarudzi akasiyana-siyana munyika ino. Vana ava varatidza nyika yose kuti havadi kusarudza rudzi …' (p. 41). [Prudence and Pfutseke Mabhunu have demonstrated the government policy of reconciliation … and co-operation of all people in this country irrespective of the cultural background. These children have showed to the whole nation that they are against tribalism …].

In another play in the same volume, 'Mbudzi Yakarasirirwa' [A Goat Sent Astray], Chakamba denounces tribalism at workplaces and its associated evils of favouritism and nepotism. He shows how a Shona manager compromises company production by employing his under-qualified nephew leaving out a highly qualified Ndebele young man. However, it is important to note that Chakamba is concerned with peace between the Ndebele and the Shona only. Europeans and people from other ethnic groups are not part of Chakamba's projected Zimbabwean identity. This is seen through the name he gives to the bridegroom. In Shona 'Pfutseke' means 'go away'. It is borrowed from the Afrikaans word *voetsek*, which means the same. 'Mabhunu' means Boers, a common way of designating 'white people'. 'Pfutseke Mabhunu' is a war name that signifies the racial and political tension between blacks and whites in Rhodesia. By using this name Chakamba may suggest that the tension between blacks and whites is not one which should also be resolved.

In his plays *Stitsha* [Stitching Things Together][2] and *Sinjalo* [We are Like That], playwright Cont Mhlanga deals centrally with the issue of tribalism. In the former, the Ndebele dramatist condemns discrimination and favouritism in the workplace, based on ethnic identity. *Sinjalo* is a satire that features two friends, Sakhamuzi (Ndebele) and Foromani (Shona) who assist each other in all the endeavours of life and satirize those who despise each other on grounds of ethnicity. In their daily conversations, the main characters, Sakhamuzi ('owner of the home') and Foromani (derived from the English word 'foreman') speak to each other in their mother tongues without any difficulties. The playwright teaches the Zimbabwean audience that there is no way it can avoid the multi-ethnic reality of its nation.

Mhlanga, Chakamba and Chimhundu's visions of Zimbabwe's ethnic identities are clearly shaped by the policy of reconciliation that was enunciated at independence in 1980. The Unity Accord signed between ZANU(PF) and PF-ZAPU in December 1987 further inspired the writers' vision.[3] Chakamba in particular wanted his play 'Kuwadzana' to project the idea that reconciliation is also in order between the blacks in Zimbabwe. This echoes what Robert Mugabe (president of Zimbabwe and the ruling ZANU(PF)) and Joshua Nkomo (president of PF-ZAPU) stated at the signing of the Unity Accord. The unity document was going to be 'an instrument for uniting the people of Zimbabwe irrespective of tribe, race or political affiliation', in order to create for future generations a peaceful and united Zimbabwe (Gowe, 1987: 11). Not unlike Sithole, Matsikiti, Nhunduma, Runyowa, Ndebele, Makhalima and Sibanda, Chakamba and Chimhundu want to stress and promote a broader identity rather than narrow ethnic ones. However, Mhlanga, Chakamba and Chimundu do so in the context of an independent post-colonial nation, rather than in the name of (Christian) humanism within a colony. They advocate the recognition of a broader Zimbabwean identity, similar to that which had concerned Ndabaningi Sithole in the 1950s when he wrote about the Ndebele society.

---

[2] *First performed by Amakhosi Theatre Productions in 1995 and subsequently screened on ZTV in 1999.*

[3] Since 1963, the two Zimbabwean nationalist parties had fought for independence separately. PF-ZAPU came to be dominated by people of Ndebele origin thereby gaining an Ndebele identity and ZANU(PF) by Shona speakers and gaining a Shona identity (Bond and Manyanya, 2003: 8). In 1980, fighting broke out between Zimbabwe People's Revolutionary Army (ZIPRA) (ZAPU's military wing) and Zimbabwe People's Liberation Army (ZANLA) (ZANU's military wing) soldiers in Bulawayo, resulting in the government unleashing the infamous Fifth Brigade to quell the rebellion (De Waal, 1990: 91). However, in 1987 the two parties agreed to unite and reconcile. In a sense, the signing of the Unity Accord indicated a broadening of the earlier policy of reconciliation, which had been viewed by most Zimbabweans as only applicable to the historical conflict between blacks and whites.

Conclusion

In this chapter, we hope to have demonstrated that Ndebele and Shona literature has, since its genesis in the 1950s, been concerned with questions of ethnicity and ethnic identity. In this body of writing, we have discerned a dichotomy in terms of how different identities are represented. While Shona novelists Patrick Chakaipa and Matthew Chikowo and their Ndebele counterparts David Ndoda and Phileos Khumalo write celebrating their own ethnic groups, the majority of writers analysed in this chapter want to celebrate and promote a broader Zimbabwean identity. The latter display a pluralistic vision, persuading their readers to renounce tribal animosity by depicting the negative consequences of ethnocentrism. After independence, the political framework adopted to transform the new Zimbabwean nation through the policy of reconciliation was the impetus behind the moralization in Ndebele and Shona literature as regards ethnic interaction. The unity agreement of 1987 further inspired Shona and Ndebele writers in that direction. The novelist Chimhundu, and playwrights Chakamba and Mhlanga in particular, disseminate the principle of the spirit of oneness irrespective of one's racial, tribal or regional identity. Matsikiti, Runyowa, Nhunduma, Chakamba, Makhalisa, Makhalima, Sibanda and Ndebele, emphasize inter-ethnic marriage as the solution to tribalism. On the other hand, Sithole, Chakamba, Chimhundu and Mhlanga – despite writing during different historical periods – all suggest that political solutions are key to problems of division and conflict. However, partly or wholly due to self-censorship and/or fear of being censored by the Literature Bureau,[4] Chimhundu and Chakamba are silent about the political and military conflicts between PF-ZAPU and ZANU(PF) during the war of liberation. They are also silent about the largely ethnically-inspired Gukurahundi crisis, which happened in the first decade of Zimbabwe's independence. The writers might have omitted these issues deliberately fearing that their manuscripts may not be considered suitable for the Zimbabwean audience by the Literature Bureau.

---

[4] *The Zimbabwe Literature Bureau was formed in 1953 as the Southern Rhodesia Literature Bureau to promote the publication of literature in indigenous languages (Shona and Ndebele). In practice it was a censorship board because it would assess manuscripts and recommend whether they should be published or not. It recommended the publication of apolitical literature and disapproved all manuscripts that it perceived as subverting the colonial establishment (Veit-Wild, 1992: 72-3). After independence it continued the same role but now promoting the publication of literature that it considered portraying the new political dispensation in a good light. It was disbanded in 1998 when its role was viewed as being outside the core business of the Ministry of Education and Culture (M. Musiyiwa, interview with W.T. Moyana, former official in the Literature Bureau, 2004).*

Chapter 6

The poverty of theory in the study of Zimbabwean literature

Maurice Vambe

Introduction: literary theory and the illusion of completeness

In this chapter I critique the application of a sociological theory to the study of Zimbabwean literature. I analyse Flora Veit-Wild's *Teachers, Preachers, Non-Believers: A Social History of Zimbabwean Literature* (1993), and Emmanuel Chiwome's *A Social History of the Shona Novel* (1996). I argue that the problem with the two critical works is that they give the impression that the literature in question is an imaginative space destroyed by the colonial structures, to a point where black identities in it are barely recognizable. In arguing so, the two critics have tended to project a single version of critical theory and attempted to 'naturalize' it as the only one that can be used to explain Zimbabwean literature. The overbearing image of colonial structures as unassailable, which the two works privilege, also threatens to foreclose debate on the multiple ways through which some works of art engaged with colonialism and its legacies. Veit-Wild's theory of historical exceptionalism and Chiwome's failure to move out of the orbit of the dominant thesis paradigm prevent the two critics from exploring the complicated ways in which the Zimbabwean authors depicted their characters' contradictory responses to colonialism and its aftermath.

In her essay, 'The Race for Theory', Barbara Christian is distressed that critics are no longer concerned with analysing literature, but with deconstructing other critics' works. This she views as dangerous to the discipline of literature in three ways. Theory is now viewed not as critical space for questioning the cultural assumptions of a world that has in Antonio Gramsci's words, not only become 'common in any given epoch' (Gramsci, 1971: 322), but a 'commodity which helps whether we are hired or promoted in academic institutions' (Christian, 1996: 149). Christian implies that critics are no longer interested in evolving new values that a rigorous explanation of creative texts might yield. In 'the race for theory the language favoured is hegemonic: it mystifies rather than clarifies social conditions of injustice, thus making it possible for a few people who know that language to control the critical space. This, according to Christian, not only attempts to deny the creative texts their various-ness and complexity, but it also fails to grasp the fact that a text or work of art might suggest a new approach that might not be adequately accounted for by the 'imposed' theory.

Most of the above concerns raised by Barbara Christian about the potential 'historic arrest' (Jeyifo, 1996:164) of critical theory during the process of decolonization are real because critical discourse is the primary medium in which literature survives (Kermode, in Jeyifo, 1996: 159). I shall underline the significance of these observations when I explore the inadequacies (what I call 'poverty of theory') of a sociological theoretical approach to the understanding of the Zimbabwean literature. I shall argue, however, that Barbara Christian's reservations on 'the race for theory' are over-dramatized. It is not possible to dispense with 'metacommentary' (Jameson, 1981: 9) or the 'criticism of criticism'. The cultural institution related to the discipline of literary theory is not innocent and has never been so. In fact, it has grown into a hegemonic cultural practice supported by 'vocabulary, scholarship and imagery' (Said, 1978: 2-3), from which statements about literature are made and views about literature are also authorized.

The race for theory is thus inevitable because it has to do with how critics shape the ethos of a particular generation, and in the process, demonstrate how a stronger interpretation can modify and challenge an existing interpretation. Once we accept the premise that critics select, order and re-arrange facts in the process of reading novels, it becomes necessary to talk of the poverty of literary theory and the illusion of literary completeness, particularly in this chapter, whose aim is to reveal and critique localized instances of the inadequacy of a sociological approach to the study of Zimbabwe literature.

The problem of historical exceptionalism: *Teachers, Preachers, Non-Believers*

Teachers, Preachers, Non-Believers: A Social History of Zimbabwean Literature was published in 1993. For a long time critics relied on Musaemura Zimunya's *Those Years of Drought and Hunger: The Birth of Fiction in English in Zimbabwe* (1982) to make sense of black fiction in Zimbabwe. Zimunya's critical forte is his understanding of the emergence of a fractured national consciousness through the prism of the images of drought and hunger. In emphasizing drought and hunger, however, he missed the potentially positive historical agency of the African people that was to manifest itself in 'songs that won the liberation war' (Pongweni, 1982) amongst other cultural/oral sites of struggle that formed unmanned spaces of African socialities in Rhodesia. Rino Zhuwarara's *Introduction to Zimbabwean Literature in English* (2001) has brought out the basic ambiguity in Zimbabwean fiction in the sense that the literature shows a desire to both rebel against and conform to colonial aesthetics. Zhuwarara's conclusions modify the picture of cultural malaise that characterizes Zimunya's work. In my own book, *African oral story-telling tradition and the Zimbabwean novel in English* (2004) I have also demonstrated how orality survived in the narrative interstices of the Zimbabwean novel with the result that that orality conferred on the novels semantic instability and the possibilities of being re-interpreted in new ways. *Teachers, Preachers, Non-Believers* may be said to have responded to the critical anomy in Zimunya's work. Veit-Wild's literary project aims to provide a 'socio-historical analysis of the effects of education, political developments and cultural policies on the literary products of a time as well as a literary analysis of these products' (1993: 5). Her search for a 'comprehensive view of Zimbabwean literature in the vernacular and in English'(5) is grounded in Abiola Irele's conception of a sociology of African literature that she quotes approvingly. This sociological approach,

> *attempts to correlate the work to the social background to see how the author's intention and attitude issue out of the wider social context of his art in the first place and, more important still, to get an understanding of the way each writer or each group of writers captures a moment of historical consciousness of the society. The intimate progression of the collective mind, its workings, its shape, its temper, these – and more – are determinants to which a writer's mind and sensibilities are subject, to which they are responding all the time and which, at a superficial or profound level, his work will reflect in its moods and structures (Irele, 1971: 16)*

Veit-Wild's major achievement in *Teachers, Preachers, Non-Believers* is in the way she provides a detailed link between black literary creations and the stultifying influences of the Rhodesia Literature Bureau on the black literary creations in Shona and English. It is also in the ways she organizes and analyses the writers of her choice in terms of social and literary generations, which she sees as enabling her to explain the 'disparity between certain distinct tendencies in Zimbabwean writing' (6). As Zhuwarara (1994) notes, Veit-Wild successfully explores the black elite's contradictory responses to colonialism.

The book gives an absorbing account of how those who

> *started writing in the 1960s occupy an ambiguous position as the first generation of writers. Their desire to preserve African values is portrayed as often being in conflict with their ambition to adapt to the colonial order, although it denied them a respectable and meaningful role, and most saw education as a means of achieving social mobility and progress (Zhuwarara, 1994: 10).*

However, a fundamental flaw that this process entails is that Veit-Wild places undue emphasis on the process of enculturation of the African writers, to a point where one is bound to question her conclusion that the influence of the Literature Bureau on the first and second generation of African writers was absolute. The notion of 'social generation', which informs her book, underestimates the fact that some writers who she places in the first generation continued to write, and their ideological vision and understanding of a changing Zimbabwean society has also been changing. Charles Mungoshi and Dambudzo Marechera are placed in the second generation in *Teachers, Preachers, Non-Believers*. What is emphasized is the perceived pessimism of their works. And yet, new critical work emerging, especially in Mungoshi's creative output, significantly qualifies the picture of cultural anomy painted by Veit-Wild. For example, Ruby Magosvongwe's (2004: 292-301) analysis of female voices in *Kunyarara Hakusi Kutaura?* [Is Silence not Talking?] brings out the power of black women such as VaNhanga to fight back restrictions imposed on women by patriarchy. Similarly, Memory Chirere (2004: 216-31) has called for a reappraisal of critiques that dismiss the character Garabha in Mungoshi's novel *Waiting for the Rain* as a social misfit (Veit-Wild, 1993: 288; Zimunya, 1982).

There are uneven levels of consciousness of class, race and ethnicity amongst the writers placed in the same generation. There are also inherent contradictions in the literary voice of an individual author, and this makes an essentialized sociological approach to Zimbabwean literature inadequate. This is the case with Chenjerai Hove's *Bones*, a novel that can be read both as a confirmation and as a critique of nationalist politics. Veit-Wild's over-emphasis on the social factors that shaped Zimbabwean literature, though useful in bringing out certain trends in Zimbabwean fiction, is cast in a deterministic way that precludes the possibility that a detailed analysis of a particular text might modify her findings and conclusions. A point in question is Veit-Wild's judicious conclusion that in *Waiting for the Rain* (1975) 'there is no way out, no hope of improvement, and no way back' (Veit-Wild, 1993: 288) just because the Old Man is 'haunted by nightmares of Death' (288) and that 'Garabha fails in real practical life' (288) while Lucifer fails to fit in either the African family or the colonial structure. A re-reading of *Waiting from the Rain* will yield the fact that the Old Man has fought in the First Chimurenga even when he and his comrades were temporarily 'defeated'. That heroic struggle cannot be wished away. Similarly, Garabha might first appear as a directionless young man but it is through his drum message that the reader is able to access and reconstruct the mythic narrative in the novel in which the nationalist discourse of resistance is embedded. Even Uncle Kuruku might on the surface appear a mealy-mouthed person, but it is he who in the text puts the problem of the Mandengu family in a clear political perspective, and also urges Lucifer to go and get the white man's knowledge so that with it the black people will fight the system. There is an acknowledgement in his wisdom that blacks will have to use some cultural resources made available by colonialism to fight the same system. Besides, his wearing of the *ngundu* – then a symbol of African resistance – shows some defiance to a system that had threatened to arrest anyone seen wearing it. In carnivalesque terms, the grammar of the messages encoded in the *ngundu* asserted black humanity at a time it was being trampled upon by the colonial system. These new readings escape Veit-Wild's analysis of Mungoshi's text. One of the reasons is that Veit-Wild expects the social aspects of the life of the author to correspond to the lives of the characters that are cast in images. Veit-Wild's sociology is as flawed as her textual analysis.

The fact that Veit-Wild focuses more on Lucifer than Garabha in *Waiting for the Rain*, and on Sam, not Sam's brothers at the battlefront in *The Non-Believers' Journey* (1980) is an ideological decision. The possible answer is that her sociological approach to the literature has sustained itself by acts of amnesia and exclusion. Grounded in the aesthetics of neo-positivism and historical exceptionalism, Veit-Wild's 'uncritical' critical work remains loyal to its middle-class origins, and consequently it searches for heroes amongst the western-educated African elites. There is thus a genuine inability in the critic to appreciate that a detailed analysis of the actual works of art can suggest new ways of understanding that same fiction. Consequently, Veit-Wild's reading of Shona and English fiction is one-sided. Part of the problem is that she is working within the limiting and limited framework of the social science paradigm in which, as argued by Simon Gikandi, any

> *implicit connection between African Literature and social science epistemology is so powerful that any suggestion that artistic production in Africa might actually work against the claims of society, history or culture is easily dismissed as a resort to formalism or the doctrine of art for art's sake (Gikandi, 2000:1).*

Veit-Wild's work takes the Shona novel as a mere reflection of the values of the author and the violent culture of colonialism. In reality, within the Shona novel colonial values were often ridiculed by authors who used modes of orality to which the colonial authorities had no easy access. The ode to Nehanda in Solomon Mutswairo's *Feso* suggests the constant trafficking of oral genres from the lived experience of Africans into the black novel. The same ode was used by black nationalists in the 1960s to mobilize Africans around the nationalist cause. Also, the contradictory structures of the mythic legend and folktale motif in *Waiting for the Rain* reveal that Mungoshi is aware that African orature cannot be used to destabilize colonialism without some of its aspects being appropriated by the system itself. Viet-Wild depicts colonial authority and its structures, such as the Literature Bureau, as unassailable. And yet, as Terence Kawadza reflects, the influence of the Literature Bureau and colonial education are exaggerated because in the actual fiction in the Shona language there are simultaneous presences of contestations against and complicities with colonialism:

> *Colonial authority was never all powerful and totalitarian. One could argue that it was the challenges, contestations and collaborations that marked indigenous textual responses to colonization. Settler state mythologies were never passively accepted. This contestation has to be identified otherwise there is a danger of constructing a culture of victimhood which only accentuates settler power and fails to see multiple responses to it (Kawadza, 2000:10).*

The 'poverty' of a sociological approach to the Zimbabwean literature as demonstrated in *Teachers, Preachers, Non-Believers* is further demonstrated by the work's under-estimation of the role of black oral forms in influencing the formal composition of the Shona and English novel. Viet-Wild is convinced that 'it must be taken into consideration that there is no direct transition from oral to written literature' (37). This comment ignores the fact that African writers from Mutswairo to Tsitsi Dangarembga were socialized into their own Shona cultural mythologies before entering European education systems, and that the influence of orature is manifested in their works in different ways. In *Feso*, allegory and clan poetry are deployed to destabilize the assumptions of a stable colonial narrative. In *Waiting for the Rain* the oral genre of the mythic legend that comprises the myth of Samambwa; the drum culture of the Old Man and Garabha; and the folktale of the Strange Bird are used in ways that depict African characters' responses as contradictory in the ways they resist, and sometimes toy with colonialism. In Dangarembga's *Nervous Conditions* (1988) grandmother's oral narrative that she tells to Tambudzai Sigauke about how the people 'without knees'[white settlers] came to take away African land paradoxically serves to undermine colonialism as well as African patriarchy's oppression of the African women. These instances of the power of orality within Zimbabwean literature have been undervalued in *Teachers, Preachers, Non-Believers*.

The problem with Veit-Wild's book is that it is 'comfortably' lodged within the social science paradigm in which all that is not put down in writing is non-knowledge, hence the failure to reveal the role of African orature in works of Shona art such as *Ndiko Kupindana Kwamazuva* [How Time Passes]. And yet, as Zhuwarara points out, in both the lives of the Shona writers and their creative output, orature 'constituted a part of the counter-culture of resistance throughout the colonial era and is an area that need[ed] to be researched more seriously than is revealed in [Veit-Wild's] book' (Zhuwarara, 1994: 11). What Veit-Wild's *Teachers, Preachers, Non-Believers* fails to come to terms with is that during and after colonialism, black orature formed a volatile cultural space that was, and continued to be used in different ideological ways by authors writing both in English and in Shona. Mnay people who have closely read *Jikinya* by Geoffrey Ndhlala will know that the novel is structured on the Jikinya folktale in the Shona oral tradition. As in the Shona oral tradition the *Jikinya* novel is a folktale of captivity and struggle for freedom. It is a folktale novel urging the Shona people to embrace tolerance and reconciliation. These deeper meanings embedded in the novel's orature would have fractured a monolithic account of Zimbabwean literature and the notion of nation that Veit-Wild would have liked to impose on the literature. Instead of recognizing the novel's oral nuances, Veit-Wild dismisses orality, and projects 'those forces that sought to maintain the repressive colonial order as forces of modernization and progress' (Zhuwarara, 1994:11).

Assigning unlimited power to colonialism enables Veit-Wild to conclude her study by saying that in Zimbabwe 'there is little of protest literature in the proper sense' (Veit-Wild, 1993: 7). Veit-Wild alone knows what is 'proper' protest literature in Zimbabwe. This strategy of discursive containment gives the sociological approach to Zimbabwean literature in *Teachers, Preachers, Non-Believers* the illusion of interpretive completeness or closure. In the end a potentially alternative literary hermeneutics in Zimbabwe that could have emerged from a thorough analysis of the interface between the Zimbabwean novel and orature is suppressed.

The limitations of the 'dominant thesis social paradigm' and the *Social History of the Shona Novel*

In the race for theory, Chiwome's, *A Social History of the Shona Novel* cannot be accused of a 'refusal… to mention specific works of [Shona] creative writers, far less contemporary ones' that Barbara Christian (1994: 149) identifies in recent post-colonial theoretical writing. The problem of the 'poverty of theory' in *A Social History of the Shona Novel* manifests itself in different forms. The declared intention of Chiwome's project is presented as self-contradictory. On one hand, the critic writes that *A Social History of the Shona Novel* aims at 'polishing up theoretical tools employed so far in the study of fiction' (Chiwome, 1996: viii-ix). To the extent that the most recent theoretical work that came before Chiwome's book was Veit-Wild's *Teachers, Preachers, Non-Believers,* one can expect from Chiwome some interrogation of the assumptions informing Veit-Wild's sociological approach. Chiwome seems to be aware of the criticism that was beginning to be leveled against Veit-Wild's work, and because of that, he is partially forced to move out of the clutches of a full-blown sociological approach to the Shona novel. Chiwome signals this intention to modify his earlier assertion of polishing up or propping up the established theoretical 'canon' when he writes that 'a socio-historical approach is employed as the methodology of handling texts' (Chiwome, 1996: ix). For him, the approach allows the researcher to focus on context without being oblivious of the literary text. The main attraction of a socio-historical approach to the Shona novel is that it brings out the extrinsic and intrinsic aspects of art and thereby gives the 'otherwise multivalent cultural, sociological, historical, creative-genetic, literary and aesthetic approaches a common philosophical base' (Chiwome, 1996: ix).

To be fair to Chiwome, *A Social History of the Shona Novel* follows the pattern suggested in his declaration of intention. Chiwome's critical work begins by delineating socio-political factors that militated against the growth of a healthy Shona novel. In his work, African tradition, colonialism and missionary education are implicated in undermining the development of the Shona novel. Colonial education is said to have thoroughly infiltrated the structures of feeling created by the Shona writers, manipulating their voices to a point where those voices became barely recognizable. For Chiwome, Shona writers operated with dissociated sensibilities and worked with borrowed values. Colonial education is depicted as being so insidious that although the Shona novelists

> *wanted to articulate their own consciousness on the one hand, … their images were manipulated to pay homage to the new culture on the other. They wanted to speak for their suffering fellowmen, yet they were*

fragmented from them. Their words were Shona while the ideas conveyed worked against the interests of the Shona. They were recipients of colonialist education which made them less sensitive to the forces underlying the reality they depicted (Chiwome, 1996: 4).

This picture of alienation of the Shona novelists from their cultural milieu by the virulent forces of colonial education is further worsened by direct and indirect colonial state intervention to control the sensibilities of the Shona writers. For Chiwome, colonial state agents manipulated the Shona novel through the Literature Bureau whose role was to direct Shona authors along 'the path of least ideological resistance to the Rhodesian government' (Chiwome, 1996: 23). Editors 'stipulated themes and techniques so that authors would not be found in prison' (Chiwome, 1996: 24). From analysing the pernicious influence of state agents on the Shona novel, Chiwome moves on to discuss how the commodification of the Shona novel by the publishing industry also underdeveloped the Shona novel. He alleges that publishers dictated what could be consumed by the reading public, who were mostly blacks of school-going age.

Credit is due to Chiwome for identifying the political forces that were ranged against the development of a healthy Shona novel. In *A Social History of the Shona Novel*, the emphasis on how different colonial stakeholders underdeveloped Shona fiction is crucial to an understanding of the ambiguities in meanings that come out of the analysis of actual texts in context. Chiwome's work is detailed, and he is aware that during colonial days in Zimbabwe, fiction was one amongst many sites of contestation, incorporation and neutralization of a potentially resistant black poetics of liberation. But Chiwome's awareness of the socio-historical factors that undermined the fruition of a healthy Shona novel has not been rid of the influence of a deterministic sociological approach. There is no denying that colonial institutions severely curtailed the potential of what might have been a vibrant Shona novel. The evidence that Chiwome gives about how a passage on the 'land question' in Mutswairo's novel *Feso* was excised by colonial editors, and how the end of Mungoshi's *Ndiko Kupindana Kwamazuva* (1975) was tampered with to conform to the Rhodesia Literature Bureau's notion of a happy ending, is too compelling to ignore. Moreover, Chiwome does acknowledge that the constraints imposed on the Shona novel 'generated a counter-culture of liberation' (Chiwome, 1996: 6) amongst blacks in Rhodesia.

But the problem with *A Social History of the Shona Novel* is that a critical reappraisal of the novels that Chiwome studied reveals that the he lacked the critical language to retrieve those moments of resistance to colonial culture. It is true that *Feso* is cited as a novel that carries the rudiments of a resistance sensibility, but this is not pursued beyond the statement that it is an allegory of resistance to colonialism. The ways in which the cryptic cultural forms from black popular memory and oral traditions are constantly being transmuted in *Feso* to offer resistance to colonial culture remain unexplored in *A Social History of the Shona Novel*. The problem with Chiwome's socio-historical approach to the Shona novel is that it is wired to the reductive assumptions inherent in the sociological approach to African literature. This sociological approach is ironically constructed around the limited theoretical claims of yet another distorted approach to literature, rooted in what Tony Bennett (1994) describes as the 'dominant thesis' notion of explicating power relations in society. In this paradigm, authoritarian institutions such as colonial structures are assigned unlimited power and are depicted as having total control over every facet of the lives of the dominated. In the political economy of the imagery of the 'dominant thesis' paradigm, the lives of the ruled are distorted, manipulated and absorbed into the systems of power to the extent that they lose autonomy and individuality.

Considered in this framework, the central thesis of *A Social History of the Shona Novel* is that there is no African space that remained unaffected by colonialism. There is in this suggestion the belief that colonial power and discourse was possessed entirely by the colonizer. In *A Social History of the Shona Novel*, the aggressive construction of the image of colonialism as all-pervasive and powerful belongs to the discourse of cultural nationalism. It accords unwarranted unities to colonialism that it did not possess. Ironically, that colonial discourse inadvertently confirms that the Shona novel and its writers are colonialism's inferior Other, and projects the stereotype of a black person as a native bereft of strategies to resist colonialism. Chiwome did not understand that the African 'Other' as a colonial creation and stereotype is a split personality within which one finds contradictory elements of resistance, ambivalence and incorporation. *A Social History of the Shona Novel* is flawed by its over-emphasis on the poetics of victimization. Chiwome identifies novelists who were co-opted at the expense of those who depicted various forms of rejecting colonial culture. And yet, a re-reading of Aaron Chiunduramoyo's *Ziva Kwawakabva* [Know Your Roots] (1977) shows that it is a critique of the educated black elites who abandoned their African families, communities and values once they were socialized into colonial education. However, the fact that Ngoni, a character in the novel, comes back to the family and communal fold radically places the novel within Amilcar Cabral's (1973) poetics and beliefs that the educated Africans had to commit class suicide and 'return to the source', which in the context of the African situation of the 1960s was to identify with the aspirations of the masses for self-rule. The reality which Chiwome's work did not explore is that in fact some of the once alienated African educated elites *did* commit class suicide and joined the liberation struggle in Zimbabwe as leaders of the struggle.

Part of the problem of *A Social History of the Shona Novel* is its judicious selection of particular novels considered representative without underlining the content of that which the novels are purported to represent. Where Veit-Wild organized her work in terms of black writers' generational responses to colonialism in Rhodesia, Chiwome reels back to the old notion inherited from George Kahari (1990) who categorized the Shona novel in terms of those belonging to the 'old' and 'new' world. What precisely these terms are supposed to mean, or what their analytical validity is meant to be is not clear. One is bound to conclude that the terms are used to serve in ways synonymous with the modernist jargon that describes social reality along the teleologies of tradition versus modernity. And yet, the question of literary representative-ness that Chiwome takes for granted in his selection of texts can no longer be taken lightly in literary theory or in criticism as narrative discourse. Hayden White reminds us that the issue of representative-ness in any selection of texts to be studied is ideologically motivated and thus highly suspect, especially where critics favour certain texts that confirm the assumptions that they already hold. For White, in literature the notion of representative-ness is brought under question, and literature's status as both evidence of the spirit of the age and the privileged interpreters of its own time and place is placed in doubt, because 'representative-ness and interpretation are no longer taken as unambiguous possibilities of texts' (White, 1987: 187).

Chiwome unwittingly betrays his prejudices by selecting and analysing those novels that openly and predictably reveal the negative influence of the colonial structures of authority on Shona fiction. On reading *A Social History of the Shona Novel*, the reader comes out fairly informed about Chakaipa's *Dzasukwa Mwana Asina Hembe* [The Beer Pots are Cleaned While the Child is Naked] (1967), in which some Africans are depicted as irresponsible since their children could go naked while the parents indulged in the unrewarding practice of beer-drinking. But Chiwome has not taken time to analyse the text so as to establish why some Africans were being irresponsible not looking after their families well. That some Africans were complicit in the designs of colonialism has not been theorized in the critic's work. Similarly, Bernard Chidzero's *Nzvengamutswairo* [Dodge the Broom] (1957) makes the reader aware of the potency of colonial education and how it prepared the likes of the character Samere to become functionaries and vectors in 'defending' the material and educational interests of the colonial order. However, Chiwome has not analysed the metaphor of the 'mutswairo' or broom and problematized why it was that some characters like Wadyazhewe needed to dodge the broom of colonial influence that had come to sweep their ways under in order to pave the way for a new colonial modernity. If one remembers that Father Biehler of Chishawasha was in 1897 petitioning his superior, Lord Grey, to authorize the killing of all the Shona people from the age of 14 (Ranger, 1967, Zhuwarara, 2001, Vambe, 2004) it becomes easier to appreciate the metaphorical meaning of Chidzero's novel. It becomes possible to read dodging the broom as a gesture of resistance to colonial misrule. These deeper layers of the Shona novel's potential meanings escape Chiwome's sociological approach.

In contrast to his critical analysis of Chakaipa and Chidzero's novels, *A Social History of the Shona Novel* reserves little space for the critical discussion of Aaron Chiunduramoyo's 1977 *Ziva Kwawakabva* [Know your Roots]. In my opinion, a detailed analysis of this text would have modified the pessimistic picture of literary malaise that Chiwome paints when he provides the reader with an uncomplicated analysis of the Shona novel.

Another conceptual problem in *A Social History of the Shona Novel* is the author's desire to correlate the historical factors that affected Shona literature to the intrinsic imagistic qualities of the Shona novel. To some extent, this is a self-defeating exercise because there is no one-to-one relationship or correspondence between the social factors and the metaphors used to describe, confirm or resist those social factors. In other words, the creative imagination of an artist is able to generate unforeseen meanings through the ways the author or artist selects, orders and deploys images and metaphors in his/her work.

To a large extent, Chiwome's reading framework excludes an alternative version of Zimbabwean reality that is not over-determined by colonial relations of production, and its modes of enunciation. The problem of narration and narrativity in the works that Chiwome concentrates on but does not exhaust is much more complicated than what is suggested by *A Social History of the Shona Novel*. In other words, if we view the notion of representation as the medium or instrument with which the conflicting claims of the imaginary and the real are mediated, arbitrated, or resolved in a discourse we begin to comprehend both the appeal of *A Social History of the Shona Novel* and the grounds for modifying its ways of explaining the fate of the Shona novel.

Because the political factors that impacted on the Shona novel are, according to Chiwome, institutional and hence putatively real, they are represented with the formal coherence of a conventional history. But how these factors are drawn into the novel to become political text has not adequately been theorized. Consequently, a single dimension in understanding the Shona novel has been proffered in Chiwome's critical work, and this aspect is about the infantilization of the Shona novel. And yet, it is possible that the same Shona novels might yield new insights and bring out different versions of realities when subjected to wider interpretive grids. This has not been considered and, as a result, just as in *Teachers, Preachers, Non- Believers*, Chiwome's *A Social History of the Shona Novel* used a sociological approach to Zimbabwean literature so pervasively to a point where fiction has been analysed as an artifact that renders visible the ideology of the ruling class.

And yet in both the experience of the black people and to some extent, in the Shona fiction such as *Pafunge* [Think of It](1972), by Thompson Tsodzo, the blacks did not at *all* times totally accept colonialism as their intellectual and moral leadership. That this point is not emphasized in Chiwome's critical work shows the inadequacies of a sociological approach in accounting for the contradictory and sometimes ambivalent responses of African characters in Shona literature. Ultimately, *A Social History of the Shona Novel* demonstrates the failure of a sociological approach to acknowledge the that critical practice is defined not so much by binary unities, but that it is radically fractured from within, and that in theory it is from these fissures that one can explain the double movement of obeisance and resistance, of opposition and complicitly in characters found in Shona literature.

Conclusion

In this chapter I have argued for the necessity of engaging in meta-commentary. Critical practice is not an innocent undertaking. It is the process where by values that often find their ways into people's lived experiences are generated, debated and naturalized as knowledge which defines people in terms of history, time and place. In many ways it dramatizes the struggle of values in the field of literature and life. It is in this context that this chapter explored the contradictions in a sociological approach to the Zimbabwean literature. This approach, as demonstrated in the critical works of Veit-Wild and Chiwome, reveals that when a theory's assumptions are not subjected to critical contestations and interrogations, the theory runs the risk of pretending to 'think' and 'know' itself as the only approach that can adequately explain literature and life. The two critics give us a one-sided version of Zimbabwe's emerging literary hermeneutics. The different senses in which these two texts may be considered theoretically impoverished sets the agenda for future generations of critics. An alternative interpretative framework would have provided the reader with complexities in ways of reading the novels. Such a theoretical framework would help us to understand that as a symbolic act, fiction is a force field where the people's identities are neither totally distorted by dominant forces nor a cultural space where it is possible to recuperate an unproblematic African identity.

Part III.

Childhood, memory and identity

Chapter 7

Writing home: inscriptions of whiteness/ descriptions of belonging in white Zimbabwean memoir-autobiography

Ashleigh Harris

In both Peter Godwin's *Mukiwa* and Alexandra Fuller's *Don't Let's Go to the Dogs Tonight* (hereafter *Don't Let's Go*), the formulation of white Zimbabwean identity is complicated by the fact that, as memoir-autobiographies, the writing of white identity is deeply entwined with the writing of self. The wealth of criticism dealing with the dialectic between personal and political memories and histories in a South African context provides some insight into the relationship between nostalgic constructions of the past, which in both *Mukiwa* and *Don't Let's Go* are developed through the narration of childhood, and Zimbabwean political history. More specifically, Sarah Nuttall provides a useful starting point for this discussion by defining autobiography as a '...public rehearsal of memory' (Nuttall, 1998: 75). This phrase implies that the narration of one's personal memory, simply as an act of remembering, or as an index to broader political history, is only ever a rehearsal, and thus can never be fixed in any one point in space and time. While this point seems obvious, the public discourses surrounding the Truth and Reconciliation Commission[1] (hereafter TRC) in South Africa seemed to urge an entire nation to a far cruder assumption that personal testimony could be the means through which national healing would occur. Testimony was constructed as truly cathartic in that it promised not only the purgation of traumatic memory, but purification through that purgation. That is to say, by speaking one's personal memory of one's experience of the past, one was contributing to the purification of an entire nation. The TRC overtly constructed itself through discourses of fixity, as its very name implies, and offered a traumatized nation the illusion that the stabilization of that past was possible.

This illusion that personal testimony will finally fill in the cracks and interstices of South African history and articulate the previously censored and suppressed

---

[1]   The Truth and Reconciliation Commission was set up by the Government of National Unity as a forum in which the human rights abuses and violence suffered and perpetrated by those in the apartheid regime could be heard and recorded publicly and officially. The commission ran between 1995 and 2002.

has been beneficial, since the entire logic of the TRC hinges upon constructing a version of apartheid as a past trauma from which the present nation can heal. This seemingly utopian construction of the 'rainbow nation' (a term utilized by government and media throughout the transition period to describe the 'new' South Africa as a multicultural and multiracial nation) – a nation in healing – is in the Aristotelian sense simultaneously eutopian (good place) and *outopian* (no place); a happy illusion, yet one that is pragmatically and politically efficacious. As Sarah Nuttall and Carli Coetzee point out, there has been a great deal of critical attention on '…the structuring metaphors that shape personal and collective memory, including the evolving metaphor of the rainbow nation, and the discourse of reconciliation' (Nuttall and Coetzee, 1998a: 5). Moreover, these utopian (master) narratives require that the '…stories of the past that South Africans are telling try in one way or another to find a place between public resistance and private healing; and between private resistance and public healing' (Nuttall, 1998: 76). Any articulation of personal memory in testimony, or in autobiography, becomes not only enunciated in the public sphere, but becomes subsumed within a broader social, political, and historical discourse of nationhood.

Just as discourses of healing and reconciliation provide a 'destination' for public testimony and narrative, so too, as Nuttall argues, does autobiography involve a '…writing from a beginning towards a destination' (Nuttall, 1998: 80). The master signified in this instance is not simply the self, but the life of the self within a broader socio-political context. Nuttall reads the memoir, as opposed to the autobiography, as a

> portion (usually an obsessive or troubled one) of a life – a pathological experience, or an experience of victimhood. This is frequently accompanied by a pressure on the ending to stage a recovery. It may have to do with a wider cultural disposition for uplifting endings, or with a culture's discomfort with untranscended tragedy – or both (Nuttall, 1998: 80).

Thus the destination of memoir, according to this formulation, is also fixed; in this instance upon redemption and healing.

Redemption itself is, of course, constructed in a variety of ways in South African memoirs, the most significant for the discussion that follows being the redemptive narrative of confession; a form mostly associated in a South African context with white autobiographies and memoirs. In his seminal discussion of autobiography and confession in *Doubling the Point: essays and interviews*, J.M. Coetzee (1992) writes of Dostoevsky's *Notes from Underground* that the underground man's

> confession [is] made via a process of relentless self-unmasking which might yet be not the truth but a self-serving fiction, because the unexamined, unexaminable principle behind it may be not a desire for the truth but a desire to be a particular way. The more coherent such a hypothetical fiction of the self might be, the less the reader's chance of knowing whether it is a true confession (Coetzee, 1992: 280).

This observation is interesting when applied to the white South African narrative of confession in the post-apartheid era. The discourses of reconciliation discussed above make possible the redemption of white guilt-laden memory: perpetuators of the apartheid regime are given the opportunity to place their narratives of self and memory within the broader socio-political discourses of reconciliation via confession. Whether we can ever know that these are true confessions or not is the source of much debate surrounding confessions of former propagators of apartheid in present day South Africa: the line between exculpation and redemption in such confessions is somewhat hazy.[2]

The ambiguity between white exculpation and redemption in narrativising the past is exacerbated in a contemporary Zimbabwean context in which Robert Mugabe's early statements of national reconciliation have given way to overt threats to white Zimbabweans' sense of belonging in the country. Mugabe's statement, printed in the *Bulawayo Chronicle* and *The Herald* (5 September, 2002), that white commercial farmers '…belong to Britain and let them go there. If they want to live here we will say "stay", but your place is in prison and nowhere else. Otherwise your home is outside the country,' is diametrically opposed to the seemingly magnanimous message of his victory speech in 1980 in which he stated:

> *Surely this is now the time to beat our swords into ploughshares so we can attend to the problems of developing our economy and our society…I urge you, whether you are black or white, to join me in a new pledge to forget our grim past, forgive others and forget, join hands in a new amity, and together, as Zimbabweans, trample upon racialism, tribalism and regionalism, and work hard to reconstruct and rehabilitate our society as we reinvigorate our economic machinery (See De Waal, 1990: 46).*

Mugabe's evocation of reconciliation in this speech was politically convenient, since it undermined the conservative white Rhodesian construction of him as 'an uncompromising terrorist' (De Waal, 1990: 6). His more recent statements, however, have allowed Zimbabweans (of all races) and the international media to return to the construction of him as an 'uncompromising terrorist'. The extent to which this construction is evidence of the perpetuation of racist stereotypes and belief systems in the western press is beyond the scope of this paper. However, the ways in which this contemporary view of Mugabe influences how white Zimbabwean identity is constructed, and at times utterly dehistoricized for an international audience, is pertinent.

Mugabe's recent statements, as illustrated in the above quotation, often evoke the ways in which Zimbabwe's complex colonial history informs the politics of white ownership of land, and white belonging on that land. Recent constructions

---

2   Mark Behr's confessional address in which he admitted to having been a spy for the apartheid regime is an interesting case in point. See Nuttall and Coetzee (1998: 2-3) for a discussion of Behr's speech.

in the western press of emigrated white Zimbabweans as exiles and refugees reinstate the significance of the relationship between white Zimbabwean identity and ownership of land. The identity of the 'exile' and the 'refugee' is one deeply entwined with the loss of land, or belonging in/on the land of one's nation of origin. This has allowed white Zimbabwean (ex)land owners to shed, along with their land, the identity of 'settler': in the past the marker of colonial occupation and oppression. Ironically then, in the loss of ownership of land the somewhat tenuous relationship between self and land implied by the word 'settler' is replaced by a seemingly authentic claim to the land as the place of origin.

This shedding of settler identity and claiming of the status of refugee is demonstrated in Chloe Traicos's controversial documentary film, *A Stranger in My Homeland* in which she presents a series of personal testimonies as a comment on the current political situation in Zimbabwe. The use of the possessive pronoun 'my' in this title indicates that Traicos is presenting her version of Zimbabwean social reality through her own autobiographical lens, and that she lays claim to Zimbabwe itself. Home, here, is presented in the language of possession, while the word 'stranger' implies displacement. In an interview about this film, Traicos goes so far as to liken white displacement and forced removal from Zimbabwe to that of the Jews in Nazi Germany. She states:

> *Hitler used the Jews, a wealthy minority group, as a scapegoat in the same way Mugabe has used the whites. Hitler told the starving Germans that it was the Jews' fault they were all starving. In exactly the same way, Mugabe has blamed the starvation of the blacks on the whites* (The Australian, *13 January 2003*).

The comparison between Robert Mugabe and Adolf Hitler is one sustained by the Zimbabwean statesman's recent infamous speech of 21 March 2003, in which he states: 'This Hitler has only one objective: justice for his people, sovereignty for his people, recognition of the independence of his people and their rights over their resources. If that is Hitler, then let me be a Hitler tenfold.' (*Mail & Guardian*, 25 March 2003). However, Traicos's comparison also parallels white Zimbabweans' experiences under Mugabe to those of Jews in Nazi Germany thereby dehistoricising whiteness in this particular context and erasing the complex history of colonization that has informed white Zimbabwean identity thus far.

This dehistoricising of race, and racial history, is further developed when Traicos goes on to state that Zimbabwe was an 'ideal place to grow up. There never was any racial tension there when I was growing up. It was newly independent' (*The Australian*, 13 January 2003). For Traicos, the idealized, deracialized, depoliticized and dehistoricized memory of her childhood underpins her belief that Zimbabwe is a nation in which she, as a white inhabitant, 'belongs'. Traicos's nostalgic construction of the past as depoliticized and without 'racial tension', and the very profound racial tensions throughout Zimbabwe's history, are so discrepant that one observes a thorough separation of her personal narrative from broader political and national ones (that is, until she is forced to leave the country at which point she inscribes her personal story into a historical narrative). Ironically, Mugabe's revocation of the discourses of reconciliation has allowed for a white re-imagining of the past that, in this instance, exculpates white Zimbabwean involvement in racial tensions through dehistoricizing that white identity. This mode of exculpation is very different to contemporary white South African narrations of apartheid in which exculpation is attained via the confessional narrative; a process of redemption which is made possible through the national discourses of reconciliation and multiculturalism.

While the political climate in Zimbabwe in 1996, the year in which Godwin published *Mukiwa*, was already one verging on crisis, it was not until 1999 that the Commonwealth press began to intensify its focus on the controversial land redistribution programme in Zimbabwe. The international climate into which Godwin's text emerged was one that had not yet been saturated with narratives of white Zimbabwean experience. Godwin made use of this international lack of information to tell what he saw as an untold story. It may be this aspect of *Mukiwa* that led Caroline Rooney to accuse Godwin of suffering from a 'saviour complex' (Rooney, 2001: 175). Godwin's compulsion to narrate the horrific stories he encounters in his service in Matabeleland must be considered against this fragile discourse of reconciliation that was undermined in the 1990s, via increasing racial tension around land issues and Mugabe's own statements about white belonging and ownership of land in Zimbabwe. It appears that *Mukiwa* writes directly into an era in which liberal white hopes for a reconciled and rehabilitated nation were beginning to waver, and new forms of inscribing white identity into Zimbabwean nationhood became necessary.

Considering this context in which Godwin writes *Mukiwa*, it is interesting to note that he opens the text with the claim '*Mukiwa* is intended as a memoir rather than an autobiography' (Godwin, 1996: Preface). This statement is in line with Nuttall's argument, outlined above, that the memoir in the Southern African context moves towards political and social redemption: Godwin clearly sees the writing of this memoir as his political and social responsibility, and believes that redemption is earned through the process of making public what he has experienced in Zimbabwe (particularly in Matabeleland).[3] This also accords with the definition of the memoir as a

---

[3] The Lawyers Committee for Human Rights report on Matabeleland states that it is home to 'the Ndebeles, or Ndebele-speaking people, who predominate in the southwest provinces of Matabeleland. Since 1982, due in large part to the presence of a limited number of insurgents in their midst, the Ndebeles have been subjected to a campaign of harassment and repression that has been scarcely distinguishable from the counter-insurgency campaign waged by the old white regime. Arbitrary arrests, detentions without charge, torture, summary executions – all have taken place on a significant scale in Matabeleland' (Berkley, 1986: 2). It was these human rights abuses and incidents of genocide (sometimes euphemistically referred to as the 'Matabele disturbances') that Godwin witnessed and felt compelled to narrative in *Mukiwa*.

[w]ritten record of people and events as experienced by the author; a form of autobiography that gives particular attention to matters of contemporary interest not closely affecting the author's inner life. It is not a formal personal history, but an assembly of memories (McArthur, 1992: 650).

However, Godwin's text is not only a memoir – it often slips into the autobiographical mode in which the writing self, or the writing of the self, seeks 'to explain and justify as well as to inform [and is] often confessional' (McArthur, 1992: 98). This slippage allows for interesting associated slippages (discussed below) between belonging and ownership; between description of landscape and inscription of the self into that landscape; between confession and exculpation and redemption; and between the writing of the experiences of the white Zimbabwean and the claiming of Zimbabwe as 'home'.[4]

Alexandra Fuller's *Don't Let's Go* is more overtly (though not entirely) autobiographical. Unlike *Mukiwa*, in which a portion of the nation's history is presented to us via an individual's story, *Don't Let's Go* offers us an individual's story set against the backdrop of a particular historical moment. The difference is a subtle one, and one that will only become clear in the discussion of these texts that follows. Fuller's text also slips, at certain points, into the modality of the memoir, and it is in these slippages that white identity is largely inscribed in her text.

In both texts, however, the most significant area of slippage, and of inscription of white identity, is between childhood and adulthood. Legitimacy and authenticity are inscribed in both narratives primarily through nostalgic representations of white childhood in Zimbabwe. It is interesting to note that both texts are marketed (predominantly for an international audience) as narratives of childhood in Zimbabwe. *Don't Let's Go* is subtitled 'An African Childhood', while *Mukiwa* carries the byline 'A White Boy in Africa'. Moreover, both the hard copy and paperback versions of both texts have photographs of the authors as children on the back cover. These titles and book covers provide a nostalgic frame for the texts, prior to the reading itself, perhaps because nostalgia gives authenticity to the inscription of the white self into the nexus of discourses that constitute Zimbabwean identity. Nostalgia for a Zimbabwean childhood allows the writer to imagine a space of political and racial innocence and naïveté; a prelapserian state of unquestioned belonging as a white child in Zimbabwe or Rhodesia. Nostalgia demarcates the space, both temporal and geographical, that delineates 'home' in both texts. Thus, while the individual's relationship with the past through memory is ostensibly personal, in both of these texts it is that memory which is crucially implicated in the inscription of the self into/onto Zimbabwe's land and history. The identification of the homeland is the metaphoric destination of both narratives, though in

---

[4] For a related discussion of self-representation and public memory in texts by Godwin, Ian Smith and Doris Lessing, see Chapter 9 of the present volume.

both instances this belonging is justified by and embedded in the narration of childhood memory. It would appear that the narration of one's childhood experiences in a place that denies one's belonging, and offers no recourse to the discourses of reconciliation and redemption through which to articulate white identity, becomes a means to inscribe one's self into the historical, political, and geographical landscape of Zimbabwe.

Mukiwa: 'The Home I Never Knew I Had'

In *Mukiwa*, white Rhodesian identity is implied from the very start with the sentence: 'It was still two years before *we* rebelled against the Queen' (Godwin, 1996: 3; emphasis added). However, the situation of childhood identity as Rhodesian is quickly framed by the child-subject's pre-political consciousness. The narrator does not only see himself as belonging to a white Rhodesian community, but also naively sees himself as a part of a black community. He says of the black policemen in search of a notorious gang: 'I knew most of them by name, but only their first names, which is what you called them by. Detective Sergeant Solomon *was my friend*' (Godwin, 1996: 13; emphasis added). Through the narrative of the child, describing the uneven power relationships between black constables and a white child *and* claiming a space of belonging to this group of people (with the words 'my friend') is made possible. The naïveté of the narrator puts him beyond reproach, and yet the broader political conditions are made clear to the reader. Godwin uses this narrative technique of childhood innocence often in the first book of *Mukiwa*, in most instances to iterate the child's sense of belonging. The child Peter accompanies Violet, the Godwins' domestic worker, to the congregation of the Apostolic Church of Africa and immediately locates himself in a position of belonging through the use of the plural pronoun:

> *Over the next few years, we Apostolics became more established and more numerous. We built a huge hut the traditional way. Working only on Sundays – we could break the Sabbath because this was Jehovah's business – we nevertheless managed to complete the project in less than two months (Godwin, 1996: 25).*

The tone of this passage is predominantly one of childish naïveté, but the subtext is a little more complex. Godwin uses a language that inscribes the white child, albeit with a hint of irony, into the black religious community. The language of naïveté coincides with the language of belonging.

The episode in which the young Peter arriving at boarding school realizes that he 'had never seen so many white children in one place before' (Godwin, 1996: 54) implies that his childhood prior to school-going was not dominated by a sense of belonging to a white community. Prior to his coming-to-awareness of white identity at a white school (in which a patriotic headmaster insists that all the students listen to Ian Smith's declaration of Unilateral Independence on the radio – Godwin, 1996: 72), the memories of childhood exist in a place beyond such racial markers, preceding the political awareness that leads to the narrator's sense of cultural displacement. This is evidenced in the episode in which Peter, as a child, writing a letter to the local *Sangoma*, addresses him as 'Mr. Wizard' (Godwin, 1996: 41): what could retrospectively be constructed as cultural displacement in this episode, is masked for the young Peter by naïveté as to his own origins. Not having the words to address a Sangoma in English does not lead him, at this point, to a crisis of displacement. It is only once he becomes entrenched in the traditions of colonial schooling in which one's cultural allegiance is marked by English hymns and songs that have little relevance in Africa, yet are ardently held to, that the crisis of belonging emerges.

This crisis is articulated as one of birth place and origins. Peter's mother tells him that he is a '*pukka* African. The first Godwin to be born out here' (Godwin, 1996: 139). Yet this does not quell the young Peter's crisis of belonging. He taunts his sister with the accusation: 'You're actually a Pom, you know'. But when she responds by calling him a rock spider, 'which was a derogatory name for Afrikaners', he ruminates:

> at least real rock spiders had lots of relatives in Africa. Uncles and aunts, cousins and grandparents, who came to visit and gave them presents. Black people all had plenty of relatives too, and they were never lonely. It made me sad that we had no relatives around (Godwin, 1996: 139).

This awareness of loneliness and displacement is exacerbated as the young Peter comes to political awareness. The racism of the character Radetski, a mine boss on the mine that Peter's father manages, alienates the narrator. Yet his, somewhat meek, attempt to distance himself from this racism through a joke that is 'supposed to show how South African law is unjust to blacks' (Godwin, 1996: 195), and thereby articulate his allegiance with the black workers in the mine, does not convince the black workers of any such allegiance. The narrator is left feeling 'hard done by and resentful', as indicated in his claim that '[you] just couldn't win, really. I felt resigned to the fact that there really wasn't much room in the middle in Africa – all sides ended up despising you' (Godwin, 1996: 195).

The young Peter's increasing sense of alienation in Africa is intensified by his feelings of displacement towards his British ancestry and culture:

> And for the first time I got a glimpse of how far we had strayed from our mother culture and mutated into this quite separate people. And I realised that was why my parents would never really consider going home to England, because England wasn't home any more, even to them (Godwin, 1996: 197).

It is because the memories of early childhood pre-exist this crisis of belonging that the narrator views his early childhood nostalgically. Yet as the narrator comes to political and racial awareness and this sense of belonging is slowly eroded away, it would appear that the nostalgia for childhood becomes intertwined with a nostalgia for the Zimbabwean landscape. Godwin begins to describe his relationship with the land as a means of inscribing himself into the landscape and thereby claiming a white Zimbabwean identity. It is interesting that it should be land, that ever contentious issue in Zimbabwean politics, that Godwin turns to as a marker of his belonging in that country. But it is not the actual ownership of land that marks belonging in this text. Indeed, the narrator's displacement is actualized by his constant physical movement: his family moves from the Eastern Highlands to Mangula, he moves from home to school in Harare, from school to training camp, from training camp to Matabeleland, from Matabeleland to Cambridge, and after Cambridge Godwin writes of his constant movements across national boundaries because of his journalistic career.

Throughout his wanderings Godwin seems to have a transitory relationship with Zimbabwean land. The political issues of land redistribution are hinted at from the very start of the text, when the attackers of Oom Piet Oberholzer, the event that begins the narrative, leave a note at the scene of the murder that reads: '*This is the work of the Clocadile [sic] Gang... We will keep on fighting until all white setlars are going and our land is returned. VIVA CHIMURENGA!*' (Godwin, 1996: 11-12). The Crocodile Gang's grammatical and spelling errors indicate their estrangement from the English language; yet that language is itself estranged from the land. In *White Writing: On the Culture of Letters in South Africa*, J.M. Coetzee states that the 'questions that trouble white South African poets above all are, as we might expect, whether the African landscape can be articulated in a European language, whether the European can be at home in Africa' (Coetzee, 1980: 167). This statement's elision of the problems of articulating an African landscape and belonging in/to that landscape is one that Godwin also makes in *Mukiwa*, although this text assumes that the English language is an adequate medium through which to describe the African landscape. Therefore, instead of belonging being marked by ownership of land, Godwin inscribes himself into the land via his descriptions of the Zimbabwean landscape.[5]

It is interesting that descriptions of the landscape in *Mukiwa* often follow the enunciation of the narrator's feelings of displacement. Shortly after being told by his parents that his family is about to leave the Eastern Highlands, Peter goes on a 'final expedition up the Chimanimani mountains' (Godwin, 1996: 166). Heading off alone, he recalls:

> *[the Chimanimani] pass was part of the ancient slave trail from the interior out to the Mozambique coast. I thought of all the thousands of slaves that must have trudged over these mountains, shackled together by logs attached to collars around their necks; wrenched from their homes and*

---

5   Terence Ranger makes a similar claim about Doris Lessing's fictional rendering of landscape, arguing that 'Lessing lays the obligations of childhood memory upon [landscape]' (Ranger, 1994: 4).

destined for a miserable life of captive toil. And now I was being wrenched from my home too *(Godwin, 1996: 166; emphasis added).*

This identification with slaves torn from their homes is followed by a lengthy description of the Chimanimani mountains which concludes with the narrator ruminating on the possibility of his being struck by lightning on the top of these mountains. In a passage that clearly inscribes his sense of belonging in this landscape, he states: 'Maybe [being struck by lightning] was God's way of ensuring that I would never leave the Eastern Highlands. I couldn't think of anywhere I would rather die than on top of the Chimanimanis. Maybe this was fate' (Godwin, 1996: 168). The narrator's description of the landscape is evoked by, and concluded with, a God-ordained belonging that is constructed as being beyond human politics, culture or language. Belonging on and to the land is, therefore, inscribed here through the dehistoricizing evocation of fate, on the one hand, and the equally dehistoricizing parallel drawn between the narrator and slaves. It would also appear that the fact that Godwin never himself owns Zimbabwean land allows him to rebuff settler identity, and its complex racial history.

This nostalgic idealization of the landscape is undermined as the adult narrator confronts personal and historical trauma. The narration of the personal trauma of the death of Godwin's sister Jain in 1978 is quickly followed in the text by the narration of the broader national traumas suffered in the 'Matabele disturbances' in the 1980s. At this point the narration of self is replaced by the need to narrate what that self has witnessed. Personal trauma seems somehow eclipsed by national trauma, and the narrator is driven by a moral imperative to tell the horrific stories of acts of genocide and to provide evidence for the existence of mass graves that have been silenced and suppressed, to a national and international audience. Ironically, as Godwin himself points out in *Mukiwa*, it is his journalistic link to the British press that makes this role possible and thus, the point at which belonging is driven not by the self, but by the needs of a broader community, is the point at which he finds national belonging. The further irony, of course, is that in discovering a place for himself in this role, he becomes 'declared an enemy of the state, *persona non grata* in [his] own home' (Godwin, 1996: 385).

This final sense of displacement leads the narrator to try to 'forget about Africa' (Godwin, 1996: 386), although, inevitably, the narrative concludes with his return to Zimbabwe and his ultimate act of claiming the nation as his home. At this point Godwin once again uses the plural pronoun to identify with a white Zimbabwean community in his statement: 'White society was seriously wounded. Peace had achieved something fifteen years of war could not. It had robbed us of our identity... Slowly the whites were undergoing a metamorphosis from settler to expatriate' (Godwin, 1996: 326). Yet, from this fleeting identification with the identity of settler or expatriate, Godwin quickly re-constructs himself as a 'returnee'. The statement, '[they] called us "returnees" and we believed in the government's policies of reconciliation – between races and between tribes' (Godwin, 1996:

327) implies that it is at the point at which the discourses of reconciliation are available in Zimbabwe that white Zimbabweans are able to claim this identity.

Godwin writes: 'I did eventually go back to visit Zimbabwe, to reclaim my past' (Godwin, 1996: 400). Return is thus constructed as a process of reclamation. It is interesting that Godwin's reclamation of what he calls 'the home I never knew I had' (Godwin, 1996: Preface) is a reclamation of memories of his childhood sense of belonging. He returns to the land of his birth and upbringing in an attempt to rediscover that land of belonging. However, the present day town of Chimanimani does not live up to his memories of the town in which he grew up (then called Melsetter): not only because certain parts of the town have fallen into disrepair, like the 'dusty' and 'airless' St George's-in-the-mountains (Godwin, 1996: 405), but because his adult experience does not allow him to see the town through the naïve eyes of the child he was. Alienated from this newly named town in which there are very few traces left of his personal and familial history, the narrator is unable to inscribe a Zimbabwean identity onto this present landscape. Instead, it is only his past, and the act of writing that past, that signifies belonging for him, since ultimately all other forms of belonging fail him.

The act of writing a portion of the nation's history *through* his own personal story is simultaneously an act of inscribing the self into that history and it is for this reason that the narrative slips between memoir and autobiography. It is in these interstitial spaces between the personal and the political, between reconciliation and political threat, between ownership and belonging and, crucially, between childhood and adulthood, that white Zimbabwean identity is located in *Mukiwa*, and it is through the nostalgic act of writing personal memories and the redemptive act of writing traumatic historical ones that this identity is authenticated.

Don't Let's Go to the Dogs Tonight: My Soul Has No Home

Alexandra Fuller's *Don't Let's Go* emerges out of a different political climate. While Godwin's *Mukiwa* may have been impelled by an urge to fill in the silences of recent Zimbabwean history, an urge that, as I have argued above, is crucial in its impact upon the author's construction of his sense of belonging in/to that country, Fuller's text is published in 2002, a year in which there was a proliferation of speech, writing and reportage on the controversial land redistribution programme in Zimbabwe. Moreover, the climate of threat for a white Zimbabwean population has been exacerbated in the last few years and the possibility of reconciliation has been destroyed. Perhaps as an act of defiance to Mugabe's insistence that white Zimbabweans all 'belong in Britain', Fuller is overt in claiming a white Zimbabwean identity from the outset. Like Godwin, she acknowledges the cultural displacement experienced by white, English-speaking Zimbabweans. Indeed, her narrative begins with statements such as 'I am the *wrong* colour', and in response to the question 'Where are you from *originally*' she responds:

I say, 'I'm African.' But not black. And I say, 'I was born in England'...But, 'I have lived in Rhodesia (which is now Zimbabwe) and in Malawi (which used to be Nyasaland) and in Zambia (which used to be Northern Rhodesia)... 'But my parents were born of Scottish and English parents' (Fuller, 2002: 8).

This list implies displacement in terms of both Fuller's own life and her lineage. She later claims: 'My soul has no home. I am neither African nor English nor am I of the sea' (Fuller, 2002: 35). Furthermore, Fuller acknowledges the difficulty of claiming African identity, as a person of European descent, given African colonial history. She states: 'how can we, who shed our ancestry the way a snake sheds skin in winter, hope to win against this history? We *mazungus*. We white Africans of shrugged-off English, Scottish, Dutch origin' (Fuller, 2002: 28). From the start of the text, the narrator's sense of displacement and non-belonging is clear, and yet alongside these statements of homelessness are statements that firmly establish Zimbabwe as the narrator's home:

In Rhodesia, we are born and then the umbilical cord of each child is sewn straight from the mother onto the ground, where it takes root and grows. Pulling away from the ground cause death by suffocation, starvation. That's what the people of this land believe. Deprive us of the land and you are depriving us of air, water, food, and sex (Fuller, 2002: 153-4).

Belonging, in this case, is closely tied to an idealized notion of land. Fuller's use of the pronoun 'we' is interesting here since she was not herself born in Rhodesia. Yet she extends this idealized construction of the relationship between birth and land to include not actual birth, but conception:

I am conceived in the hotel (with the casino in it) next to the thundering roar of the place where the Zambezi River plunges a hundred metres into a black-sided gorge. The following March, I am born into the tame, drizzling English town of Glossop. The plunging roar of the Zambezi in my ears at conception. Incongruous, contradictory in Derbyshire at birth (Fuller, 2002: 33).

This statement implies alienation from her actual birth place and identification with her place of conception. Moreover, the place of conception becomes the landscape through which Fuller claims a home for her 'soul': 'I plucked a new, different, worldly soul for myself – maybe a soul I found in the spray thrown up by the surge of that distant African river as it plummets onto black rocks and sends up into the sun a permanent arc of a rainbow' (Fuller, 2002: 35).

Yet having made this claim for her African soul, Fuller spends a large part of her narrative pointing out how vulnerable and lonely her childhood as a white child in Africa seem to her. The text begins with Bobo's (Fuller's nickname as a child) fear that there is a 'terrorist under the bed' (Fuller, 2002: 4-5); a fear that is not simply the imaginings of a child, as we see when Bobo is expected to know how to load and shoot a gun at a very young age. Unlike Peter Godwin's childhood belief that he belonged in and with a black community, Fuller's childhood self is constructed as feeling alienated when her school becomes racially integrated: she is teased by black children about her sunburned skin – ' "Argh! I smell roasting pork!" they shriek' (Fuller, 2002: 7) – and claims: '[we] are among two hundred African children who speak to one another in Shona – a language we don't understand – who play games that exclude us, who don't have to listen to a word we say' (Fuller, 2002: 151).

The Fuller family's movement from one farm to another exacerbates this sense of displacement and alienation. The land that they farm is never a source of stability for them since they are constantly uprooted; moving from Karoi to the Burma Valley farm called Robandi, from Robandi to Devuli, from Devuli to a tobacco farm in Malawi, and from Malawi to Zambia. The family thus interact with the land that they farm more as *bywoners*[6] than as land owners and as their relationship with the land becomes increasingly transitory, the landscape is described as increasingly hostile. Karoi is described as having 'some lift off the sunburned lowveldt. But not enough so you'd notice' (Fuller, 2002: 40). The Burma Valley 'represented the insanity of the tropics so precarious for the fragile European psyche. The valley could send you into a spiral of madness overnight if you were white and highly strung. Which we were' (Fuller, 2002: 47). Devuli is described as 'an uncomfortably hot place bordering on oppressive' and is declared 'Not Fit for White Man's Habitation' on a 1920 map (Fuller, 2002: 166). In Malawi the 'land bleeds red and eroding when it rains' (Fuller, 2002: 237) and Lake Chilwa is described as being 'less a lake than a large, mosquito-breeding swamp' (Fuller, 2002: 236). The increasing hostility of the African landscape seems to parallel the Fuller family's sense that the Zimbabwean nation is increasingly hostile towards them as white farmers. Robandi is 'designated as one of those that, under the new government, may be taken away (for nothing) or bought (at whatever nominal price) by the government for the purpose of "land redistribution"' (Fuller, 2002: 155).

Given the link that Fuller draws between birth and land, it is not surprising that the deaths of the three Fuller babies are connected to the family's losses of land. The Fuller's second child Adrian's death from meningitis leads them to leave Rhodesia; their fourth child Olivia's death by drowning follows swift on the heals of their arrival at Robandi; and the loss of their fifth child in childbirth seems to be attributed to the loss of Robandi. In each case it is Africa that claims the lives of these babies. Yet, for Fuller, the personal trauma of these terrible losses roots the family firmly in Africa. The land that takes these children is the homeland; not through a nostalgic memory of childhood or idealistic reinvention of the relationship to that land, but through the personal trauma experienced there.

---

6   *Bywoners* is an Afrikaans term commonly used to refer to tenant farmers.

Indeed, the personal traumas make an entirely nostalgic memory of childhood impossible. After Olivia's death the narrator divides her childhood into two halves: '[the] first half is the happy years, before Olivia dies' (Fuller, 2002: 95), the second after the baby's death. The first half of the narrator's childhood is associated with a naïve Rhodesian nationalism and childhood belief in white belonging, stability and superiority in that country:

> We'll be Rhodesian forever and ever on top of the roof driving through mud up the side of the mountain, through thick secret forests which may or may not be seething with terrorists, we'll keep singing to keep the car going. "We'll keep them north of the Zambezi till that river's runnin' dry! And this great land will prosper, 'cos Rhodesians never die!" (Fuller, 2002: 96).

This nationalist song presents the belief that the land will prosper in white hands. J.M. Coetzee's argument regarding nostalgia for the prospering land in Pauline Smith's *The Beadle* provides a useful parallel. He states that the

> farm Harmonie becomes a kind of Eden, producing a modest abundance...in prelapsarian innocence... The farm of Harmonie, at the heart of the valley, is presented as the culmination of a historical tradition. Indeed, there would be nothing in The Beadle to indicate that Harmonie is not the end of history – the achievement of an ideal equilibrium or stasis or finality in social relations such as could survive forever – were it not for a pervasive tone of nostalgia, hinting that the idyll of Harmonie belongs to the past (Coetzee, 1980: 67).

It is this place of prelapsarian innocence, in which 'good' farming reaps abundant rewards, before Olivia dies, before Robandi is lost, that Fuller's narrative views nostalgically. At the close of the text the Fuller parents settle on a fish farm, and Alexandra and her sister settle in marriage. These settlings coincide with the family's acceptance of their personal losses and realization that their idyll of the past can never be returned to. Settling comes at the point of acceptance, yet the personal traumas of the past fix the family in Zimbabwe, despite the fact that at the close of the text Bobo's sister Vanessa is the only family member actually living there.

In Fuller's text the writing of childhood memory is personally, rather than historically, redemptive. I would argue, against the claim printed on the back cover of the text stating that *Don't Let's Go* is about 'living through a civil war and coming to the realization that the side you have been fighting for may well be the wrong one', that there is little evidence in this text to suggest that Fuller undergoes any major political epiphany. Unlike *Mukiwa* in which Godwin overtly engages with the relationship between political context and selfhood and perhaps only discovers an interstitial space in which to inscribe white identity, *Don't Let's Go* seems to subsume political context under the autobiographical narrative of the white self. This may occur because the possibility of racial reconciliation has been foreclosed by the time Fuller writes this text. Thus, a very different mode of writing white Zimbabwean identity can be seen to emerge alongside, and perhaps because of, the international media's construction of white Zimbabweans as victims of, and in, their 'homeland'. Fuller, living in the United States, clearly writes into such constructions since her text articulates white Zimbabwean identity through a discourse of victimhood: an articulation that is in danger of obfuscating the complexities of Zimbabwean racial history.

In both *Mukiwa* and *Don't Let's Go to the Dogs Tonight*, the claiming of white Zimbabwean identity is a complex process in which the tensions between belonging and ownership, between displacement and settling, and between personal and national memories and histories are negotiated. Whiteness has a somewhat ambiguous space in this discursive matrix; veering between these binaries and never settling comfortably in any singular or fixed position. The negotiation of this terrain is framed by the public discourses that construct Zimbabwean whiteness nationally and internationally: both texts claim Zimbabwean identity despite, or perhaps because of, Mugabe's injunction to the contrary. In both texts it is the writing of the memories of childhood, whether nostalgic or traumatic, and descriptions of childhood belonging, that ultimately allows the authors to inscribe their identities as white Zimbabweans into that country's history, and permits them to write Zimbabwe as 'home'.

Chapter 8

Children of resistance: childhood, history and the production of nationhood in two Zimbabwean novels

Robert Muponde

Children played a central and active role in the liberation struggle in Zimbabwe and elsewhere in Africa. In Zimbabwe (then Rhodesia), the brutality of the colonial government's armed forces created a great determination on the part of nationalist guerrillas to fight, and change things. They 'actively recruited schoolchildren by making them more conscious of the poverty and misery of their situation and telling them that there was a way out and that they could fight for better conditions' (Zimfep, 1992: 22). Similarly, Victoria Brittain and Abdul Minty (1988) link the repression and activism of children in South Africa to the policies of apartheid, which induced in children the feeling that a war had been declared on them by the state. In *Ngunga's Adventures*, set in war-torn Angola, the Angolan writer Pepetela depicts conditions of war that transform the thirteen-year-old hero, the orphan Ngunga, into a combatant and an amalgam of Pan-African childhood experiences in the colonial worlds. He is at once 'the child of Africa' who 'goes to school in Soweto' and 'studies his people's oppression in the townships of Namibia' and 'shares his people's struggle and emergent organizations in the liberated villages of Zimbabwe' (in preface).

Researchers have not always looked for the transformations in creative agency that children in war represent. What has caught the attention of some is the spectre of 'plundered childhoods' (Maxted, 2003), and an unrelieved fatalism which sees children as having 'been the pawns of the mighty ever since Herod slaughtered the Innocents' (Acker, 1986: 11), hence the enormity of their suffering in war (Machel, 2001). Writers such as Alison Acker (1986) and Roger Rosenblatt (1984) have, on the other hand, attempted to study the varied nature of children's autonomy in war situations, and find that each situation produces its own version of agency. While for Rosenblatt the 'ardent, monotonous nationalism' of Palestinian children 'offered them a purpose for living, where much else in their lives had tried to take all purposes away' (1984: 94), the children in Alison Acker's book 'are not just victims; many of them are actively trying to change their own lives and those of others, in societies where this attempt is dangerous' (1986: 15).

In this chapter I look at how the space of war converts the symbolism of childhood into a social structure within which is rehearsed the imaginings of the foundational moments of the Zimbabwean nation, in two Zimbabwean novels: Wilson Katiyo's *A Son of the Soil* (1976) and Ben Chirasha's[1] *Child of War* (1985). I look specifically at how, in these texts, childhood as an invented 'social structure' and 'social artefact' (Postman, 1994: xii) convenes the 'in-tales' (Donald, 2000: 26) of a predetermined national history in two narratives that are replete with the metaphorics of war and nation-forming. I argue that the mediated childhoods in both novels are 'more than the sum of our memories' (Bachelard, 1971: 126). They are, rather, sets of archetypes erected to shore up a vision of an emerging nationhood constructed around the tropes of 'son of the soil' and 'child of war' which assumes a unified identity of 'children of resistance'. The twin tropes, which link childhood inextricably with the 'soil' and 'war', point to what Gaston Bachelard theorized as a distinct 'new found childhood' (ibid: 126), a 'distinctness of a beginning' (ibid: 124), and a specific 'cosmicity of childhood' (ibid: 126) associated with the birth, struggle and emergence of the Zimbabwe nation.

A Son of the Soil

Wilson Katiyo's novel tells a story of the stresses and struggles of growing up in colonial Rhodesia. Alexio, the novel's hero, is the only child of a couple plagued by miscarriages. His father dies in mysterious circumstances. His mother refuses to be taken as a wife by Gomo, her husband's brother, and is chased away from the village. Gomo, keen to deprive the mother of any contact with her son, and also unable to take care of the boy, sends the three-year-old Alexio away. He is taken care of by Gomo's daughter Rudo, a domestic worker in Salisbury (now Harare), the capital city. Alexio is forced out of the city at age five by Rudo's employer, a white settler, for having fought with the white woman's two children. Rudo takes Alexio to a farm school in Macheke to live with Chipo, her young sister. Here at age six, he is nearly murdered by Chipo's father-in-law, for having witnessed the latter killing his wife. He is returned to Gomo, who arranges to have the boy taken care of by a brutal childless couple, the Murimis. After five years of slavery in their fields, Alexio is again sent back to his village. He finally confronts the abusive Gomo, and leaves for Salisbury, the capital, for Rudo, education and work. Lost in Salisbury, he meets Sam, a young boy who initiates him into political consciousness. Later, Alexio, still a schoolboy, is harassed by the colonial police, tortured and detained without trial. A white expatriate couple, Paul and Sarah Davies, drive him back to his village where he immediately joins the first group of guerrilla recruits. The story ends with the first gun fight between colonial soldiers and the African guerrillas, which coincides with the first cries of Alexio's baby.

---

[1]   Ben Chirasha is the pseudonym of Shimmer Chinodya, the author of the award-winning novel *Harvest of Thorns*.

A Son of the Soil depicts a childhood that is not only a condition but a history. Recollections come 'structured by ideology and discourses' (Middleton, 1992: 21) that seek to mark out the child as an instance of historical continuity and therefore a structure of perception. In the novel, the colonial encounter is likened to continuous misfortunes; hence childhood is both a life-threatening experience, and a stage for new beginnings. Musaemura Zimunya views Alexio as 'a heroic seeker of freedom' (1982: 95) and believes that his childhood is '[f]rom the start [...] marked out by fate for a heroic quest for truth and freedom' (ibid: 94).

The recollection of Alexio's childhood is structured into a history and ideology that establishes cyclic links with a broken heroic ancestry. Sekuru, the Old Man, narrates the disastrous encounters with colonial agents at the end of the nineteenth century. He tells how a man called Shonga was killed, in the first uprising against white settlers, 'with his fingers still clawed around the neck of a white man' (21). Shonga turns out to be the elder brother of Sekuru's father. Sekuru himself is Alexio's grandfather. Sekuru dies after having foretold the birth of Alexio. His illness and death coincide with the cultural confusion in the country as represented by the influence of the mission school and church, as well as the miscarriages and pregnancy of his daughter-in-law:

> *There was nothing particularly unusual about the fact that at the same time Sekuru was so ill, one of his daughters-in-law, Tendayi, the wife of Rugare, the old man's only son with his late third wife, was pregnant. This was her fourth pregnancy. Unfortunately, the other three pregnancies had all ended as miscarriages. Everyone in the village was hoping this time she would have the baby. (26)*

Rugare had deserted his traditional culture and became a Christian. The miscarriages that his wife Tendayi suffer are viewed as punishment for turning his back on his culture. It is only when Rugare became 'disillusioned with Christianity' (29) and went to make peace with his father Sekuru, that he is rewarded with a boy child, Sekuru's last conditional gift to the erring couple. Sekuru admonishes the couple: '[The spirits of the ancestors] are not pleased, Rugare... You can't go on defying their will any longer. You have to mend your ways. Take this as a warning' (31).

Despite the warning, Rugare and his wife convert to Christianity soon after Alexio is born. They change his name from the 'pagan' Shona Chikomborero ('a blessing') for the new and 'civilized' Alexio (32). However, Rugare is stricken by a bolt of lightning while trying to rescue Alexio from an ancestral black snake that was licking the face of the baby in the fields. He dies on the spot.

Alexio's cyclic links with history and spirituality inaugurate the birth of a new warrior spirit whose key trope is 'son of the soil'. Alexio's birth is equated to the resurrection and animation of subterranean life forces of his society; in this sense he has a Christ-like significance to his community. '[The people] all tend to agree about one thing: there had to be something more than a mere coincidence between Sekuru's death and the birth of the child on that same day' (32).

Alexio's childhood can be taken as a symbolic form of spirit possession, a reconstitution of a dialogue with the heroic past, carried through the spaces of war in which the subject reconfigures and launches the race. It is a childhood in which the ego of the race remains indissoluble (see Walcott, 1995: 371) and seeks to authenticate itself, and a new capacity to aspire for a renewed quest for autonomy, unity and identity resonates with the cultural nationalism of the epoch.

Alexio's joining the armed struggle is both a spiritual and physical journey to reconnect with roots and to seek new routes for the national struggle. An unnamed figure approaches Alexio in the mountains, and has special words 'to say to Chikomborero Shonga' (147) – note how he reverts to his ancestor's name Shonga as well as the first name that links him to his ancestral spirits and the circumstances of his birth. The unnamed visitor proceeds to isolate the significance attached to Alexio in the armed struggle: 'The rest of the warriors will be fighting for our country. But you, Chiko, grandson of Sekuru, a descendant of Shonga, will be fighting not only for our land but for your village as well. Fight well!' (147).

The circle closes; the circumstances of Alexio's birth are replicated, only this time, in place of the ailing and dying Sekuru, it is the country that is symbolically under the extreme strain occasioned by colonial rule and is in need of relief. When, soon after Alexio joins the young guerrillas in the mountains, 'a fierce gun battle was raging just outside Makosa's village when the first cries of a baby were heard' (147), there is a sense of history repeating itself. The war has come to symbolize birth, in the same way Sekuru's death on the day Alexio is born is a sign of continuity in the cycles of life.

The liberation war is central to an understanding of how the Zimbabwe nation is forged and imagined. The throes of birth and death amalgamating in the sounds of gun fire and Alexio's baby institute imaginaries of pain and pleasure, birth and death, blood and soil, childhood and age at the core of the values of the embryonic nation. The cries of the baby symbolize the purity and pleasures and hopes of the new nation which the guerrillas' guns seek to realize in the space of war. The space of war allows an expanded sense of childhood and its agentive role in the stimulation of memory and history, and the imagining of the driving forces and scope of the nation in suffering and at birth. On the other hand, childhood as history is structured into a deterministic tale of resistance against colonial brutality. Alexio's childhood is situated in the 'complex network of in-tales' (Donald, 2000: 26) of history which 'represent a nesting of origins' (ibid: 26). The 'in-tales' are interconnected histories which build a sense of common fate and destiny. These stories, as narrated in folk tale form by Sekuru, prefigure the form of the nation. This form is adumbrated in a structure that encapsulates a complex mix of linearity and circularity.

Katiyo's novel has a tripartite structure, with the three parts titled 'In the Beginning', 'Discovering the Time' and 'Closing a Circle'. It is a structure that lends itself to a linear model of narrating the nation and its origins. Musaemura Zimunya (1982) understands the linearity of the story to relate to three significant phases. In the beginning is the story of Sekuru, 'a source of family and national history and fountain of cultural consciousness' (95) and an archetypal figure in Zimbabwean literature. In Sekuru's story are the seeds of national consciousness. In 'Discovering the Time' Alexio is portrayed as a 'representative of a large group of people who are outraged by their fate' (95) in a colonial setting. In 'Closing a Circle' Alexio not only discovers institutionalized racism, jail and police brutality, but decides to shatter the circularity of the story of oppression by engaging the oppressors on the battlefield as a guerrilla. He becomes a 'son of the soil' when he decides to close the circle through armed combat. In becoming a guerrilla, he embodies and enlivens the narratives of Shonga, his warlike ancestor; the heroic story of Chief Chuma; and the prophetic story of Sekuru. These in-tales do not only speak of the nexus between childhood, history and resistance, but provide a complex texture and webbing to the nation-space as articulated by the metaphor of Alexio's childhood. The narrative structure of the novel alludes to 'an immense potential for cultural regeneration and national resurgence' (Donald, 2000: 27), while the scenes of childhood it stages renew visions of nationalist unity and ancient heroism.

The structure of the novel is given force by the 'pattern of eternal return and guarantee of heroic triumph' (Donald, 2000: 25) that a circular model of history projects. Drawing from the folkloric tradition that informs the novel's structure, it is not difficult to make links between the circular story with its tripartite settings and the motif of eternal return to origins. The structure of the story confers 'a sense of inevitability – and therefore "naturalness" – on the prospect of the hero's success' (Donald, ibid: 26). Donald believes that the use of the folktale genre 'in itself implies a cultural continuity, a seamless link between the past and present' (ibid.), making the novel a tempting model to the 'nationalist visionary' (ibid.).

It is in this sense that Alexio's childhood becomes a prototype of heroic triumph in the established nationalist historical model. His childhood represents the nesting of received notions of identity and belonging, which Chief Makosa celebrates and authorizes when he calls him a real son of the soil. These notions are rooted in the trope of 'the soil', which Nyenyedzi, the patriot in Yvonne Vera's *Without A Name* (1994) believes is inescapable. He speaks to Mazvita, his girlfriend, who has decided to abandon the struggle for land:

> *'It is like that with the land. It holds and claims you. The land is inescapable. It is everything. Without the land there is no day or night, there is no dream. The land defines our unities. There is no prayer that reaches our ancestors without blessing from the land. Land is birth and death. If we agree that the land has forgotten us, then we agree to be dead.' (Vera, 1994: 33)*

In the writings of the early Zimbabwean nationalist Ndabaningi Sithole, the modes of belonging which define the native-subject relate exclusively to 'those who were possessed by the Soil, and those who possessed it' (Sithole, 1977: 19). It must be clear that 'those who possessed the Soil' are sons of the soil only when they seek to 'retrieve this lost possession' (Sithole, ibid.) from the stranger-other, the white man. The stranger-other is defined as a misfit in the social and symbolic conditions that the practices of '"real" belongingness of the belongers' (Hammar, 2002: 214) create. The 'outsiderhood' of the stranger-other arises out of a lack of what Amanda Hammar called 'intangible intimacies of history' (ibid: 228) from which self-defined 'original' settlers derive their 'authenticity and authority'(ibid: 214). This 'insiderhood' is what Alexio's childhood is made a symbol of when he decides to join the armed struggle as a son of the soil. The 'us' and 'them' dichotomy that arises creates what Margery Hourihan (1997: 3) considers an 'adversarial way of perceiving the world [which] means that conflict is seen as natural and inevitable.' Yet, in Katiyo's novel, it is not always clear what direction the sense of inevitability of conflict would have taken: the text suppresses several possibilities of childhood.

Most pointedly, it glosses over intra-cultural violence. The failure of tradition, represented by Gomo, unleashes mindless violence on the child Alexio. First, he forcibly separates Alexio from his mother and sends him away to his daughter Rudo in Salisbury. When Rudo can no longer take care of Alexio, she hands him over to her young sister Chipo, who in turn hands him back to Gomo. For reasons of space, a single example of the trauma that characterizes Alexio's childhood while in the hands of his own people will suffice.

Gomo sends six-year-old Alexio to a slave-breaking neighbour Murimi so that the latter could foster the boy and send him to school, responsibilities Gomo had divested himself of. On the very first day of meeting Murimi, Alexio is inducted into a work ethic which involved working from dawn to midnight: and then going to school in between. On one occasion Murimi asks the little boy to drive cattle:

> At about sunrise, both Alexio and the oxen were very tired.
>
> "Give me the whip!" shouted Murimi.
>
> Alexio thought Murimi was going to give him a short rest. He handed the whip over. Murimi gave the boy a couple of lashes around the legs.
>
> "That should wake you up a bit!" he said and threw the whip back at Alexio.
>
> Finally the oxen could barely walk. (61)

Alexio rationalizes this suffering and views it as important for his future: 'Although he hated being over-worked, he realized that he was gaining a capacity for work which would prove useful in the future. And anyway, he had no choice. Gomo had clearly told him that if he left Murimi, that was the end of his schooling' (63).

Zimbabwean critics Musaemura Zimunya (1982) and George Kahari (1980) minimize the impact of such insensitive and dehumanizing episodes, while privileging the narrative of liberation and the anti-colonial war. It may be useful to ask questions about whose interests are being served here. Zimunya praises Alexio for being '[q]uite the opposite of Lucifer' in Charles Mungoshi's *Waiting for the Rain* (1975), whom he deeply loathes for his 'misanthropic selfish intellect' (ibid: 93) because he decides to rebel against the desolate misery of his community. In Alexio's childhood, Zimunya sees a 'more socially and historically fulfilling vision of the educated elite' (ibid: 93) as they relate to the nationalist struggle for independence. On the other hand, Kahari seeks to mythologize Alexio's childhood by linking his suffering to that of the 'wonder boy' of magic tales, who would emerge out of his tormented life to free his family and society. Understood within this mythology, Alexio's childhood represents redemptive suffering, his traditional society being the site for preparatory suffering, which is consummated in a higher order of suffering (the war for national independence). Kahari compares Alexio's progress in his journey to national liberation with the dream journey of Christian in Bunyan's *The Pilgrim's Progress*, and notes similarities in the 'snares, pitfalls and stumbling blocks' (ibid: 129) that both characters encounter. The gloom of Alexio's narrative is dispelled by the suggestion that it could be socially and historically fulfilling both in the context of the national liberation struggle (Zimunya) and folklore (Kahari).

The narrative 'refigures the past, broadening the visions of national identity that history is so often called upon to authorise' (Donald, 2000: 32), but there is a sense in which, as it expands the space upon which to lay claim on a broader, homogeneous national identity, through the trope of 'son of the soil' and 'war', it seems to contract the reach of diverse childhoods and identities. The desire to convert childhoods into a philosophy, a social idea and social structure which serves the determinism of the brand of nationalism espoused by Ndabaningi Sithole (1977) and Musaemura Zimunya (1982) limits the questions those childhoods could ask about the very society that makes them such a social idea. In this sense, what may be questioned is a nationalist vision which translocates one boyhood trauma (of tradition) and transmutes it into an all-consuming higher kind of trauma (of colonialism). Furthermore, in *A Son of the Soil*, the 'Martian landscapes' (Middleton, 1992) of the liberation war, and the tropes of 'son of the soil' and 'child of war' upon which the war revolves, are spaces for particular gendered childhoods, which limits the participation of women (for example Joy, Alexio's childhood sweetheart and bearer of his child at the end of the novel) as invented symbolisms of fertility/virility and continuity of the male combatants.

Child of War

The hero of Ben Chirasha's *Child of War* performs acts of journeying quite dissimilar in form to the one embarked on by Alexio Shonga, but shares the symbolic infrastructure in which Alexio's childhood is produced. *A Son of the Soil* ends with Alexio entering the war as a guerrilla. *Child of War* begins with the child-hero Hondo Tapera entering the same war as a collaborator, runner and spy for the guerrillas, and ends with the end of the war in 1980. Hondo, like Alexio, is an orphan, the only boy in his family. The conditions and causes of his orphaned state are dissimilar to Alexio's – Hondo's father is killed by a white farmer, while looking for his stray ancestral bull. Hondo's mother is loving and responsible. What is comparable is the situatedness of Hondo's childhood within a symbolic resistance whose tropes are 'son of the soil' and 'child of war', with the inclusion of a dream-story which marks a kind of cyclic journeying and enmeshment within the emerging nation-space. The dream-story is a conduit of ancestral memory and network of dialogic intercourses with a deep-rooted genealogy of anti-colonial resistance. The knot of symbols of childhood, history and resistance that the dream-story becomes is given expression by the all-powerful metaphor of land as history and nation. The dream-story is a confluence and expression of the same forces and symbols that knit the destinies of 'sons of the soil' with the soil, the land, and ascribes to them the monolithic identity of 'children of resistance'.

Hondo Tapera, whose Shona name means 'Watch out, war is upon us', or literally, 'We are finished by war', resides within the symbolic conditions animated on the arrival of the guerrillas in his village. The story begins with Hondo's encounter with the guerrillas in the 1970s when he is herding his father's cattle. He expresses familiarity and kinship with the guerrillas, although he is seeing them for the first time: 'But I was not afraid, somehow. I had heard too much about the war to be afraid. Everyone in our village knew that the fierce war of liberation raging throughout the country would one day spill over the borders of our village' (1). His recognition of the guerrillas, and immediate acceptance of them factors into his relationship with them what James Garbarino et. al., (1992: xi), in their discussion of children's coping strategies in community violence, called a ' them" is "us"' identification, as opposed to the adversarial 'them' and 'us' which constitutes the relationship between the colonial agents and Hondo Tapera's people. It is an identification which is strengthened by the maturation of a political consciousness which results from children's feeling their 'historical and deeply-rooted identities threatened' (Cairns, 1996: 108). In this situation, children support 'doctrines offering a total immersion in a synthetic identity' (Erikson cited in Cairns, 1996: 108). Hondo Tapera, thirteen years old, and in grade seven, is already politically decided when he meets the guerrillas. When they ask him: 'Do you know why we are here, Hondo?' (2), he answers 'To free the country' (3).

The recruitment of Hondo into the war project, as I have suggested, is at first on two levels. His name suggests a narrative of war, and 'this way of naming the child is a politically symbolic act and may well be instrumental in constructing the child's political views from birth' (Cairns, 1996: 126). The murder of his father by Farmer Taylor provides a *prima facie* experience of violation and victimization. Ed Cairns (1996: 130), however, argues that '[v]ictimization does not have to be personally experienced in order for it to lead to politicization. Vicariously experienced victimization may also have this effect', and may result in the subject carrying out a private war of revenge and succeeding in 'releasing an enormous personal pressure' (ibid: 130) by shouldering the burden of altering the hostile circumstances that led into the victimhood of others. In the case of Hondo Tapera, his role in the struggle is already decided also by the inherited folk-memory of heroism of his ancestors and dispossession by the stranger-other, which is linked to the emergence of the guerrillas. It is through him, as a child, that the symbolic system of his society is activated, armed and deployed. Immediately after Hondo agrees to be a *mujibha* (collaborator/spy) for the guerrillas, he has 'a strange dream' (5) in which he hears 'the noise of drums and singing in [his] ears. The noise was distant, rising and falling with the wind' (5). The drums are articulate inanimate presences of the culture that link Hondo with the past and present. They are part of the raft of symbolic manifestations of a repertoire for the constitution of an archetypal childhood. Hondo is imaged as the connection between the present and the past in two ways. As a child, he is a medium of his ancestors' dreams, and therefore mediates between the living and the dead. His great-grandfather, the man he sees in the dream soon after the sound of the drums, is a veteran of the First Chimurenga of the 1890s, and Hondo 'inherits' the war from him. The second connection is that Hondo's slain father continues the war against Farmer Taylor through the son. There is therefore an instance of double possession when Hondo is shown a vision of both his father and his great-grandfather, both victims of settler occupation, in the dream. The war against white settlers becomes part of the family myths, of which Hondo is an expression. Family myths, according to Maureen Slonim (1991: 11),

> *stress that the family can always be counted on for comfort and support, no matter what the circumstances. Through family myths, ancestral figures, especially grandparents of the same sex, often become a major part of a child's imaginative life and may even serve as role models. [...] This family identity then becomes incorporated into the child's personal sense of identity.*

It is interesting how Hondo, the child, calls into being an antecedent symbolic system of dreams and ancestry, while simultaneously embodying the eternal childhood of the race, which is mediated and renewed at multiple levels in the story.

In the dream-story, Hondo stalks a man who wore nothing but a sheepskin round his loins: 'He carried a spear in his hand and a bow and quiver of arrows on his back' (5). This man, who 'was not very old', is a warrior of the 1890s. He resembles the guerrilla commander that Hondo meets in the village, 'fairly tall, slim and athletic' (1). The man Hondo encounters in his dream is 'lean and strongly built' (5). He, like the guerrilla commander, recruits Hondo into the raging war. First, he anoints Hondo as heir to the war: '[...] slowly, he took out his snuff box and tipped some snuff into his palm and mine. I sneezed several times when I took up the snuff, and hot tears squeezed out of the corners of my eyes. He laughed gently at me and rubbed more snuff into my hair' (5). The man is shot and killed by the white settlers. Before he dies he gives Hondo 'an arrow from his quiver to make me go away. Still I sat there, watching him. He gave me two more arrows and placed his spear at my feet. [...] At last he lifted his snuff box from his side and placed it in my hand' (8). This ritual of ancestral passage over, Hondo 'was the only living soul in this valley of death but [he] was reluctant to leave him [the dead ancestor]' (8). Immediately, the settlers' wagons roll back towards him, to continue the war with the heir of black resistance, the child. While this gesture may appear only symbolic, it is true that the Second Chimurenga war of the 1970s was fought largely by young people, many of them as young as Hondo. By accepting the arrows and snuff from his dying ancestor, Hondo is immortalizing a vision and inheritance of war, and extending a genealogy of black resistance against colonialism. It is also important to note that when the guerrillas enter the village, the first person they meet is Hondo, the child, who in the dream-story is stranded in the valley of death, but stands by his warrior ancestor. The guerrilla commander explains the revenge plot against Farmer Taylor, using the trope of the orphaned child, Hondo, as the rallying call for the war.

Recreated in *Child of War* are the founding imaginaries of Zimbabwean nationalism, which are played out in the space of childhood. 'Children of resistance' invoke the 'native-subject' of the land through spirit possession, dreams and myths, and define the dispossessed victim as exclusively a black person. These imaginaries are more than inventions of the Zimbabwe nation. They are at the very core of the post-war nation's politics.

It is the status of the 'child of war' which is not sufficiently debated in post-war Zimbabwe. *Child of War* makes interesting reading in the sense that, on the one hand it celebrates the deployment of a deeply historically and spiritually embedded social structure of childhood in the war, and on the other hand, it suggests a critique of the ambiguities of the spaces of war. There is a contradictory sense of 'war' at the end of the novel, and a suggestion of altered continuity in the social institution of childhood.

It is not that 'the charm, malleability, innocence and curiosity of children are degraded and then transmogrified into the lesser features of pseudo-adulthood' (Postman, 1994: xiii). It is, rather, that childhood 'is constituted at a particular moment in time and point in space' (Prout and James, 1990: 29), in which various discourses constitute various childhoods (27), 'each and all of which are "real" within their own regime of truth' (ibid.).

Childhood is a social structure, constituted in symbols that reveal the nature of the community that makes use of such childhoods. It is in the ways that children, 'as a social institution that exists beyond the activity of any particular child or adult' (Prout and James, ibid: 28), alter the social institution which constitutes their identities while reproducing them that *Child of War* differs from *A Son of the Soil*. In *Child of War*, there is a sense in which 'War and violence have set in motion processes of social change' (Maxted, 2003: 68), not only in terms of the altering of the social structure when independence is attained and small pieces of land are redistributed to the peasants, but in terms of 'the political voice' (Maxted, 69) that childhood represents.

Having been tortured and bombed, and witnessed brutal murder at the hands of Rhodesian forces, Hondo begins to question the post-war scenario:

When I could walk, Rindai [his friend] took me to the mountain to show me the guerrillas' graves. [...]

They had put large, flat rocks round the guerrillas' grave [sic] and planted a wooden cross in the middle. It was a mass grave, they were buried together in six square metres of earth. The air was so still, the leaves so green that I gasped at the cruelty of war and the heartlessness of those who caused wars to be fought (96).

The seeming neglect of the war heroes by those who led the struggle remained a critical issue in Zimbabwe, but Hondo is suggesting a redefinition of hero when he says 'The whole exercise of identifying them exhausted me. [...] All that mattered now was that whoever they were, they were buried in the soil they had fought to free' (96-97).

Specifically, Hondo wants to know whether the guerrilla commander, now presumed dead, acknowledged him as a 'child of war': 'Maybe I will meet him one day and he will recognize me. And maybe he will shout my name, sling his gun over my shoulder and call me a child of war' (100).

It is easy to appreciate Hondo's desire to be factored in the national memory, having been central to the redefinition of colonial space both as a social actor and a rallying key trope of the national struggle itself. Terence Ranger (1985: 292) writes about how the former *mujibhas* were told that 'politics is a business of the grown-ups' and how the election of village committees 'was an opportunity to put youth in its place' after the war. This was because post-war society was eager to neutralize 'the power exercised by the mujibhas during the war' (ibid.). Pamela Reynolds (1996: 53) notes a similar trend in post-war Zimbabwe: 'As communities began realigning power structures after the war, children were firmly placed back into the niche of childhood.' In *Child of War*, Hondo says: 'I am repeating the class I was in last year, at the same school' (99), where of course he is stripped of his war-time powers. Again, the child's role in the post-war space is to reactivate memory, and insist on being central to the new forms of political participation because, as Julia Maxted puts it, 'debates about those forms are debates about the nature of citizenship, responsibility and the morality of social action' (2003: 68). The cycle of folk-memory, which carried the symbols of a long genealogy of war, is continued in Hondo, this time mildly subversive of the emerging social order.

Conclusion

Both *A Son of the Soil* and *Child of War* help us to reflect on the nexus between childhood, history and resistance in ways that bring to light the versions of childhoods that are central to the construction of notions of belongingness in a nation-space. The character of the symbols of childhood prove that childhood, like adulthood, is in a state of 'continual becoming' (Archard, 1993: 36), susceptible to the exigencies and contingencies of a social order. As a condition and a history, childhood in *A Son of the Soil* and *Child of War* can be invented, deployed and redeployed to serve as the rallying call for the war. As post-war communities begin to realign power structures, the institution of childhood is also altered, making the social idea of childhood elastic and malleable.

The war is just one of the many spaces that define a specific, usable version of childhood. The space of childhood in war teems with symbolic instances of rootedness and belongingness. It is a shunting yard of tropes that work as a template in the production of unified national identities, which are woven into a powerful imagined 'family' of 'children of resistance'.

The staged fiction of 'family' is conjured by the cycles of inherited folk-memory, replete with what Stephen Daniels (1993: 5) theorized as the constituent elements of national identities: '"legends and landscapes", [...] stories of golden ages, enduring traditions, heroic deeds and dramatic destinies located in ancient or promised home-lands with hallowed sites and scenery.' In both novels, the 'symbolic activation of time and space [...] gives shape to the "imagined community" of the nation' (ibid.). Each childhood carries with it a predominantly 'genealogical "ethnic" national identity' (Daniels 1993: 4), traced from a heroic male ancestry. Alexio traces his heroism to his ancestor Shonga and to Sekuru, while Hondo Tapera locates himself within the sacred landscape and genealogy begun by his great-grandfather, and continued through his father.

The idea of 'children of resistance' traces its genesis to a patriarchal lineage, making childhood stand for instances of founding moments in a long history of decolonization, from which the new nation descends. The childhoods depicted in *A Son of the Soil* and *Child of War* are near perfect models of a politically convenient social structure from which the imagined singularity of national formations can be projected. They are instances of new-found childhoods and boyhoods that could serve as pliant templates of a stable nationalist memory and narrative. These boyhoods will not be Alice Miller's (1990) reformed Biblical Isaac, who would question his sacrificial role in the service of patriarchy and its wars. For Alice Miller, the new Isaac, 'with his questions, with his awareness, with his refusal to let himself be killed – not only saves his own life but also saves his father from the fate of becoming the unthinking murderer of his child' (Miller, 145). But these 'sons of the soil' are not the new Isaacs: they are, as Franklin Abbott (1993: 4) puts it, 'too dutiful to save their own lives.' The murmurs of despair that Hondo Tapera expresses about the destructiveness of the war are not accompanied by a revalorization of the ascription of 'child of war', a label which he cherishes as an elevated identity. Alexio is happy to be among the young recruits in the mountains, and participating in a mythical circle which connects the birth of babies (the *métier* of women left behind the war) with the founding of the nation in an armed revolution (the forte of men). This will be left to other writers and characters, who, excluded from the dominant national symbols and culture, seek to explode the myths of 'children of resistance' and explore altering versions and subversions of childhoods.

Chapter 9

Self-representation and national memory: white autobiographies in Zimbabwe

Anthony Chennells

The narratives and diaries of missionaries, travellers and hunters make up the early published accounts of Zimbabwe and many such books appeared both before and immediately after the British South Africa Company's invasion of 1890. Livingstone's *Missionary Travels and Researches in South Africa* (1857) was the earliest of the missionary books and provided a model for his successors. Extracts from the journals of Robert Moffat describing his first journey into Matabeleland were published in 1856 in *The Missionary Magazine* which also published accounts both of his subsequent journeys and the experiences of the London Missionary Society agents at Nyati. Thomas Morgan Thomas's *Eleven Years in Central South Africa* (1873) described the early years of the Nyati mission. Baldwin's *African Hunting and Adventure from Natal to the Zambesi* (1868) and Selous's *A Hunter's Wanderings in Africa* (1881) were among the earliest hunting narratives. Books that describe the occupation of Mashonaland include Selous's *Travel and Adventure in South-East Africa* (1893) and Leonard's *How We Made Rhodesia* and experiences of the 1896 risings were recorded in texts such as Selous' *Sunshine and Storm in Rhodesia* (1896) and Baden-Powell's *The Matabele Campaign 1896* (1897). Almost invariably these early writers plotted their lives and travels in the South-Central African interior as imperial romances. The form of these writings may be autobiographical but they are not offered as documentations of unique experiences. The constraints and imperatives of British imperial culture are recognisable as soon as the British reader identifies the romance tropes of the narrative and anticipates the disclosures that these presume: the male author's rationality shapes and connects the items that constitute the incoherence of African life. His narrative gives these a form that they could not have without him. He invokes science to categorize and name what he is observing whether these are rocks, plants, animals or people and science's detached objectivity convinces the reader that he is describing what he encounters with truthful precision and thus has the authority to control the meanings of what he has seen. As narratives of control, the travel journals anticipate the more pervasive control which colonialism will one day assume over Africa's random existence. The autobiographer is the fixed point of his observations just as one day the colonial metropole will be the fixed point of an Africa newly knowing itself as one item within a global, imperial order. Fulford and Kitson (1998: 4) quote Marlon B. Ross's remark that throughout the nineteenth century the individual's narrative increasingly contributes to a sense of national identity. Ross argues that 'the Romantics... help prepare England for its imperial destiny. They help teach the English to universalize the experience of "I"'. In Rhodesian and Zimbabwean autobiography, the referents of the narratives change as the imperial nation is replaced by local nationalisms. The early autobiographical narratives contributed to the larger imperial narrative. When the same documents and books were published and read in Rhodesia after the Second World War in the Oppenheimer Series that published the Moffat and Nyati journals, or the Rhodesiana Reprint Library, they helped to constitute a discrete white Rhodesian national identity shaped by its own narratives. For some Rhodesians, this identity was validated in 1965 by constitutional separation from Britain. Dan Wylie (2002: 102) remembers during the Liberation War that to 'subscribe to [the Rhodesiana Reprint Library] [felt] like a mild act of patriotism. One could find there unlimited justification for present attitudes'.

Georges Gusdorf (1980: 29) observes that '[a]utobiography is the second reading of experience and it is truer than the first because it adds to experience itself consciousness of it.' Albert E. Stone (1982: 7) points to one reason for our interest in people writing about their lives when he remarks that '[a]n autobiographical act...makes the writer at once the creator and recreator of his or her personal identity.' Stone, of course, knows that identity derives from many sources, takes many forms and is read in multiple ways. Individual identity can derive as much from the historically produced collectives of which we are a part as it can from genes and personal trauma, but for Stone the personal finally shapes autobiography (1982:17-18): 'Embedded, therefore, in conscious generalizations about historical experience will be preconscious utterances from the inner darkness of the psyche... How, then, to understand autobiography as both representative cultural history and stubbornly singular story[?]'

The romance emplotment of the travel narratives is evidence of how the narrators place themselves within the public domain or how the singular story is rendered as part of a representative cultural history. Narrative always imposes some public constraint on the freedom of the imagination, but I have a particular difficulty in imagining how 'the inner darkness of the psyche' is the authorizing provenance for autobiography in Africa, since few African writers whatever their racial, ethnic or regional origin are unaware of the importunities of a collective that has (or at least demands) their allegiance. That African cultures refuse autonomy to the individual is a claim often made to distinguish Africa from the West, and Kwasi Wiredu (1998: 311) provides a stereotype of traditional African philosophy with his claim that 'a human person is essentially the centre of a thick set of concentric circles of obligations and responsibilities matched by rights and privileges revolving round levels of relationships.' In Zimbabwe, the autobiography as an account of the typical became a medium of black writers when Zimbabwean nationalism was using published narratives to help form its consciousness. Nathan Shamuyarira (1965), Ndabaningi Sithole, Lawrence Vambe (1972) and, immediately after independence, Maurice Nyagumbo (1980) recall how racial insult, poverty and the frustration of educational ambition constrained their lives within Rhodesia. These men do not offer their life stories as unique, but rather as representative of the material and spiritual dispossession of an entire people which explicitly justifies the collective political action in which the authors are engaged when they write their autobiographies or when they include autobiographical material in theoretical works.

In an essay on African-American writing, David Palumbo-Piu (1996: 211) argues that '[t]he ethnic narrative presents an occasion for a subversive revision of the dominant version of history'. 'Dominant historical referents' have silenced the voice that only now can be heard and in ethnic autobiography there can be found 'an imaginative invention of a self beyond the limits of the historical representations available to the ethnic subject'. This formula applies to the early black Zimbabwean autobiographies: the dominant version of history was authorized by whites, and a black person, in the act of writing, established him- or-herself as an authorizing subject subverting a presupposition of white history that there were no alternative and valid black perspectives which whites did not command. The 'dominant historical referents' around which white historical narratives were organized were the only referents that mattered.

This has now changed. The current dominant version of history within Zimbabwe is the self-serving historical memory of Zimbabwe's ruling party, ZANU(PF), and insofar as the historiography that informs white memories opposes it, in contemporary Zimbabwe white autobiography has become an ethnic narrative in Palumbo-Piu's sense. One could also argue, however, that the numerous black-authored histories that deny ZANU(PF)'s historiography invent selves beyond the limits of current and dominant historical referents and therefore conform to Palumbo-Piu's categories of minor histories, refusing a black particularity, a single black subjectivity. An obvious example is Joshua Nkomo's autobiography that begins with his crossing into Botswana in 1983, when he was 'driven into exile from Zimbabwe by the armed killers of Prime Minister Robert Mugabe' (2001:1). The revised edition that I am quoting from was published after Nkomo's death while he was serving as one of Zimbabwe's vice-presidents, a detail that reminds us that the ruling party's history is not an uncontested recall of the past but, like all national histories, a story of exclusions and inclusions depending on the political exigencies of the moment.

Not only black African societies valorized the community above the individual. Colonialism imposed its own communal imperatives and settler communities were urgent in their demands for conformity. When colonial or imperial autobiographies recall the self's activities, they simultaneously reveal how the settler or imperial collective knows and imagines itself. The primary signifier of a colonial identity was race, although what race signified differed between colonial systems and sometimes carried different significations within the same system. By 1940 different meanings attached to what being a black African meant in Northern and Southern Rhodesia for example. Whiteness is also an unstable signifier. In Rhodesia, settlers of British origin grudgingly accorded whiteness to Jews and Afrikaners although the phrase 'poor white' was used to describe many of the latter, a qualification that prevented too intimate an identification.

Autobiography, however, is never likely to be a wholly accurate recall of the subject's past or what his or her responses were in each successive experience. That autobiographies are plotted so that they conform to a narrative convention is indeed one reason for doubting that they are accurate in recalling what the subject experienced. John Smith Moffat, one of the first London Missionary Society agents at Nyati, realized that accommodating a narrative to suit a particular genre probably falsifies. Writing in 1861 to J.S. Unwin, Moffat confesses '[o]ne is so tempted to write *for effect*. I fear, judging from personal observation, that five sixths of the *interesting* narratives in missionary periodicals are mere romances' (Wallis, 1945: 151).

As we live through the shifting certainties of our lives, each one of us experiences multiple selves that correspond with the various stages we are living through. If the authoring self is significantly different from the earlier self that the author is remembering, what authority attaches to the author's memories? Is there in each one of us a self that simply accrues experience to its own being? Or do we not comprise multiple selves produced by multiple experiences? Dorothy Driver (1995) adds to the multiplicity of selves accrued over the disjunctions of a lifetime by postulating multiple synchronic selves. In an essay on *The Cape Journals of Lady Anne Barnard*, Driver (1995: 46) identifies in Barnard's writing 'different facets of the self, as if the different speaking positions that constitute her subjectivity are engaged in negotiation (or contestation) with one another, the self engaged in dialogue with an "otherness" within'. Driver coins the term 'self-othering' for this process. She takes issue (1995: 47) with 'a current critical fashion which denounces – with extraordinary ease – white South African writing for an apparently self-assured deployment of racist stereotypes'. Barnard's journals, Driver argues, 'rather than simply reproducing established categories of gender, race and class... show ideology *in construction* in eighteenth-century South Africa' (1995: 46). She gives additional profundity to this insight when she rejects the stasis of the stereotypical colonial self and other and argues instead that 'stereotypes, like other linguistic moments, are sites of contestation, discursively produced rather than simply borrowed from a convention always already in place' (1995: 47). This moves beyond a determinism that sees the text as mechanically reproducing established ideological norms and allows us to see instead how such norms are negotiated and (to use her own word) 'unsettled'. If one can demonstrate that an autobiographical text is produced through negotiations between different facets of self, self and identity are rendered even more problematic terms than I have implied.

In Zimbabwe, where a short twenty-four years has reduced an arrogant and politically all-powerful white elite to an anxious and embattled minority, the idea of a stable white-colonial identity is untenable. As questionable is the idea of a single black Zimbabwean identity that commands a single black subjectivity. The leadership of any successful revolution almost invariably fails to retain the ideological rigour that inspired it during the armed phase of the struggle. Notoriously, after the fighting has ended, revolutionary vanguards transform themselves into new elites and sometimes into new classes so that conditions for new conflicts between themselves and the mass of the people are soon in place. In Zimbabwe, the new elite is a new class and invokes a shared racial identity with the mass of the people only when it perceives its interests as a ruling class to be threatened. Mugabe has promised us his autobiography when he retires. Will this recount the experiences of a stable self in possession of a single identity and driven by a single ideology or will new identities respond to the radical reconfigurations of racial power of the past forty years in Zimbabwe? I am stereotyping both black and white Zimbabweans in the Zimbabwe of 2003 (the time of writing), but stereotypes are as Driver reminds us, 'linguistic moments'. My stereotypes are constructed from the linguistic terms 'minority', 'resistance', 'vanguard', 'elites', 'mass of the people' and 'class', which belong within a Marxist discourse, and which like all discourses is constantly changing the conditions that it chooses to address as they in turn change the possibilities which the discourse defines.

Ethnicity has a place in the creation of Zimbabwean literature where Shona, Ndebele and white-authored texts are studied as discrete literatures. Only perhaps some black-authored novels and poems in English are almost uncontroversial nationalist texts. The history of Zimbabwean whites, however, shows that ethnicity does not refer to some racial or regional minority forever marginalized in its subalternity and subverting in its writing a stable and dominant group. This is additionally confirmed when one considers the complexities of Ndebele identity. Depending on the circumstances, 'Ndebele' can denote people of Zulu origin or include the others who historically were incorporated into the Ndebele state which before 1890 was the most powerful political institution on the Southern Zambezian plateau. Joshua Nkomo was a Kalanga and therefore of a lower caste within the hierarchies of the nineteenth-century state but for much of his political life when he was not a national leader, he was regarded as *the* Ndebele leader. Lindgren (2002 :124-7) argues that the ZANU(PF) atrocities in Matabeleland in the 1980s forged for the first time an Ndebele-Kalanga unity that not even ninety years of white rule achieved. Ethnic minorities in Zimbabwe include people, both black and white, who previously exercised tyrannical power and controlled the production of public memories.

I have emphasized this point in order to allow me to qualify and make use of Palambiu-Pio's theories of ethnic autobiography. Palambiu-Pio (1996: 211) argues that if an ethnic history is 'to carve out an area for revision...[it] must legitimate itself by laying claim to a firmer epistemology than that claimed by the dominant history.' Perspective informs epistemology and conclusions as to whether one or other perspective can lay claim to a firmer epistemology can be at best tentative. What we can be sure of is obvious: when an ethnic history arrives at conclusions that cannot be accommodated within a dominant history, two contradictory discourses generated from different sites within a society provide opposing readings of the same events. Palambiu-Pio (1996: 212) points out that 'the particular politics of ethnic memory' grow out of the 'epistemological crisis that is opened up with the "death" of the project of modernity' and inseparable from this crisis are the 'truth claims of any minor history and ...of the status of the personal within the politics of history'. One project of modernity is, of course, nationalism and its enabling historical narratives that assume a single teleology for the largely diverse elements that constitute a nation. White Rhodesian history is modernist in this sense but so is the history promoted by ZANU(PF). The latter may be a dominant history but it is also an ethnic history because, although it claims to be nationalist, it promotes the power of particular factions, regionalisms and ethnicities. In Zimbabwe, minor and major histories have swapped places and probably will swap places again although it is extremely improbable that a history produced by white memories will ever again be dominant.

* * * * *

The texts that I have chosen for analysis are all autobiographical, but they employ widely different narrative forms that locate the personal in quite different ways within the politics of white Rhodesian history. These differences enable me to show the diversity with which the personal can invoke ethnic or indeed national memories and can subvert stereotypes of the white settler. Ian Smith's *The Great Betrayal* (1997) insists that justice and pure rationality were inherent in Rhodesian nationalist ideology; the betrayal of his title refers principally to the withdrawal of South African support for Rhodesian independence but it also signifies the moral deviance of anyone who recalls the Rhodesian past in terms different from his own. Smith's narrative observes the nineteenth-century conventions of realism (as did the early travel writers) in which the narrator is assumed to have no biases either ideological or personal. He is a detached, objective observer, his prose a transparent medium for the certainties of the past that he accurately recollects. Much of Peter Godwin's *Mukiwa* (1996) shows traces of white Rhodesian nationalist romance but a historiography of either the white collective or the personal, which shows a triumphant Rhodesian ordering of black disorder, was impossible after 1979 and satire displaces Godwin's romance. This formalism is more interesting for my purposes than the exaggerated claims of his importance or the several inaccuracies in Godwin's story. Doris Lessing is not only profoundly self-conscious in her acts of remembering, but is also aware of the problems of autobiography in ways that Godwin and Smith are not. For Lessing, the whole autobiographical exercise is inseparable from invention: '[W]e make up our pasts,' she writes (1994: 13). 'You can actually watch your mind doing it, taking a little fragment of fact and then spinning a tale out of it'. The certainty with which Ian Smith claims to recall the events of his life suggests that he would have no idea what Lessing is talking about. Smith inhabits a stable world that is destabilized only by other people's lies or treachery. He does not doubt for one moment that his memory can sift the real and the fanciful, the truth from the lies. Lessing's *The Golden Notebook* is one of the great monuments of British modernism and it is not surprising that her autobiography should refuse to register an easy equivalence between an event and its textual representation.

In Smith's *The Great Betrayal* the personal is the collective. When he returns home after the Second World War, he realizes (1997: 27) that home is 'even better when one is a member of a close-knit family built around worthwhile traditions... [G]reat nations are built on the foundations of great families'. Family becomes a trope throughout Smith's story: Britain's kith and kin in white Rhodesia upholds those values that made Britain great, and in denying Rhodesia its independence, Britain is betraying its own traditions of heroism and honour. Two men who approach him to replace Winston Field as leader of the Rhodesia Front are described as 'by birth such true-blue Britishers' but Rhodesians by choice. They were much decorated in the Second World War and 'were the calibre of men who had made Great Britain great' (1997:60). Halfway through the book he returns to this idea and quotes from Kenneth Young's *Rhodesia and Independence*: '"the spirit and courage that made Britain great were not extinct; they had emigrated"' to Rhodesia (1997: 150). The heroic individual and the family true to its traditions are metonymies of Rhodesia, and Rhodesia itself upholds British traditions that are no longer a part of British memory. Smith writes his life as a story of personal and national betrayal and the two are inseparable. His voice *is* the voice of white Rhodesia.

Smith's autobiography is the story of the death of a nation and this inevitably raises the question of who is in and who is out of the nation. He refers to blacks as 'tribesmen' (1997: 75), a word that suggests that they are outside the common run of humanity – although sometimes he uses 'African' to mean 'black' (e.g. 105; 149). This was a liberal usage in the 1950s and 1960s but inappropriate at the time when Smith was writing and when whites, quite correctly, were insisting that they too were Africans. In the opening chapter (1997: 1-8), significantly entitled 'Growth of a Nation', Smith outlines what is in effect the sub-text of his account of what went wrong: there were simply too few whites in Rhodesia and when the going got tough, they left. He argues that the 'greatest mistake' that the South African National party made when they came to power was to halt Smuts's immigration plan: 'It was a decision made in haste by people who lacked the wisdom and foresight which comes with experience' (1997: 5). If immigration had not been checked, South Africa's white population 'would have been around 15 million, instead of 6 million... And of vital importance, with the population ratio of white to black being 1:2, as opposed to the present 1:5, the political problem would have been significantly reduced.' (Ibid.) The political problem of

Southern Africa is simply that there are too many blacks and too few whites. As his story proceeds, Rhodesia can on occasion become more inclusive. Through intelligent planning on the part of the Rhodesian government, Smith notes (1997: 149) the development of a black middle class with 'a growing number of black people joining the ranks of the wealthy, owning modern houses and employing their own servants, whereas a few decades previously they themselves had been servants'. This, he explains (1997: 150), is part of 'an evolutionary process' for 'if people tried to run before they could walk, they invariably tripped'. Who exactly the previous generation of blacks were servants to, or what they were before they were servants is not revealed. Perhaps it is too obvious.

Lessing (1994: 229) tells young English people that they will understand how colonials thought about the 'Colour Bar' if they look at old copies of *Punch* with its endless 'jokes about comic housemaids and the absurdities of the working classes'. The same contemptuous distancing is present both in colonial racism and pre-Second World War middle-class representations of the 'lower classes'. Blacks, whether middle class or 'tribes-people', are never securely located within Smith's nationalist discourse, however. He writes of the 1975 Victoria Falls conference that this was 'a meeting of Rhodesians discussing a constitution for Rhodesia' (1997:178), but as the conference gets underway a distinction is made between Rhodesians and black nationalists. 'On the one side we had Vorster coaching the Rhodesian team, and on the other Kaunda (and Nyerere) coaching the black nationalists. The Rhodesians would play according to the rules of the game, but what about the black nationalists?' (Ibid.) Smith shapes his story in a succession of clichés that constitute his homespun philosophy: 'the rules of the game', 'not running before you can walk', 'hearts and not heads'. If the happy family is his model of the nation, its informing ideology is common sense. That common sense is culturally constructed and invariably privileges the person who claims to possess it, is not something that Smith's narrative is able to acknowledge.

Stone (1982: 13) claims that 'Behind historic identity, lurks another "self" whose psychic structures and states reveal themselves symbolically through language. In fact autobiography's coded imagery speaks more truly than literal renditions of experience for it suggests patterns of deep continuity within personality.' In *The Great Betrayal*, it is impossible to distinguish between Smith's historical identity and a psychic self encoded in language. His story is how he and many other white Rhodesians knew their continuities, but an unsympathetic reader can trace in it a succession of blunders: trusting that the British would abide by verbal agreements, the futility of UDI, believing that Portugal could hold onto Mozambique, that South Africa was willing to sacrifice its interests to support Rhodesia and that whites would stay. The only continuity is Smith's capacity to misinterpret the context in which he is acting so that each new situation as it rears up takes him by surprise.

His biggest error was to believe that Britain still thought of itself as an imperial nation. Engaged in redefining its nationhood within the shifting alliances of Europe and the United States, Britain saw Rhodesia as a nuisance and Smith's 'psychic self', encoded within the language of imperialism, an anachronism. Shortly after the Lancaster House conference has ended, he records a conversation with Rowan Cronjé, who had been in his cabinet. Cronjé tells his leader that his 'record was exceptional, unequalled in the latter half of this century, and that [his] composure and dignity over this latest disgraceful episode would be recorded in history.' A group of young people had told Cronje that Smith 'was one of the few constant factors they could find in this world' (1997: 331). Smith has explained (1997: 329) that 'Vorster [and] the South Africans were working hand in glove with the front-line states' and that Cronje, an Afrikaner, should be his praise singer demonstrates what Rhodesia's independence should have signified not only in Southern Africa but in a Commonwealth corrupted by communism and by people whom Britain's weakness has thrust into premature nationhood. Encoded in Cronjé's words are those values that Smith believes Rhodesia represented: dignity and constancy to the best of Western Christianity in the face of unprincipled betrayal. Only once is he more than a voice for Rhodesia and becomes an agent in his own right. Quoting Cronjé he writes (1997: 331) 'I was the person responsible for creating this incredible nation.' Throughout most of the book, there has been no Smith without Rhodesia. Here there is no Rhodesia without Smith. My list of Smith's blunders and the way which Smith writes about himself or records Cronjé's opinion of what he and Rhodesia meant confirm Driver's remarks about stereotypes as discursively produced sites of contestation.

Godwin's *Mukiwa*, as its subtitle – *A White Boy in Africa* – implies, sets out to tell the story of a typical white-African childhood, although there is in fact nothing typical in his childhood. Few childhoods include attendance at post-mortems; a ring-side view of a neighbour's body after he has been ambushed and stabbed; climbing a tree to cut down the body of a suicide; and watching women gathering to kick and abuse a dead leopard which has eaten one of their children. These contacts with violent death were a consequence of his mother's position as medical officer at Melsetter and his father's management of a Manyika tea and timber estate. They were not a function of growing up in Africa although some reviewers found in the book confirmation that Africa is an inherently violent continent. When he is a child, Godwin's family drives down to lunch in the Save valley which for the child is a hot and hostile world quite different from the green and misty mountains of the southern Eastern Highlands where his early childhood was spent but which the early days of the Liberation War had already made dangerous.

> *I longed to live in a safer place... where there were no scorpions or lethal snakes, or rabid jackals to bite me, or mosquitoes to infect me with cerebral malaria, or tsetse flies to give me sleeping sickness. A place free of the tokalosh [sic], and the muroyi – the evil African witch; a place where there were no tsotsis setting fire to the forests or killing Europeans for the Chimurenga.*

> *From the books I'd read, and the pictures I'd seen, and the films I'd watched, I thought maybe that place was England, a gentle deciduous place where man had tamed nature and moulded it to do his bidding. (1996:138-9)*

The opposition between a violent Africa and a gentle England which people have shaped to accommodate them is a conventional trope of the imperial romance. Disease, wild animals, gross superstition and people violently rejecting the gifts of English civilisation are the metonymies of the violent continent. If *Mukiwa* is plotted as romance, it is because such disorder requires control and for much of his autobiography Godwin is controlling Africa either through language or more literally as a member of the British South Africa Police. Through the voice of his parents he offers another and more conventionally Rhodesian view of England: '[My parents] said it was much better over here in Africa now. That England was small and grey and wet and full.' And Godwin's mother takes him on her lap and says, '"You're a *pukka* African. The first Godwin to be born out here"' (1996: 139). The England and Africa of his parents' remarks are stable and from them a settler colony and a new nationalism can be imagined. Even after UDI and its claim to affirm white Rhodesia's nationhood, Godwin recalls his ambivalence about how far he really belonged. At one point he acquires an Afrikaner girlfriend and envies the unquestionable African-ness of Afrikaners (1996: 187). An English cousin comes to stay, sporting a loincloth and an 'Afro' hair-do. Not surprisingly cousin Oliver stands out in Mangula where the Godwins are living, but through him, Godwin gets 'a glimpse of how we appeared to the outside, of just how far we had strayed from our mother culture and mutated into this quite separate people' (1996: 197). These competing texts and perspectives authorize a self that is constantly changing until the subject of the autobiography becomes an unanswered question of who is self and who is other.

His autobiography traces Godwin's growing realization that as a white person, he does not belong in Zimbabwe, and an Africa that resolutely and successfully rejects the invader is one possible signifier of the Africa of his sub-title. Satire in the sense of circumstances overcoming ideals has replaced the earlier romance. When Godwin returns from Oxford to an independent Zimbabwe, he briefly plays with the journalist stereotype of whites in Africa: he recalls tennis parties and swimming in his parents' Chisipite garden. 'The restaurants were cheap, and the beer was cold and plentiful, sanctions were over, petrol rationing had finally been lifted, and noone was shooting at us. For the first time we were enjoying the country without a conscience. We were no longer in charge and, frankly, it was a relief.' (1996: 328-9) This is agreeably complex writing and its complexity refuses to attach a single meaning to Africa. Godwin appropriates an expatriate's or tourist's detachment that neither feels responsibility for the Zimbabwean past nor expects to live out the consequences of present errors. The moral burden that is lifted from Godwin is that of being in charge, and the preceding chapters of his story have shown how Rhodesia demanded that young white men learned to shoulder the responsibility of being white, male and Rhodesian. He is relieved that he is in a space that, if not amoral, possesses no moral imperatives.

The description of the good life for whites in Africa precedes the peripeteia of Godwin's narrative. While he is working as a clerk in a Harare law office, he discovers, with the help of appalled Ndebele civilians and Catholic missionaries, the barbarity of the Fifth Brigade during the *Gukurahundi*.[1] Godwin's encounters with the thuggish soldiers manning road-blocks, his witness of torture as a routine means of political control and his claim to have discovered the mass graves in the disused mine-shafts at the Antelope Mine force him to realize not only that the civilian population is being terrorized but that thousands of people are being murdered. Knowledge of evil creates its own moral imperatives, if only the obligation to let other people know what is happening. One of the charms of the exotic is that it makes no moral demands on us. Not being in charge rendered Zimbabwe exotic for Godwin. The final Matabeleland scenes refuse him his right to detachment. Does he feel obliged to reveal what is happening in Matabeleland because a crime against humanity is taking place and he is obliged to protest in the name of humanity? In Zimbabwe, his race no longer imposes specific responsibilities on him. As a white, he does not control the public narrative. Or has he made the transition from Rhodesian to Zimbabwean and a revelation within that transition that he is still involved with the fate of all other Zimbabweans whom the state has identified as its enemies? His involvement with them is not as a responsible authority but potentially as a fellow victim.[2]

Godwin retains a precise control over the shifts in his choice of genre – his story is shaped as carefully as a novel – and the closure of *Mukiwa* recalls us to the earlier imperial romances. At the end of the book, Godwin places himself at the memorial erected by whites to recall those whites who were killed in 1896 in the Filabusi district. Two of the dead on the memorial are registered only by their surnames and Godwin ruefully observes: 'Imagine that, fighting for Queen and country, and then no one can even remember your bloody name' (1996: 418). The disclosure here is not about shared humanity or being a Rhodesian and an African. We are returned to empire, and satire registers futile deaths among the many loose ends of imperialism's grandiose schemes. The next paragraph contains the literal closure of the autobiography. Filabusi is in the Manduna chieftainship and as Godwin turns to leave the memorial, lighting forks above him and he 'wondered briefly whether Chief Maduna's ancestral spirits were going to strike down another white man before he could bear witness.' (Ibid.) Does another white man bearing witness suggest that the function of texts like *Mukiwa* is to testify to the Matabeleland massacres? Or is the *Gukurahundi* a metonymy for

---

[1]   When the government used the presence of a handful of dissidents in Matabeleland as an excuse to massacre thousands of civilians. Most Zimbabweans, black and white, chose to remain unaware of what was happening in Matabeleland during those years.

[2]   For a related view of Godwin's ambivalence towards a Zimbabwean identity, see Chapter 7 of this volume.

Africa's savagery that once again has escaped the control of rational Europe and it is that savagery to which Godwin's story bears witness? However one chooses to read those final paragraphs, the triumphalism of both the imperial and Rhodesian nationalist romances has been left far behind.

John McCallister (2001: 14) describes *African Laughter* in which Lessing recounts the first four visits she made to Zimbabwe after independence as her 'deconstruction of travel writing', because she refuses to 'take [...] imaginative possession of [place] through a triumphantly coherent, commanding gaze'. *Under My Skin*, Lessing's subsequent work of non-fiction, deconstructs Zimbabwean autobiography. At first sight, it is a work of realist autobiography in which she recreates her identity within the specific contexts of her early life. We are told of her parents' backgrounds, her infancy in Persia and the family's immigration to Rhodesia where they experienced the poverty that was typical of many whites on the land in the 1920s and 1930s, her antagonism to her mother, the schools she went to, her marriages, her identification with communism and finally her departure for England. If the personal and public are one in Smith's autobiography, Lessing gestures towards something like Stone's 'psychic' self. The book ends (1994: 419) with her thinking that she has 'done...with the tentacles of family. I was born out of my own self... I was not going home to my family, I was fleeing from it'. This is immediately qualified and the qualification is the final example of the many destabilizations of realism throughout the book. The claim to be fleeing into an individual identity is wrong, Lessing writes, but it is not untrue. It is merely the truth of the moment: how 'I experienced myself then.' The larger experience that the book has revealed is that she is 'slotted into place, a little item in a tree of descent' from her parents and their ancestors whose lives she has told or speculated about. She has been made by them and by Persia, England and Rhodesia and when she encounters (1994: 408) English women locked into the British class system, she understands 'how fortunate [she] was to have been brought up in Africa and not in the Home Counties. These women seemed to [her] ignorant, innocent, insular.' Lessing realizes (1994: 148) that '[t]he democratic spirit of the Colony was too strong' for her 'mother's preoccupation with nice and less nice people, with commonness' to have had any effect on her. In spite of her desire to escape from Rhodesia and its racism – she qualifies her remark about the colony's democratic spirit with a parenthetic 'Democratic, that is, for the whites' – she was for nearly thirty years of her life a Rhodesian. It was not an identity of her choosing but as she remarks, it is 'the human condition...to be trapped by circumstances' (1994: 120).

When Godwin and Smith speak of being Rhodesian, they are always conscious of race, although Godwin registers race more complexly than Smith does. Lessing explicitly rejects race as the shaping principle of her story (1994:113): 'Did we talk about the Africans? – the blacks – the "munts" – the "kaffirs"? Not much. They were there taken for granted... I don't propose to elaborate on white settler attitudes, there's nothing new to say about them. My *African Stories* describe the District – Southern Rhodesian farms at that time.' This is not an evasion. She does not direct the reader to her African stories or the 'Children of Violence' sequence out of a desire not to repeat what her readers know or to distance herself from the Lessing of the 1950s. In an autobiography that recognizes the fallibility of memory, she remarks (1994:162) that in writing *Martha Quest* she was 'being a novelist and not a chronicler. But if the novel is not the literal truth, then it is true in atmosphere, feeling, more "true" than this record, which is trying to be factual.' Not only are fact and truth distinguished but what is factual in Rhodesia or Zimbabwe is qualified: 'That is from a white point of view.' In later life, she meets a man who had been a black child in the district when she was growing up. His memories are of moving 'from farm to farm... [T]o him all the farm compounds were the same – poor, ugly, badly built.' He and Lessing cannot share the same memories of Rhodesia.

James Clifford (1988:173) says of Michel Liebris's *L'Afrique fantôme* that '[i]ts poetics are one of incompletion and process... Interrupting the smooth ethnographic story of an access to Africa, it undermines the assumption that self and other can be gathered in a stable narrative coherence.' Similarly, *Under My Skin* cannot be read as a smooth account of a radical female consciousness caught up in a racist colonial institution, a story of escape from colonialism's racialised dualism of self and other. Lessing recalls numerous selves including their own 'self-otherings'. In the situations that she recalls there are multiple possibilities both for herself and for Rhodesia. One of the possibilities within the latter was of course Zimbabwe, which briefly – but only briefly – was an inclusive nation, a triumphant closure to Rhodesia, before the conflicting interests of region, ethnicity, race and class created a nation whose history can be related only as a story of 'incompletion and process'. Speaking of a landlady obsessed by theft, murder and rape by black men, Lessing remarks that '[i]f large numbers of people are mad in the same way, it is not recognized as madness' (1994: 267). That remark could apply to contemporary Zimbabwe but also to any political cause with which we once identified and which we now regard as absurd. Forms of madness in her story are white Rhodesian racism from which she distanced herself and the communism with which she became involved. Her loathing of Rhodesian racism (1994: 265) 'would be commonplace in a couple of decades' and yet at the time it made her one with 'misfits, eccentrics, traitors, kaffir-lovers'.

Lessing argues (1994: 395) that it was the stupidity of white 'Authority' that created a militant nationalism. While Communist theory was solemnly designating 'Black Nationalism...a reactionary deviation' (1994: 394), the Rhodesian authorities were forcing blacks to aspire to an alternative nationalism by excluding them from the Rhodesian nation. This was a literal exclusion during the 1948 general strike (1994: 395), when the whites set about 'starving their rebellious subjects into submission' by locking the gates of the Location. This provided the dreaded nationalist '"agitators"... [with] captive, frightened audiences' who over five days became 'increasingly angry crowds [as they] listened to inflammatory descriptions of their situation'. Lessing, the ex-Communist, has moved us very far from the determinism of historical materialism. Stupid white blunders create black nationalism.

Both Lessing's life and Rhodesia's history consist of choices that could have been different and, if they had been made, would have had different consequences. Public and private choices are supported by convictions held with passionate intensity that are simply discarded to be replaced by other convictions defended with equal passion. I suggested at the beginning of this chapter that plotting a South-Central African journey as imperial romance writes an apparently unique act as culturally representative. Because Lessing's sense of who she was is as elusive as the accuracy of what she recalls and the provenance of her own memories, her story cannot be accommodated within a formal emplotment. The classical genres of romance and satire are as absent in Lessing's book as they are present and used to give form to the informing ideologies of Godwin's and Smith's autobiographies. The Rhodesia of Lessing's autobiography is not the exclusive and homogenous family of Smith's recollections or the violent place that Godwin recalls from which whites have been excluded. Lessing refuses the constraints of narrative genres because her Rhodesia is more diverse than theirs. Where she deals with what are seen as stereotypes in colonial writing, we can see them being constructed, contested and transformed. Neither she nor the place she recalls is locked into categories whose meanings are fixed. When asked whether *Martha Quest* was autobiographical, Lessing's reply is that she tried 'to take the story out of the personal into the general. ...[and that] "If [she] had wanted to write an autobiography...[she] wouldn't have written a novel"' (1994:160). The 'facts' of the 'chronicler' are as a result closer to our stumbling experience of our pasts than the general truth that a novel provides.

Part IV.

Imagining the spaces of belonging

Chapter 10

'Mind has mountains': poetry and ecology in eastern Zimbabwe

Dan Wylie

One of the icons of our European presence in Zimbabwe – then Rhodesia – with which I grew up in the 1960s was a small bronze statue which gazed out from the heights of Christmas Pass above the eastern border town of Umtali (now Mutare). It represented a young white boy (with whom I immediately identified), an obviously older black servant ('Jack') curled obsequiously around the white boy's knees, and a little dog, 'Vic'. The boy was Kingsley Fairbridge, one of the area's earliest colonial settlers, and its first prominent white immigrant poet.

The statue might be seen as a synecdoche of a network of frontier conflicts: racial, political, social, aesthetic and ecological. From this Mutare Heights viewpoint one can see the constructions and scars of the multiple influences on Zimbabwe's historical life, from clashing and overlapping geological upheavals to the ugly russet scars on the Nyarusengeri ridge marking a now defunct 'security road', carved out along the border in the 1970s by the Rhodesian military as a futile anti-guerrilla measure. Almost beneath the statue's feet, amongst the granite boulders of Murahwa's Hill, remained Iron Age, even Stone Age, rock paintings and tools, traces of a rich and obliterated culture of hunting-and-gathering, shamanistic dance and, no doubt, unwritten poetry. A few kilometres eastwards, the stubborn pimple of Cross Kopje, surmounted by an extravagant monument to the dead Rhodesian soldiery of World War One, marks the border with Mozambique. That largely arbitrary line (it only tentatively converges with the north-south run of Zimbabwe's Eastern Highlands) was negotiated between Cecil John Rhodes and the Portuguese in 1891, splitting river-valleys, mountain ridges, ecosystems, and individual Manyika families, indiscriminately down the middle. Due south, one looks over the mushrooming satellite townships around Weirmouth, towards Rowa and the turbulent, impoverished hills of Zimunya Communal Area, rural home to Musaemura Zimunya, one of the poets I will concentrate on. The sometime home of another poet, Noel Brettell, lies a similar distance due north, beyond nearby radio masts, in the historically largely white-occupied region of Nyanga (formerly Inyanga). Nyanga remains distinguished by upmarket hotels, extensive plantations of wattle and pine, and a national park surrounding the country's highest peak, Mount Nyangani. The park was named after Rhodes himself: he had taken a particular fancy to the area's elevation and beauty and set aside 82,000 hectares there for his personal pleasure. He called it the sanatorium of Rhodesia (Cherer-Smith, nd: 128).

Mountains have an interesting aesthetic power-relation with empire. My sweeping gaze has been, in its way, imperial, echoing a passage written by Kingsley Fairbridge himself, surveying the landscape from much the same point. In 1897, he wrote, he could look down on 'Findlay's trading store and Russell's two huts' and 'on the flank of the vast Inyamutshura range were Fisher's huts'. Beyond these scraps of civilization, Fairbridge frowns darkly, 'it was all wilderness' (Fairbridge, 1974: 10). 'Wilderness' is laden here with aesthetic, racial and topographical tonalities. In selecting one's cultural salients, then, physical vantage-point is all: it is in this sense (with apologies to Hopkins), that 'mind has mountains'.

None of the frictions hinted at in this toposcopic sketch – black/white, immigrant/autochthon, rural/urban, exotic/indigenous, agricultural/wild, local/ global – is irrelevant to an appreciation of the region's poetry, and especially to an ecologically-orientated appreciation. Nor, conversely, is poetry irrelevant to understandings of local ecologies from socio-political or biological perspectives. Poetry remains a relatively neglected area of study in Zimbabwe. Equally thin is study of the inevitable embeddedness of that poetry within its environmental envelopes. The cityscape environment has received most attention, perhaps – not least because of the cultural prominence of that rather overrated maverick, Dambudzo Marechera. This chapter will, I hope, provide the beginnings of a counter-balance to that 'urban drift', and stimulate further work in the invigorating field of ecologically-orientated criticism. While southern African landscape studies are well-developed (see Coetzee,1988; Darian-Smith et al.,1996; Bethlehem, 1997; McGregor,1995; Moore, 1998 and 1988a, and Schmidt, 1995), their human-geographic or anthropological bias remains to be linked to and amplified by literary and related aesthetics.

An ecologically-sensitive literary criticism thus goes beyond merely noting the presence of the natural in a body of literature, whether as historical evidence, setting or symbol; and beyond merely designating Poet X or Y a 'nature poet', or not. It rather attempts to assess and explain the place of that literature within the ecosystems of its time. Robert Mugabe's tragically botched 2000-2003 land reform drive – a product of all the conflicting histories pencilled in above – is a salutary reminder that, above and beyond politics and putative reversals of historical abuses, the natural ecologies undergird all our human activities, and will, in some form, outlast us all. Ecocriticism examines, on the one hand, the contribution of the work to general awareness of its environment, as a reflection of pragmatic practices of, say, land-use, racial attitudes, or conservation of wildlife. (See Glotfelty and Fromm, 1995; Bate, 2001 and Tallmadge, 2000). Such practices, explicitly or subconsciously, are deeply informed by particular *aesthetics*; poetry is one medium in which such aesthetics are openly expounded, embodied, or challenged.

Ecocriticism also tries to unearth, from behind the omissions and rifts of the work itself, evidence of unspoken or unrecognized ecological dynamics, not in a merely historicist or scientific mode, but as a means of explaining the cultural values, limitations and effects of the work's aesthetic itself. There is no landscape that is not also a culturescape (Adorno, 1970: 94; see also Baker and Biger, 1992; Barnes and Duncan, 1992; Meinig, 1979 and Schama, 1995). Likewise, no animal, plant, bird or insect – co-inhabitants, even co-creators of that landscape – is in-scripted (or encrypted) without aesthetic or iconic import. At the same time, however – this is crucial to my approach – nature's language is not propositional (Adorno, 1970: 109). There is no natural language *within* the terrain; there are only more or less socially coherent, accepted or historically localised descriptive languages, none intrinsically more authentic to the *terrain* than another, but each authentic to the psychic *landscape* they express. This chapter compares the work the Shona poet Musaemura Zimunya – locally-bred but globally enculturated and urbane – with an English-born immigrant poet N. H. Brettell. It will be seen that the two poets' aesthetics of inscribing both an ecology and a home – of expressing in-dwelling or exile in topographically adjacent areas of Manicaland province – both clash and overlap.

Cultural touchstones

Two literary touchstones provide some background to a comparison of Zimunya and Brettell. In the first touchstone, Aaron Hodza and George Fortune's *Shona Praise Poetry* (1979), the name Zimunya is mentioned only once, in a reference to the early chief from the Umtali district from whom both the present Communal Area and the poet derive their name (Hodza and Fortune, 1979: 178). Chief Zimunya belonged to a swathe of complexly inter-related but scattered people who take as their totem *Soko*, the monkey or baboon. Other groupings in Zimbabwe take *Shumba* (lion), or *Tembo* (zebra), for their identifying totem (Shona *mutupo*); the animal is (or was once) subject to special taboos prohibiting clan members from eating it. Though impossible to document or quantify now, the taboos doubtless had direct ecological effects. The pervasive presence of the totem in thought and life is often expressed almost as if the animal is a medium through which to communicate with the ancestors underground (Shona *pasi*); its characteristics provide a base for describing the clan's identifying qualities, praised in Shona oral poetry. Each unique set of clan praises (Shona *nhetembo dzorudzi*) contributes to the praise of the natural creation as a whole. The poetic results are rich in allusion, close observation, obvious knowledge of intricate ecosystems at work, self-referential humour, and the sacralising of a set of inextricable relationships between climate, symbolic animals, and humanity. The following is a rendition of the 'Praises of Baboon':

Masters of the forests.
Those who make the rain to fall.
And who make all kinds of caterpillars come.
Sons of the Leader of big groups.
Their young clinging on to their backs.
Those of the long faces.
Smooth as a log without any bark.
Watchmen...
Animal almost human.
Knowing where the wild plums and the wild loquats are.
(Hodza and Fortune, 1979: 213)

Lest we fall into over-romanticizing some putative pre-colonial pastoral, we should remember that these same baboons would have to be fought off the people's grain-crops, that other creatures would be hunted or exterminated without compunction, and that, albeit at a level commensurate with low population densities and limited technology, the landscapes shared by humans and baboons would have been modified by human presences over centuries. Nevertheless, with such praises and prayers the people cushioned themselves against the ravages of drought, disease, human enmity, and marauding animals, sometimes sheltering in the declivities of the very mountains and forests which frequently frightened them. The relationship with mountains especially is both fraught and beneficent, life being lived mostly between them, where cultivation and clear grazing could be created or found. The ecological taboos, spiritual associations and pragmatic safeties of the forested hills would play important roles in the Chimurenga war of the 1970s (as several of Musaemura Zimunya's 'mountain poems' show; see Zimunya, 1982b; Pongweni, 1982 and Lan, 1985).

Not altogether unlike European conqueror-surveyors, Shona peoples like the Chihota clan (who originated also from the Mutare area) expressed profound attachment to particular geographical features in names (once as new as any English imposition) and in the rhythms of ancestral journeying:

Kindly done, people of Zomba.
And you have done kindly, Those who lie along the way.
Kindly done, those who lie at Tsoka;
at Mahwemachena;
at the pool of the lady Senwa.
(Hodza and Fortune, 1979: 145)

This reveals, amongst other things, a native ecology of relative mobility, characterized by specific modes of agriculture, uses of 'wild' resources, expressions of spirituality, and conceptions of ownership – all of which was comprehensively ignored by settler legal machineries, most notoriously the Land Apportionment Act of 1930, which violently carved up the space of the colony.

The settler apportionment of land had its own aesthetic basis and history, as evidenced by our second touchstone, John Snelling's anthology of *Rhodesian Verse* (1938). This collection of 72 poems by 26 white writers bears all the hallmarks of a half-hubristic, half-cringing colonialist attempt to create a sense of emergent nationhood. Its foreword, by no less a personage than the Governor of Southern Rhodesia, Sir Herbert Stanley, is couched in the euphemisms which conventionally mask the violence of conquest. Stanley evokes, instead, the glamour, courage and tenacity of settler achievement, and sets it against the background of 'the mystery of African life, dark and amorphous to the white man's ways, set in a scene lovely in light, colour and form.' (Snelling, 1938: 7).

The antithesis of 'dark and amorphous' indigenous people and vaguely 'lovely' landscapes governs much of the poetry in the volume, as it would govern much of the practical manner in which the whites apportioned, used, saved or destroyed various parts of the land they had occupied. Furthermore, a persistent attachment to English poetics is evinced by most poems in the anthology (a number you would never guess related to Rhodesia at all). Governor Stanley recognized that this produced a comfortably 'familiar ring' (7). Perhaps understandably, no immigrant European could spontaneously shed his literary heritage. Arthur Shearly Cripps, the main contributor to the volume (thirteen poems) and the author of its introduction, wrote that it was 'Books [that] have helped me most to see the sacredness and the beauty around me in African country-life' (Snelling, 1938: 17). A poetic aesthetic does not arise unmediated from the landscape itself, but out of precursor aesthetics: hence the poetries of Cripps, Fairbridge, Brettell, Zimunya and Marechera alike, share the wrestle between multiple blanks and possibilities, between identifying with the indigenous oral modes or with the written English ones, and trying to forge new hybrids appropriate to the uniqueness of each experience.

What kind of 'sacredness' and 'beauty' did Cripps see? It was (he quotes Burns) 'the simple joy the country yields' (Snelling, 1938:19). Cripps slips in some stiff criticism of the opposing *aesthetics* of the government's policies: 'Surely the time has come in Southern Rhodesia', he trumpets in a footnote, 'for some common action to be taken *by beauty-lovers* against such obvious eyesores (so wanton and detested) as Native Departmental Ribbon Development of our Africans villages' (Snelling, 1938: 18n; my emphasis). Cripps's beauty is peasant, pastoral, ecologically-integrated, even moral – and associated with 'our unspoilt granite hill-country' (note the 'our') (Snelling, 1938: 18). He grieves that the glory and loveliness of old Africa have been passing away at a great pace (ibid.); he is keenly aware that the natural ecology is being plundered, and that native customs and the natural order are intricately interlaced:

> The m'sasa bushes on the sand-veld so bright in their September Spring-tints – with leaves crimson and purple-brown, rose and copper – are not likely all to be cut down or grubbed for many a long year yet.

And at least the blue and golden skies of day and those blue and silver
night-skies, in which the stars, watching over Africa, slumber not nor
sleep, are too far out of reach for Africa's gold-seekers and diamond-
hunters and Big-Business agents from overseas to get at them, and spoil
them. (Snelling, 1938: 18-19)

Self-consciously 'poetic' diction, nostalgia for lost pastorals, and the dismissal of modernity, work together to fashion, even in Cripps's alert if wayward mind, a vacuity of description in which any sense of a locally specific ecology is smothered. As Mary Louise Pratt has written, 'Redundancy, discontinuity, and unreality are the chief coordinates of the text of Euroimperialism' (Pratt, 1992: 2). Nevertheless, English poetic dictions, backhandedly and projectively, but *authentically*, acted both as a shield and as an assertion of the new manliness, the muscular Christianity, upon which the European presence depended and defined itself. The radical contradictions inherent in this work *were* the colonial identity.

For the poets were not all immune to transcultural influence. As Cripps recognized, Kingsley Fairbridge is perhaps the poet of Snelling's anthology who goes furthest in assimilating the local into his diction, creating works awkward but vivacious, observant though still Kiplingesque in narrative colour. His poem Bongwi (Baboon) reads interestingly alongside the Chihota praises already cited:

A haunted soul put under ban,
    A hunted beast that has to roam
The voiceless image of a man
    With neither speech nor home –

Upon the summit of the height,
    Where only wind-swept lichens grow,
Bongwi, lit by the dawning-light,
    watches the plain below.

Fierce eyes, low brow, protruding mouth,
    Short hands that twitch and twitch again,
The hairy gargoyle of the South -
    A man with out a brain;

Upon the highest krantz he waits... (Snelling, 48)

An echo of an individuated Cripps-like exile is associated with mountain eminences: Fairbridge senses the human/baboon conflict – Bongwi's mates are all engaged in wrecking the fields of corn and making off with the stolen feast – and makes an aesthetic identification with what the baboon sees from his elevated post: 'the breaking morn,/ ... the soundless blue/ The golden distance of the dawn' (Snelling, 1938: 49). Idyll, it seems, demands generality, vacuity, mist, pure colour. Yet this is not mere blindness, or detachment. It is in its way an active extraction of that which is *readable* in terms of conventional English verse: the books dictate, in part, what is seen. Other parts of the terrain were at first literally unreadable, because as far as the immigrants could see, the land boasted no antecedent texts. Yet such purity, such ignorance of ecological and political dynamics, is precisely what constitutes the powerfully emotive, emergent sense of belonging, all the more powerful for feeling simultaneously under threat.

It is not only the baboon which is 'voiceless' here, 'without speech or home': it is the poet-in-the-landscape. Nevertheless, the language is unstable: readability evolves, beginning to emerge in the interpolation of local words (Shona *bongwi*, Afrikaans *krantz*; it is an irony that English people found Afrikaans words more 'authentic' than their own). This is evidence of subversive transculturation (Pratt, 1992), as much as of imperial appropriation. Nor is it merely colonial; it is also existential: Fairbridge's stance is as ambivalent as his Shona counterpart's, involving recognition of the baboon's near-humanity, which simultaneously provides the leverage to assert that which makes the poet *more* human (the brain, the poetic voice itself).[1] In encountering the baboon and his uniquely-contoured hills, the identity of the speaker is also being re-created. Conversely, Fairbridge cannot resist defensively translating the creature into familiar terms of Northern-hemisphere myth (gargoyles), just as the dawn incongruously 'throbs with Aeolian song' from the throat of a fish-eagle (Snelling, 1938: 48). There is here, in short, no single workable ecosystem of language-space: identity, for the present, is constituted by the very rifts in the poetry.[2]

Where the forest ended

Introducing Snelling's anthology, Arthur Shearly Cripps expressed a desire to see soon an equivalent Africans Poetry Anthology (Snelling, 1938: 16). He could hardly have anticipated Musaemura Zimunya's free-verse poems, let alone Marechera's anarchies; or the 1981 anthology, *And Now the Poets Speak* (Kadhani and Zimunya), in which liberation poets evinced no gratitude for colonial education whatsoever; or even Colin Style's major anthology, *The Mambo Book of Zimbabwean Verse in English* (1986), which included a comprehensive range of black and white poets from the nineteenth century to the present. Yet, paradoxically, Cripps would have identified keenly with Zimunya's castigation of the moral ills of the city.

The cover of Zimunya's early collection, *Thought Tracks* (1982b), bears a photograph of two little boys splashing in a stream beneath a towering, typical Manicaland granite batholith. Zimunya's poetry – as encapsulated in the title of his best-known collection, *Country Dawns and City Lights* (1985) – evinces a powerful split between the nostalgia for that rural childhood and the grimy allure

---

[1] Compare this with Zimunya's poem 'Men and Monkeys' (Zimunya, 1993:22), which deals with the same human/animal interface.

[2] Something more ecologically aware emerges in Fairbridge's 'On the Veld', not in the Snelling volume (see Fairbridge, 1974: II 74).

of the city. Even poems ostensibly of 'pure appreciation' are riven with estranging imageries drawn from industrial worlds, as in this description of 'Mountain Mist':

> There like a pangolin he silently crouches
> Grips the victim and gently stretches
> His body over the mountain's green carpet
> With his colour a lovely cream. (Style, 1986: 355)

While the imagery generally expresses knowledge of a local ecology, intrusively modern references ('carpet' and, later, a millipede's 'wheels') create a certain dissonance: this is no more a winsomely isolable world of independent 'Nature' than that depicted by Fairbridge. Other dissonances are striking: the characterization of the tranquillity as 'oceanic'; the contradictory gentleness and forcefulness; the comparison of mist caressing mountain to sex: 'Arched solidly he remains/ Like a pangolin during a mating season' (Style 1986: 355). These features are as symptomatic of an inner condition of visionary disruption as Cripps': Zimunya is – has become – no more capable of finding that authentic language of ecological integration than the white interloper.

This is not to deny Zimunya's capacity to find a relatively untrammelled beauty in the landscapes of his childhood. As he has said of his home area:

> We would go up mountains herding cattle and would look down as though we were in an aeroplane and would see the beauty of those rolling fields. You could see where there was forest, where the forest ended, you had the red of corn ripening, golden colours and so forth. And also, if you looked at the mountains from the land, they had their own beauty ... there was always this amazing visual beauty. (Wild, 1988: 56-7)

Strikingly, Zimunya's aesthetics echo those of his European counterparts in their antithesis of cultivated land and forested mountain: one is viewed at some distance from the other – even as if from an aeroplane, a comparison which enacts precisely the dissociation of the Western-educated, well-travelled academic from a vanishing cultural ecology. Indeed, Zimunya turned rapidly to writing explicitly about this eco-cultural transition in poems which Flora Veit-Wild, for one, finds rather too gauchely moralising (Wild, 1988:10).

The ecological ramifications of white rule were unavoidable, particularly in the wake of the Land Apportionment Act. Most newly instituted 'Tribal Trust Lands' (TTLs), including Zimunya, were agriculturally poor, and though several subsequent additions were made, the imbalances remained massive. By 1970, TTLs covered 53 per cent of the country, but housed 4.4 million people; the 47 per cent reserved for white occupation, by contrast, housed only some 32,000 whites and perhaps a million transient and dependent black workers (Riddell, 1978: 34). Heavily over-populated by both people and animals, the ecological condition of the TTLs deteriorated. It was a 'white wisdom' in my youth that the desertification of the TTLs was the direct result of black stupidity and destructive traditional agricultures;[3] in fact, it was the result of enforced changes in agricultural practice from relatively ecologically undamaging shifting subsistence and transhumance to over-crowded, static, market-driven modes. Even in Musaemura Zimunya's childhood, the landscape must have been seriously modified and already deteriorating. The theme surfaces in a number of poems which reveal how he, like other black Zimbabwean poets, was now finding it as difficult – aesthetically, pragmatically, spiritually – to locate his true roots, as almost any immigrant. Zimunya himself characterized his poem 'My Home' as 'crucial in that passage from the sheer aesthetic pleasure of observing nature around oneself to an awareness of the terrible condition that we were living in, in that beautiful land' (Wild, 1988: 57). The poem opens in a condition of deracinated doubt:

> I live in the highlands
> encompassed by great green ridges
> where is my home,
> in the heart of the storms of the world?
> Is this my home? (Wild, 1988: 70)

He answers himself in the positive – 'Brother, it is' – out of some lingering sense of communal, familial security, as well as one of a continental imaginary: it 'beats with/ the whole of Africa's pulse.' For all its symbolic efficacy in the face of colonial invasion, this is a fraught move, smudging as it does the cultural and ecological specificities of the place itself. A related blurring (or amplification) occurs in the second section (ibid.). Zimunya here turns the image of storms towards a positiveness reminiscent of 'Mountain Mists', but in his modulation into sea imagery again both recharges a localised perception of landscape and reveals his wider worldly experience:

> Upon those storms and billows of mountains
> capped with the surf of transient mists,
> whale-like woolly objects slumber,
> crowns of bulky trees sway...
> ... in the grace of breathing breezes.

In a manner similar to the white poets we've already looked at, the nostalgic is pushed into a register of vagueness, strongly contrasting with the greater specificity afforded by the third section's invasion of

> ...rude young girls from the city
> gurgling and giggling
> swayed by mini-morals
> clothing the old chaste tradition
> with everlasting defilement. (Ibid.)

---

3   Alexandra Fuller makes a similar observation in her autobiographical *Don't Let's Go to the Dogs Tonight*. For a discussion of Fuller's attitude to land, see Chapter 7 of this volume.

In this image of modernity's violation of the local, Zimunya introduces the image he paints of dissolute city life in other poems. The rural idyll is no longer attainable, if indeed it ever existed, and he accepts it in its full panoply of contradictions, all its mingled 'odour of life' (ibid.).

In 'No Songs' (Wild, 1988: 69), Zimunya expresses his deepest political and existential despair over the triply interlinked ecological loss of natural denizens, spirits and agricultural productivity: 'Where shall we find the way back?' Of course there is no way back; his imagery turns almost Dantesque ('So we live outside the burning flames of our thirst/ we live the lives of locust-hunting rooks') before expressing the final hopelessness in terms, partly, of wildlife at once predatory and lost:

> the day we shall know the way back
> to the caves of the ancestors
> the lion tongue of death will be licking
> the last gush of blood from our souls.

It is only to the hills of his childhood that Zimunya can still look for hope, as, in a symptomatic mixture of the domesticated and the wild, he has a vociferous rooster (Shona *jongwe*, a liberation-war rallying-icon) crowing towards the future from the ancestrally-named and humanised hilltops of home:

> So stand on one leg on the mountain of Chitungwiza,
> erect and high on the boulders fontanelle...
> Echo the overdue Hope
> until Vhumba and Matopo answer... ('Rooster'; Zimunya, 1982b: 105).

Listen for the undertones

Noel Brettell (1908-1991) is of an earlier generation than Zimunya's, but their work overlaps in both time and geography. The cover of Brettell's *Selected Poems* (posthumously compiled in 1994) inadvertently echoes that of Zimunya's *Thought Tracks*: a monochrome impression of one of Brettell's many water-colours of the Nyanga area, entitled 'Elephant Rock, Honde Valley', displays a massive buttress of granite deserving both the epithet 'dramatic' and the nineteenth-century 'sublime'. Here, geology is inescapable, the naked foundation of being and thought. Where Zimunya's poetry arcs into alienation from the natural, Brettell's moves in closer to it, though hardly Romantically. Steep declivities, hills, and waterfalls provide Brettell with a vertiginous correlative for unexpectedly nihilistic thought.

In his tightly-crafted verse (it is usually *verse*: rhymed, rhythmical, stanzaic), Brettell has perhaps come closest of any immigrant poet to forging a new language which actively restructures one's view of Zimbabwe's mountain landscapes. It's not entirely free of the English-isms of which Brettell accused Cripps; nor is it particularly replete with local argot. Neither usage is as much to the point as the sense of a life lived searchingly through language, into and out of that terrain, in that ecology of interfusion which is what constitutes the experience of home.

Some of Brettell's poetry, drawing strongly as it does on those other hill-poets Wordsworth and Edward Thomas, may appear superficially Romantic in the vernacular sense: slightly wistful, nostalgic for the loss of an environment never actually possessed, in mutually beneficent relationship with the natural. This is a mistake. 'On an Inyanga Road' is a poem dedicated to Edward Thomas (1878-1917), the bleakly pastoral English poet whom Brettell never met but deeply admired. The poem is sinewed with a tough realism tightening, at times, to an apocalyptic pessimism. It is about hill-climbing, time, estrangement, and poetic inheritance: Thomas and Brettell walk the same kind of path, thirty years and six thousand kilometres apart. Brettell is keenly aware of the impress of ancient and foreign mythologies on his own perceptions of Nyanga:

> The blue scythe of his [Thomas's] eyes would slice the mist
> The Merlin's isle I've sought in an alien sun
>
> And like him, never found, losing my way, myself.
> On we go, on and up. The track is harsh with flint,
> Diamonds but quartz and turquoise scraps of delf,
> His the edged splinter, mine
> The agate curious grain of serpentine.
> Through the black pines the constellations glint
> And scrawl their heartless theorems on the sky. (Brettell, 1994: 15)

Brettell's meditation is at once on his relationship to the imaginative legacy of European myth; the craftsmanship of Thomas; and the solid land before him. He finds himself distanced from his mentor by the very physicality he so closely observes in the stones at his feet, by the loss of a previous self impelled by the strange environment, by a sense of a radical cruelty in that environment. So there is some recrudescence of the beauty/threat tensions implicit in earlier settler poetry, but on a far more conscious level. It is captured in the image of the 'black pines', trees at once alienating and as alien as he is, an imported forest which nevertheless signifies a cosmic moral abyss. The awareness of the loss of young ideals makes the close observations both possible and necessary; it's a quality of attentiveness without which a sense of home cannot mature. This poem ends ambivalently, the speaker overwhelmed by mountainous questions, still torn between Haggard-inspired fantasies of exotic otherness and attachment to the homeliness of old England:

> The final hills arch their enormous crests,
> Stretch their black necks up to the steepest pitch
> Of the worlds utmost gable: to Sheba's Breasts
> Or Mother Dunch's Buttocks[4] – which? (Ibid.)

---

4   This distinctive landmark in the Sinodun hills of Wiltshire is mentioned in Thomas's poem 'Lob' (Thomas, 1997: 41).

If this evidences a certain elision of autochthonous presences, another effect is to make the actual English hills as fantasial, distant and important as the imagined ones. In part it is this layering of the English folktale – and a vocabulary drawn from English regional, rural dialect – which makes Brettell's relationship with his local Zimbabwean ecology distinctive. But his use of this and other literary or mythological reference is reflexive in a way that is paradoxically both inclusive and self-limiting. In 'Duiker Doe', for instance, Brettell characteristically begins with literature – the story of an old half-pay sea captain who, mid-shave, spotted a unicorn 'across the satin bay' and abandoned the squiredom he had made in order to pursue it. Brettell, next morning, in his own Nyanga squiredom, looks up from *his* shaving to see

> Not a unicorn
> But a duiker doe who primly prunes my roses,
> With sly prehensile lip fumbling the shoot and thorn:
> Ear-flick and nostril-twitch the lurking fear discloses
> With tight-strung nerves across composure drawn.
> Rosebud and honeysuckle fed, mild sybarite... (Brettell, 1994: 22).

The duiker, while unthreatening to the poet himself, is nevertheless iconic of the wild invading the imported garden, but also feeding off it, establishing a new kind of ecological relationship. Often one senses Brettell himself, like the duiker, 'Tiptoe[ing] between alarm and appetite', finding the Nyanga wilderness simultaneously beautiful and pulsating with existential threat. He tries to identify with – imagine – the duiker's inner being, its 'Quick flux of fear and feed'; he reads its emotions through its physical movements; and he queries what it is that drives life itself, the force that unites his own being with the animals:

> Instinct, hallucination – what is it comprehends
> Behind my still mirror while the shadows creep? (Ibid.)

'Instinct, hallucination': these are indeed the poles of the phenomenological apprehension of any ecology. Brettell consistently views the landscapes and its denizens through his reading, but he uses it to make them imaginatively his own. Animals are read through literature – the antbear through Webster ('Antbear'; Brettell, 1994: 39), a cobra through the legend of Medusa ('Spitting Cobra'; Brettell, 1994: 50) – but in alliance with a concreteness of observed detail that grounds the myths themselves as a strange new presence. If this concrete African wild thing-ness represents a truth beyond the foreign and the literary, it's a harsh one that dives, and blinds, and kills ('White Harrier'; Brettell, 1994: 23); yet the implication throughout is that the literary is less a shield against it than a way of integrating it into an evolving sense of both the ecology and the poet's own identity. It takes, as he wrote, years of waiting and expectancy (Brettell,1981: 130).

One of Brettell's concerns is to mediate between the languages of England and Africa; more importantly, however, he wants to assert the necessity of art in the face of death. He does this through a vision of the natural, the very strangeness and wildness of which alerts him afresh to his own limitations and possibilities. Thus, for instance, in 'Wind and an Eagle Owl' (Brettell, 1994: 20), the compassionate necessity of killing an eagle-owl smashed against a fence complexly parallels the aftermath of a domestic quarrel. Mountains also become correlatives of emotional states. An early poem, 'The Summit' (Brettell, 1994: 40-1), Herbert-like in its gentle economy, celebrates the attainment of love in the image of reaching a mountain-top – but the drop beyond also figures the uncharted territories of the relationship's future, and the advent of death itself:

This is our wanted world,
　　Our guerdon, bliss,
All we had hoped, contrived,
　　Narrowed to this.

But, through the sentried rocks
　　On the top crest,
Our shadows, thrown ahead
　　From the red west,

Lean over a far gulf,
　　Unmapped, unmade,
Valley of shadowy woods,
　　The last decade,

And, catching the wild light
　　Of day's overspills,
Chins cupped in hands and knees drawn up,
　　The ultimate hills.

In the alignment of the dialect word ('guerdon') with the fantasy, opposed to the 'unmapped', the 'wild' and the 'woods', Brettell enacts a peculiarly colonial unfolding of images. While it would be facile to read this too narrowly as political, the reference to 'sentried rocks' is interesting, inasmuch as militaristic imagery recurs elsewhere in his poems. In 'Moon' (Brettell, 1994: 43), a thin sickle of moon, 'the last sad remnant of discarded truth' is besieged by, from 'the purple ambush of the clouds,/ Gun-toting gangs of wild dishevelled light'. (It is almost prescient of the guerrilla attack that forced the Brettells off their Nyanga plot in 1979.)

Brettell also evinces a strong sense of the human war on Nature, a world increasingly under stress and siege (Brettell, 1981: 60). In 'No Road to Xanadu' (Brettell, 1994: 46), wild animals destroying crops are imaginaries even as they wreak their damage. They are already becoming the absent beasts of dream, just as much as those extinct animals still propping up European coats-of-arms, 'Glimmering through the nightmare fog/ In gilt and gules on gay heraldic gates'. The conception of a Nature distinct and separable from humans is an illusion: rather, nature includes the human imagination, and its characteristics only come into being through the vision of human artistry.

It is appropriate, perhaps, to end with one of Brettell's moving elegies to his wife, a poem entitled 'Wild Orchids', set at Nyanga's Chirwe Falls:

At the edge of the day, on the edge of a cliff,
we stood beside them, small circle of flowers.
Below our feet, the slender stream fell headlong
Shattered in spume... (Brettell, 1994: 52)

In the wake of loss, the drop of the falls mirrors the poets despair:

Speak to me, love: keep my feet to the earth,
Lest, hung for an instant on the falcon's wing,
I drop – to what? (Ibid.)

All the poems discussed here are about this: 'keeping one's feet to the earth'. I have extracted only one cluster of concerns from these poets' more complex *oeuvres*: the imagistic role of mountains, and some of the underlying aesthetics informing attitudes towards them. This thread can act, I hope, as synecdochic of a more pervasive concern with being at home in a natural environment whose ecological well-being is under threat everywhere. It seems appropriate to conclude with Musaemura Zimunya's words recognising the ecological intersections between politics, poetry and place, the ways in which foreign imposition robbed one of a sense of a literary home, and the ways in which land and psyche are inseparably bound in one's inner 'exploration':

Our environment had no African landscape in it, and one has been at pains to find in African literature ... the sense of genii locus *which we find in Aimé Césaire's* Return to my Native Land. *Zimbabwe, in particular that part where I was born, is so topographically dramatic that one cannot afford to miss the physical dimension in one's exploration (Zimunya, 1982b: x).*

Chapter 11

The eye of the nation: reading ideology and genre in a Zimbabwean thriller

Ranka Primorac

> *The world that surrounds the thriller hero is always opaque.*
> Jerry Palmer (1978: 58)

> *Detective narratives are constructed in relation to one of the most important self-referential systems of modernity: the law.*
> Scott McCracken (1998: 59)

1.

This chapter offers a reading of the genre/ideology interface in the Zimbabwean novel entitled *Detective Ridgemore Riva*, written by Rodwell Musekiwa Machingauta and published in Harare in 1994.[1] Although, as I hope to show, Machingauta's narrative is textually interesting in itself, the analysis that follows seeks to situate the novel within the larger field of Zimbabwean fiction and, by doing so, to contribute towards re-configuring some of the established perceptions which govern the study of Zimbabwean writing. In such a context, my aim is threefold. Firstly, I wish to argue that there is an urgent need to study the *generic* properties of Zimbabwean fiction (rather than referring to all long fictional narratives as simply 'novels'). My second aim is to indicate that generic similarities between texts may be seen to extend across the barriers of language and race, which still conventionally organize the study of Zimbabwean literature. And thirdly, I hope to show that the historical achievement of those Zimbabwean writers who have, unlike Machingauta, achieved international recognition, and have entered the contemporary 'postcolonial' (that is, global) literary canon, cannot be properly appreciated without studying the local (intertextual *and* social) contexts from which their work originates, and which include texts like Machingauta's.

I have argued elsewhere (Primorac, 2003) for the need to re-think conventional categorisations of post-independence Zimbabwean fiction which are guided primarily by categories stressing the race of authors ('white' and 'black' fictional

---

[1] I here understand 'ideology' in the Bakhtinian sense, as a pattern of evaluative accents configuring the combination of discourses that make up a novel.

traditions) and the language of texts (English, Shona, Ndebele). A key problem with such approaches is that they pay insufficient attention to novelistic genre. One of the outcomes of this is the fact that Zimbabwean post-independence popular-genre novels in English have so far (to the best of my knowledge) escaped critical attention altogether. While it is certainly true that the generic properties of fiction in African languages need to be discussed in more detail, George Kahari (1995) has at least drawn readers' attention to the fact that some novels in Shona and Ndebele may be described as thrillers or stories of detection. In contrast, no critical mention has been made of the locally published, English-language popular genre novels, although a substantial body of such novels is in existence. Research into Zimbabwean Anglophone fiction has, so far, dealt exclusively with the output of the writers who have appropriated and re-shaped elite novelistic genres such as the *Bildungsroman* or the modernist novel. Some of those writers – Dambudzo Marechera, Tsitsi Dangarembga, Yvonne Vera, and others – have become internationally prominent, winning literary prizes and seeing their works published and translated outside Zimbabwe. Their texts have sometimes been compared (if not uncritically, then certainly somewhat unreflexively) to 'postcolonial' writers from other nations (see, for example, Veit-Wild,1999; Flockemann, 1992; Uwakweh, 1998). My reading of Machingauta's texts is performed in part against the background of canonical Zimbabwean novels, with which it shares the space-time of origin. I would also argue that juxtapositions of Zimbabwean novelistic texts motivated by a national historical perspective enable us to appreciate in more depth not only Zimbabwe's *literary* history, but also wider Zimbabwean social and discursive trends. This is illustrated by a brief comparison between Machingauta's text and another Anglophone Zimbabwean thriller, published in the same period.

2.

The back cover of *Detective Ridgemore Riva* describes its author as a professional schoolteacher; my copy states that the novel went into a second printing in Harare in 1996. *Detective Ridgemore Riva* is a Zimbabwean version of the thriller; the hero's surname (Shona for 'trap') alludes to his skill in catching offenders and bringing them to justice. Its narrative is based on what Jerry Palmer (1978) has described as a dominant procedure of the genre: the combination of an abominable conspiracy that threatens the well-being of the community, and an individualistic hero who averts it by a combination of reasoning and physical intervention.[2] The novel's narrative – filled with surveillance, counter-surveillance,

---

2   I rely on Palmer's definition and description of the thriller throughout this article. He collapses (to my mind, convincingly) the generic distinction between 'hard-boiled' thrillers and classical 'whodunnits', and sees both as belonging to the thriller genre. 'If there is any difference between Holmes and his modern counterparts', he states, 'it is in the balance between logical inference and physical intervention in the course of events' (Palmer, 1978: 102).

car-chases and minutely described martial-arts action – relates the story of how Ridgemore Riva, the diminutive agent working for ZSAO (the 'Zimbabwe Secret Agency Organization' – Machingauta, 1994: 5) recovers top-secret documents stolen from Zimbabwe's Ministry of Home Affairs.

The novel's plot is constructed around three waves of watching and following. After being assigned the case of the missing documents by his Chief, Murwira, Ridgemore Riva goes to work undercover at the Ministry of Home Affairs. There, he draws a complex diagram of the missing files' movement and discovers that they were stolen from the computer room, where they were waiting overnight 'for their computerization' (12). He goes to the computer room under a pretext, and while he is there, one of the Ministry's employees *looks* at him with 'what seemed to be an interest' (24). Riva follows him and another man on foot and in a taxi, and is led first to a family house in Glen Norah, on the south-west outskirts of Harare, and then to a block of flats in the Avenues, near the city centre. After watching the block of flats disguised as a drunk, Riva again follows the men who emerge from it. They spot him, and there is a fight in which one of them is wounded.

Riva's next lead comes at Parirenyatwa, the Harare hospital where the wounded man is taken. One of the doctors there *appears* to Riva suspicious (86). At the same time Riva is himself subjected to 'interested scrutiny' by a patient on a nearby bed (84). Events linked to these two men eventually lead Riva to two more private houses in Harare. One contains a secret room, with 'walls covered by various sophisticated instruments with video screens all over the place. There were three computers which were numbered SA944, SA945 and SA946' (93). The other, in the southern suburb of Hatfield, also contains surveillance equipment and what appears to be 'a data processing room' (115-16). Both are centres of a South-African-based 'gang' of spies, whose aim is to destabilize Zimbabwe's economy. The identity of Riva's enemies is announced in the first half of the book (60), and is based on the South African number-plate of one of the cars Riva has followed.

After killing several gang members and setting himself up as bait (in the course of the novel, Riva and his helpers kill over 20 people in a matter of weeks), Riva's final stroke of luck comes when he catches a white man with sandy hair '*looking* fixedly at him' (132, emphasis added) in a city-centre café, where he has gone after posting a love poem to his fiancée Martha. Riva again follows, locates another suspect, and survives a final showdown during which the doctor from Parirenyatwa hospital reveals himself (in a conventional, final villain self-revelation) to be one of the leaders of a sinister organization called 'Central Valuable Information Conveyancing System' – CVICS (172). 'With this network,' he tells Riva, 'we can obtain any type of information we require or stay cool, depending on what I want which will be determined by the political climate' (172). Riva kills him, is promoted, and returns happily to Martha who is waiting for him at her parents' house.

Despite its generic competence, the plot movement of *Detective Ridgemore Riva* often seems arbitrary, the writing style ungainly ('From the corner of his right eye Riva could see the doctor who did not notice him or pretended not to, if at all he did' - 86), and characters' words and motivations naïve. (When arriving at the Ministry of Home Affairs for the first time, Riva tells the receptionist: 'I have come here on a secret mission, sir' -8; after the discovery of complex spying equipment, 'one of the agents who specialized on computers pointed out that even if a computer was disconnected, information which it possessed would not be lost' - 96). However, readers familiar with Zimbabwe might be struck by several other aspects of the narrative.

Firstly, the novel, set in and around Harare, is scrupulously exact when it comes to detailing Riva's movement through the streets, parks, shopping centres and open spaces of Zimbabwe's capital and its environs. The detective's trail is so meticulously and consistently described that it may be followed on a map of the city. Those who choose to do so will discover that both Riva and his opponents (no matter how rich, powerful and racist they are meant to be) avoid the city's opulent (and traditionally predominantly white) northern suburbs.[3] Part of the enjoyment of reading this novel may therefore not lie merely in following the unfolding of the plot, but also in *visualising* this unfolding in places with which readers may be familiar.

Furthermore, Riva eats local food ('sadza with meat and vegetables' - 132) and – both at home and in his car, while working – listens to local popular music with strong nationalist overtones.[4] When in a tight spot, he remembers his ancestors (166), and when faced with death he thinks of the many freedom fighters who died in the war of independence (167). The novel positions Riva unmistakably as 'a man of the people': a member of Zimbabwean black professional elite who defends the interests of ordinary citizens and the Zimbabwean nation. He himself identifies his duty repeatedly in nationalist terms: '"Let the dog die. He's foolish and deserves to die for he has sinned before all Zimbabweans including himself", Riva said to himself' (33). 'Surely how can a person in his right mind betray his own motherland for the sake of a few thousand

---

[3]   In residential terms, Harare is still to an extent racially divided along colonial lines. The novel's action takes place around the city centre and in areas such as Glen Norah, Hatfield, and Msasa. Riva himself lives in Dzivaresekwa. The northern-most parts of Harare covered by the plot are Eastlea and the Avenues; there are also out-of-town excursions to Chegutu and along Bulawayo and Beatrice Roads.

[4]   The novel mentions *Usandisiye* [Do not desert me] by Simon Chimbetu (17); *Bangaza* [possibly a corruption of 'Bangidza' – a Shona praise name] by Ephat Mujuru (46); *Shinga mwana wedangwe* [Be brave, first-born] by Simon Chimbetu and the Marxist Brothers (50); an mbira song 'from the Mujuru family' (79), and Thomas Mapfumo and the Blacks Unlimited (156). These are actual musicians and existing songs, well known in Zimbabwe. Simon 'Chopper' Chimbetu is a war veteran with strong links to the ruling party; Mujuru's mbira music is associated with both 'tradition' and revolution, and Mapfumo is, of course, the master of Chimurenga music. I am grateful to Paul Danisa, Alison Nyoni and Praise Zenenga for conversations about the music and musicians in *Riva* .

dollars? It's just like stabbing oneself in the heart with a hot spear' (97). This may be another factor contributing to some readers' identification with the hero and with his victory at the novel's end.

It is precisely the kind of nationalist ideology underpinning this novel's ludic (entertainment) function, and the manner in which this ideology articulates itself through the conventions of a popular genre, that makes *Riva* a worthwhile object of critical attention. Riva's nationalism is shared by his boss, Murwira, and the Minister of Home Affairs: 'He could not understand how a right minded person could allow his [sic] country to be used in this way for its destruction which may lead to his as well as his fellow citizen's death' (96). The question of how best to defend the nation and its institutions is, in fact, present in the text throughout. At the text's very beginning, as a sort of a prelude to the main narrative, two employees of the Ministry of Home Affairs, Terrence and George, debate the merits of democracy vs. dictatorship. ('"The only problem that is prevailing, one that is very difficult if not impossible to eradicate is the untrustworthiness and lack of commitment to one's duties and country." George gave a philosophical explanation to his friend.' - 4). The rest of Machingauta's novel may be read as a resolution of the questions raised in this prelude. In the world that Terrence and George inhabit, defending the nation is first and foremost a masculine affair.

The only female character prominent in *Detective Ridgemore Riva* is Martha, Riva's fiancée.[5] She conforms to the 'traditional' model of feminine behaviour by cooking for him, and living with her parents while waiting for their marriage. When it becomes likely that Riva's enemies might kidnap or harm her (129), Martha becomes a symbol of the nation that he is protecting: he can only return to her after the threat to the motherland is removed. She, however, does not herself participate in removing the threat. According to the typology of thriller characters elaborated by Jerry Palmer, she is an Amateur – a character helpless in the face of conspiracy, whose fate is decided by the outcome of conflicts entered into by Professionals, such as Riva and his enemies (see Palmer 1978: 7-15). (Palmer's third type, the Bureaucrat, is here represented by the inept employees of the Ministry, and by the law. I return to this below). When Martha worries about his safety, Riva consoles her with the words: 'Thank you very much, darling, for fearing for me, that's what real love is like, but don't forget that I can also be as dangerous as anybody else. I am a man, dear' (82). And to be 'a man' in the world of this novel means to possess determination, dedication to patriotic/ professional duty (both Riva and his boss pointedly go without proper rest for long periods of time -52, 65, 119), physical toughness and fighting skills. It also, of course, means being good at detection. But although there are some echoes here (at the level of motif) of the 'whodunnit' – Riva, for example, makes good

---

5   The only other two women mentioned in the text are Sithembile, an 'attractively ugly and tall lady' with a sonorous voice who is assistant to the Minister of Home Affairs (9), and a female police officer at Machipisa police station, who gratefully accepts a two-dollar tip from one of Riva's helpers (139).

use of his magnifying glass in Chapter 9 – the kind of detecting he practises does not rely on deduction, psychological analysis or even evidence examination.[6] When he is not following suspects or physically fighting them, Machingauta's hero practises his craft by simply looking around him.

The brief plot summary given above purposely underlines the fact that the narrative movement of *Detective Ridgemore Riva* hinges on instances of a character *appearing* suspicious, or simply *looking* at the detective. Each time, the suspicion turns out to be well founded. In the world that Riva inhabits, no truth is really hidden: suspects and witnesses are not characters with secret lives for Riva to disentangle in order to get at the one secret he is interested in. All he has to do is look about – and the enemy becomes visible. Even the slightest suspicions of guilt are confirmed, because the assumption is that the enemy is always *present*, and always *looking back*, and will be unnerved by the investigator's presence and gaze. Looking has, of course, always been associated with detection: not for nothing did Pinkerton's detective agency choose an open eye as its logo. But in Machingauta's novel, the characteristic opacity of the world of the thriller, referred to by Palmer, has been replaced by near-transparency. Typically, '[a] world which is riddled with conspiracy is opaque: things happen that are only very partially comprehensible. When conspiracy is compounded by treachery, the world is extra-opaque.' (Palmer, 1978: 39). In Machingauta's novel, conspiracy *is* accompanied by treachery. Yet guilt is manifest to the eye of the Professional. And there is, to be sure, nothing 'private' about this eye: the detective takes on the role of the ever-vigilant *official* observer, the eternally open eye of the nation.

In Chapter 8, Riva visits Parirenyatwa hospital incognito, and while he and other agents disguised as doctors observe the enemy agent who is a patient, other enemy agents, disguised as doctors and patients, watch *them*, and later kidnap Riva in front of the building. In Chapter 11, Riva and his colleagues stalk a house in Hatfield, only to find out on entering that they had been watched from the inside. When he decides to use himself as bait, Riva simply sits down in the middle of a wood and waits for the ever-present enemy to appear. The final confrontation in Chapter 18 is initiated in the same manner. In Chapter 13, Riva wishes he could *see* every single Zimbabwean – the better to protect them: 'Riva wondered why photographs of all citizens of Zimbabwe as well as duplicates of their identity cards were not yet in the library' (137).

The identity of the enemy Riva and his allies are confronting is established at the beginning of Chapter 4. This is also a moment when the narrative focus shifts temporarily from Riva to Murwira: 'Murwira had been very much excited by Riva's

---

6   The species of ratiocination typical of Riva is exemplified by the following passage: 'He let his mind dwell on her for a while as he secretly watched her. Could she be the one who had stolen the papers? Riva asked himself, but no sooner had the question come than a reply appeared in his mind. It could possibly be her. Her maturity could mean nothing and could have been used as a weapon to try and avoid speculation. But she could be as innocent as she looked, who knew besides herself and God?' (21).

quick findings about part of a gang of South African secret agents who were greatly wanted by the state for destabilizing the peace in Zimbabwe' (60). Although the text does not explain at this point how Riva has reached this conclusion, Murwira accepts his 'quick findings' and the narrative asks its readers to do the same. In the model of post-colonial Zimbabwe constructed by *Detective Ridgemore Riva*, the identity of those behaving badly is, to an expert observer, obvious as a matter of principle.[7] Investigating a crime does therefore not involve exposing a reality obscured by appearances: it simply means correctly interpreting appearances to the uninitiated.

In this surface-bound world, looking sometimes takes the place of talking: in Chapter 8, Riva maintains secrecy by communicating with fellow agents through winking. This is symbolic: in *Detective Ridgemore Riva*, dialogue is used sparsely. When characters do talk, their exchanges are often one-sided, and never yield new insight or information.[8] In conversation with his boss and fellow agents, for example, Riva usually overrules their opinions (119, 122, 144). All physical confrontations with enemy agents – on Bulawayo Road in Chapter 3, in front of the house in Eastlea in Chapter 9, and on the grounds of the house in Hatfield in Chapter 11 – take place in complete silence. Riva, of course, wins them all. But although some of his opponents are wounded rather than killed, they are not questioned afterwards (Riva himself remarks on this - 124) – and neither are, at any time, the employees of the Ministry of Home Affairs (99).

On the rare occasions when dialogue between Riva and members of the opposing side does take place, it is either inane (as in a hospital toilet in Chapter 8), or it implies a previously existing, non-verbally arrived-at understanding. (When Riva chooses to expose himself to danger at Cleveland Woodlot in Chapter 12, a stranger emerges from among the trees and tells him: 'I won't tell you who I am for I am quite sure that you already know me' - 125). When, finally, gathering verbal information becomes indispensable, Riva and his foils resort to torture.

The final five of the novel's eighteen chapters alternate between two parallel narrative lines: one (Chapters 14, 16 and 18) relates the course of the final confrontation between Riva and the leaders of the South African spy gang, at a hotel outside Harare. The other (Chapters 15 and 17) narrates in considerable

---

[7]   Whether Riva qualifies for the status of 'post-colonial detective' is an open question, as is the adequacy of the definition of the term offered by Ed Christian. He specifies that 'post-colonial detectives are always indigenous to or settlers in the countries where they work; they are usually marginalized in some way, which affects their ability to work at their full potential; they are always central and sympathetic characters; and their creators' interest usually lies in an exploration of how these detectives' approaches to criminal investigation are influenced by their cultural attitudes' (2001: 2). Riva is certainly indigenous to the formerly colonized country where he works. He is, however, in no way marginalized – precisely the opposite. Whether he is perceived as sympathetic would depend on circumstances to do with individual acts of reception.

[8]   See, as a point of contrast, the role dialogue plays in the work of Arthur Conan Doyle (on this, see Fowles,1980) or Elmore Leonard.

detail the manner in which 'tall and muscular' (73) secret agent Katsande and his colleague Agent 129 torture some of the suspects Riva captured previously. A useful contrast to these chapters is provided by James McClure's detective novel *The Steam Pig*, set in the 1970s South Africa and originally published in 1971. *The Steam Pig*, too, contains an episode of suspect torture. But McClure refers to the details of the procedure only metonymically, and it leaves his detectives feeling drained and ambivalent.[9] Machingauta's Katsande, on the other hand, positively enjoys the experience, and the novel relates it in full. In Chapter 13 we are told that Riva knew that 'Katsande enjoyed torturing his victims especially when he knew that the person he was dealing with was guilty' (136). Two chapters later, the narrative has presented the reader with no evidence on which Katsande could base such knowledge in this particular case. Nevertheless, he and Agent 129 cut a Zimbabwean suspect's buttocks with a razor blade, burn the wound, whip him and scald him with boiling water.

Chapter 17 shows why this is necessary. The two white South African citizens that Katsande questions next conform to this novel's stance on the limited usefulness of dialogue by answering questions evasively and refusing to admit that they are spies. They also taunt their interrogators by referring to a need for democratic questioning procedure. This infuriates Katsande, who delivers a long, ironic speech on the obviousness of their guilt:

> Let us leave that issue of our good and democratic neighbour South Africa and concentrate on the issue that has brought us all here. It's obvious that you are not a South African Spy as we had earlier on thought. We had forgotten that the country is a very good neighbour, which is not aggressive and bent on causing turmoils to it's [sic] neighbours. Since our independence in 1980 we never had any problem with South Africa. It assisted us greatly in our economy and defence in order to maintain our hard won sovereignty. As a country opposed to racism and fascism, it helped us greatly by training guerillas as well as arming them in order to fight the Smith Regime (162).

The speech continues for three more paragraphs: Katsande mentions South African interference in the affairs of Mozambique and the training of Zimbabwean dissidents. When the accused man continues to deny guilt, Katsande again switches to violence. The man must be guilty because he is South African, and all of 'these racists' (167) are the same. Talking to them is a waste of time because '[i]f all the prisoners refuse to co-operate it means we will lose, and this will look as if we captured the wrong people. We need to extract the truth from them' (158). And so the circle is closed: if detection means spotting the obvious truth, interrogation means extracting it from the pre-

---

9   'Every sordid item now declared itself in stark relief against its own sharp shadow; the coffee cups, the hose pipe, the crumpled packets, the wet towels, the plastic duck.' (McClure, 1993: 104).

designated enemy by whatever means necessary. The main obstacle that Riva and his collaborators face in doing this is the law.

In Chapter 3, Riva tells his boss disparagingly: 'You know what kind of judicial system we have in this country. The [accused] man may appeal against conviction and even sue me for defamation' (52). In Chapter 17, Katsande – as if in answer to the dilemma of Terrence and George from Chapter 1 – delivers several invectives against the legal state.

> *"Damn the bloody fucken law" Katsande said stamping hard on the floor with his left leg, his face frowning with anger. "Why then do we defend the country when its laws are at times against us and in support of the very people who want to destroy it? At times I wonder whether some of our laws were not imposed on us to please certain organizations or outside countries (158).*

As Scott McCracken has remarked, it is obligatory for a detective and his allies to position themselves in relation to the law, and since the days of Sherlock Holmes it has been commonplace for the heroes of crime fiction to find themselves outside it. In constructing a morality, which has little in common with the ethics that are publicly admitted to regulate society, and which disregards, among other things, the due process of law, *Detective Ridgemore Riva* is in keeping with the conventions of its genre. But in the Anglo-American thriller, the hero functions as a leader who disregards rules imposed on the majority only in order to ultimately establish the conditions for following them. 'His job is, essentially, to carve civilization out of the wilderness, to act in an emergency solely on the strength of his own intentions, to *create* a society that can develop the rule of law' (Palmer, 1978: 84). Riva differs from this in two respects. Firstly, as I have tried to show, he is at home in 'the wilderness' which, for him, has lost most of its opacity. And secondly, as the above extract from Katsande's speech indicates, the novel represents the process of law as essentially formalistic (Bureaucratic) and therefore *un-Zimbabwean*. If '[w]hat the thriller hero does is to save society from conspiracy: in other words, in each novel *he re-founds the state*, he prevents society from returning to the wilderness from which it supposedly came' (Palmer 1978: 85), then the ideological stance of *Detective Ridgemore Riva* deviates from the template of thriller ideology by implying the possibility of a permanently law-less state, a 'wilderness' protected solely by silent, professional watchers. The state that Riva and his helpers symbolically re-found is a dictatorship.

Furthermore, and perhaps even more importantly: in basing its own morality on the us/them, good/bad, and insider/outsider binaries – by insisting, that is, on an always *already existing* group of *external* enemies, whose subversive activities may be taken for granted – this novel is also participating in a specifically local (Rhodesian/Zimbabwean) popular-literary tradition, or textual formation. Its outline can here be sketched only briefly.

3.

In Chapter 14 of Edmund Chipamaunga's 1983 novel *A Fighter for Freedom*, set in the 1970s Rhodesia, the hero Tinashe Gari discovers a secret boardroom in the family house of a white Rhodesian, Mr Null. The house turns out to be the seat of WITE INTERNATIONAL, a 'sanctions busting and secret military planning unit' (Chipamaunga ,1983: 314). The setting of an international organization's headquarters in a private house is replicated by the Harare base of *Riva*'s CVICS, and Mr Null himself (of whom Tinashe thinks: 'You obviously don't belong this side of the Limpopo' - 312) would not seem out of place in Machingauta's gang of spies. *A Fighter for Freedom* has received some critical attention as a war novel (see Kaarsholm, 1989 and 1991, and Chapter 1 of this volume). Critical texts, however, do not mention the fact that Chipamaunga's freedom fighter is also a spy (in the novel's Part III) and a detective (in Part I). When he faces extreme danger in the final chapter of Machingauta's novel, Ridgemore Riva draws a parallel between himself and a guerrilla: he 'found solace in that many freedom fighters died for the independence of the country. He also saw it worthwhile to sacrifice himself it if meant rescuing his country from it's [sic] aggressive neighbour, since many people had shed blood for the country's independence' (Machingauta, 1994: 167). In textual and generic terms, the parallel is apt: both the detective and the war hero are constructed within the masculinist, bipolar logic I referred to above.

The same logic applies in the popular novels published in Rhodesia in the 1970s by white settler authors. Peter Armstrong's *Operation Zambezi* has also been described as a war novel (Chennells, 1982). And yet it is related to the thriller in that it deals with a large-scale military operation mounted by internationally *isolated* Rhodesia and designed to thwart a Communist-inspired *conspiracy*; appropriately, one of the sub-plots underpinning the main story is about a bank robbery. Its omniscient narrative voice resembles the voice of *Riva*'s agent Katsande in that it lectures the readers on the pernicious influence of 'outside countries', whose propagated opinions are *evidently* wrong. The only difference is that here the enemy organisations are those of the African 'terrorists':

> *That which the world regarded as a race war with the oppressed black man fighting for his rights against the white supremists [sic] was nothing of the sort. The propaganda put out by the terrorists and their Communist backers conveniently and successfully made the claim that they were fighting for the rights of the downtrodden majority, but this took no cognisance of the fact that Rhodesians had accepted the need to transfer power to the Africans in the country (Armstrong 1979: 15).*

Similar passages may be found in Daniel Carney's *Under a Raging Sky*, whose narrative combines the themes of the war novel and the mining novel (a South African genre premised, like the thriller, on a celebration of competitive individualism – see Hofmeyr, 1978). The same is true of several other popular novels published by settlers in Rhodesia (for a list, see Primorac, 2003). Moreover, Emmanuel Chiwome has found what sounds like the same partisan, propagandist ideology in war novels in indigenous languages, published after independence by authors such as Vitalis Nyawaranda, Aaron Moyo, Munashe Pesanai and Raymond Choto. (Due to Rhodesian state censorship, novels in indigenous languages could not mention the liberation war before independence.)[10] Interestingly, Chiwome links these texts' apparent naivety (a trait discussed above in connection with *Riva*) to the influence of orature:

> The partisan nature of the accounts is captured and reflected in the published fiction under discussion. It is one of the hallmarks of Zimbabwean nationalist fiction in African languages. The war rhetoric acquires its character from orature. When it is rendered in novels, it appears rather superficial and naïve because of the way it frequently dispenses with realism (Chiwome 1998:17).

Because he is concentrating on the interface of orality and literacy, Chiwome does not discuss other generic components of these war novels.[11] George Kahari and Flora Veit-Wild have, however, made passing mention of the pressure exerted by crime-fiction genres on the Zimbabwean novel in indigenous languages. Kahari (1995) includes 'The Detective-Cum-Thriller Form' and 'The Thriller' in his typology of Shona fiction, whereas Veit-Wild (1992) comments briefly on the popularity in post-independence Zimbabwe of James Hadley Chase[12] and other authors of western Anglophone thrillers. Both authors comment on the moralising tone of Shona thrillers, and remark on the bipolar (good vs. evil) nature of this moralism (see Kahari, 1995: 213-217, and Veit-Wild,1992: 70-71). Although neither author draws parallels between Shona and English-language texts, or between the pre- and post- independence historical periods, their observations, in combination with those of Chiwome (1998) and Primorac (2003) indicate that such parallels may exist.

Clearly, there is much that is as yet unknown about the generic characteristics of Zimbabwean novels. Yet there is evidence that a segment of the multi-lingual corpus of Zimbabwe's popular fiction endorses and promotes a particular kind of patriarchal, bipolar and inward-looking nationalist discourse, and that this discourse transcends the boundaries of language and race. Texts such as these, characterized by the 'ideological single-toned quality', have famously been called

---

[10] For a brief discussion of a Shona thriller, see Chapter 5 of this volume. In a text such as this, the ideological properties typical of orature, Literature Bureau-sponsored fiction and the thriller genre would appear to collude.

[11] He does, however – and perhaps not merely coincidentally – say that the authors of Shona *romances* (Patrick Chakaipa, Canisius Zharare and others) 'create interesting thrillers' from the vital energy that their characters have at their disposal. See Chiwome, 1998: 16.

[12] This popularity is given a fictional illustration in Chapter 14 of Yvonne Vera's *Without a Name*, in which Joel – the casual, urban-based lover who refuses to support the heroine's child – is seen reading a James Hadley Chase novel.

monologic by Mikhail Bakhtin (Bakhtin, 1999: 83). In a discussion of monologic literature, Bakhtin stresses that, in such texts, '[t]he idea, as a principle of representation, merges with the form' (83). The thriller form is, by definition, monologic: the detective's world-view is dominant, and superior to all others: it is the vehicle of the novel's moral stance, and is constructed as the exclusive focus of readers' admiration.[13] Although in the Zimbabwean context it is generally more profitable to think in terms of a confluence of formal-ideological strands (not all of them written) rather than 'pure' generic form, it is possible to state that several Rhodesian and Zimbabwean popular novels have appropriated aspects of the Western thriller and incorporated them into vehicles for monologic and violent local nationalist ideologies. In Rodwell Machingauta's *Detective Ridgemore Riva*, the presence of the dominant procedure of the genre, and its appropriation/modification in order to accommodate such an ideology, is particularly clearly visible.

In a long essay on discourse in the novel, however, Bakhtin (1987) explains how textual (novelistic) monologism is always both threatened and inflected by an ambience of polyphonic (or: heteroglossic) language.[14] Novels by canonical Zimbabwean writers such as Dambudzo Marechera, Tsitsi Dangarembga, Yvonne Vera, Chenjerai Hove, Shimmer Chinodya, Alexander Kanengoni and others construct polyphonic forms of expression that resist and subvert the appropriations of popular genres such as those described above. It seems to me, as indicated at the outset, that this form of resistance is an important aspect of Zimbabwean writers' historical achievement, and one that is easily missed if canonical texts are seen in isolation, or chiefly in juxtaposition with similar texts from different (albeit postcolonial) contexts. A brief survey of key texts reveals that there are, in fact, thriller-like elements in several canonical Zimbabwean texts in English. A character who is a spy features importantly in Dambudzo Marechera's *The House of Hunger* (1978). There is a mystery surrounding the heroine's parentage in Yvonne Vera's *Butterfly Burning* (1998), and the hero's parentage in Chenjerai Hove's 1996 novel *Ancestors* (both are solved at the novels' ends). The entire central part of Shimmer Chinodya's *Harvest of Thorns* may be read as an exploration of the mystery that the youthful hero faces at the end of Chapter 13, namely: what is 'a child of the soil'? (Chinodya, 1989: 97-99). Furthermore, it could be argued that, in these three texts, there are social forces at work that 'conspire' against the central characters and their communities. But of course, Marechera's, Vera's, Hove's and Chinodya's novels are not thrillers. Their heroes and heroines are not detectives; more importantly, the 'conspiracies' they contain are not constructed as discrete

---

[13] Jerry Palmer offers a remarkably Bakhtinian formulation of this point in a discussion of how characters function in thrillers: 'It is not true ... that character portrayal and the thriller are incompatible; but it is certainly true that one cannot have a *multiplicity of characters all protrayed with equal emphasis, so that none of them has a monopoly on perspective.*' See Palmer, 1978: 112 – 113, emphasis added.

[14] For a complex example of such contestation, see Chapter 2 of this volume.

events that can be 'solved' – or even represented – in any kind of a non-contradictory or 'ideologically single-toned' manner.

Having said that, there also exist in Zimbabwe popular texts and thrillers that resist the extremity of *Riva*-like ideological monotone. In Paul Freeman's thriller *Rumours of Ophir*, published four years after *Riva*, a brave and thoroughly Zimbabwean detective unmasks and thwarts a complex conspiracy executed by external agents. Freeman's detective, special investigator James Carter, resembles the pre-independence thriller heroes created by Peter Armstrong and Daniel Carney not only in being a ruggedly individualist white male, but also – in a conscious textual nod to the mining novel – in his reliance on the help of an old-time white miner in the process of detection. The crime itself is a series of murders motivated by a race to access a vast treasure of hidden gold, located somewhere in the Zimbabwean countryside. The novel resembles *Riva* in conveying a strong sense of Zimbabwean space: it unfolds in recognizable locations in and around post-colonial Harare,[15] and evokes much closely observed local detail. ('Carter's Peugeot spun dizzily from the empty Parkade onto deserted Sunday streets where learner drivers were being put through their paces without fear or hindrance to themselves or other motorists' – 61; 'In a homesick imitation of an English country pub, a yoke hung from the ceiling... - 78). But there are also significant differences.

The series of murders that the novel traces is committed by a trio of 'coloured' (mixed-race) Mozambican brothers, formerly 'MNR bandits' (46). Their racial 'in-betweenness' points to a key point of divergence between Freeman's novel and Machingauta's. Although Freeman's Mozambican villains resemble Machingauta's South African spies in being non-Zimbabwean citizens, the world of *Rumours of Ophir* is not easily reduced to a series of *Riva*-like binary identity markers (black Zimbabwean patriots vs. foreign white enemies, active men vs. passive women, etc). The list of place-names in which *Rumours* is set includes both former colonial ghettos (Mbare) and elite white enclaves (Borrowdale), as well as the liminal urban spaces such as the racially mixed suburbs of Marlborough and Arcadia. Also in contrast to *Riva*, the music that accompanies parts of Carter's investigation is pointedly represented as hybrid.[16] Although Freeman's detective is a white man, he is aided by a diverse group of characters, who, between them, combine a variety of race, class, gender and age-related traits. Carter's primary helper is Julia Machaya – a tough young black former prostitute. The pair is supported by

---

[15] The novel refers to the suburbs of Borrowdale, Marlborough and Arcadia, the high-density area of Mbare and its bus terminus, the Sheraton and Monomatapa hotels, the city centre and the central urban area called The Avenues, and intersperses references to actual places with invented place-names that mimic real ones, such as Lendale, The Mashumba Mine and Mount Longden.

[16] In an early chapter, an old street beggar sings 'a religious song in Shona, incongruously to the tune of Auld Lang's Aye' [sic] (54; see also 213); later, in a city hotel, the 'soft strains of a Beethoven piano sonata floated down from the mezzanine where an old black pianist with white woolly hair allowed his fingers to flitter and skip almost magically across the keys' (66).

Julia's father – the trench-coat wearing police chief Tatenda Machaya – the grizzled ex-Rhodesian miner Ronald Grenville and the meticulously professional black policeman Kelvin Gotora. Carter himself is a widower and no longer a full-time detective: his former boss Machaya has pulled him out of retirement into which he was forced after he lost control of himself following the killing of his black wife Maria.

In addition to this, *Rumours of Ophir* is populated by an even more varied throng of minor characters: the Afrikaner mine manager Van Rooyen, the urban Madam Big Betty Mlambo and her 'girls', a smart young female receptionist at the Harare Sheraton, Carter's tantrum-prone, mixed-race teenage daughter Emily, the corrupt Mbare policeman Colin Chiwoko, the white owner of a private plane on his way to a lakeside holiday, Australian tourists, a pornography-loving American expatriate, rioting university students and many others. In this novel, the possibility (contemplated by Riva) of all Zimbabweans being clearly visible, definable, and reduced to a series of photographs seems unthinkable, and neither are ordinary Zimbabweans (Palmer's Amateurs) represented as passive recipients of the Professionals' protection: they all have agency, and they all influence – no matter how indirectly – the outcome of the investigation.

All this would be impossible both in a pre-independence thriller and in the black-and-white world of *Riva*. *Rumours of Ophir* is a novel that revels in variety and difference, and it explicitly designates plurality as a key characteristic of the Zimbabwean nation. In an early conversation with Tatenda Machaya, Carter makes the following remark about a suspect, commenting on the fact that he is an expert in Portuguese history: 'Armitagere isn't a very Portugese sounding name.' (52). His boss's answer firmly dissociates this novel's ideology, and its understanding of what it means to be Zimbabwean, from all such essentialisms: '"Carter isn't a very African name," retorted Machaya drily' (ibid.). In a further contrast to Machingauta's novel, Freeman's key suspects (the mixed-race divorcee Cecilia Drake, her black admirer Josiah Zulu and the white male academic Professor Armitage) are all directly linked to key national institutions – a national heritage museum, the University of Zimbabwe and the National Archives. Ultimately, the originator of the conspiracy – the Mozambican killers' taskmaster – is to be found occupying a prominent position *within* the nation, rather than somewhere outside it.

This is not to say that the 'us' vs. 'them' polarisation is not prominent in *Rumours of Ophir*. But it is *not* immediately obvious who 'they' – the originators of the conspiracy – are. In its opacity, Freeman's world conforms to Palmer's description of the thriller genre, and his detective differs from Ridgemore Riva in that he cannot rely on simply looking around him in order to find out the truth about the crime he is investigating. The novel situates Carter within a complex, non-transparent Zimbabwe, complexly related to the outside world and its own colonial and pre-colonial pasts The text places special emphasis on the racial tensions in the post-colonial society, and repeatedly refers to the need to overcome them. Carter thinks about his dead wife in the following terms:

He wondered again at the possibility of his having wasted much of his life. His marriage to Maria had left him rebuffed by his parents and many friends and colleagues. Even black workmates and black acquaintances often treated him with a disrespectful familiarity that bordered on contempt. And now, with Maria gone, her face had become vague and indistinct in his memory, like a visage on a worn coin – a black face that because of its blackness he had been expected by his white peers to despise. It all seemed so ridiculous. (145)

In an earlier chapter, he worries about his daughter: 'If only she could get the chip off her shoulder about being coloured. The common expression to degrade those of racially mixed parentage was that they were neither fish nor fowl, yet, thought Carter, she should be able to revel in her dual heritage, not feel shamed by it' (60). Racial tensions also surface in professional relationships: on first welcoming Carter to the scene of one of the crimes, his black colleague Kelvin Gotora casually enquires whether one of the other black policemen had shown signs of racism:

Gotora gave back the ID card. "You've gone up in the world I see, Jim. Did my sergeant tell you we were here?"

"Yes, he did."

"I hope that wasn't a problem. He sometimes has trouble relating to the long-nosed brethren." (82)

Such divisions, however, have to be overcome if the case is to be solved and the conspiracy thwarted. The investigating team must work together and, despite their many differences, *share information* if they are to succeed. Carter makes his worst mistake at the moment when he breaks the promise to co-operate that he has given to Gotora earlier: 'Common sense gave way to egoism and selfishness. He did not want to share the climax of the investigation with more people than he had to' (151). This way of thinking imperils the entire investigation, and nearly gets Carter and Julia killed. Carter is later sharply criticized by his team of helpers, and is only able to solve the case after he has learned a key lesson: 'From now on it's co-operation all the way' (183). If, in his manner of relating to the conspiracy, Machingauta's Riva may be said to bear a distant resemblance to the lone, 'hard-boiled' detectives created by Dashiell Hammet and Raymond Chandler, then the collective effort of detection in Freeman's novel resonates with an earlier text – Wilkie Collins' *The Moonstone*. In the Zimbabwe that is imagined in *Rumours of Ophir*, no *single* 'eye of the nation' could possibly be anything but blind.

The parallel between the two novels may be taken a step further. Situating Machingauta's and Freeman's narratives in the context of the widely publicized historical events of twenty-first century Zimbabwe helps us to discern how popular texts such as these may be 'pressed into service politically' (Glover and Kaplan, 1992: 221) by emergent official discourses and their counter-discourses.

Machingauta's novel may be read as a rehearsal of the violence and lawlessness of what the Zimbabwean ruling party has called the 'Third Chimurenga' – the 'fast-track' alienation of privately-owned farmland and the weakening of the legal state justified by a narrative of the ongoing battle between internal patriots and external enemies. Seen from that perspective, the diversity of Zimbabwean identities represented in Freeman's text is an expression of the pluralistic and tolerant Zimbabwean society that many, after independence, had hoped for, and had seen emerging. In that respect, the two novels could not be more different – except for one detail.

When, at the end of *Rumours of Ophir*, the originator of the conspiracy is discovered to be an academic working in a government-related institution, he and his collaborator are not publicly named or prosecuted, and the impending scandal is hushed up by the government. Thinking about one of the victims, Carter asks himself: 'What justice had there been for Martin Chisunga?' (218). Just like in *Riva*, the due process of law does *not* take place. 'And what happens' – the disillusioned detective asks his boss Tatenda Machaya – 'if I go to the press with the true story?' The answer he gets is, 'The government will deny it.' (Ibid.). Those who were surprised by the seeming suddenness of the events surrounding the 'Third Chimurenga' may have done well to read popular novels: Zimbabwean thrillers, it seems, gave plenty of warning.

Chapter 12

Inside the city: reassembling the township in Yvonne Vera's fiction

Sarah Nuttall

Literary critics have to date celebrated various forms of innovation in Yvonne Vera's work – its post-realist style, its articulation of women's voices and its engagement with questions of memory, space and trauma. Questions of selfhood and its articulation have been at the centre of this work (see, for example, the essays in Muponde and Taruvinga, 2002). Less attention has been paid to the undergirding or underwiring of that selfhood by the objects of urban space as such, or to the ways in which urban subjects and objects mutually constitute each other. Critics have hardly begun to draw out, that is, the assemblages of city and township in Vera's work, and the ways in which they constitute, are constituted by or even exceed, the construction of subjectivity in her writing. By 'assemblages' I mean structures that are put together and are also continually being remade and reassembled in both historical and psychic time. Vera builds city spaces in her fiction, constructs the city, revealing as she does so, its materiality. This may be through her attention to roads and streets, less as backdrops to the unfolding narrative than as themselves the holders (as well as shapers) of biographies and social lives, and also through her focus on the 'things' which make space urban, and are therefore part of the formation of urban subjectivity. Thus her work has a great deal to tell us about citiness and subjectivity, about the production of the urban, including the city as an African metropolitan form. It helps us to explore the ways in which urban space, and in particular the agglomeration of 'township' and 'city' specific to southern African countries such as Zimbabwe and South Africa, give rise to assemblages of citiness. Deleuze and Guattari suggest that an assemblage is constituted by 'lines of articulation or segmentarity, strata and territories; but also lines of flight, movements of deterritorialization and destratification. Comparative rates of flow on these lines produce phenomena of relative slowness and viscosity, or, on the contrary, of acceleration and rupture' (Deleuze and Guattari, 1987: 3-4). While for them, assemblages are that which combine a 'regime of signs' (ibid: 83), I am interested in considering here what both assemblages of citiness and urban objects might look like beyond the implicit immateriality of the sign as such.

The assemblages of citiness I will be analysing here are constructed by, and themselves construct, infrastructures of the self. Infrastructure, as AbdouMaliq Simone has argued, can be understood in physical terms – as reticulated systems of roads and grids in specific ensembles. But, he shows, we can extend the notion of infrastructure to people as such:

> African cities are characterized by incessantly flexible, mobile and provisional intersections of residents that operate without clearly delineated notions of how the city is to be inhabited and used. These intersections [depend] on the ability of residents to engage complex combinations of objects, spaces, persons and practices. These conjunctions become an infrastructure – a platform providing for and reproducing life in the city. (Simone, 2004: 1-2)

The 'infrastructure' that Simone writes about can be taken as assemblages, both non-human and human, which cannot be holistically assembled or fully critically disassembled, but can only be provisionally and inventively reassembled. This chapter explores, as Simone does, different kinds of 'infrastructures', with particular emphasis on the links between the different infrastructures of on the one hand the interior of the self, subjectivity, and on the other, the urban interior, the 'inside' of the city, the city spaces that Vera builds in her fiction. These infrastructures together, soul, flesh, matter, urban space and things, emerge, as I will show, as a fragmentary if unified assemblage.

I am suggesting then, that while critics have so far been captivated by the life of the subject, the fate of individuality and the vicissitudes of consciousness in Vera's fiction, we might equally ask about the ways in which citiness itself and the material cultures on which it relies impress themselves upon her literary imagination. How, in other words, does her writing work to imagine the materiality of city and township and how does it render a life of things urban, in order to reveal how human subjects and material objects in the city constitute one another? There are a number of ways in which to imagine the life of things. One way, as opened up by Appadurai (1986) and Kopytoff (1986) is to think in terms of the making of things: that is, their circulation, exchange value and the uses to which they are put. Moreover, one could think under this rubric of the manner in which they come to be discarded, turned into waste (which can then, often, be re-utilized, suggesting that things do not die – or at least causing us to wonder what might constitute, in this instance, the death of things). A second approach to the life of things, however is the one that will be pursued in this chapter: that things constitute more than objects, with a use value, as such, and that they have an aesthetic life. It is the intersection between the life of things, the life of the self and the life of the city that will be explored here.

The chapter aims to draw out the above themes in relation to Vera's novels *Butterfly Burning* (1998) and *The Stone Virgins* (2002). *Butterfly Burning* is set in the city of Bulawayo and its township, Makokoba. Most of the story takes place along a single street, Sidojiwe E2, and the street itself is part of the imaginative life of the novel. *The Stone Virgins* is set, in the opening and closing chapters, in Bulawayo, and the city in this novel frames the trauma that occurs outside it, a bus ride away, at Kezi. Below, I begin by making some brief remarks about the historical production of Bulawayo and Makokoba as urban forms. I do so in order to draw out aspects of late colonial culture in Zimbabwe, the complexity of its modernity, and also to highlight the citiness of the township, on the one hand, and of the ways in which the township gradually comes to disassemble and reassemble the city, on the other.

Initially, the 'township' and the 'city' were conceived of as separate, if connected, urban formations. The township, home to black residents, would service the white city. Vera's fiction shows, firstly, that the production of the city as a practice could more easily be found within township culture than within the sterile conceptions of citiness produced by colonial constructions of city space and personhood. She also shows how township practices of citiness come to shape, though often in circumscribed ways, and as forms of protest, the colonial and post-colonial city. One of the ways I explore these issues is by focusing on infrastructure, objects and things and the modes of engagement with the city that they suggest. I consider, that is, how things structure relations to urban space in these novels; how, propelled by a new responsiveness to form as such, we might bring to the surface the economies of sense and structure at work in Vera's writing, writing which draws out, rather than obscures, encounters with the physical world.

In considering the emergence of Bulawayo and Makokoba as urban forms, it is important to see the extent to which, whereas the colonial project intended to implement a centralized view, a totality (within what was a 'totalitarian' project), with its neat symbolic and economic distinctions between various races and spaces (city and township) and different (material and human) infrastructures, it nevertheless became an impossible project which gave way to a fragmentary world. It was the modernity of the colonial city which produced it as a city of fragments, and which made the work of assembling, dis-assembling and re-assembling so important. Makokoba, first known as the Location, was laid out on a Municipal plan with 'cottages' – and roads – in straight lines on a grid pattern. African-owned buildings which got in the way of this linear pattern were removed. (Ranger, forthcoming: 65) Terence Ranger notes that everything had been done, to sweep away the impression of an African landscape which the Location had presented earlier in the twentieth century, with its clusters of huts in compounds; its winding paths; its patches of maize; and its cattle grazing on the Commonage (ibid: 66). Africans were not allowed to build their own houses, despite their obvious desire to do so, and complained that 'in the Location we have but two rooms, there is no door between these two rooms, only a gap in the wall, and the dividing wall does not reach the roof' (ibid:

70).[1] 'Municipal cottages' were built, which, despite their rustic name, were small brick boxes, packed tightly together, with inadequate partitions between their two rooms, no ceilings and unplastered walls. Nevertheless they were 'finished' and thought to look civilized by contrast to African buildings in progress.

What we might also draw out from a historical perspective is the imbricated relationship between township and city, in part because of their physical proximity to each other. Ranger suggests that Bulawayo's social topography was unique amongst urban centres in Southern Rhodesia, or even in Southern Africa as a whole. Whilst its heart was a 'European town' along the lines of Salisbury or Johannesburg, its agglomeration very much resembled the 'dual town', possessing within itself both what he calls colonial and indigenous elements (ibid: 117). It was this proximity, which produced a duality that left colonial culture in Zimbabwe particularly insecure about spatial segregation and led to specific kinds of oppression of black people. The spectre of the growth of a skilled African artisan class in Bulawayo was consequently strongly resisted by whites (ibid: 21). Driving licenses were denied to Africans and everything was done to handicap African carpenters, shoe-makers and so on in the Location (ibid: 22). The notorious 1894 law banning Africans from walking on the pavements of the city was the more extreme example of colonial insecurity and neurosis – a case of what Ranger calls 'pavementia' (Ibid: 59). Nevertheless, writes Ranger, the Location represented the nearest thing to black citiness.

Butterfly Burning

Butterfly Burning begins with a sequence describing black men who construct and maintain the city. Barefoot, they use sickles to cut the grass along the roadside. Arms moving quickly, their bodies curved, palms bleeding, they twist the grass together, roll it into a mass, gather it into heavy mounds to be carried away the next day. The work of maintaining the roadside is 'not their own. It is summoned' (Vera, 1998: 2) but 'the ordeal is their own' (ibid: 3). The sequence recalls a later one in which we are told that:

> *For almost twenty years Fumbatha has done nothing but build, and through this contact, Bulawayo is a city he understands closely, which he has held brick by brick, on his palm, felt the tension of effort over his back. He has held this city, without a clear emotion of anger or love; with an unresolved abandon. He has watched each building acquire its own mood, the darkening walls where the factory smoke has tarnished the*

---

[1]   Ironically, at first, 'white man's' Bulawayo was a mere shanty settlement. 'Grass Town' was made up of shelters and cabins thatched with straw. By 1894 it was decided that 'straw houses' were dangerous, both symbolically and practically – symbolically because they seemed to show that whites were no different from blacks, and practically because they offered a fire hazard in a city which had twice before been razed to the ground (ibid: 3).

> paint, where the train smoke has built over the front building of the
> railway station. He has built. When he is dead, his hands will remain
> everywhere. (20)

Fumbatha has performed the work of assembling the city and knows its built
structure intimately. The work of assemblage is physical ('the tension of effort')
and emotional, a work of both 'anger' and 'love' ('He has held this city...with an
unresolved abandon'). The work or labour of making the city is affective and
contradictory. The assembled city is a space of subjectivity ('Bulawayo is a city he
understands closely') and a city which writes itself in his imagination ('He has
watched each building acquire its own mood, the darkening walls where the
factory smoke has tarnished the paint...'). It is also a legacy of a kind ('When he
is dead, his hands will remain everywhere') – but what sort of legacy is it, this city
which Fumbatha authors but can't own? Rather, perhaps, we could say that
Fumbatha encrypts himself onto the city in the act of building it, and in so doing
leaves traces for the future. Buildings, physical structures, become markers which
contain and display the city's unconscious. In this case, the city produces the
body as infrastructure as well as the body in the infrastructure: his hands are
both tools in the making of the buildings and parts of his self that will remain
within them. In both passages above, people and things appear in terms of making
and using in the colonial city. In such a city, people are themselves sometimes
perceived as things, at other times, the distinction is well-kept. Both occupy the
realm of utility: in both passages, people are both being used and being useful.
Yet the distinction between use and affect is also erased or complicated here:
people, and things, are both used and are the subjects of affect or sentiments,
and the body is always also the archive of the city.

Assembling the city is also that which has to be healed and that healing is to be
found in *kwela* music, which itself carries in it the history of the city, a history of
both violence and desire ('Kwela means to climb into the waiting police jeeps. This
word alone has been fully adapted to do marvellous things. It can carry so much
more than a word should be asked to carry; rejection, distaste, surrender, envy.
And full desire' - 3). Kwela is played in the township, which is 'inside' the city itself:

> Bulawayo is this kind of city and inside is Makokoba Township where
> Kwela seeks strand after strand of each harsh illusion and makes it new.
> Sidojiwe E2, the longest street in Makokoba, is fresh with all kinds of
> desperate wounds. Bulawayo, only fifty years old, has nothing to offer
> but surprise; being alive is a consolation (3).

In a more complex matrix of assemblage, the township is inside the city and
inside the township is kwela music. Inside the township, inside kwela, is the
wound ('Sidojiwe E2, the largest street in Makokoba, is fresh with all kinds of
desperate wounds'). Yet just as histories of violence and desire go together, so
the wound is also, as we will see, the place from which to create in the city. Thus
it is that the wound is also imbricated with joy, a joy that permeates the sound of

kwela and of the narrative, which is also the tale of death and self-destruction. Vera is interested in complex emotional assemblages which pervade and themselves shape the city. While she depicts the physical work of assembling the city, the labour of the novel itself is also to construct images and memories that assemble the city into imaginative being.

In the opening sequences of both *Butterfly Burning* and *The Stone Virgins*, Vera builds the story of black subjectivity in relation to the experience of walking in the street. It is the biographies of road-space that provides the scaffolding for the stories of selfhood that she develops. In particular it is the distinction between walking in the city and walking in the township that she draws out at the beginning of *Butterfly Burning*:

> *Bulawayo is not a city for idleness. The idea is to live between the cracks. Unnoticed and unnoticeable, offering every service but with the capacity to vanish when the task is accomplished. So the black people learn how to move through the city with speed and due attention, to bow their heads down and slide past walls, to walk without making the shadow more pronounced than the body or the body clearer than the shadow. It means leaning against some masking reality – they lean on walls, on lies, on music...The people walk in the city without encroaching on the pavements from which they are banned. It is difficult but they manage to crawl to their destination hidden by umbrellas and sunhats which are handed down to them for exactly this purpose...They understand something about limits and the desire that this builds in the body (3-4).*

Walking here is a means of moving through the city, and involves living between the cracks, the capacity to vanish (when not offering a service), to slide, and walking in such a way as not to supersede shadows themselves. Walking in the city, too, is finding something to lean on (walls, lies, music), to find relief in. The paraphernalia of whites (umbrellas and sunhats) become means for black people to decentre, detract from their own presence in the street. What black people come to understand is the relationship between 'limits' and 'desire'. None of these practices of walking reflect those identified by de Certeau in his essay 'Walking in the City' (1984) nor those of Benjamin's figure of the flâneur. Rather, Vera's narrative is built upon an often largely unspoken infrastructure of constraints, which in turn structure practices of walking in the city. Here, modes of inhabiting the city by walking through it are differently structured, and map the alternate routes of the black city subject. Moving through the city, here, suggests a certain fugitiveness in motion, and a contrast is drawn between the solidity of the built structures and the fragility of lives lived between the cracks.

Vera goes on to describe how, once black people arrive back in Makokoba, Sidojiwe E2 is flooded with kwela music, and here by contrast, 'the distinctions [are] always unclear, the boundaries perpetually widening'(4). Whereas in the city everything is bounded by rules and categories, life on the township street is allowed to burgeon in its complexity – including the full complexity of living in the city itself. Boundaries 'widen' and understanding gives way to confusion ('The music brings 'understanding, then, within that, other desperate confusions' - 4). It is on Sidojiwe E2 that one 'flees from an image reflected from translucent shop-windows' and contradicts oneself ('...a brief resolve not to bend. Then saying yes' (ibid.). The body is addressed 'in its least of possible heights' and 'there is no expectation of grace' /(ibid.). In the township, the activities of self-making emerge: it is here that the remaking of the self can begin, as well as the chance, the need to escape the self, here where the self is found reflected back, where the self is presented as that which one wants to escape, to be something different from. It is here, in this 'location', that one faces the contradictions of who one is, both musters and then lacks the courage to be someone. If we take it that the city is the place of self-making, or at least the place where the confrontation of the self with numerous other selves is likely to be at its most fundamental, then in Vera's fiction it is the township, and not the 'city', that embodies citiness as such.

In the making of this complex urban subjectivity, kwela, symbolizing violence and love, limits and desire, understanding and confusion of living in the city, is 'pulled back from the police jeep' and comes to represent 'freedom and style and survival'(5). Township life in all its contradictions, as it is lived on Sidojiwe E2, is explicitly identified by Vera as the city: 'This is the city and the pulse of possessing desire' (5). The township inhabits the city, occupies its subjective centre, becomes a city form.

Almost all of the story of *Butterfly Burning* is set on Sidojiwe E2. The road, that is, forms the infrastructure of the narrative, is the geometry to the action, the undergirding which connects lives, imposes selves on others and others on selves. The township road, moreover, is Deleuzian, symptomatic of the rhizomic city, a space of surface and leakage.[2] It is here that Fumbatha wakes in the night to the sound of a van speeding past, and loses his father, arrested by the colonial authorities, to become 'a prisoner...a stranger'(11). It is here, too, that children watch people being consumed in an oil fire disaster, prefiguring Phephelaphi's own death as she sets herself alight at the end of the novel: they see 'bodies vanishing in flame, the miraculous vanishing of the living' and then 'retreat into Sidojiwe E2 where they close their eyes and rest' (17). Phephelaphi, herself born of 'a kind of frenzied city-love'(35), decides to live with Fumbatha on Sidojiwe E2 in the year 1946 ('1946 was fast pace and promised a sultry escape' - 26). The longer she lives on this street, the more Phephelaphi becomes compelled by it: 'Sidojiwe E2. Each day Phephelaphi grows more curious about its lure and commands, its absent urges. How can you trust another's hunger, another's tumult and desire: the strength of it, the force of it, the courage not in it?' (38).

---

2   For Deleuze and Guattari, the rhizomatic structure is characterized by connection and heterogeneity: 'any point of a rhizome can be connected to anything other, and must be. This is very different from the tree of root, which plots a point, fixes an order' (Deleuze and Guattari, 7).

On the street, desire and its hungers, trust and courage, or the lack of it, play themselves out. The street embodies emotional life; the confusions of self and other are played out here. It is here, too, that Phephelaphi, 'mad with hope' (51), walks along Sidojiwe E2 to visit Deliwe: 'She is wearing a flaring white skirt underneath which is a stiff petticoat which she has dipped in a bowl of warm water thickened with sugar and then ironed it hot till it dried. A white butterfly, her waist a tight loop' (54). It is her hope, her burgeoning sensuality, as much the first inklings of how to love herself as much as or more than meeting the desire of others, of men, that will consume her, finally, in flame, in her butterfly dress, on Sidojiwe E2. The promise of the street, of Sidojiwe E2, is the promise of the city, a promise to which Phephelaphi but not Fumbatha, responds. Fumbatha, we are told, 'mistrusts the city which does not understand the sort of triumph a man and woman can find and share in their solitude' (60). 'He wants to love her without risk, but Phephelaphi had been born in the middle of Makokoba' (60). Even from the time that Fumbatha and Phephelaphi first meet, it is clear that it is the city which will be the locus of their desire and which will frame their story. Phephelaphi meets Fumbatha at the Umguza river, where she has been swimming. Fumbatha sits on a rock on the side of the river, which is opposite the city. Phephelaphi swims towards him from 'the city side'. Of the river we are told: 'On the other side of the river [from where Fumbatha is sitting], the city is a commotion of activity. The city has swallowed the river' (19). The city, then, has subsumed the river, and Phephelaphi, in her city-self, has in a sense swallowed Fumbatha emotionally, and inspired his (doomed) love for her.

In the course of the novel, Vera works with the idea of the story of the city that people tell. She writes about those who occupy the waiting rooms of the train station, those who have come to the city, to find it out, unearth it, wait to gain access to it, and describe the city in detail to new arrivals. The emblems of the city which they first register are:

> the heels of black women clicking red shoes against the pavement and holding matching bags close to their bodies clad in tight slacks; the smoothness of transparent silk blouses swishing against black skin, bras and ultra-sheen pantyhose; black women's faces turned white and soft like milk, smooth (47).

In addition, they describe Western cowboy movies in the city hall, teacups, daily newspapers and white men with batons patrolling the city streets. The city, then, is, first, the place where the relationship between people and things (clicking red shoes, matching bags, tight slacks, ultra-sheer pantyhose) produce changes in the constitution of urban subjectivity. In particular, the relationship between the remaking of women's bodies and commodities seem to signify the city form. New needs and desires develop, what once were thought of as luxuries becomes necessities, meanings become invested in commodities, imaginative possibilities expand and 'intricate emotional and intellectual investments' (Burke, 1996: 6) are made by individuals within the new commodity cultures. The history and meanings of these commodities, Tim Burke observes, are often 'hidden in the unspoken parts of everyday life' (ibid: 9). Commodities are not only colonial capitalism's resources for domination ('black womens' faces turned white') but testimony to 'less visible and more uncertain changes in identity' (ibid: 10). The history of city things is about change and modernity (films, newspapers, teacups) and also always has an undercurrent of violence, a violence aimed at curtailing black peoples' engagement with and investment in metropolitan modernity.

On Sidojiwe E2, urban life, just as in Bulawayo itself, is increasingly saturated with things, things which evoke memories and become filigreed to points of self-making:

> *An orange dress. A dress bought a Baloos Stores one new year's day just across the road when the shop-owner has to leave suddenly and sells every item for twopence: dresses and khaki shorts, shoelaces, candy cakes, Eat One Nows, Afro combs, folded Swiss knives, Lion matches, Andrews' Liver Salts, Star Cigarettes, Golden Syrup, Minora Razors, Vanishing Pond's, Vinolia Soap, Roll-On, and Bata Tender Foots. Twopence for Tender Foots: black encasing shoes with the thick black rubber right around the edges and soft maroon soles that smelt, well, like that (37).*

What do these assemblages of objects stand for? They embody an era, invoke a vivid memory, inhabit a language of proper names which seem to contain and produce meanings within and beyond the consumable items that they are. They hold and produce a certain 'consciousness' of their own, superceding the traditional, modernist critical gaze on the consciousness of subjects. Consciousness and subjectivity are mediated through the relation with things, and between things themselves. People and things, subjects and objects, mingle in a non-dialectical way, melt into/onto each other. Subjectivity itself appears as being built and refashioned through the intersection of subject and object, person and thing. The passage reveals not only the sheer materiality of objects, but also the materiality of memory as such (partly represented in the artefact that is the novel itself).

While the passage above emphasizes the materialities of culture and the biographies of objects as memory-deposits and complex assemblages of use and signification, the following passage, capturing the nature of the love between Fumbatha and Phephelaphi (a love which will later extinguish itself), reflects a more enigmatic readings of objects, household objects here, decisively dislodging them from the history of their use as such:

> *They forgot the walls thin like lace. They remembered only the shapes of teaspoons they had lost and replaced and lost again, whose every curve and shape they heaped to spilling with generous portions of either sugar or salt. That part they remembered well. A slim flat handle of a spoon*

> *which they caressed with thumb and forefinger and held gently down*
> *from sugar bowl to cup to quivering lips. The rest they did not remember.*
> *Once, perhaps, the curved spout of a teapot. They were indifferent to*
> *any other memory, especially thin walls and neighbours holding their*
> *own breath and waiting to witness what they never tired of hearing over*
> *and again, however painful, their own lonely distance reach a pitch louder*
> *than the fearless fulfilment of these two (40-41).*

Here, the shape of a teaspoon, a sugar bowl or the curved spout of a teapot comes to stand for, and becomes a means of creating, their own private world. They evoke the substance and erotics of their love; become part of, but do not fully amount to, what Robert Muponde calls 'conscious strategies to live the body in its fullness'(Muponde, 2004), in spite of, and because of, the thin walls of the house, built as we have seen to colonial specifications, and the chances these offer to neighbour's prying. In particular, the passage above is about how memory attaches to certain things, so that the things become vivacious fragments, intimate but unassimilated into a whole.

Urban interiors, in both *Butterfly Burning* and *The Stone Virgins*, become places in which to reclaim and express subjectivity, even if the life of the road outside is always part of what it is to be 'inside'. The inside of rooms, and the things that they contain, offer an urban aesthetics of the self. Building on Kopytoff's (1986) and Appadurai's (1986) notion of object biographies, Silverstone and Hirsch (1992) point out that objects tend to develop more than one biography, and therefore more than one symbolic path of meaning. In the process of developing multiple biographies, fields of what Helen Meintjies calls semiotic friction can arise around objects (Meintjies, 2001: 352). In other words, the various symbolic meanings with which objects are imbued do not necessarily cohere. The symbolic associations of the objects can operate in opposition to one another, resulting in a process of 'symbolic rubbing' that charges objects with a potency greater than they would have were their meanings uncontested (ibid: 352). So, for example, whereas elsewhere in the novel, a teacup is a symbol of city-life which those coming to the city for the first time must take pains to describe since it belongs to another world – 'to describe a teacup, that is something else, it is necessary to creep up and peep through windows or wander into the First Class waiting-rooms in order to say saucer with the right meaning' (47) - in the passage above, the paraphernalia of tea drinking (teaspoons, a sugar bowl, a teapot) represents an alternate biography for (these two) people in the city. This activity of recomposition or reassemblage opens up alternate modes of engagement with the city as things, such as 'tea things', suggest divergent relations to urban life, selfhood and space. Processes of living, forms of life, are experienced and enacted through relations with things. These things become the material infrastructure of subjectivity.

Assembling the self in the city, itself a site of assemblage, is ultimately, in *Butterfly Burning*, a matter of living and its opposite, dying. Vera often refers in this novel to the life form, forms of life, or to what we could call practices of living themselves. In Bulawayo, 'being alive is a consolation' (3). The phrase is an ambivalent one. It suggests that all one can expect, given the conditions of being (the oppressive and difficult lives that black people live), is to be alive. At the same time, 'being alive' contains within it, or is made to contain in this novel, the possibility of life in its fullness, its joy, its desire, the capacity to be oneself. Elleke Boehmer (2003) writes how Vera's ceaseless mixing of unadorned plain nouns and abstractions produces a style and offers a peculiarly appropriate vehicle for the articulation of yearning. Vera, too, Boehmer remarks, is fascinated with repetitive, non-object related activity (such as the process of living or 'being alive' itself) and with the movements of music. In *Butterfly Burning*, Kwela music is 'lively, living' (3). Vera writes: 'Living is a matter of keeping everything intact, her mind together too because there is so much living to be done' (71); and: 'inside their room they have carefully selected some pictures to make their living valid' (71). Life, then, becomes that which has to be kept intact, which has to be done and which has to be 'made valid'. How truly alive you are is also how trapped you can be in 'the minute details of living'(117) and how close you can come to death.

Once Phephelaphi has performed an abortion on herself with a large thorn, she wonders at 'the purpose of being alive and so unchosen, so unspecial, so forgotten, so dead...everything beating loudly just to remind you how truly alive you are, how trapped in all the minute details of living' (117). 'Life', in the novel, is frequently enmeshed with death, and this may indeed be part of the 'surprise' of being alive in the city. Dead men hang on a tree like fruit. A woman swallows a needle and dies with the thread sticking out of her mouth. Another woman carries her husband's corpse in a wheelbarrow. Getrude dies a dramatic death at the hands of her white lover. The styles of dying, the spectacles and excesses of death, just as the styles, spectacles and excesses of life, are generated in large part by (colonial) citiness itself. In the end, being trapped is being without the skill and passion and intimacy of a deep living which in this novel results in an extraordinary act of dying, as Phephelaphi, butterfly in a white dress, is burning.

The Stone Virgins

Vera's most recent novel *The Stone Virgins* begins, like *Butterfly Burning*, with an intense engagement with roads and street-spaces. That it should do so is not unexpected, since, as we have seen, such spaces in Rhodesia/Zimbabwe have always been highly symbolic and contested spaces. The book begins as follows:

> Selborne Avenue in Bulawayo cuts from Fort Street (at Charter House) across to Jameson Road (of the Jameson Raid), through to Main Street, to Grey Street, to Abercorn Street, to Fife Street, to Rhodes Street, to Borrow Street, out into the lush Centenary Gardens with their fusion of dahlias, petunias, asters, red salvia and mauve petrea bushes, onward to

the National Museum, on the left side. On the right side, and directly opposite the museum, is a fountain cooling the air; water flows out over the arms of two large mermaids. A plaque rests in front of the fountain on a raised platform, recalling those who died on the Wilson Patrol...Selborne Avenue is a straight unwavering road, proud of its magnificence. The first half, beginning at the centre of the city...(3).

In describing the infrastructural matrix, the spine, of the city thus, Vera maps out the very idea of colonial city space. The names of the streets, the institutions and sites to which they give rise (Centenary Gardens, National Museum, military plaques, fountains) and the assumption of centrality all fill out this map. Vera goes on to describe Selborne Avenue as 'the most splendid street in Bulawayo and you can look down it for miles and miles with your eyes encountering everything plus blooms'. Thus you pass the Selborne Hotel (1897), Meikle's Department Store, the Ascot Shopping Centre and Race Course and finally the secluded streets of the suburbs of Hillside, Riverside and Burnside – 'named after English poets – Kipling, Tennyson, Byron, Keats and Coleridge'(Vera, 2002: 4-5). The street becomes a metaphor for the colonial gaze itself: 'Before all that, Selborne Avenue is straight and unbending, it offers a single solid view, undisturbed'(5). It is a gaze which as we have seen, will fail in its long-term project, producing fragmented spaces, objects and selves.

Selborne also carries you 'straight out of the city limits and heads all the way to Johannesburg like an umbilical cord', so that part of Johannesburg, its 'joy and notorious radiance' is in Bulawayo, measured in the 'sleek gestures' of migrant labourers who travel back and forth between the two cities. These labourers have learnt something more 'of surprise, of the unexpected: of chance'(5). They have learned a practice of urban being derived from elsewhere, a practice derived from vocabularies of challenge and scorn. 'They can challenge the speculative, the hostile and suspicious enquiries about their presence in the city, and this, without flicking an eyelid'; 'they click their fingers, move one knee forward, and dance mightily'; 'what they touch, they sing of with scorn; what they scorn, they do not touch'(5). Their attitudes are materially embedded in the display of an assortment of objects. On Lobengula Street in Makokoba, 'the last road before you touch Fort Street and penetrate the city', the returned migrants wear 'indolence, scorn and well-decorated idleness, cobra-skin belts and elephant-skin hats, topped with exciting layabout tones, why not, what with their cross-belts pulling up their waistlines when it suits them, on an afternoon'(6).

These assorted objects, adornments, are 'buoyed', Vera tells us, by the built infrastructure of 'double-doored wardrobes, metal single beds, paraffin stoves and display cabinets lined with silk flowers, teapots, breakable plates' (6). New styles, new assemblages of the self, emerge from a transnational urban imaginary. Preben Kaarsholm (1999) remarks how this imaginary, encompassing Bulawayo and Johannesburg, has been fostered not just by migration but by language networks and resistance traditions (nationalist political organizations in Bulawayo were historically close to the ANC and shared many of the congress movement's basic outlooks, contributing to a political tradition unique in Zimbabwe). Moreover, the two cities have long occupied a common cultural field or corridor: Dorothy Masuka became a star in South Africa; Mbube choirs and jazz bands from South Africa have travelled north and inspired imitations and elaborations; Bulawayo drama groups looked South to the performance energy of theatre in Soweto and other townships and made the interaction between the two societies part of their field of representation.

The symbolic as well as material infrastructural grid of the city in *The Stone Virgins*, then, is one in which colonial trajectories give rise to a new urban migrant culture, and which are crossed by large townships streets, such as Lobengula Street (the name itself deeply symbolic of Zimbabwe's pre-colonial history) via which black inhabitants 'penetrate' the city itself, again not only in material terms according to an unequal and racially based colonial hierarchy but also in ways that institute certain forms and practices of citiness as such. The city, Vera writes, revolves in sharp edges, roads cut at right angles, so that the edge of a building is a profile, a corner, 'ekoneni'. Ekoneni is a rendezvous, a place to meet. Here you linger, ambivalent, 'permanent as time'. You are in transit. The corner is a 'camouflage, a place of instancy and style; a place of protest' (10). A corner means a chance to strike a pose, or disappear – or form a subculture. Here you can assume a cowboy pose, for instance, derived from Sunday afternoon Westerns, in so doing creating a wide berth for yourself, making space where your options are otherwise circumscribed. How you turn a corner, and what a corner comes to mean has everything to do, then, with assembling the self in the city. The city is where these practices of self-assemblage are honed and developed. The other place of self-making in the city is the photo studio. At Kay's Photo Studio on Jameson Street (versus at African Photo Studio on Lobengula Street and 11th Ave),

> the self that you have prepared all week and now set free falls into the palm of your hand as easy as morning, your finger is curled tight over the slim, long stem of the glittering glass, your eyebrows are pencil sharp and the smile you have prepared in the mirror hanging behind the door is not all tucked right at the edges, almost not there but your head is as far back on your shoulders as it ever could be. You are looking just fine; the city is part of you (12-13).

By the last chapter, the city has changed. Independence has been won. Black mannequins have appeared in the windows of Edgars. Recently employed black bank tellers and trainee managers step out onto the streets. Black customers step up to the front entrance of these banks and walk into the regulated air 'with a look of both pleasure and amazement' (149). The sound of the bell which rings at noon fills the city, and 'gives it an alertness, a sense of expectation'. Back copies of *Drum*, *Moto* and *Parade* are available for sale on the streets. Cephas moved from the township to a flat in town, 'partly to prove to himself that independence has really come, to share in its immense promise, in its cityscape' (161). Nonceba, deeply traumatized by the murder of her sister and her own mutilation during the Matabeleland war during the 1980s, comes to live with him at No.341 Kensington Flats, in the heart of the city. She unlocks the blue painted door, and enters:

> *She turns on the light, then reduces the brightness. The apartment has a parquet floor that spreads from the small corridor into the lounge, and two bedrooms interfacing, a bathroom, a balcony. From the corridor, there is an arched entrance leading to the kitchen. Inside the kitchen a small fridge, an electric kettle, pots and pans, a double sink. A stove. There are fitted cupboards, inside them plates, pans, and cooking ingredients. A pantry to the extreme left, extending full height to the pine ceiling. Nonceba slips the package of small fruits from her arm into a basket near the sink, on her left is a small breakfast nook along one side, with a bench attached to it, and two free chairs facing the wall, which have covers of red and white fabric. A broom closet (152).*

What is described here could be seen, first, as the material infrastructure of an increasingly middle class urban life: a light switch with a brightness control, a parquet floor, separate bedrooms, an arched entrance to the kitchen, a fridge, electric kettle, double sink, a breakfast nook and a broom closet. Yet here, too, the ordinary – that is, the ordinary dimensions to a middle class life – also becomes somewhat otherworldly; domestic objects are here, one feels, not entirely domesticated. This is because we see them through the eyes of Nonceba, in her trauma. They take on a particular quality as material fragments because of the landscape of violence that has preceded her presence amongst them.

The description intimates the violence of war, which precipitates a particular quality to it. This quality derives from Vera's subtle intimation of both time and space. The pace of the narrative, its temporality, is more deliberate, deliberated, than in earlier passages in the novel. Moreover, although Nonceba occupies the flat, is inside it, and is alongside the objects, the domestic infrastructure, she also views them from a distance, the quality of her observation of them reveals a gap between her and them. This gap is the profound dissociation between the events of the past and present she finds herself in, the temporal delay of the trauma itself. Nonceba is grateful to Cephas for his 'imprecise distance' (154), and it is this imprecise distance which marks the passage as a whole. She is both present and not, both are in the present but subsumed in the past ('Their thoughts are absorbed by the full weight of the past... The past for them is so much heavier than the present; it exists with an absolute claim' (155), especially the despair that they feel over the death of Thenjiwe.

> *She bends down to open the fridge door. She takes a bottle of orange crush, a glass from the cupboard above her, and carries both out of the kitchen into the lounge. She slides onto the three-seater couch and places*

her drink in front of her on the coffee table. She places a coaster underneath the glass. There is a small side table in the same room with a telephone on it. Two small windows look out down to a large square where a rotating clothes line is positioned, she can look out to the balconies of the other apartments, which house pot plants, some outdoor chairs (152).[3]

Since domestic objects and spaces reveal, in her relationship to them, her stress and anxiety, we can see that they represent something larger and perhaps stranger than the history of a culture of consumption. Bill Brown argues that we should sacrifice the clarity of thinking about things as objects of consumption, in order to see how our relation to things cannot be explained by the cultural logic of capitalism – freeing objects from their domestic human context and enabling them to achieve a formalism that obfuscates any exchange or use value that the objects may have (Brown, 2003: 9). Thus he confers on them an aesthetic value, through encouraging us to discover a kind of 'thingness' to them, obscured by their everyday use as objects. Following Brown, we could say that Vera offers us, in the two novels examined here, ways of beginning to understand both how subjects occupy material culture, and how there may be forms of possession that are irreducible to ownership.

Conclusion

In this chapter I have explored some of the ways in which urban space in Vera's novel gives rise to assemblages of citiness, and how township practices of citiness come to shape, in myriad ways – whether through forms of labour, leisure or protest – the colonial and post-colonial city, in this case Bulawayo. Citiness has been shown to be, in Vera's novels, an assemblage of people and objects, and urban colonial and postcolonial experience to be non-dialectical: subject and object, person and thing, that is, melt into and onto one another. This may constitute a schizophrenic or at least fragmentary relationship to life worlds and their surrounding materialities. Subjectivity itself is built and refashioned through the intersections of subject and object, person and thing.

Vera's assemblages of urban objects and things, as I have attempted to draw them out here, offer us important new terrain as literary critics. Though the literary criticism of the past decade has been newly attuned to image culture and the logics of vision, it has hardly begun to bring material culture into full view (and though cultural studies has helped to put material culture on the critical map, it

---

[3]   The passage could be related to what Vera has said in an interview: Experiences are not always flowing, non-fragmented, but floating. I'm fascinated with the individual, especially the woman, especially the woman in Africa, and how they are forced to endure without having a nervous breakdown – because they cannot afford it. But they collapse inside and I'm keen to capture that collapse (Muponde and Taruvinga, 2002: 223).

has generally done so when it relegates literature, or the literariness of the literary, to the periphery). Brown observes:

> *The criticism of the past decade has been profoundly successful in showing how literary texts exhibit multiple modes of fashioning the identity of subjects (national subjects, gendered subjects, hybrid subjects), but the identity of objects has hardly been voiced as a question* (ibid: 17).

Vera's work can be taken as a meditation on the poetics and politics of objects, and how selves as things can be used to mutually think one about the other. Beyond objects per se, however, she explores the potency and affect of things, that which is excessive in objects, as what exceeds their materialization as objects or their mere utilization as objects – their force as a sensuous, metaphysical and aesthetic presence. As such, her writing helps to uncover what we might term the material infrastructures of urban subjectivity itself.[4]

---

[4]   I would like to thank Isabel Hofmeyr, Robert Muponde, Ranka Primorac and Juan Obarrio for their comments on a draft of this chapter.

Part V.

Writing, history, nation

Chapter 13

Some thoughts on history, memory, and writing in Zimbabwe

Kizito Z. Muchemwa

I.

Zimbabwean fiction, in both the white and black traditions, embodies a convergence of history, memory and imaginative acts in search of individual and group identities. This convergence of history, memory, and writing often deconstructs and contests archival practices which seek to capture and freeze the past through officially sanctioned discourses. Official history is selective and supportive of the status quo. This chapter offers some thoughts on ways Zimbabwean fiction and auto/biography written in English set out to contest official narratives of the past in order to open new spaces for the re-creation of cultural memory, revisions of the past and re-inscriptions of identity.

Both memory and history deal with the past. Zimbabwean novels, stories and autobiographies written in English abound with characters trapped by history. Texts such as Yvonne Vera's *The Stone Virgins* (2002) or Tim McLoughlin's *Karima* (1985) – both dealing with Zimbabwean wars – represent racial, gendered, and ethnic groups that have been left out of official narratives. On the other hand, in texts contributing to the Zimbabwean nationalist narrative (found in the black literary tradition) there is an insistence on memory as a sacred set of absolute meanings, owned by a privileged ethnic group. The production of this memory of exclusivity is found in the nationalistic epic narratives of Solomon Mutswairo, who is not so much a father of the Zimbabwean black novel in English (Vambe, 2001) as the literary originator of an unproblematized and ethnic nationalism. When so considered, memory becomes a set of instruments used to exclude and expel the undeserving from the ancestral house. Ancestral memory, initially appropriated to interrogate colonial misrepresentations of the black 'other', now reveals its inability to provide adequate sites for the creation of a multi-ethnic, post-colonial national identity. In such a context, autobiographical writing – especially when combined with journalism, as in the case of Peter Godwin's *Mukiwa: White Boy in Africa* (1996) becomes an effective way of countering false mediations and incomplete representations found in official historical narratives. In *Karima, Mukiwa, The Stone Virgins* and other such texts, writers resist the slipping into oblivion of unacknowledged, unspoken, and unwritten traumas of history.

II.

History relies on documentary evidence but the process of producing and preserving documents is often owned and controlled by powerful groups. In Zimbabwe, historical events have gone unreported or under-reported. It is this creation of absence in history and memory that informs much of Zimbabwean literature. Imagined narratives establish hidden clues, stories and documents, allowing writing to adopt the excluded and rejected, to enlarge on that which is originally consigned to footnotes, and to open new vistas on recorded events and historical personages. Yvonne Vera in particular demonstrates a mistrust of academic history and openly admits to distorting it artistically (Ranger, 2002b). The uses to which history and memory are put have a bearing on constructions of identity. Texts considered here demonstrate how history and memory can be used to maintain racial, ethnic and gender privilege. This misuse is marked by either destroying or hiding sites of memory, denying the other the right to speak for itself, adopting strategies of false representation and illegitimate mediation, and 'disappearing' the other. This has been a characteristic of Zimbabwean colonial and post-colonial history especially during times of war.

Zimbabwean fiction consistently makes use of biographical and autobiographical modes. Not only do writers use fiction to interrogate facts found in historical narrative; they also seek to collapse boundaries of discipline and genre that separate history and fiction. Matthew Henry demonstrates the dynamic ways in which the American novelist E. L. Doctorow explores the interstices of history and fiction. Doctorow collapses and blurs boundaries between these two modes of narrative in order to achieve 'historical consensus or imaginative re-interpretation' (Henry,1997:133). Doctorow, in his own words, privileges fiction as 'a kind of speculative history, perhaps a superhistory' (ibid.). Zimbabwean literature veers between these two ways of treating recorded historical facts.

Although the black and white traditions in Zimbabwean literature rarely write to each other and often write across each other, their apparent ideological and stylistic isolation masks the sharing of common concerns. The texts considered here, although often quite different in style and imaginative conception, reflect a preoccupation with history and memory that deserves attention. Stanlake Samkange's *On Trial for My Country* (1966), Charles Mungoshi's *Waiting for the Rain* (1978), Dambudzo Marechera's *The House of Hunger* (1978), Tim Mcloughlin's *Karima* (1985), Chenjerai Hove's *Bones* (1988), John Eppel's *The Giraffe Man* (1994), Peter Godwin's *Mukiwa* (1996), and Yvonne Vera's *The Stone Virgins* (2002) are shaped by history (both written and oral) and respond to it. For writers such as these, who work against the foundational grain of nativist aesthetics (to use a metaphor derived from Marechera's *The House of Hunger)*, history is an unavoidable prison-house from which to escape.

Such writers often use post-modernist techniques that convey a sense of escape from the entrapment of language, traditional cultural memory, and history. Marechera fractures language, not on the level of syntax but on the level of metaphor where his imagination dredges the violent and disgusting images that may assail the reader's sense of decorum. For Marechera it is the decorous that is stultifying, that in its pretence of order violates the individual's agency and power of self-representation and self-creation. *The House of Hunger* challenges linear perceptions of history, which close off possibilities of re-conceptualising causality. Memory, both private and communal, is about celebrating specific aspects of the past. By unifying different temporal zones, memory energises the past to inform the present and shape the future. Memory locates and constructs group and individual identities in a time continuum. A concern with ancestral memory arises out of the need to repair identities damaged by colonialism. Texts such as those discussed here contest primordial and essentialist models of identity. Zimbabwean black writers who come after Samkange and Mutswairo treat ancestral memory with ambivalence.

III.

Seeking to retrieve ancient traditions that are older than the imperialist imposition, these writers ironically reject the nativism and patriarchy they discover. In a world bereft of ancestral memory, Marechera writes about painful recent pasts by invoking images and symbols that articulate the fragmented character of these pasts. Marechera's fiction deals with the immediate past, not recollected in tranquillity but remembered with excruciating disgust and horror. The focus on marginalized groups in novels by Hove and Vera reveals how both written colonial history and the black oral tradition are often involved in similarly stressing a monolithic past and memories that either reduce to subsidiary roles or consign to oblivion the pasts of women, children and those who are not indigenes of the country. Ways of remembering and forgetting the past are probed. This probing is singularly absent in the current official obsession with history that has seen an alarming rise in the production of patriotic packages of the past.

Secrecy guards the skeletons in the nation's cupboard. The forces of silence are the taboos that prohibit public exposure of rape, incest, and murder in families. That which is hidden from public scrutiny cannot be spoken and cannot be written. The word that is taboo carries the extreme experiences of rape and incest that patriarchal history and memory gloss over. Rape and incest – as Vera's work so powerfully shows – violently destroy language and human victims who are left with no words to mediate physical and psychological horrors. In *Under the Tongue*, victimhood, representation, and mediation are themes that develop from the trope of the tongue. Traumatic experiences of violence, rape, and incest trigger claustrophobic introspection and silence.

IV.

In the black tradition, spirit possession is used as a strategy of recovery of the tongue and explains the fascination with ruins and graveyards. Spirit possession, although largely conceived in terms of passivity, does, in principle, allow for the coming to life of suppressed discourses and identities. The backward migration of the spirit allows it to rediscover that which has been lost and discarded, those aspects that are too horrific to integrate and accept within a modern consciousness. In *On Trial for My Country*, *Waiting for the Rain*, *Bones*, and *Under the Tongue*, the forgotten dead kinsmen or kinswomen seek justice. The spirits of the dead haunt individuals, families and communities. These are avenging spirits that demand remembrance, recognition, and re-incorporation into cultural memory. Bantu cosmogony suggests various outcomes in spirit possession: a momentary transformation of personality, a return to the past, a resurrection of the dead, and a metaphoric death of the living. No one meaning is allowed to be dominant as all four meanings are simultaneously present at any given time. These outcomes of spirit possession are metaphors of suppressed discourses. These discourses contain memory and history. To allow these discourses to be rehabilitated is to allow memory and history pushed to the periphery to be relocated to the centre.

In the early pages of *On Trial for My Country*, Stanlake Samkange refers to spirit possession to achieve a number of things: to give authority and authenticity to the black version of history, to show that the technology of writing is not the only way of capturing and maintaining cultural memory, to show that the exclusion from the technology of writing does not entail loss or absence of history and memory, and to demonstrate the antiquity and sacredness of history and memory. Hove's poetic prose in *Bones* relies very heavily on oral mnemonics and motifs to demonstrate these purposes, although there is no direct instance of possession in this novel. The black characters are ordinary peasants excluded from Western formal education and the settler culture of writing, an exclusion that leads to reliance on traditional Shona discourse that resists the monologic fixity of the written world of coloniality. In foregrounding orality in *Bones*, Hove challenges the authority of the written word in the creation of texts, canons, history and memory. And yet, although closely associated with the classical Shona oral culture, *Bones* illustrates the point that monologism is also found in oral societies. The novel is about the patriarchal truncation and repression of cultural memory. The narrative voices of women show the extent to which cultural memory in traditional African culture is associated with silencing strategies that have robbed women of the power to speak for themselves. To escape the cruelties, deprivations and injustices of colonialism is to enter a world that is older than colonialism. Ironically this ancestral past represses women.

V.

Books by white Zimbabweans McLoughlin, Eppel and Godwin do not foreground issues of gender that are found in fiction written by black writers. Rather, they interrogate the place of whites in a changing historical environment. Before independence this probing of memory and history to prepare for the re-inscription of white identity in Zimbabwe was carried out in McLoughlin's *Karima*, a novel about the war of liberation. Stylistically, *Karima* is an ambitious and experimental novel that seeks to address the problems of representation of the other in African literature. McLoughlin uses a dramatic technique, in which asymmetrically arranged scenes establish contrast and comparison of parallel worlds that tragically collide when they are forced to meet beyond the pretence and paternalism of master-servant relationships. *Karima* shows that different racial groups inhabiting the same country interpret events in different ways, and this accounts for the racialized sites of memory and history.

The settler government as depicted in *Karima* has provided the post-independence black government with ready models for the use of propaganda to stem the tide of history and to create and sustain a monolithic, racist, and privileged but unsustainable collective identity. In *Karima* radio is used to engender a trite, saccharine, masculinized and racialized patriotism. Programmes are so structured that no contrary voices are heard, thus create a stultifying and dangerous parochialism. Newspapers and television have also been subverted to serve narrow ethnic interests that masquerade as national ones. To counter white propaganda that has appropriated the public space available for the creation of racial memory, black characters use village meetings, modern orality, and songs of liberation.

While McLoughlin's *Karima* focuses on the collapse of pasts and memories and stands at the edge of an as yet undefined national identity, John Eppel's *Giraffe Man* and Peter Godwin's *Mukiwa* examine spaces for the articulation of a non-racialized post-independence national identity. The autobiographical mode allows these writers to use details from personal lives that are linked to the colonial history of the country, in order to trivialize colonial memory. Eppel's riotous comic imagination unmasks the pretentiousness of pioneer settlers. White colonial education, made to transmit the cultural memory of the white settler, is shown to be tragicomically inadequate in preparing the white child for the reality of the post-colonial nation.

In Godwin's *Mukiwa*, on the other hand, it is the post-colonial government that stands guilty of evasion, distortion and misrepresentation in dealing with the tragic history of the civil war of the 1980s. Misrepresentation of a people's history and memory is synonymous with distortion, evasion, and destruction of truth. The narrator's return to the locations of specific historical crimes – the killing of civilians in Matabeleland – is also an imaginative return to a past that, although under siege, can be retrieved. Wanton physical destruction of sites of memory is a facet of genocide. Writing then becomes a mnemonic device of preserving lives that are 'vulnerable, exposed and hopeless' (Godwin, 1996: 320). Godwin the investigative journalist shows how genocide, as embodied by the Belaghwe concentration camp, seeks to minimize the scale and destroy the evidence of its own criminality. The Antelope Mineshaft becomes a sinister site for the disappearance of people, history and memory and a dark symbol of a regime's ultimate control over bodies. People die without proper burial, without dignity, unremembered. There is a bitter and complex irony in the fact that this unmarked site is adjacent to the memorial of the whites that fell during the Matebele War of 1893.

VI.

The last part of Godwin's autobiography and Yvonne Vera's novel *The Stone Virgins* share the same setting and use the same stories of horror of the civil war in Southern Matebeleland. In the novel, those directly affected are given the power to speak for themselves and there is no authorial intervention in the mediation of their horrific experiences. Vera fearlessly confronts the problems of mediation and representation of horror. The novel gets its title from San rock art: Vera goes beyond the limits of Shona and Ndebele mythology, to the San antecedents of Zimbabwean history and memory. The Gulati hills are a site of the convergence of ancient and modern history and memory, and also of violence, religion and art. As a writer, Vera consistently uses her imaginative ability to evoke a living past, to will into life nuances of thought and emotion, to capture the rhythm and spirit of past times. She has said: 'I'm writing, in a way, the biographies of unknown women, but I'm also interested in our national history, so they are always against the backdrop of a particular time' (Bryce, 2002: 223).

In Vera's texts, history is the dynamic particularity of the moment that reveals the connectedness of times, people, thoughts and feelings. Her fiction is constantly showing how the past violently intrudes into the present, and shapes it. The novels *Under the Tongue, Without a Name* and *The Stone Virgins* are texts of trauma that precisely focus on the violence of history and memory in colonial and post-colonial Zimbabwe. The first two deal with the violence linked to colonialism and the liberation war. Their ability to forge counter-memories and counter-histories is in itself liberating. *The Stone Virgins* traverses the same terrain, situated this time within the post-colonial dream of a free nation. The ancient virgins depicted on the rock of one of the caves in the Gulati hills link with the modern victims of secular sacrifice, Thenjiwe and Nonceba, to form a pattern of violence that erupts during troubled periods of history.

Memory and history mean different things to the different characters in Vera's story. Cephas, the archivist, is a keeper of public records who is objective, academic and emotionally distanced from the material collected. Archivists preserve documents that have a bearing on public life and believe in the power of written documents to salvage stories and memories from the forces of oblivion. Yet Cephas Dube resembles a psychoanalyst drawn into the aspects of the national tragedies that at first he learns about from a distance. In the novel's final chapters, Vera deploys the trope of the archivist to focus on the ethical dilemma in writing about genocide – the intrusive nature of such writing, its voyeuristic character and art's inability to stop the carnage while watching and using it as raw material.

When it comes to the other characters, more directly involved in the violence that the novel represents, Vera uses names to indicate the ironic ways in which historical context determines their fate. Thenjiwe ('trusted one'), brutally murdered, is a victim of a tragic lack of trust and a missing of opportunities at both the individual and national level. Sibaso ('make fire') represents both the creative and destructive aspects of war. The two aspects of 'fire' need to be understood and reconciled within the national psyche. Sibaso, an ex-combatant turned dissident, is a tragic figure shaped and distorted by violence. Zimbabwe's primordial history frightens him – 'all over the inside of these walls of Mbelele was a thundering testimony of sorrow to rival our own' (Vera, 2002: 94). But this apprehension does not arrest Sibaso's descent into lunatic violence. He becomes a prisoner of this memory of violence. Vera comes very close to forgiving the rapist and killer by direct personal motives in the crimes he commits, and by placing him too closely to myth: 'I too have come from beneath, the earth, uprooted, like the rocks' (Vera, 2002:130). She turns him into an elemental object ejected from the bowels of the earth by the cataclysmic eruptions of war – beyond healing or redemption, the opposite of Cephas the archivist, who represents the spirit of restoration.

VII.

Any study of memory, protocols of national remembrance, history and writing in Zimbabwe depends on how far back one is prepared to go into the past, on the politics of inclusion or exclusion, on the identification of national myths, and on isolating and analysing continuities and discontinuities. Race, ethnicity, and gender have always marked boundaries of memory and history in Zimbabwe. Ancestral memory re-traces an ethnic black history and identity to a mythic time that excludes those who arrived into the country in the nineteenth century. Texts in the white tradition can only trace memory back to the period of hunters, traders, missionaries and prospectors. However, the significant point of departure for white writers is the arrival into the area of the Pioneer Column, that point of intersection of two cultures that has ensured that, for both of them, nothing would ever be the same again.

With the destruction of the white racist political order, it became possible to envision memory as common and multi-faceted. Yet the enforced recourse to an ancestral memory marks the continuity of an ethnocentric Shona ancestral imagination that has threatened to subsume the memory of other ethnic groups in this country. Whites, 'coloureds', Asians, and black immigrants cannot occupy the spaces opened up by myths of indigeneity. The disrupted memories of groups that have recently migrated to Zimbabwe cannot go beyond their point of intersection with the group that claims privileged ancestral heritage. Foundational myths have, despite progressive and recuperative intentions, an unfortunate habit of othering, and evicting the other from the father's house. The texts examined in this chapter, although emerging from traditions that differ in style, address the same historical experience.

Chapter 14

Yvonne Vera: rewriting discourses of history and identity in Zimbabwe

Lene Bull Christiansen

My title suggests that Vera, who is one of Zimbabwe's leading authors, can be read as engaging in what will here be termed 'the discursive field of national history and identity' in Zimbabwe and that her novels can therefore be analysed from the perspective of political discourse analysis. Vera's writing has been praised for its feminist breaking of the taboos of a male dominated society (see, for example, Wilson-Tagoe, 2003 and Primorac, 2001) because she 'gives voice to previously suppressed narratives and brings into focus fissures in the nationalist discourses of power' (Muponde and Taruvinga, 2002: xi). This point has especially been made in reference to *Nehanda*, in which Vera rewrites historicist accounts of the First Chimurenga from a feminist point of view. This analysis focuses on *Nehanda* (1993) and *The Stone Virgins* (2002), and it is inspired by the ZANU(PF) government's monopolization of the discursive space of national history and identity in Zimbabwe (on this, see Raftopoulos, 2002 and 2003, and Chapter 15 of the present volume). It seeks to describe the relationship between literature and the politics of national identity by focusing on the way history symbolizes national identity and accordingly can be utilized in political discourses of inclusion and exclusion. The literary narratives and the political discourse are here analysed as deriving from articulations of the nation's history within this discursive field of national identity; articulations that define the nation as a temporal and spatial agent; that is, as an 'imagined community' (Anderson, 1991: 6, 24-7, 145; Bhabha, 1990: 2-3).

Two arguments are made from this analytical perspective. Firstly, that *Nehanda* represents a feminist nationalism, which draws on the same eternalising spiritual narratives of the nation, as the current 'Third Chimurenga' discourse of ZANU(PF); a narrative strategy that represents the Zimbabwean nation as an eternal community forged in the struggle against colonialism. Secondly, that *The Stone Virgins* can function as an opening of the discursive space of national identity by forming a counter discourse to ZANU(PF)'s appropriation of national history because it is voicing the history of the Matabeleland genocide (see Catholic Commission for Justice and Peace, 1997, and Alexander et al., 2000) and because it rewrites the spiritual temporal schema of the novel *Nehanda*. It is suggested that it does so in such a way that it disrupts the imaginary spiritual connection between the first anti-colonial wars in 1896-7; the so-called First Chimurenga, and the Second and Third Chimurengas, which sustains ZANU(PF)'s political discourses.

In ZANU(PF)'s discourses of national history and identity the 'birth' of the Zimbabwean nation under colonialism has become a symbolic point of reference for representations of the nation's history because of the colonial definition of the nation's space and time. Since before the liberation war national symbols such as the role of the spirit medium Nehanda in the First Chimurenga[1] have in Zimbabwean nationalism functioned as symbolic defiances of colonialism in cultural as well as in political representations of national identity.[2] Hence, African nationalist discourses in Zimbabwe have represented the national community as deriving from a pre-colonial community and an eternal national spirit. Accordingly, in ZANU(PF)'s discourses of history the anti-colonial struggle defines the national community, and therefore the liberation war and the 'liberators of the nation' are ascribed a privileged position in these discourses. Thus, ZANU(PF) has used a specific narrative of the liberation war to delimit the nation's imagined community discursively by defining different agents in relation to a schema of inclusion and exclusion (see Dorman, 2003). By declaring a 'Third Chimurenga', which is defined as a final de-colonization, ZANU(PF) defines itself as the liberator of the nation and its political opponents as agents of the colonial oppressors. This discursive appropriation of the First Chimurenga and the liberation war articulates the history of the First Chimurenga and the liberation war into a temporal schema that equates the Chimurengas with an on-going struggle against neo-colonial forces. The opposition, the white commercial farmers, the independent media and intellectual critics of the ZANU(PF) government are therefore represented according to the schema of inclusion and exclusion as subversive agents, who are aligned with the former colonial masters. They are said to attempt to overthrow the legitimate heirs to the rule of the Zimbabwean nation, namely ZANU(PF) and President Mugabe, who is in his own words 'a bigger person' (Latham, 2003) because of his historical authority as the liberator of the Zimbabwean people (see also Mugabe,

---

[1]   The role of the spirit medium Nehanda in the first anti-colonial war has gained a mythic status partly because of the use the liberation armies made of her story during the liberation war in 1965-80. Thus, her famous statement: 'my bones will rise to win back freedom from the Europeans' (quoted in Lan, 1985: 6) became a rallying cry for the public mobilization of the nationalist movement during the war, just as Terence Ranger's (1967) account of the first anti-colonial wars is said to have been a source of inspiration for the liberation armies.

[2]   See for example: Ranger, 1967; Pongweni, 1982. Mutswairo's novel *Feso* (1957) describes an idyllic pre-colonial golden age as a time of prosperity when the Africans lived in harmony with nature and the ancestral spirits. This version of pre-historical Zimbabwe functioned as an articulation of a societal utopia towards which the nationalist movement would work.

2002a and 2002b; News 24, 2004; wa Mirii, 2004). Thus, in ZANU(PF)'s political discourses President Mugabe's authority relies on defining the present time as a state of emergency, which is signified by the war against the neo-colonial forces that threaten the Zimbabwean nation with regression into a colonial state. In that way the Third Chimurenga discourse deems the current 'state of the nation' irrelevant for political debate and the government unaccountable for its mismanagement of the country, because the prime objective of the government is to defend the nation against the neo-colonial enemy (Sylvester, 2003: 44-6).

The novel *Nehanda* and the Third Chimurenga discourse

A reading of the novel *Nehanda* which locates it in the context of the political discourses of ZANU(PF) as outlined above, is here proposed in order to analyse the novel as an anti-colonial critique and as a representation of a 'spiritual temporality' ascribed to the anti-colonial struggle. It points out how Vera through *Nehanda* makes common cause with an African religious world-view in order to propose a different kind of national narrative. Nana Wilson-Tagoe has called this narrative 'a re-invention of Nehanda', which constitutes 'a subversive act and that imagines the possibility of rupture in the social order' (Wilson-Tagoe, 2002:162). This is, according to Wilson-Tagoe, 'potentially revolutionary' because it 'paves the way for a possible re-construction of leadership, authority and the social order.' (ibid:163).

It is here argued, that Vera's narrative of Nehanda subverts a male dominated version of Zimbabwean nationalism and replaces it with a feminist nationalism, and that it can do so because Nehanda is an already established icon in Zimbabwean nationalism. In Vera's representation Nehanda personifies national history through a historical narrative of the nation which installs Nehanda's spiritual temporality as the catalyst in national history. Thus Vera's spiritual history of the First Chimurenga, can be analysed in light of what Homi Bhabha has termed 'a pedagogical narrative of the nation' (Bhabha, 1994:140-6), and that this interpretation of the nation's temporality also forms the narrative structure behind the nationalist discourses of the ZANU(PF) government in its ongoing Third Chimurenga.

Nehanda is in the novel described as a liminal figure who connects her people with the spiritual reality of their ancestors. The novel contains an account of this liminality. It describes how Nehanda possesses a dead and a living part. Her dead part is seeing and has knowledge of the history of her nation. Her living part will die, but this death is represented as the stepping-stone for the return of Nehanda as a stronger and more powerful spirit of war, and in this second coming the nation gains hope:

> *She has travelled long distances through time to meet this vision for the future: She knows that her own death is inevitable, but sees its significance to the future of her people.*

In the future, the whirling centre of the wind, which is also herself, has collapsed, but that is only the beginning of another dimension of time. The collapse of the wind, which is also her own death, is also part of the beginning, and from the spiralling centre of the wind's superimposed circles another wind rises, larger and stronger. Hope for the nation is born out of the intensity of newly created memory. The suffusing light dispels all uncertainty, and the young move out of the darkness of their trepidation, into the glory of dawn. The trembling wind asserts its eternal fury, and it will not be dominated, or destroyed (Vera, 1993:111).

In Vera's description of the First Chimurenga and the spiritual reality, the birth of the nation is eternalised in the spirit of struggle against oppression. There is a cyclical rebirth of the nation, which is generated from the spiritual realm, signified by the wind:

The birds fly out of the trees bearing signs that send new hope to the ground. It is always in a state of creation, and of being born: the legend-creating wind gives new tongues with which to praise it, and new languages with which to cross the boundaries of time (ibid:112-3).

Vera's inscription of the Nehanda figure into this religious temporal schema affords the national symbol an eternity that is also ascribed to the nation. In this spiritual narrative there is only one force which leads to the destruction of colonial rule: the spirit of the struggle that drives the people. This spirit is eternal, and therefore Nehanda's death at the hands of the Europeans is not a spiritual death. In Vera's representation, Nehanda surpasses the moment of her own death and becomes the driving spiritual force behind the greater battle of the 'Second Chimurenga' i.e. the liberation war. In other words, in Vera's spiritual history Nehanda's bones rose to win back freedom form the oppressors.

Through the discourse of the Third Chimurenga, ZANU(PF) claims that the colonial occupation is a recurrent threat. This is at times stated in the religious language of African spirituality. The chairman of the Media and Information Commission, Tafataona Mahoso, has gone so far as to state that the British Prime Minister Tony Blair is a spirit medium for the 'evil spirit' of the coloniser Cecil Rhodes, and a spiritual temporality is also utilized in the political discourses that draw on the symbolic field offered in the spiritual narratives of the First and Second Chimurengas. Accordingly, President Mugabe is claimed by Mahoso to have spiritual gifts that enable him to identify the 'true spiritual identity' of his opponents. In this capacity he is being aligned with Nehanda: 'So, old Mugabe is not the person of Robert Mugabe. Rather it is the powerful, elemental African memory going back to the first Nehanda'.

The relationship that is established between President Mugabe and the spirit of Nehanda is claimed to be of a spiritual nature. President Mugabe is ordained by the spiritual power and thus gains authority through the connection with the higher spiritual reality. So, Mahoso's description of President Mugabe's spiritual authority installs President Mugabe in the already existing narrative of a spiritual connection between the First, Second and Third Chimurengas. It ascribes him an authority not just as a hero from the liberation war, but as a metonymy for the very spirit of the struggle. This narrative strategy is aimed at dismantling discourses which oppose President Mugabe's contemporary political authority by claiming that he was indeed a liberation war hero, but that he is not fit to lead the country now. By declaring a renewed struggle against colonial oppression and installing President Mugabe as an eternal spiritual leader, his contemporary authority is restored. As such, the notion of a spiritual temporality is essential because it serves as the link between past, present and future and makes it possible to deem the government's present mismanagement of the country irrelevant to political debate.

As mentioned earlier, an affirmation of national identity in relation to this spirituality appeared in nationalist discourses even before the liberation war. Nothing suggests that Vera's rewriting of the history of the colonial encounter has been adopted by the ZANU(PF) government. However, the spiritual temporality of *Nehanda* revitalizes the idea that even though the spirit medium Nehanda was killed, the spirit Nehanda did not die; it is living as the whirling wind of the Zimbabwean anti-colonial struggle. The Third Chimurenga discourse of ZANU(PF) appropriates the very notion of the nation as born in the spirit of the struggle against colonialism, drawing on a wide field of nationalist articulations of a spiritual temporality. Like Vera's feminist nationalism, the discourse of the Third Chimurenga draws strength from the imagery of an African spiritual reality that renders the Zimbabwean nation eternal and naturally existing outside of the realm of the social construct of the nation state. However, it is argued below that Vera's use of the symbols of Zimbabwean nationalism and her representation of the nation's spiritual temporality has changed, and is rearticulated in *The Stone Virgins*.

The counter-discourse of *The Stone Virgins*

The Stone Virgins can be read as engaging the official narratives of Zimbabwean history on two levels: a straightforward level where the official silencing of the Matabeleland genocide is being challenged by Vera's voicing of the atrocities; and a level where Vera rewrites her narrative of the spiritual reality of the anti-colonial struggle from the novel *Nehanda*.

The Matabeleland genocide was perpetrated under the 1981-7 so-called '*Gukurahundi*', a campaign to 'sweep out the rubbish'[3] from the newly created

---

3   The word 'gukurahundi' means 'early spring rains' and had earlier been used by ZANU in their electoral campaign under the slogan 'The Year of the People's Storm' or 'Gore reGukurahundi'. In the way it was used by Mugabe in relation to the campaign in Matabeleland, it was taken as meaning to 'sweep out the rubbish'. (Alexander et al., 2000:191).

Zimbabwean state. The Korean-trained Fifth Brigade was deployed in Matabeleland in the campaign that President Mugabe described as an act of self-defence on the part of the Zimbabwean people. The Ndebele-speaking part of the population was seen as the constituency of ZANU's long-time rival ZAPU and dissidents from the newly-formed Zimbabwean army, whom Mugabe accused of attempting to bring about a secession of Matabeleland.[4] Thus 'written out' of the nation as enemies, the population of Matabeleland became subject to a reign of terror, which was aimed at supporters of ZAPU, but in practice targeted the whole Matabeleland population.[5] As a consequence of the Gukurahundi, the leader of ZAPU Joshua Nkomo gave up political opposition to ZANU(PF) rule in 1987 and signed a unity accord. This practically dissolved ZAPU in a merger with ZANU(PF) and left political opposition in the hands of civil society organizations and the independent media, who tried to keep Mugabe accountable for the atrocities of the Gukurahundi. However, under the token of unity and in a remarkable act of reinscription, Mugabe called on the people of Matabeleland to forget the antagonisms which the state had propagandized only months before. As unity became the key signifier of national identity, the Ndebele were once more perceived as part of the Zimbabwean people. Therefore, importance was placed on remembering ZANU(PF)'s role in the liberation war, and accordingly forgetting its role in the Gukurahundi. ZANU(PF) history became the history of the nation, and other versions of history, be it the achievements of ZAPU and ZIPRA during the war or accounts of the Gukurahundi, were deemed anti-national and a breach of the unity of the nation (Sylvester, 2003:35).

President Mugabe had not at any stage been prepared to discuss the methods deployed by the Fifth Brigade. The Catholic Commission for Justice and Peace presented him with an account of the Fifth Brigade's violations of the civilian population in Matabeleland as early as 1983, but he was not prepared to enter into dialogue with them.[6] Quite to the contrary, after the unity accord in 1987, Mugabe began to refer to the recurrent memories of the Gukurahundi as 'ugly history'. Ugly history was articulated into the schema of inclusion and exclusion

---

[4] The nationalist party ZAPU and its armed wing ZIPRA had had their main constituency in the Ndebele-speaking areas in the south western part of the country during the liberation war. In the political unrest after independence ex-ZIPRA guerrillas deserted from the joint Zimbabwean army. Mugabe interpreted these desertions as a militant uprising and thus instigated the 'Gukurahundi' in Matabeleland. See: Alexander et al. (2000:180-1, 189-203); Meredith (2002: 60-4).

[5] See: Catholic Commission for Justice and Peace/Legal Resources Foundation (1997); Alexander and McGregor (2001:513); Alexander et al. (2000:189-203); Alexander and McGregor (1999:244-54); Sylvester (2003:34).

[6] This report was followed up by the Catholic Commission for Justice and Peace in the report Breaking the Silence (1997), which is still controversial because it highlights the violence of the Fifth Brigade by describing how bodies were still to be found in mass graves in Matabeleland years after the 'reunion' of ZANU and ZAPU. These disclosures brought to light the 'ethnic' wounds which, the report stated, were far from healed in the unity process. (Meredith, 2002:68).

in official nationalism. Those who aired ugly history were dismissed as agents of the external enemy, because true Zimbabweans were said to be able to distinguish 'real differences' from historical divisions that were overcome by the unity accord (see Chapter 15 of the present volume).

In this manner, unity was installed as the sign by which memories of the violent past could be turned into an obligation to forget. This discourse relies on a narrative strategy of the progression of the nation. The violence of the past is perceived as a stepping-stone on the way towards unity and is therefore both remembered and forgotten (Anderson, 1991:199-200). The discourse of unity is connected to the discourse of the Third Chimurenga in the current political discourses of ZANU(PF), as unity becomes the sign of the struggle against colonial oppression. In this way, any opposition that can be interpreted as instigating a threat to the nation's unity can be inscribed into the schema of inclusion and exclusion.

This analysis of *The Stone Virgins* argues that the novel engages this discourse of national unity; 'breaking the silence' by voicing versions of the nation's history that the government has invited the Zimbabwean people to forget. It does so by articulating a number of different versions of the nation's history, which are narrated from different points of view that cannot be merged into a single narrative of the nation. One of these stories, which Vera has chosen to depict, is the Fifth Brigade's torture and murder of the Kezi storekeeper Mahlathini:

> *Mahlathini, long the storekeeper of Thandabantu Store has died. Those who claim to know inch by inch what happened to Mahlathini say that plastic bags of Roller ground meal were lit, and let drop bit by bit over him till his skin peeled off from his knees to his hair, till his mind collapsed, peeled off, and he died of the pain in his own voice. [...] the soldiers had walked into Thandabantu towards sunset and found over twenty local men there, and children buying candles, and the old men who should have been at that ancient Umthetho rock dying peacefully but preferred the hubbub at Thandabantu and therefore went each day, all these. The soldiers shot them, without preamble – they walked in and raised AK rifles: every shot was fatal (Vera, 2002:121).*

By insisting on time and narrative space for stories of this kind in healing the wounds of the nation, Vera opposes the obligation to remember and forget the Matabeleland genocide in the way that is dictated by the government. Instead, she suggests an attempted closure or healing of the wounds of the nation through the narrative of the historian Cephas who nurses Nonceba, a victim of the conflict, back to health while he is also working at restoring the nation's past (Vera, 2002:165). This is described as a process which works against the absolute claims of the departed:

> *The mind is buried in its own despair, but they survive, day to day, in their friendship. The past for them is so much heavier than the present; it exists with an absolute claim. To sip some tea, to pass the sugar, their*

fingers meet: memory. A delicate act of forgiveness; to be alive at all seems a betrayal. They should have saved her, even by their will alone. This is their preoccupation, and they acknowledge it, and live within it, somehow (Vera, 2002:155).

Time and narrative space for healing the wounds of the war as well as the Gukurahundi are thus suggested by Vera as a means of living with the memories; not forgetting them.

The Stone Virgins is divided into two parts: '1950-1980' and '1981-1986' – i.e. before and after independence. The first part the novel describes the hopes the people of Matabeleland attached to independence:

A burden lifts as a new day appears. This new day, A place to start again, to plant hope and banish despair, to be restored. Everything has changed. Day is light, not heavy; light as a leaf. [...] They sing earth songs that leave the morning pulsating. [...] Voices rise to the surface, beyond the dust shadows which break and glow, and lengthen. They will not drown from a dance in the soaring dust – the memories of anger and pain. [...] All that is bright among them is brighter still: the sky, the altars in Gulati, hope. A wind sweeps through the hills, their voices, their bodies in chorus (Vera, 2002:45-6).

Yet, these hopes are devastated in the second part of the novel which sets off in Bulawayo:

The war begins. A curfew is declared. A state of emergency. No movement is allowed. The ceasefire ceases. It begins in the streets, the burying of memory. The bones rising. Rising. Every road out of Bulawayo is covered with soldiers and police, teeming like ants. Road blocks. Bombs. Landmines. Hand-grenades. Memory is lost. Independence ends. Guns rise. Rising anew. In 1981 (Vera, 2002:59).

Vera describes this renewal of war as 'bones rising', which refers both to the legend of Nehanda and to Vera's own representation of this legend. This signifies a break away from the spiritual temporality in *Nehanda* because in Bulawayo after independence the bones that rise represent Shona 'quasi-nationalism' (for a description of this 'dark side of nationalism', see Werbner, 1996: 197-205). The above passage therefore alludes to a change from *Nehanda* to *The Stone Virgins* in Vera's use of the historical narratives of the connection between the First and the Second Chimurengas. Independence, which should have been the signifying moment in Zimbabwean history, is in Vera's account turned into an interim where the hopes and dreams of the people of Matabeleland are articulated but immediately shattered. Instead, Vera depicts this in terms of what Bhabha has called the unequal interests of the people (Bhabha, 1994:142-9, 153-5). She inscribes a disjunctive moment in the pedagogical narrative of the nation by iterating the divisions of the past, which the nation's people are obliged to forget

(Bhabha, 1994:160-1; Anderson, 1991:199-200). Vera rearticulates the significance of independence not as a moment of release, but as a moment of anticipation and instead installs 1981, when the war begins again, as a defining moment in the national narrative. The unison of the ceasefire is represented as an illusion, as the nation does not progress from the moment of independence but rather regresses into war. The two periods into which the novel is divided, therefore, represent the narrative of the nation as divided into a united and a divided period. Before 1981 the national hopes and dreams were still intact, the 'rain' (the spirit of the liberation war) opened the eyes of the people (Vera, 2002:40-1), but after 1981 the rain did not come (Vera, 2002:117-8).

The Stone Virgins may thus be intertextually linked with the novel *Nehanda*. When read in relation to the 'spiritual temporality' of Zimbabwean nationalism, *The Stone Virgins* appears to be a rewriting of the vision of the connection between past, present and future, which was portrayed in *Nehanda*. Vera recycles the imagery of a spiritual reality and turns it into a broken and fragmented narrative of the spiritual temporality of the nation. *The Stone Virgins* represents the spirit of the anti-colonial struggle as far less glorified. This stands in contrast to the triumphant spirit of the anti-colonial struggle in *Nehanda*. In *The Stone Virgins*, the narrative of the triumphant spirit of the anti-colonial struggle is turned into a narrative of a distorted reality where rape is mistaken for lovemaking, and where the 'hero' guerrilla soldier is ostracized from society and lives a half life of sacrilege and desiccation of kindness as a cruel parody of Nehanda's role in *Nehanda*.

An example of this is the difference between Vera's use of the metaphor of spiders in *Nehanda* and in *The Stone Virgins*. In *Nehanda* the spirit Nehanda is likened to a spider as a symbol of the turning of time, and as knowledge of the past and the future, which is being woven into the spider's web (Vera, 1993:89-93). The spider stretches its legs into the future and resembles Nehanda's role as a liminal figure that resides both in the future and in the immediate struggle: 'The spider weaves silence out of patience. Sending spindly legs into the future, it weaves all of time into its hungering belly' (Vera, 1993:89). While this spider-Nehanda signifies the anti-colonial struggle, in *The Stone Virgins* the spiders appear in the murderer Sibaso's narrative of the liberation war and also signify the connection between past, present and future. However, Sibaso does not articulate one single narrative of the spiritual temporality of the Chimurengas; instead he describes numerous spiders. These are different from each other and stand in contrast to Vera's use of the spider in *Nehanda*. Sibaso's spiders offer no coherent vision of the narrative of the nation. Vera blurs Sibaso's version of 'a perfect truth' as what remains is a multiplicity of versions of the connection between past, present and future in the nation's history of struggle.

Sibaso's broken dreams are illustrated through his tale of a spider which he finds when he revisits his home in Bulawayo. Here he finds his old copy of Solomon Mutswairo's novel *Feso* (Vera, 2002:109). *Feso*, in which Mutswairo articulated the utopia of the pre-colonial golden age that the nationalist movement saw as an inspiration for their own struggle (Kaarsholm, 1989a:34), had originally inspired Sibaso to join the liberation struggle. Between its pages he finds a crushed spider that has been weighed down by time. The spider's legs, which in *Nehanda* were pointing to the future, are here associated with the past, and the web representing the disappointed vision from *Feso* is broken:

> *For this spider, a rainbow has broken its web. In war, time weaves into a single thread. This thread is a bond. Not all bonds are sacred. The present is negotiable, the past, spider legs which were once needles. [...] I lift the sheet and this shape falls off the web of words, a fossil floating in noon light, perforated like a dry leaf. I wonder if spiders bleed before dying, before drying.*

> *[...] Of all continents, only Africa has known the crushed solitude of a dead spider. Charcoal perfect (Vera, 2002:111).*

Sibaso's nationalist dream has died, and is preserved as a fossil – a perfect vision without vitality. What remains of his vision of the past and the future is but a crushed, dried and transparent outline.

Sibaso is also linked to spiders in the eyes of his victim Nonceba:

> *Spider legs, he insists. In my fear of him I envy this kind of perfect truth which sounds exactly like a well-constructed lie. While he closes his eyes I have the sensation that I am drowning, and see a multitude of spider legs stretch into the darkness. That is the other strange fact about spiders, their ability to walk on water while humans drown, he says (Vera, 2002:73).*

In the novel, Sibaso's 'perfect truth' comprises a number of other spider-images, which may be linked to articulations of the connection between the past, present and future. These do not resemble the spider-Nehanda in *Nehanda*, or the spider he finds in *Feso*. One is like a crane fly, another is a venomous spider and a third devours its partner during mating. They occupy the same post-war temporal space, yet their differences are striking. The venomous spider weighs down on Sibaso, and makes him fear its ability to inflict harm (Vera, 2002:96). The thin post-war spider has long thin legs; ready to disappear. It inhabits the margins, creeps in corners and it dies outside of time (Vera, 2002:76). It appears that Sibaso's narrative of these two spiders is directed towards specific articulations of the connection between past, present and future after the liberation war, just as the spider, which Sibaso found inside *Feso*. The narrative is, however, deliberately blurred and incoherent with no references to specific actors, ideologies or discourses of history.

In *The Stone Virgins* the spiritual narrative of the nation has become blurred, fragmented and broken and, as such, it does not correspond with any nationalist version of the nation's temporality. Sibaso has the role of an anti-hero, at once the narrator of the spiritual reality but also the perpetrator of the defining act in the novel; namely the respective murder and rape of the sisters Thenjiwe and Nonceba. From his point of view this act is perceived as a re-enactment of an ancient virgin sacrifice; an idea which he has fostered in his refuge in the sacred caves of Gulati:

> *I place my hand on the rocks, where antelopes and long-breasted women stand together. Tall women bend like tightened bows beneath a stampede of buffalo while the rest spread their legs outward to the sun. [...]*
>
> *Disembodied beings. Their legs branch from their bodies like roots. The women float, away from the stone. Their thighs are empty, too fragile, too thin to have already carried a child. They are the virgins who walk into their own graves before the burial of a king. They die untouched. (Vera, 2002:94-5).*

During the rape of Nonceba Sibaso thus envisions these stone virgins and likens the virgins of the cave to Nonceba who is in his arms:

> *He thinks of scars inflicted before dying, betrayals before a war, after a war, during a war. Him Sibaso. He considers the woman in his arms.*
>
> *He sees her dancing heels, her hands chaste dead bone, porous thin, painted on rock. Her neck is leaning upon a raised arrow, her mind pierced by the sun. She is a woman from very far, from long ago, from the naked caves in the hills of Gulati. She does not belong here. She bears the single solitude of a flame, the shape and form of a painted memory.*
>
> *He thrusts the body to the ground: a dead past (Vera, 2002:71).*

In this scene, described in Chapter 6 from Nonceba's point of view and in Chapter 7 from Sibaso's, Vera depicts an interaction between the victim and the dissident which appears as a parody of a dialogue. That is, this rape scene is set in what can be termed a non-dialogical space, where the interaction between points of view is impossible. The rape is, seen in that way, a perversion of dialogue, as the context and the characters' points of view distort the possibility of a meeting of minds in dialogue. The individual voices ascribed to Nonceba and Sibaso are depicted as monologues that occur in the same time and space. In this space the 'dialogue' is distorted by their different points of view, and by the context of the violence Sibaso inflicts on Nonceba. She does not understand Sibaso; all she understands is to fear him and his ability to inflict harm. The perversion of dialogue in the rape scene displays violence as a 'language', which was instituted in the difficult interactions between the guerrillas and the civilian population during the liberation war.[7] This can be described as a culture of violence, which is an ultimate discursive perversion that is outside the realm of a dialogical space,

---

7   Different kinds of counter insurgency violence had been instituted by the Rhodesian forces and guerrilla soldiers during the liberation war in order to secure support from the civilian population. See Werbner (1996:194); Moore (1995:376-9).

because, as the rape scene displays, the monologues of the characters do not interact, the interaction in the scene is that of violence and desecration.

The figure Sibaso in *The Stone Virgins*, who in view of the spiritual temporality of *Nehanda* should represent 'Nehanda's bones risen' because he has participated in the de-colonization of the nation, can in the light of the above be viewed as a cruel parody of the spiritual battle represented in *Nehanda* as he associates the rape and murder with the spiritual reality. The spirit of the nation, which in *Nehanda* was borne out of the anti-colonial struggle, is in *The Stone Virgins* rearticulated as a grim apparition that has become distorted during the liberation war. Sibaso's role in respect to the virgin sacrifice of Thenjiwe and Nonceba appears to be a mockery of a parallel to Nehanda's role in the novel *Nehanda* as he represents the idea of desecration and violation of kindness:

> He [Sibaso] has to crouch, and his body soon assumes a defensive attitude; the desire to attack. If he loses an enemy, he invents another. This is his purge. He is almost clean. He seems to have a will, an idea which only he can execute. Of course, this idea involves desecration, the violation of kindness (Vera, 2002:74).

The liberation war and the wars of the African continent are a wind, which has swept over the land as in *Nehanda*, but it has not brought with it the social utopia of Nehanda's vision of the ripe valley in the future (Vera, 1993:112). The way in which Vera uses the wind as a symbol of the spirit of war has changed in *The Stone Virgins*. Whereas in *Nehanda* the wind signified Nehanda's role as the liberator of the Zimbabwean people, it is disturbingly violent in *The Stone Virgins* and it hurts Sibaso who associates the wind only with death:

> Everything I fear has already happened. I do not fear what has already happened; not the ungraceful arm of history, not recent and touchable deaths. [...] In the darkness a wind builds, whipping through the trees. It moves against my cheek and throws wild dust into my eyes, hard and sharp grains like bits of ground bone. If I close my eyes I can tolerate this rough exposure, it is a merciful burial (Vera, 2002:97).

As Sibaso hides out in a bomb crater among dead dissident guerrillas, his internal monologue reflects the way in which the war and the wind have hardened his mind. This wind is a burial; not a birth as one would expect in relation to Vera's use of the wind in *Nehanda*. In Sibaso's narrative of the liberation war and its aftermath the spirit of the liberation war is associated with dying. The wind of the history blinds Sibaso as it throws 'grains like bits of ground bone' into his eyes. This blinded 'hero' stands in contrast to the seeing Nehanda who asserted the eternal fury of the nation in *Nehanda*. Accordingly, Sibaso's version of lovemaking, the rape, is in his narrative offered not only as a parallel to the history of his own nation, but also as a parallel to the African continent in disarray – and, again, uses a spider as a basic image:

There is a type of spider which changes colour when mating. It devours its own partner and rolls him into a fine paste. With this it courts its next partner. It offers him this round, perfectly prepared sacrifice in exchange for a brief but sweet liaison. This kind of spider hangs between trees and can only be viewed in the light of a full moon. Such a spider possesses a valuable secret, the knowledge that love cannot be founded on mercy, but that mercy can be founded on love. It knows the true agony of ecstasy, that violence is part of the play of opposites, and that during war, there are two kinds of lovers, the one located in the past, and dead, the one in the future, living and more desirable. The past is a repast, the future a talisman. This kind of truth also belongs to the fantasy of a continent in disarray (Vera, 2002:76).

In conclusion: the unison voicing of national identity, which the unity discourse of the ZANU(PF) government represents, is fragmented in *The Stone Virgins* both by the direct descriptions of the atrocities of the Matabeleland genocide and in Vera's creation of the polyphonic narrative space. Vera's representation of the violence in Matabeleland is not an authoritative or closed articulation of history; rather the narratives are personal and cannot be merged into a unison articulation of history. Her rewriting of the spiritual imagery of the novel *Nehanda* in *The Stone Virgins* rearticulates her own spiritual temporality of the nation as well as other uses of this narrative of the nation, as her imagery of the nation's temporality no longer forms a coherent vision of an eternal national community. Rather, time for memory and healing as well as an opening of the discursive field of national history and identity are in *The Stone Virgins* suggested as means of articulating a more viable multi-voiced narrative of the nation.

Chapter 15

Rule by historiography: the struggle over the past in contemporary Zimbabwe[1]

Terence Ranger

Introduction

When I retired from my Oxford Chair in 1997 I went to the University of Zimbabwe for four years as a Visiting Professor. In the first year I was asked to second mark final examination papers in African historiography and in the modern history of Zimbabwe. It was a chastening and illuminating experience. In the historiography paper every student denounced 'nationalist historiography' – history in the service of nationalism – and instanced me as its prime practitioner. Fortunately, they all said, the sun of political economy had risen and made the past scientifically clear. In the modern Zimbabwe history paper, however, students without exception wrote intensely nationalistic answers with barely a trace of political economy.

In the next three years I was myself generously allocated by the History Department the task of teaching African historiography and the modern history of Zimbabwe. I tried to complicate things in both courses. In the historiography course I tried to explain that political economy in its turn had come under very heavy criticism and the students and I struggled with post-modernity and post-coloniality. I also tried to explain the difference between writing 'nationalist historiography' and the 'history of nationalism'. In my own case, I maintained, my first two books about Zimbabwe – *Revolt in Southern Rhodesia* and *The African Voice in Southern Rhodesia* – had been 'nationalist historiography' in the sense that they attempted to trace the roots of nationalism; they were historicist in so far as they presented narratives leading to its triumphant emergence. But my more recent books, particularly those on Matabeleland, had been histories *of* nationalism as well as histories of religion and landscape and violence. Nationalism as a movement, or set of movements, and as an ideology, remains central to contemporary Zimbabwe and still requires a great

---

[1]   A version of this chapter appeared in the *Journal of Southern African Studies* 30 (2), 2004. The editors thank the publishers, Taylor and Francis, for their permission to republish.

deal of rigorous historical questioning (see Ranger, 1967; Ranger, 1970; Ranger, 1999 and Alexander et al., 2000).[2]

When it came to teaching the modern history of Zimbabwe, therefore, I tried to complicate things by asking a series of questions which opened up the apparently closed issues in the ZANU(PF) narrative of the past. I tried to show that Rhodesian colonialism had been more various – and often more internally contradictory – than the nationalist narrative allowed (Bhebe and Ranger, 2001). I drew upon the work of Brian Raftopoulos to explore the tensions between nationalism and trade unionism. I sought to re-open many of the 'contradictions' within liberation history – the so-called Nhari rising, the assassination of Herbert Chitepo, etc. I argued that Robert Mugabe's dominance of ZANU(PF), complete though it has seemed since 1980, could not be dated back earlier than 1977. I spent a good deal of lecture time on the events in Matabeleland in the 1980s – on which I had been researching and writing. More generally I explored the many and varied sources of the authoritarianism of the nationalist state in post-independence Zimbabwe. In seminar presentations I raised questions about topics outside conventional political history – on landscape and religion and urban culture.

Meanwhile, as I was exploring with the students the history of nationalism and proposing other topics of study, I was enormously impressed with the vitality of historians, economic historians and archaeologists at the University of Zimbabwe. A generation of scholars had arisen which did not envy their fellows who had gone into business or politics. They wanted nothing more than to be successful researchers and publishers, respected by their peers and by Africanists internationally. These young Zimbabwean scholars were able to go beyond the agendas of nationalism. The archaeologist, Innocent Pikirayi (2001), for example, declared that there was now no need to combat colonial myths about Great Zimbabwe or to write of African 'empires' where none had existed. The time had come to ask new questions about environment and landscape and symbol (see Pwiti, 1997). A new school of Zimbabwean urban historians was emerging.[3] One of them, Ennie Chipembere (2002), took the complexities and contradictions of white Rhodesian politics seriously for the first time since 1980. Gerald Mazarire (2003), given the responsibility to develop oral history after the death of Professor David Beach, argued that the political focus on empires, states and chieftaincies had distorted interpretation of oral tradition and suggested instead an approach based on historical geography. (For a constructive criticism of 'political' oral historiography, see also Pikirayi, 1999.) Sabelo Ndlovu (2003) began to apply Gramscian theories of hegemony to the Ndebele State; Enocent Msindo took up issues of ethnicity and particularly of Kalanga identity.[4]

---

[2]　In August 2003 University of Zimbabwe Publications issued Terence Ranger, ed., *Nationalism, Democracy and Human Rights*, a set of essays exploring the authoritarian turn of nationalism in Zimbabwe and very much 'history of nationalism' rather than 'nationalist historiography'.

[3]　Two urban history workshops have recently taken place at the University of Zimbabwe. At each some ten young Zimbabweans presented papers.

[4]　Enocent Msindo is registered for a doctorate at the University of Cambridge.

Senior scholars, like Professor Alois Mlambo and Professor Brian Raftopolous, gave an intellectual lead through their own research and writings, particularly through their explorations of urban and labour history and of political economy. The University of Zimbabwe has some twenty scholarly manuscripts, including an important collection on Zimbabwean political economy, ready for publication. When I made my second retirement in June 2001 a research seminar was organized as a farewell gift at which some thirty scholarly papers were presented by historians, archaeologists, students of religion, and members of the departments of literature and languages.

So when I came to reflect on my return to the University of Zimbabwe thirty five years after I had first taught there it seemed to me that if one of my hopes in the early 1960s had been dashed, the other had been exceeded. The emancipatory potential of Zimbabwean nationalism, in which I had so confidently believed, had not been fulfilled. But I could not have foreseen in 1963, when I was removed from Rhodesia and from the University College, a future in which there would be over ten thousand African students at the University of Zimbabwe, all with high A level entry qualifications, and in which research and scholarship would be so thriving. As I thought that I might perhaps venture upon an academic autobiography it seemed to me that I would not locate the golden age of African historiography in the past, as other pioneers have done. For me it seemed that the golden age was here and now, at the University of Zimbabwe in the opening years of the twenty-first century.

When I came to deliver my valedictory lecture at the University of Zimbabwe on 31 May 2001 under the title 'History Matters', I proclaimed the potential of this emerging Zimbabwean scholarship. I also located two circumstances under which historical scholarship was crucially important. The first – which I had myself encountered in Rhodesia in the 1950s and 60s and in Matabeleland in the 1980s and 90s – was when people had been denied a history. But you could have too much history as well as too little. You could have too much history if a single, narrow historical narrative gained a monopoly and was endlessly repeated. In Rhodesia in the 1950s and in Matabeleland in the 1990s it had been necessary to remedy a deficiency. Now it had become necessary to complicate over-simplifications; to offer a plural history. Academic history was in difficulty in South Africa, I said, because it did not seem important enough. In Zimbabwe, by contrast, history seemed enormously important. The question was – which history for what Zimbabwe.[5]

---

[5]   My Zimbabwean colleague, Josephine Nhongo Simbanegavi, author of *For Better or Worse? Women and ZANLA in Zimbabwe's Liberation Struggle* (Nhongo Simbanegavi , 2000) and now researching on 'trans-national women' and 'nationalist men', is currently spending her sabbatical at the University of Lesotho. She arrived there to find that the government of Lesotho had suspended all grants to Humanities students on the grounds that their subjects were useless. Dr Nhongo Simbanegavi had begun to campaign with the slogan 'History Matters'. The Britain Zimbabwe Research Days on June 12 and 13 2004 at St Antony's College, Oxford, are on the topic 'What History for Which Zimbabwe?'. I hope that it will lead to a publication.

The emergence of patriotic history

It is only just over two years since I gave my Zimbabwean valedictory lecture but things have changed a great deal in that brief time. I have come to realize that it was foolish for me to separate the growth of nationalist authoritarianism from the growth of historical scholarship at the University of Zimbabwe and to deplore one and celebrate the other as though they could be disconnected. The University of Zimbabwe today is very different even from the University of Zimbabwe two years ago. It has been torn apart by student and faculty strikes; by police repression; by the collapse of funding. Many of the young historians I celebrated in my valedictory lecture are no longer at the University of Zimbabwe and some of them not in Zimbabwe at all. They remain determined to research and write but they will no longer do so as a collectivity. The History Department cannot this year offer an MA course. Some of the senior academics, whose example has been so important, have left or are leaving for universities elsewhere. Much of this is the result of Zimbabwe's dire economic crisis and affects academics in all subjects. But there is a particular challenge for academic historians.

There has arisen a new variety of historiography, which I did not mention in my valedictory lecture. This goes under the name of 'patriotic history'. It is different from and more narrow than the old nationalist historiography, which celebrated aspiration and modernization as well as resistance. It resents the 'disloyal' questions raised by historians *of* nationalism. It regards as irrelevant any history which is not political. And it is explicitly antagonistic to academic historiography. 'The mistake the ruling party made', says Sikhumbizo Ndiweni, ZANU(PF) Information and Publicity Secretary for Bulawayo, 'was to allow colleges and universities to be turned into anti-Government mentality factories'.[6] Out in the ZANU(PF) countryside university history has become deeply suspect.[7]

I first became aware of the full force of 'Patriotic history' when I returned to Zimbabwe for the six weeks running up to the presidential election of February 2002. In a personal report on that election I wrote that:

I want to begin discussing the elections by talking about history. You will say that this is because I am a historian. But I don't think anyone could fail to notice how central to ZANU(PF)'s campaign was a particular version of history. I spent four days watching Zimbabwe television which presented

---

[6] *Chronicle*, 26 April 2001.

[7] One of my history students at the University of Zimbabwe went to teach at a secondary school in Matabeleland. He found there was no history taught there and was tasked instead with teaching Business Studies. Then, however, the Minister of Education decreed that history must be taught in every school. But my student found this far from an advantage. His headmaster told him that in order not to attract the hostile attention of the war veterans he must stick very closely to the official line: 'Whatever you do don't tell them any of the things you were taught at the university'. He told me later that his pupils regarded history lessons as mere propaganda but they loved business studies where 'you can say anything'.

nothing but one 'historical' programme after another'; the government press – the Herald *and the* Chronicle *– ran innumerable historical articles ... Television and newspapers insisted on an increasingly simple and monolithic history ... Television constantly repeated documentaries about the guerrilla war and about colonial brutalities ... The* Herald *and the* Sunday Mail *regularly carried articles on slavery, the partition, colonial exploitation and the liberation struggle. I recognised the outlines of many of my own books but boiled down in the service of ZANU(PF) (Ranger, 2002a: 60).*

This condensed resistance history could be communicated at various levels, from the relatively sophisticated to the crudely racist. The essential message was spelt out by Godfrey Chikowore in an article in the *Herald* of 16 February 2002 entitled 'Defending our Heritage. Armed Struggle should serve as Guiding Spirit'. Each presidential candidate, said Chikowore, 'should produce manifestos which spell out clearly that they are going to uphold Zimbabwean values and heritage and restore a sense of patriotism among Zimbabweans':

Zimbabwe is the product of a bitter and protracted armed struggle. That armed struggle should serve as the guiding spirit through the presidential elections and even beyond. The right to choose a president of one's own choice should not be considered as a mere exercise of a democratic right. It is the advancement of a historical mission of liberating Zimbabwe from the clutches of neo-colonialism. Any other wild illusion about it constitutes a classic example of self-betrayal and self-condemnation to the ranks of perpetual servitude. The stampede for democracy should not undermine the gains of the liberation war.

Meanwhile in August 2001 the Zimbabwe government had instituted youth militia camps which were intended to establish the basis of a compulsory National Service scheme. There were many statements that the main function of these camps was to teach 'patriotic history'. Not only had universities and colleges become 'anti-Government mentality factories', but parents and teachers generally had failed to pass on the inspiration of the liberation struggle. Now, therefore, the revolutionary spirit would skip a generation. As the *Herald* reported on 28 January 2002: 'The Government will soon make youth training compulsory for all school leavers to instil unbiased history of Zimbabwe.' The youth were recruited as warriors into the 'Third *Chimurenga*' – the First *Chimurenga* having been the 1896-7 uprisings and the second having been the guerrilla war of the 1970s. They became a militia available to discipline their own parents; to attack MDC supporters; and to intimidate teachers and other educated civil servants in the rural areas.

Teaching in the youth camps was crudely rudimentary. As a recent report on youth militia training by the Solidarity Peace Trust explains:

there is overwhelming evidence that the youth militia camps are aimed at forcing on all school leavers a ZANU(PF) view of Zimbabwean history and the present. All training materials in the camps have, from inception, consisted exclusively of ZANU(PF) campaign materials and political speeches. This material is crudely racist and vilifies the major opposition party in the country ... The propaganda in the training camps appears to be crude in the extreme. One defected youth reported how war veterans told trainees that if anyone voted for the MDC, then the whites would take over the country again. They were also told that the whites used to kill black people in the 1970s by pouring boiling beer onto them, and this would happen again if the MDC won the election. A youth militia history manual called 'Inside the Third Chimurenga' gives an idea of the type of 'patriotism' that is instilled in the camps. The manual is historically simplistic and racist and glorifies recent ZANU(PF) National Heroes along with the land resettlement programme. It consists entirely of speeches made by President Robert Mugabe since 2000, among them his addresses to ZANU(PF) party congresses, his speech after the 2000 election result, and funeral orations for deceased ZANU(PF) heroes ... The MDC is said to be driven by 'the repulsive ideology of return to white settler rule' ... According to youths trained in the camps ... this was the sole source of written information on Zimbabwean history used in the training process.[8]

While at this crude level the MDC was simply being demonized in the run-up to the elections – as it has been since – Chikowore was using more sophisticated arguments in his *Herald* article. While Mugabe drew deeply upon the revolutionary past, the MDC, he said, had abolished history, proclaiming its irrelevance in an 'age of globalisation'. They merely promised prosperity and were prepared to 'reverse' Zimbabwe's history in order to achieve it, even if this meant 'turning Zimbabwe into a British and American overseas territory'. 'The Zimbabwean public has to be assured', wrote Chikowore, 'that this group has no history that could logically confirm its credibility for the Presidential crown.'[9]

The election, therefore, was history versus 'the end of history'. Tsvangirai was regularly mocked, not only for having failed to take part in the guerrilla war but

---

[8]   Solidarity Peace Trust, 'National Youth Service Training. "Shaping Youths in a Truly Zimbabwean manner". An overview of youth militia training and activities in Zimbabwe', 5 September 2003. The Solidarity Peace Trust was established in 2003 and consists of church leaders in Zimbabwe and South Africa. Its report on the militias is endorsed by the Crisis in Zimbabwe Coalition, the Zimbabwe National Pastors Conference, the Ecumenical Support Services and other organisations. The report does not focus on 'patriotic history'. Its main purpose is to show that 'the reality is a paramilitary training programme for Zimbabwe's youth with the clear aim of inculcating blatantly anti-democratic, racist and xenophobic attitudes. The youth militias so created are used as instruments of the ruling party to maintain their hold on power by whatever means necessary, including torture, rape, murder and arson.' But 'patriotic history' is important to the church leaders because they believe that youth can only behave in this way once they have been 'thoroughly brain-washed'.

[9]   *Herald*, 16 February 2001.

also for having failed to understand history, which amounted to more or less the same thing. 'The depth of his knowledge of our history is so shallow that it is frightening', wrote Olley Maruma.[10]

This unprecedented historiographical barrage in the weeks before the presidential elections produced some cries of protest. The most eloquent and deeply felt came from Innocent Chifamba Sithole, writing in the *Financial Gazette* for February 14 to 20, 2001. Sithole protested against 'narrowly defined definitions of Zimbabwean nationalism':

> Big brother has wrenched open the archives [wrote Sithole about the nightly televised scenes of war-time atrocity] and history cringes into the vulnerable system of mere signs and symbols of ink on paper, of recorded image and sound on films. The nation is daily bombarded with grim images of grotesquely mutilated and decomposing black bodies from the liberation war, falling like boulders from the cliff of the television screen. [It is] an attempt to edit the nation's collective memory in order to rewrite the history of the struggle for independence ... By virtue of being the government of the day ZANU(PF) has access to and control over the recorded signs and symbols that denote and connote our history as a nation ... Central to ZANU(PF)'s election campaign is the political commodification of the legacy of the liberation war. Amid the choking fumes of aggressive political campaigns, history lets out a piercing wail as Big Brother relentlessly attempts to weave past, present and future into his person.[11]

The Authors of Patriotic History: Veterans, Robert Mugabe and Tafataona Mahoso

The history instructors in the youth militia camps are war veterans and it has been suggested that 'patriotic history', with its focus on violent resistance, is the result of the re-emergence of the ex-guerrillas at the centre of Zimbabwean politics. Thus Norma Kriger writes, in her new book on war veterans, that the recent prominence of the ex-guerrillas is a return to the politics of immediate post-independence. The rhetoric of patriotic history displays 'the same dynamic that I have shown characterized the relationship between veterans and the ruling party in the context of working out the legacies of the [1980] peace settlement: often simultaneous conflict and collaboration as party and veterans manipulate one another, using violence and intimidation and a war discourse,

---

10   *Herald*, 12 February 2001. Maruma was attacking Tsvangirai for saying that ZANU(PF) wanted to turn Zimbabweans into peasants. '70 per cent of the black people *are* already peasants'. They were made so by the colonial regime. ZANU(PF) aimed to make them 'independent agricultural producers'.

11   Many of the films being shown on ZTV had been made by the Rhodesian army for a 'shock and awe' campaign in the 1970s.

to advance their respective agendas ... Contemporary politics in Zimbabwe recalls the early post-independence years.' Kriger finds that 'ZANU(PF) and the war veterans have shown remarkable consistency in their power-seeking agendas, their appeals to the revolutionary liberation war, their use of violence and intimidation' (Kriger, 2003: 208).

On the other hand Luise White, in *her* new book on 'texts and politics in Zimbabwe' notes that the 'patriotic history' of the early twenty-first century is different from the ZANU(PF) rhetoric of the early 1980s.[12] It is wider in some ways since the mobilized war veterans now include ex-ZIPRA guerrillas and even ex-dissidents, who in the 1980s were being hunted down by the Fifth Brigade. Joshua Nkomo, who fled for his life in the 1980s, is regularly celebrated on ZTV today as 'Father Zimbabwe'. It is narrower in other ways since hardly anything is now said about ZANU(PF)'s modernising, reconstructing and welfare agenda which was such a feature of the party's rhetoric in the 1980s. 'Patriotism' does not seem to include Socialism, for instance. But White also notes another major shift:

> *Zimbabwe has been given a new history in which it was a British colony until 1980; moreover the British still meddled, still broke promises and still tried to control the country. This rhetoric was constant in ZANU(PF), perfected by the often-used slogan 'Zimbabwe will never be a colony AGAIN'. This new colonial history sits awkwardly beside the history of settlers, dominion status, and the Rhodesia Front's renegade independence. (White, 2003: 97).*

White is right about the importance of this 'new colonial history' – during the presidential campaign it often seemed that Robert Mugabe was campaigning against the man he called 'Tony B-Liar' rather than against Tsvangirai. In speech after speech Mugabe barely mentioned Tsvangirai but hammered home the simple message that Zimbabwe was Zimbabwe, not Britain.

These changes – the inclusion of ZAPU and ZIPRA, the focus on Britain as colonial power – needed imagining and making. It is the ex-guerrillas who have been teaching 'patriotic history' to youth militias – and occasionally to headmasters and teachers brought into the camps for crash courses. So we need to examine how the war veterans have processed this new history. Jocelyn Alexander and JoAnn McGregor (2003) have begun to do this by exploring the way in which ex-ZIPRA guerrillas have remade their own very distinctive history, as it was defiantly expressed in the 1980s, so as to fit with the combined 'patriotic history' of today. If there are gains to ZAPU pride now that Joshua Nkomo is safely installed in the

---

[12] A major difference, of course, is that the policy of Reconciliation in the early 1980s meant that the violence and brutality of the Rhodesian army was played down then while it is being played up now. In many ways the atmosphere of state media discourse in Zimbabwe today suggests that Zimbabwe is in the immediate aftermath of a liberation struggle rather than twenty three years away from it.

national heroic pantheon,[13] there are also losses to ZIPRA's own self-image of a uniquely disciplined and rational army. Their revolutionary history has now been combined with and made part of the once despised history of ZANLA indiscipline and adventurism. This redefinition has also set them against the majority of their own Sindebele people.[14]

There needs to be similar work on ZANLA veterans. But if the veterans are teaching history in the militia camps, their text book is a collection of Robert Mugabe's speeches, *Inside the Third Chimurenga* (2001). I want here to explore Mugabe as historian.

What is fascinating is that in the last two or three years Mugabe has been celebrated primarily in this role. An outstanding example is the novelist Alexander Kanengoni's essay in the *Daily News* of 12 April 2003, 'One-hundred days with Robert Mugabe'. Kanengoni is an ex-ZANLA guerrilla whose outstanding novels of the liberation war certainly have not celebrated Mugabe. His last novel *Echoing Silences* did not mention Mugabe at all but ended with a ghostly *pungwe* at which the dead heroes, Chitepo and Takawira, mourned the betrayal of the revolution.[15] Yet Kanengoni has emerged as an outspoken advocate of the Third Chimurenga. In his 'One-hundred days' Kanengoni described how he had 'lived with Mugabe for over three months, eating from the same pot, perched on the top of the same hut to thatch it, slept in the same room at a remote base called Saguranca in central Mozambique in 1975, and the man left such a deep impression on my mind – nothing will erase it.'

---

13   The death and burial in Heroes Acre of Joshua Nkomo's widow, MaFuyana, has given a recent opportunity for the new patriotic rhetoric. The *Chronicle* of 21 July 2003 recorded that: 'The whole country (as one family) converged at the national shrine to pay their respects to their dear Mother of the Nation'. Like every other Zimbabwean she was 'a carrier of a unique culture, specific to the Zimbabwean society'; the 'consolatory speeches' at Heroes' Acre emphasised that 'naturally our destiny is different' from any other nation's. MaFuyana, though, had differed from all other Zimbabweans by bringing her role as an 'African mother' to a national height. Throughout the 1980s she had striven to bring about unity between ZAPU and ZANU(PF). Through her influence 'both parties acknowledged that Zimbabwe was a sovereign country which belonged primarily to our indigenous Zimbabweans. This experience reflected the deeply engraved morality of an accomplished motherhood by African standards in Mama Fuyana which compelled her to reflect diplomatically beyond the family circles, in constructive national terms as well'. She represented 'the sacredness and mightiness of the Zimbabwean culture, which Zimbabweans first, with others to follow, have the right and privilege to develop.' Zimbabwean universities needed to teach students about her so as to develop 'well conceptualised educative materials on outstanding national personalities ... [to be] systematically developed in the curriculum in a bid to reinforce the question of national identity'.

14   In March 2002 I met in Bulawayo the ex-ZIPRA directors of the Mafela Trust, a body concerned to preserve and record ZIPRA's history. Their main concern was to make videos of ZIPRA's revolutionary role so that these could be shown on ZTV along with the videos of ZANLA forces.

15   For a more detailed discussion of Kanengoni's literary work, see Chapter 1 of the present volume.

Kanengoni describes how Mugabe arrived at 'the secluded Frelimo base' to find it in turmoil. The Frelimo base commander, Kanyawu, had received an instruction 'from above' to send all the ZANLA guerrillas 'back to Rhodesia because our colleagues in Zambia had killed Herbert Chitepo.' Mugabe asserted his authority and told the commander that 'we would rather die than give the Rhodesians the immeasurable pleasure of killing us'. Then he 'quickly organised political lessons for us that he personally conducted'.

And what were these political lessons at a time of acute crisis? Kanengoni tells us that they were about land and violence:

> Mugabe took us through the lessons: the history of Zimbabwe ... and all through that rather academic process, there was not a single book, a single piece of paper, a single pen. What I found quite fascinating about him was how he had his facts at the tips of his fingers ... When I look at him now – 23 years later – the man has not changed because what he told us then, he is telling an entire nation now.[16]

The greatest admirer of Mugabe as a historian – and his interpreter to the world – is Dr Tafataona Mahoso, now chairman of the Media and Information Commission and a weekly columnist in the *Sunday Mail*.[17] In his column of 16 March 2003, Mahoso argued that the Mugabe demonized in the Western press was not the 79-year-old President as an individual but the embodiment of pan-African spirit:

> Mugabe is now every African who is opposed to the British and North American plunder and exploitation ... So, old Mugabe here is not the person of Robert Mugabe. Rather it is that powerful, elemental African memory going back to the first Nehanda and even to the ancient Egyptians and Ethiopians who are now reclaiming Africa in history as the cradle of humankind ... The Zimbabwe opposition and their British, European and North American sponsors have exposed themselves as forces opposed to Mugabe as Pan-African memory, Mugabe as the reclaimer of African space, Mugabe as the African power of remembering the African legacy and African heritage which slavery, apartheid and imperialism thought they had dismembered for good ... It is not accidental that both the opposition to Mugabe and its sponsors sought to denigrate African liberation history as out-moded and undemocratic traditions.

---

[16] In 1977 Robert Mugabe at last became the elected leader of ZANU. During that year the party periodical *Zimbabwe News* articulated his views. The July 1977 issue was devoted to 'ZANU and History'. Mugabe's own contribution argued that 'the spirit of ZANU' had been present throughout the history of Zimbabwe, wherever and whenever there had been patriotic resistance to foreign intrusion. In that sense what Mugabe was writing then in Mozambique 'he is telling an entire nation now'.

[17] Mahoso also took part in the weekly 'National Ethos' programme on ZTV, described by unsympathetic commentators as 'a televised version of Mahoso's Sunday Mail articles', designed to 'propagate a primitive and exclusivist nationalism that clearly fails to seize the popular imagination'. In October 2002 ZTV's own monthly survey revealed that this was the least watched of all its programmes. *Independent*, 25 October 2002.

The west stresses mechanical, even computerised, recall in the place of what Mary Daly calls 'deep ancestral memory'. In the place of original elemental memory which reconnects the once disconnected and liberates them, the west now prefers speed and efficiency which are often mistaken for information and knowledge. What the west takes for memory is mechanical recall, superficial regurgitation of formulaic catechisms which are taken out of context because they must be both uni-polar (centralised) and globalised – rule of law, transparency, free enterprise and human rights.

By contrast to this mechanical, artificial 'memory', Mugabe represents 'deep ancestral memory'. And this allows him to penetrate below the apparent surfaces of world affairs. Younger Zimbabweans do not associate Britain with colonial exploitation because Ian Smith was in revolt against the British crown and a British governor presided over Zimbabwean independence. Mugabe understands the underlying British responsibility for the loss of Zimbabwean land. Younger Zimbabweans accept Colin Powell's appointment as US Secretary of State as a sign of American pluralism and democracy. Mugabe knows that there have always been house-slaves complicit with the slave owners. So when Mugabe attacked Britain and the US at the Johannesburg earth summit on 25 February 2003,[18] Mahoso proclaimed in the *Sunday Mail* that the speech was an expression of deep ancestral memory and more important than any speech by Martin Luther King:

The earth cannot be saved without authentic life rituals. Such life rituals were impossible in the presence of two evil spirits whom most youngsters could neither identify nor recognise. The most aggressive demon was that of apartheid founder Cecil John Rhodes. It appeared in the most aggressive, photogenic, restless and boyish body of British Prime Minister, Tony Blair. In place of Rhodes's vision of capturing and controlling Africa 'from Cape to Cairo' it now brought the new slogan of 'the conscience of the world' with Africa having been reduced to a mere 'scar' on that conscience.

The second demon, Mahoso continued, was that of 'the US founding slave-master, Thomas Jefferson'; of his half-caste bastards and Uncle Tom house slaves. Colin Powell was 'the evil spirit medium of Washington and Jefferson'. It took an elder, in touch with the ancestral spirits, to recognize these re-incarnated demons since only the elders 'possess the wisdom and memory deep and long enough to recognise the slave master in Colin Powell and the pirate invader in Tony Blair.'[19]

---

[18]   For a Zimbabwean report of his speech see the *Chronicle*, 26 February 2003.

[19]   *Sunday Mail*, 8 September 2002. In practice it was not only the young who failed to perceive the connection between Tony Blair and Cecil Rhodes. As the local historian of Matabeleland, Pathisa Nyathi, remarked in the *Sunday Mirror* on 18 November 2002, 'my cousin out at Sankonyana does not even know there is a country somewhere known as Britain. The last white man he saw was a Rhodesian soldier fighting freedom fighters.' Nyathi's cousin, in short, knows about Rhodes and Rhodesia rather than about Blair and Britain. Mugabe's speeches have been designed to remedy this ignorance.

Within Zimbabwe, 'patriotic history' has seemed indefensibly narrow, dividing the nation up into revolutionaries and sell-outs, in the spirit of Didymus Mutasa's remark that he wished that only the seven million revolutionary Zimbabweans could remain, or of Robert Mugabe's demand at the 2003 Heroes' Days ceremony that the opposition must 'repent' and declare its commitment to the continuing revolution before any unity talks could begin.[20] Mahoso, however, portrays Zimbabwean patriotic history as an all-embracing pan-Africanist ideology. He also takes care to do what Mugabe does not often bother with – namely to attack the propositions of what he calls 'bogus universalism'.[21] In reality, argues Mahoso, it is a-historicized globalized morality which is divisive and narrow.

In a series of *Sunday Mail* articles Mahoso has warned against 'the threat of false universalism'. In an article under that title on 26 May 2002 Mahoso took on the two major cultural institutions of Zimbabwean civil society, the Harare International Festival of Arts and the Zimbabwe International Book Fair. What was missing from the Arts celebration was 'African culture as strategic unhu/ubuntu, African ethics.' The Best 100 African Books awards in Cape Town, that 'anti-African city', would become 'African culture without its soul'. Both events were manifestations of 'the problem of false universalism which in the context of imperialism, means the false liberalism of the white man which is used strategically, by arch-racists, as a Trojan horse against revolutionary ubuntu'. The inspiration of the 100 Best Books project was the historian, Ali Mazrui, whom Mahoso described as 'head of a US institution which generates deadly ideas, from an ubuntu point of view, concerning global culture.'[22] Analysing a typically paradoxical Mazrui lecture from a ZIBF publication, Mahoso finds it guilty of 'deletion' of the factors of imperialism and racism; of 'reductionism'; of 'false analogy'; and above all of 'false universalism' which adopts 'the white liberal view of the world as the only model of civilisation' and this dooms most of the world to poverty and impotence.

Having thus taken on the man often introduced at the Book Fair as 'Africa's leading historian', Mahoso went on in succeeding articles to demolish other pillars of Zimbabwean civil society. In one he attacked Zimbabwean churches for accepting neo-liberal and a-historical definitions of human rights[23] which had become, in his view, the ideology of the latest form of right-wing Christianity. In another he

---

20 A powerful expression of this view is Caesar Zvayi, 'Opposition MDC must embrace national values', *Herald*, 2 October 2003. Zvayi cites Mugabe to ask the MDC: 'Are you a willing traitor and second executioner of these heroes, willing posthumous betrayer of their cause?'

21 Mugabe did briefly address these in a passage of his Johannesburg speech. 'We get globally villagised under false economic pretences. We are cheated to believe that we shall all be equals in that village'. See also his speech to the Non Aligned Summit at the end of February 2003. *Chronicle*, 26 February 2003.

22 Mahoso names Mazrui's institution as the Institute of Global Cultural Studies.

23 'Right-wingers seek to hijack churches', *Sunday Mail*, 15 December 2002. Mahoso complained that 'no African church or religious movement is described in our media as part of "civil society" ... unless it has adopted the views of its Western sponsors.'

repudiated 'liberal' protests of press censorship and repression in Zimbabwe. These were based, he wrote, on narcissism:

> The narcissist replaces the real world of history and society with what he/ she thinks ... in contrast to the African who says 'I relate, therefore I am.' [There is] a compulsive desire to lie in order to protect the unipolar view of the world. History is treated either as useless or dangerous because it uncovers uncomfortable relationships of slavery, colonialism, apartheid and genocide. Yet we must always look at that history.[24]

Mahoso found on the part of the Zimbabwean opposition and its foreign sponsors 'a compulsive need to lie and to escape from history'.[25] In this way he claims Mugabe and ZANU(PF) as custodians of history and depicts the MDC as representing a-historical globalization.

ZANU(PF)'s ministerial historians: Chigwedere and Mudenge

I remember being chided by Victoria Chitepo in 1980 for having helped to produce so many Zimbabwean historians when Zimbabwe needed men and women of a more practical bent. I jokingly replied that there were so many historians in the cabinet and in charge of public institutions that the new Zimbabwe was an experiment in rule by historiography. It is not a joke which seems so funny now, and some of those early historians are dead or gone. Some still remain, however, and two in particular have contributed to the current Zimbabwean debate about history. One is the Minister of Education, Aeneas Chigwedere. The other is the Minister of Foreign Affairs, Stan Mudenge.

Chigwedere is the author of several books on Zimbabwe's pre-colonial history, including the *The Roots of the Bantu*. As he says, in dedicating the book to me, he took History Honours in the early days of the University College of Rhodesia and Nyasaland.[26] *Roots of the Bantu* is an exercise in what Mahoso calls *'unhu/ ubantu'*. It begins with a dedication by Chigwedere:

> If it be the will of the common ancestors of the Black African Community both at home base (Africa) and overseas, ordained that I be their instrument for unravelling their history and culture in the interest of their progeny, I thank them for the energy, will-power and inspiration they infused into me.

---

[24] *Sunday Mail*, 4 May 2003.

[25] Mahoso includes bodies like the Zimbabwe Democracy Trust and the Zimbabwe Crisis Network among those who seek 'to escape from history' and describes their human rights protests to international bodies as a-historical appeals to bogus universalism.

[26] I reproduce the terms of the dedication here in the interests of showing the relation between the new patriotic history and earlier nationalist historiography. Chigwedere says that I inspired him to research through my 'own untiring work on behalf of both Zimbabawe and black Africa.'

Chigwedere's contribution to the current debate, however, has been rather different. In July 2001 he published *British Betrayal of the Africans. Land, Cattle and Human Rights. Case for Zimbabwe.* Chigwedere effectively uses the 1919 Privy Council decision that the Crown owned all the land in Rhodesia by 'act of conquest' to demonstrate that Britain had always had primary responsibility for the alienation of African land. As one reviewer remarked, the book also reveals the trickery and violence of that 'devil', Cecil Rhodes:

> *Lobengula even wrote to Lord Knutsford, the Colonial Secretary, but it seems that his lordship was also in cahoots with Cecil Rhodes. As the story develops, it is amazing just how almost everyone involved in the story is in cahoots with the devil (Mufuka, 2002).*

The oddity has been that Chigwedere's book has barely been noticed in Zimbabwe and is not to be found in bookshops. The *Herald* did not review it until 28 June 2003, though then it declared it a 'marvellous book' presenting readers with 'the true history of Zimbabwe highlighting the real facts as done by the British imperialists.' The reviewer explains:

> *It becomes obvious that to direct the fire against the local commercial white farmers is to direct the fire against the wrong enemy. The settler was only an agent. The proprietor and culprit was and still remains the British and their government ... This book is an asset for all Zimbabweans and to the future generations (Tshaya, 2003).*

The reviewer tells readers that the 'volume can be obtained from the Ministry of Education, Sport and Culture'. And it is in his role of Minister of Education that Chigwedere has done most to advance patriotic history and to combat 'bogus universalism'. Before Chigwedere became Minister of Education, Unesco and Danida had collaborated with the Ministry to produce a series of textbooks on *Education for Human Rights and Democracy in Zimbabwe.* Several Zimbabwean teachers from Education Colleges were employed to write History text books for Forms 1 and 2 and for O level. Hundreds of thousands of these beautifully produced books were printed in 2000. They represented universalist history at its best, containing a great deal of comparative material on Nazi Germany and Soviet Russia; on slavery in Ancient Egypt and the Americas; on colonial repression and nationalist aspirations for liberty; on the slow emergence of international conventions on human rights.

Despite all the money and time spent on these texts, however, they remain in the warehouses, while patriotic history texts are being distributed to the schools. It is easy to see that Mahoso would detect 'bogus universalism' in these human rights text books. They stress the value of Commonwealth monitoring of Zimbabwean elections. They describe the rejection of the draft constitution in the February 2000 referendum as a 'triumph for democracy'. They also contain passages critical of traditional Zimbabwean society. The Forms 1 and 2 text says that 'the slave trade may not have affected the Zimbabwe community in ancient times but slavery did. At Great Zimbabwe chiefs were expected to bring enough people to build a portion of the wall. Although this was called persuasive force, in real terms it was slavery'. The section on minority rights describes the Kalanga, Shangaan, Tonga and Venda peoples of Zimbabwe as 'vulnerable, marginalised and discriminated'. There is a passage on sexual abuse of children in Zimbabwe, though the O level text remarks that 'abusing women is not a monopoly of Zimbabwe alone'.[27] These texts are not being distributed; Human Rights are not to be taught in Zimbabwean schools; but Chigwedere has instructed that history is to be taught everywhere.

Mudenge, who has a doctorate from SOAS, is a more sophisticated historian. While he was Zimbabwe's representative at the United Nations he wrote and published an excellent history of the Munhumutapa state between 1400 and 1902 (Mudenge, 1988), which was very well received by professional historians and has become the standard work. As Minister of Foreign Affairs, of course, Mudenge has been regularly involved in contemporary historical debate. Recently, however, he has drawn upon his historical data to paradoxical effect. Addressing senior army, air force and police officers in Harare, Mudenge told them that it did not matter that Zimbabwe had been suspended from the Commonwealth:

> *A nation must not only recall its glorious past but must also know its sad and humiliating history and draw lessons from it ... Zimbabwe was once a Portuguese colony before the British came, yet the majority of Zimbabweans are not aware of this part of the country's history ... Zimbabwe became a Portuguese colony in the 17th century after Munhumutapa Mavura Mhande, the then ruler of the country, signed a treaty of vassalage to the Portuguese crown.*

What the *Herald* called a 'revelation' was likely, it said, 'to trigger debate on whether Zimbabwe should consider joining the community of Lusophone countries, a grouping of former Portuguese colonies, as a way of widening its areas of diplomatic participation'.[28]

Patriotic history and the pre-colonial past

Mudenge was not only speaking as foreign affairs minister, longing to widen diplomatic participation. He also gave a message of warning to the MDC:

> *Both the sovereignty of the state and the institution of Mutapaship suffered a mortal blow from which they never really recovered. Depending on foreign influence to come to power has a costly price tag, often too dear for the nation, and sometimes even for the puppet.*

---

[27] I owe my sight of these texts to Mary Ndlovu.

[28] *Herald*, 21 October 2003.

And though patriotic history is so focused on Rhodes and the British and the First Chimurenga of 1896 it does appeal also to an earlier Zimbabwean past. Perhaps the best example of this is the televised ceremony presided over by Robert Mugabe at which two halves of a long separate Zimbabwe bird were re-united, one half having been returned to Zimbabwe by the German government.

The 'multi-million dollar ceremony' aroused much criticism even in Zimbabwe. 'It was quite noble for the German government to return the Zimbabwe bird carving', wrote Fidelis Mashavakure to the *Standard* on 6 June 2003. 'Surely the bird is of some historical significance to present day Zimbabweans and generations to come'. Yet the government had 'over-dramatised' the event:

> It was astonishing to see women religiously kneeling down in honour of a stone carving. It was even more astonishing to see the President lead the gathering in sloganeering over the carving. Does the carving belong to ZANU(PF) or Zimbabwe. The millions of dollars used for this event could have bought food for starving people ... State television and radio could have been used for covering reports on the concerns of the impoverished population.

But it was criticism in the South African press which outraged the Zimbabwean government. The *Sunday Times* in South Africa satirized the ceremony, saying that Mugabe had a 'bird in his head'. Outraged, the Zimbabwe Minister of Information, Jonathan Moyo, himself responsible for co-ordinating the patriotic history campaign in Zimbabwe's media, sent an official protest to the South African government. The re-uniting of the bird had been 'a historic moment in the reconstruction of the country's heritage' and for the ceremony to be 'ridiculed and insulted by a newspaper is mind-boggling'.[29] Mahoso seized on the occasion:

> The white racist columnist, Hogarth, wrote a column called 'Our Bob's got birds on the brain', which was a savage attack on the entire African process of 'remembering', that is the process of remobilising African memory by reconnecting symbols, communities, movements and people as the South's answer to Northern driven globalisation, reviving their memory of a world without apartheid.

The West feared this process, hence the destruction of Iraqi antiquities and 'spitting' on the Zimbabwe bird.[30]

Joost Fontein's recent Edinburgh doctoral thesis, 'The Silence of Great Zimbabwe', offers a fascinating analysis of the current historiographical struggle over the monument. He argues that the African peoples who live around Great Zimbabwe are just as much excluded from it today as they were by Rhodesian curators. Today the monument is interpreted by elite nationalists and by academic

---

[29] *Sunday Mail*, 25 May 2003.

[30] *Sunday Mail*, 1 June 2003.

archaeologists who jointly ignore the sacredness of Great Zimbabwe to the locals. Fontein describes how local spirit mediums, in alliance with ex-combatants, have constructed their own 'African memory'. Theirs, too, is a kind of patriotic history, and certainly a product of 'deep ancestral memory'. But they have been given no role in the elaboration of the patriotic history of the ZANU(PF) regime (Fontein, 2003).

The ceremony of the re-uniting of the Zimbabwe bird, though it took place after Fontein completed his thesis, fits perfectly into his argument. The present academic curator of Great Zimbabwe, Dr Edward Matenga, is author of *The Soapstone Birds of Great Zimbabwe. Symbols of a Nation* (1998). It was Matenga who publicized the existence of the lower half of a Zimbabwe bird in the *Museum fur Volkerkunde* in Berlin and who proclaimed: 'Zimbabwe has a plan to recover the specimen in Berlin and allow it to return home to roost!' Matenga's book has a foreword by Stan Mudenge, who hails it as a contribution to 'authentic national history'. (See Matenga 1998: vii, 62). The recent ceremony was a fulfilment of Matenga's agenda as well as of Mugabe's and Mudenge's.

There are other signs of tension between a local, radical, war-veterans' agenda and the agenda of state patriotic history. In early 2002, for example, war veterans in Matabeleland launched a campaign for the removal of Rhodes's grave from the Matopos. The veterans' leader, Andrew Ndlovu declared that 'we cannot find peace when we are keeping a white demon in our midst. It is the very core of our problems. His grave should be returned to the British'.[31] Ndlovu's demand seemed the logical conclusion of Mugabe's ancestral vision of Rhodes as a demonic spirit continuing to possess Tony Blair! And indeed this sort of patriotic demand is continuing to be made in the state press. On 29 October 2003, for example, Caesar Zvayi renewed the call for Rhodes to be removed:

> The Matopo Hills, which today are a tourist attraction ... were a very sacred shrine in the pre-colonial halcyon days and believed to be the earthly residence of God and his high priests and priestesses ... This was the sacred Njelele, Matonjeni, Mabweadziva, Mwarindidzimu, which today has been desecrated as the burial place of a white bandit, who was rabidly racist ... Can the powers that be please do something about this sacrilege and mollify the spirits of the land.[32]

Yet here arises one of the paradoxes of patriotic history. Mahoso is hostile both to the colonial legacy and to bogus universalism. But the one international agency he admires is UNESCO, remembering its attempts to create a new international

---

[31] 'ZANU(PF) crusade threatens monuments', *Standard*, 28 April 2002. I quote and discuss this demand in 'Mugabe versus Rhodes: The Uses of Colonialism in Zimbabwe', international conference on Rhodes, His Networks and Their Legacies', St Antony's, Oxford, 1 December 2002.

[32] 'Colonial Monuments a Shame to Pan-Africanism', *Herald*, 29 October 2003.

information order and how these led to attacks on UNESCO by Britain and the United States. As Fontein shows, Zimbabwean archaeologists and oral historians have taken a leading role in the development of UNESCO's new doctrine of 'cultural landscape' as a key criteria for the declaration of World Heritage sites. And on 3 July 2003 the World Heritage Committee of UNESCO endorsed the Zimbabwe government's application and carried through the inscription of the Matopos Hills as a World Heritage site.[33] As the non-government Sunday paper, the *Standard*, tactlessly but triumphantly reported on 6 July: 'Matobo Hills, where Cecil John Rhodes is buried, have won UNESCO's World Heritage listing'. And the listing does indeed mean that Rhodes's grave is safe.

Robert Mugabe's address on 29 October to the 14th General Assembly and Scientific Symposium of the International Council on Monuments and Sites, meeting for the first time in Africa at the Victoria Falls, presented an altogether more sophisticated version of patriotic history and its relation to world heritage:

> *Zimbabwe was committed to preserving its heritage ... Zimbabweans had, through the agrarian reform programme, found joy because their greatest heritage – land – had been returned to them. 'Now that land has returned to the people, they were able once more, to enjoy the physical and spiritual communion that was once theirs. For it must be borne in mind that the non-physical or intangible heritage is an equally strong expression of a people, manifesting itself through oral traditions, language, social practices and traditional craftsman-ship'. The objectives of ICOMOS were synonymous with Zimbabwe's philosophy. Cde Mugabe said Zimbabwe valued Heritage so much that even the graves of the country's colonialists such as Cecil John Rhodes were being preserved. 'We accept history as a reality'.[34]*

Patriotic history and academic history

Zimbabwean patriotic history, then, is a complex phenomenon. It ranges from the brutal over-simplifications of the militia camps, through presidential campaign speeches, through the work of ministerial historians, to the sophistications of

---

[33]   The issue of cultural landscapes and world heritage with reference to the Matopos is discussed in Terence Ranger, *Voices From the Rocks* (1999). Fontein's thesis contains a final chapter based on research at the UNESCO headquarters in Paris.

[34]   'Land greatest heritage', *Herald*, 30 October 2003.With the proclamation of the Matopos as a World Heritage site something of the same combination of interests which Fontein has documented for Great Zimbabwe is emerging. Not only Rhodes's but Mzilikazi's grave is sited in the Heritage area. On 7 August 2003 Jackson Ndlovu, Librarian and Oral Historian at the National Museum in Bulawayo, delivered the annual Lozikeyi Lecture in the Bulawayo National Gallery. Entitled 'Breaking the Taboo: Mzilikazi's Grave and National Heritage' it was an eloquent demand that the grave become a public focus for Ndebele nationality sentiment, for Zimbabwean national sentiment and for world history.

Mahoso, and to addresses to world conservationists. It is equally variously propagated – in courses taught by war veterans in the camps, in collections of Mugabe's speeches, in Chigwedere's syllabi and textbooks in the schools, on state television and radio, and in the writings of Mahoso and others in the state-controlled press. As we have seen, it is proclaimed as a remedy to the failures of parents and teachers and especially of universities to instil the revolutionary spirit. As we have also seen, in moments like the Zimbabwe bird ceremony or the declaration of the Matopos as a World Heritage site patriotic history and academic archaeology fit together very well.

The academic custodianship of National Museums and Monuments seems assured. But what are the intentions of the various makers of patriotic history towards the lukewarm universities? Here there is certainly pressure from below. There is a good deal of evidence that there is a project to take patriotic history all the way up from the militia camps to the universities. Headmasters and College lecturers, if not yet university professors, have been instructed in patriotic history by war veterans. The radical veteran, Joseph Chinotimba, told headmasters in Masvingo that 'to be in harmony with the government you must go for the training. You can only be patriotic if you undergo this course.'[35] War veterans have taken over entry procedures at Teacher Training Colleges so as to ensure that only their candidates are accepted. Courses in journalism are to be restricted to entrants who have completed militia training. It has also been announced that only those who have completed national service will be accepted into polytechnics and universities or as entrants into the civil service. And in November 2002 it was declared that all tertiary level students would be obliged to take a compulsory course in patriotism, to be called for some reason National Strategic Studies: 'The course will cover topics such as the history of the liberation struggle, nationalism, the importance of the land reform programme and other related matters.'[36] In March 2003 there was an attempt to launch such a course at the Bulawayo Polytechnic. Students at the Poly declared a boycott of all courses and asked for support from all other tertiary institutions so as 'to save tomorrow's generation from brainwashing'.[37]

And yet one wonders whether the Zimbabwe government will really try to carry these policies through. At the moment there are not nearly enough – let alone enough qualified – National Service graduates to fill all tertiary places. If they are to have any effect, courses in National Strategic Studies will have to be taught by competent lecturers. It seems more likely that the government will try to co-opt university history lecturers and to establish a relationship with them like that between Mugabe and the Museum staff at Great Zimbabwe. There are some signs of this. At Heroes weekend in 2003 the *Chronicle* deplored the ignorance amongst youth about Zimbabwe's liberation:

---

[35] 'National Service for Teachers', *Standard*, 12 August 2002.

[36] 'Government to introduce patriotism courses', *Independent*, 29 November 2002.

[37] 'Students reject National Service Lectures', *Daily News*, 1 March 2003.

> *Sadly, a major stumbling block in this regard has been the dearth of books that give a true account of our history, especially the history of the liberation war. We have relied too much on books written by hostile and clearly biased white supremacists who have often wrongly depicted the liberation struggle as a war between barbaric black Africans and white Rhodesian emissaries of civilization. As long as all story-tellers remain bigoted and narrow-minded whites, there will never be a black hero.*

The editorial ends with a mingled entreaty and invitation: 'What are the level-headed historians in Zimbabwe doing about this? Surely they cannot sit and watch while racists distort the history of our people for cheap political gain. Remember, truth hates delay.'[38]

As though in response to this entreaty it was announced on 16 October 2003 that 'a partnership agreement aimed at gathering and documenting the country's history' had been signed by the National Archives of Zimbabwe, the Department of National Museums and Monuments of Zimbabwe and the University of Zimbabwe's history department. The project is entitled 'Oral History: From the First to the Second Chimurenga'; it is a 'response to a challenge thrown to the three institutions by President Mugabe to record for posterity the facts of the national struggle.' The Secretary for Home Affairs, Melusi Matshiya, said that the results 'would be made available to future generations through the Liberation War Museum to be constructed at the National Heroes Acre'. The chairman of the UZ History Department, Dr Ken Manungo, said: 'We hope we will have maximum co-operation from the Government as there is nothing more important than being available to tell what happened.' Manungo said he was 'grateful to the Government because they are going to fund this project'; History students at UZ 'will carry out the necessary interviews and research'.[39]

Depending on how it is carried out and presented this could be a perfectly valid research project.[40] But it obviously has a very different emphasis from the series of projects carried out at UZ in the 1990s under the rubric of 'Democracy and Human Rights', directed by Professor Ngwabi Bhebe and funded by SAREC. It is still more different from the 'post-nationalist' historiography, which was beginning to emerge at the university in the early twenty-first century.

Patriotic history, nationalist historiography and the history of the nation

If the editorial in the *Chronicle* offered a role to 'level-headed' black historians, it strikingly ignored the contributions already made by Zimbabwean nationalist

---

[38] 'Lest We Forget', *Chronicle*, 10 August 2003.

[39] 'Project seeks to document Zimbabwe's history', *Herald*, 16 October 2003.

[40] For a recent fascinating collection of interviews with ex-combatants which offers a complex, non-heroic view of the liberation war see Musengezi and McCartney (2000).

historians and historians of the nation. It is certainly not true, for example, that there is nothing to read about the liberation struggle except books by white historians, leaving aside for the moment whether these have all been 'bigoted, narrow-minded and racist'.

The best book on the war is in fact the work of Zimbabwe's most distinguished and productive historian, Professor Ngwabi Bhebe (1999). Bhebe is indeed the outstanding example of a scholar who has written both nationalist history and the history of the nation. It cannot be said that Professor Bhebe has been cast aside in Zimbabwe's era of patriotic history. He is, after all, Vice Chancellor of the state university of the Midlands. Still, it is significant that the *Chronicle* chose to ignore his work. Professor Bhebe's nationalist historiography and still more his history of the nation is *too* level-headed and inclusive to be what the paper is looking for.

Plainly I ought to confront the *Chronicle's* attack on 'bigoted and narrow-minded' white authors of the books which Zimbabwean students read about the First and Second *Chimurenga*. I was in Bulawayo when I first saw the editorial and my first impulse was to write a letter to them asking, 'Do you mean me?' But then I thought they probably did. And yet patriotic history's relationship with my work is more complicated than merely saying it is 'white' or, heaven forbid, 'British'. The *Chronicle* itself, for instance, carried a whole page article in 2002 showing that 'historians' confirmed the government's case on land alienation. It drew heavily on my *Voices From the Rocks* and from the collaborative *Violence and Memory* to show that 'even' a white historian had documented evictions from the land. Of course it did not make any use of the last parts of these books which deal with the Matabeleland repression in the 1980s and with the failure of the Zimbabwean government to re-distribute the huge areas of land which fell into its hands in southern Matabeleland in the mid 1980s.[41]

Yet sometimes even the last part of my writings gets in. In June 2003 the *Herald* carried much to my surprise a whole page entitled 'Ranger re-examines colonial myths'. It turned out that this had been lifted from the Heinemann African Writers website and was something I had written at their request as background for readers of novels by Zimbabweans. The first two-thirds of my 'social history' documented the force and fraud of Rhodes, the seizure of the land, the rise of nationalism, etc. So far so good. But the *Herald* made the mistake of printing the

---

[41]   I tried to enter these considerations into the historical debate about land in a letter to the *Daily News* on 12 April 2000. 'In Matobo district the great majority of former white-owned farms and ranches have been in the hands of government for nearly 15 years. Therefore, if there has not been a just redistribution of land in this part of Matabeleland South, this has not been because of white farmers or British vested interests. It has been, alas, because the people in power have used the land for their own profit rather than for the relief of ordinary people and their cattle herds ... The people of Matobo are still waiting.'

final third, thus presenting its surprised readers with 'the horrors of independence'; with the Fifth Brigade 'savaging the civilian population'; with the rise of a vigorous civil society and a critical church; with 'the megalomania of an aging and unpopular president'. My piece ended:

> *The confrontation between the old revolutionary rhetoric (and history) and the new realities of a complex plural society threw Zimbabwean intellectuals and artists into turmoil. Their whole approach to Zimbabwe's national identity and to its history had to be thought through all over again.[42]*

Rethinking Zimbabwean history

Patriotic history is more complex than it at first appears and even on occasion – as with Mugabe's speech to ICOMOS – flexible. Nevertheless because of its narrow focus it has a certain force and simplicity. Critical responses to it have been much more scattered.

Some critics have focussed on Mugabe's appeal to pre-colonial glories. Many stress the gulf between this appeal and the sterile unprofitability of national monuments. Patriotic history elevates Great Zimbabwe but also, they say, empties it and devalues it. The hostility to whites aroused by patriotic history lessons in the militia camps – which has led to attacks on roadside curio sellers because they cater for and attract whites – has depressed the tourist trade:

> *'Great Zimbabwe is now just a heap of stones with no benefit for us', cursed the empty-handed Jerina, as she arrived at home, her arms folded behind her back. A few kilometres away from her hunger-stricken homestead, a disappointed fisherman folded his nets ... When things were normal this was the time for him to cast his nets at the shores of Lake Mutirikwa in anticipation of a major catch that would meet an ever increasing demand for fresh fish. 'Will Great Zimbabwe ever rise and be great for us?' the fisherman muttered to himself ... It was not only Jerina and the fisherman who went home empty-handed ... In fact it is now the order of the day for drought wracked villagers in Chief Mugabe's area in Masvingo who were earning a living through selling their various wares to tourists who thronged the Great Zimbabwe monuments on a daily basis to explore the mysteries buried at the world acclaimed heritage site. The villagers ... now sing the blues as the monuments have lost their lustre ... Tawanda Magara, a stone carver, said GZ now had a different meaning to him altogether. 'In the past when we saw the GZ monuments we realised that we would always make money since visitors would always come to discover the mystique*

---

[42] *Herald*, 17 June 2002.

associated with them. Now we see them just as any other heap of stones. They don't make any difference to our lives.[43]

Others have criticized the disproportionate focus the Mugabe regime has placed on 'heritage' in the midst of economic crisis. 'Patriotism' and 'Heritage', they say, are 'the last refuge of the scoundrels' who are ruining the nation. In May 2002 a Zimbabwean in the diaspora, Dr T. Mangwende, cited Dr Johnson's definition in his response to criticisms made by Mugabe of 'young professionals who have forgotten that it was ZANU(PF) that liberated the country'. Mangwende admitted that he was himself a beneficiary of the 'splendid efforts in education during the early 1980s' but declared himself grateful that these were now 'helping me see through your ruinous policies'. Mangwende claimed that all Zimbabweans were 'number one when it comes to patriotism' but that ZANU(PF) itself was dealing in 'rubbished patriotism ... used to justify the training of wholesale murderers':

It is a sheer waste of time and resources to set up colleges to supposedly teach 'patriotism' to the youth when the teacher needs intensive lessons in 'patriotism' ... The President knows more than anyone else that the country is in a mess and there is no point in touring the ruins to assess damage ... Still on the subject of 'patriotism', some young Zimbabweans referred to the other half of the recently returned bird as 'just a piece of stone'. Yes, it is patriotic to refer to this 'half' as just a piece of stone given the situation that Zimbabweans find themselves in. If a country is ravaged to the point that it cannot provide basics to its citizens, cultural symbols are the first to lose their value and meaning.

The true symbols of the new Zimbabwe were queues and Mugabe ought to visit them. 'I wish the President well in his tour of man-made ruins'.[44]

It is not only the pre-colonial emphases of patriotic history which are criticized. Its account of the 'Second *Chimurenga*', the guerrilla war of the 1960s and 1970s, is also repudiated:

Every day in the state-controlled media one hears of distortions of the history of this country ... We are frequently nauseated by endless propaganda about how freedom fighters were always winning battles against Rhodesia forces and how lots of helicopters and planes were downed during such engagements. A lot of young men and women sacrificed their lives for this country but that is no reason to lie that an

---

43 Walter Marwizi, 'Great Zimbabwe now just a pile of Stones', *Standard*, 21 June 2002. For similar reports on the Matopos –'stakeholders in the Matopo National Park said removal of Rhodes's body to pave the way for the resettlement of landless people would render the Park worthless' – see 'Tourist arrivals at Matopo cut by half', *Financial Gazette*, June 6-12 2002.

44 D.T.Mangwende, 'Patriotism does not equate to training murderers', *Daily News*, 31 May 2003.

> *outright military victory was achieved on the battlefield in 1979 [when] not even a single settlement, including those at the borders had fallen to the liberation forces [and] white farmers were able to continue farming even in the remotest hot-spots ... War is a serious affair with a high price to pay ... Real heroes do not lie and trivialise the pain of war.*[45]

The narrowness of patriotic history and its division of Zimbabweans into revolutionaries and 'sell-outs' has been attacked by many critics, not least, as we have seen, by the church leaders in their condemnation of the youth militia. Its narrowness in other ways has also been effectively condemned. In August 2003 Erikana Haurovi wrote to the press to bemoan 'the high levels of environmental degradation which are occurring everywhere'. These demanded practical solutions, but 'Zimbabwe has adopted a strange paradigm in solving its environmental crisis':

> *I have noted with great amazement the fact that whenever people sense danger they are reminded of some historical achievement. People are forced to remember the harshness of the historical colonial past whenever some crisis emerges. [Yet] a degraded environment will never recover despite the high level of praise it receives. Such an environment can never offer subsistence to man despite the level of high political achievement which may have occurred in the area two to three decades ago. The indoctrinative sentiments being echoed by the State propaganda machinery seems to be telling the country that no matter how degraded your environment is, political history will save us.*

Haurovi found that all 'state channels of disseminating information' were 'singing the same chorus in unison, elevating political history as an indisputable saviour'. But 'let us protect our environment first and then enjoy talking about our political history. Political history is nothing when we are living in misery and uncertainty.'[46]

But these varying criticisms do not amount to an alternative historical narrative capable of displacing patriotic history. Their authors share Zichanaka Munyika's hope in a future 'when ZANU(PF)'s stranglehold on Zimbabwe will end and the history of this country will be debated freely by all shades of opinion for the benefit of our children'.[47]

There are signs, admittedly, of more systematic historiographical dissent. One of these centres around the events of Matabeleland in the 1980s, part of the past which patriotic history excludes. As Mugabe himself declared in December 2002: 'Whatever remains were historical differences. These remain as history of our country and we can't bring ugly history into the present affairs and rewrite that

---

[45]   Letter from Zvichanaka Munyika, *Independent*, 14 February 2003.

[46]   *Standard*, 3 August 2002.

[47]   *Independent*, 14 February 2003.

ugly history. No.' Instead ZANU(PF) has sought to turn December 22, the day of the Unity Accord between ZANU and ZAPU in 1987, into a national anniversary (Mhizha, 2002). In response, the Zimbabwe Liberators Peace Platform, the organization of critical ex-combatants, has announced that Unity Day should be kept as a day of national mourning. Max Mnkandla, information secretary of the Zimbbabwe Liberators Peace Platform, called on Zimbabweans 'not to be fooled into celebrating an accord which legitimated the slaughter of their kith and kin'. Instead of expensive celebrations 'an upright government' would spend money on exhumations and reburials.' History itself needed to be exhumed. On December 22, said Mnkandla, 'we shall be in our black robes, remembering those who perished and lie in mass graves'.[48]

And if Matabeleland in the 1980s is one of the large omissions of patriotic history so, too, is the history of the towns and of the trade unions. Patriotic history sees townspeople as 'those without totems' and the state press from time to time carries bewildered articles about why urban populations are so unpatriotic. The role of trade unionism is largely excluded from the new narrative of nationalism. The most articulate protest against these exclusions has come from the veteran journalist, Bill Saidi. Saidi quotes from a ZAPU central committee report in 1984: 'In the period leading up to the first national organization of resistance to colonial rule, the workers of Zimbabwe led the way to unity in their struggle to form the first trade unions'. According to ZAPU, 'this development of a working class was an important foundation for the resurgence of the people's resistance ... The workers have fought many battles and taught the people many useful lessons. One of these lessons was the value of unity'. Yet, says Saidi, after the 1987 Unity Agreement the workers dropped out of political discourse. How, he asks, 'did the workers lose out? ... Today the most important people to ZANU(PF) are not the workers but the so-called war veterans.'[49]

The MDC emerged from the trade union movement and obtains most of its support from the towns. One might have expected it to have developed a counter-narrative against patriotic history which re-instated the workers and made urban history once again central to Zimbabwe's modern experience. One might have expected it also to try to overcome what Brian Raftopoulos has diagnosed as the main weakness of the trade unions in the 1950s and early 1960s, namely their

---

[48] 'A time of national mourning', *Standard*, 24 December 2002. The *Daily News* on 20 February 2003 carried a two page spread on Matabeleland rural memories of the 5 Brigade killings in the 1980s. The 80-year-old Moffat Tshabangu declared: 'The events of those years will forever remain etched in our minds. It is a story I will tell my grandchildren and great grandchildren so that they can fully understand the history of this country. All the things they read about in the country's history books are pure, refined nonsense meant to placate the egos of ZANU(PF) chefs'. Another villager, Kennias Ngwenya , hoped that history was still alive. 'As for those who participated in the murders, may God make the memories of our dead linger for ever in their minds'.

[49] 'Bill Saidi on Wednesday', *Daily News*, 10 July 2002.

failure to articulate rural grievances and aspirations. Then this weakness allowed political nationalism to dominate and eventually to absorb radical trade unionism. Today the divergence between an urban MDC and a rural ZANU(PF) yawns dangerously wide. But the MDC has made very little of trade union or worker history, perhaps because it believes that it already enjoys the support of the towns and of labour. Nor has it made much of a show of articulating rural grievances and aspirations. It does not possess a coherent land policy. It has been all too easy for ZANU(PF) to depict the MDC as globalized and a-historical.

In any case ZANU(PF) controls all television and radio; now, with the closure of the *Daily News*, it commands virtually all the press; and it is able to determine what kind of history is taught in schools. It is virtually impossible for critics to develop a counter-narrative in any systematic way. The spokespeople of Zimbabwean civil society, however, increasingly feel the need for this. The Crisis Coalition and the NGOs have appealed to international norms of human rights: precisely those, in fact, that Mahoso has criticized as bogus universalism. It is not a policy which has worked, as the recent refusal of the United Nations Human Rights Commission to discuss a motion censuring Zimbabwe reveals all too clearly. In the week of this refusal a spokesman for the Crisis Coalition told a gathering in London that it was essential to develop a new narrative which rooted human rights in Zimbabwe's own history.[50]

Conclusion

It must have become clear that history is at the centre of politics in Zimbabwe far more than in any other southern African country. But how can academic historians make an impact in the debate? Let me return at the end of this review to the University of Zimbabwe and to its aspirant pluralist and post-nationalist historians. These have refused to go on radio or television. But if their voices have not been heard as advocates of patriotic history, they have not been heard in any other way either. Zimbabwe is a country in which books have much less effect than radio, tv or the press.[51] But even if academic books and articles made an impact the University of Zimbabwe is effectively gagged. Printing costs have risen so

---

[50] There have been some attempts to do this in the independent press. On 17 April 2003 the *Daily News* carried a feature entitled 'Yet another gigantic ZANU(PF) failure'. The failure was ZANU(PF)'s betrayal of the democratic aspirations of nationalism. 'When we embarked on the liberation struggle in the 1950s, the main aim was to create an environment where the black majority could have equal opportunities ... The core of those objectives was for the SRANC to acquire power to improve the lives of the people. What occurred thereafter is history whose culmination was the birth of the nation of Zimbabwe'. Yet the people's lives have not improved and they have been given no opportunity to shape their own future.

[51] The Czech ambassador, coming from a country whose authoritarian regime took books very seriously, used regularly to ask me about *Violence and Memory*, with its account of the 5 Brigade, 'Have their been any repercussions?' There have been none.

rapidly that the UZ publications department cannot afford to publish any of the admirable monographs and collections it has accepted without massive subsidy. Among other things this means that a very large edited collection on Zimbabwe's political economy remains unpublished. Even my own edited collection, *Nationalism, Democracy and Human Rights* – which might be said to provide some of the building blocs for a counter narrative – has only seen the light of day after two successive subsidies. And even then only 100 copies have been produced! The university's journal, *Zambezia*, has not been published for several months. All the external agencies which used to subsidize research and publication have withdrawn. The university is mute.

When I retired from the University of Zimbabwe in 2001 I agreed with two of the university historians that we would jointly write a single-volume history of Zimbabwe. No such book exists and even in today's economic conditions it would sell. We have not written it yet and it is obviously both a very difficult and a very significant time in which to attempt it. But I hope that either we, or somebody else, will soon make that attempt. It might provide an alternative to patriotic history.

Bibliography

Abbott, Franklin (ed.), 1993. *Boyhood: Growing Up Male, A Multicultural Anthology*. California: The Crossing Press.

Archard, David, 1993. *Children: Rights and Childhood*. London/New York: Routledge.

Acker, Alison, 1986. *Children of the Volcano*. London: Zed Books.

Adorno, T W. 1970. *Aesthetic Theory*. London: Routledge.

—— 2003. *The Jargon of Authenticity*, trans. Knut Tarnowski and Frederic Will. London: Routledge.

Alexander, Jocelyn and McGregor, JoAnn, 1999. 'Representing Violence in Matabeleland, Zimbabwe: Press and Internet Debates' in Allen, T. and J. Seaton (eds), *The Media of Conflict: War Reporting and Representation of Ethnic Violence*. Zed Books: London.

—— JoAnn McGregor and Terence Ranger, 2000. *Violence and Memory: One Hundred Years in the 'Dark Forests' of Matabeleland*. Harare: Weaver Press and Oxford: James Currey.

—— and JoAnn McGregor, 2001. 'Elections, Land and the Politics of Opposition in Matabeleland'. *Journal of Agrarian Change* 1 (4): 510-33.

Alexander, Jocelyn, 2003. '"Squatters", Veterans and the State in Zimbabwe' in Hammar, A., et al., op.cit.

—— and JoAnn McGregor, 2003. Veterans, Violence and Nationalism in Zimbabwe. International Conference on Violence and Memory. Emory, September.

Amani Trust/IRCT, 2003. *The Role of Militia Groups in Maintaining Zanu PF's Political Power*. Harare, March: Amani Trust.

Anderson, Benedict, 1991. *Imagined Communities*. London: Verso.

Appadurai, Arjun. 1986. *The Social Life of Things: Commodities in Cultural Perspective*. Cambridge: Cambridge U. Press.

Armstrong, Peter, 1979. *Operation Zambezi – The Raid Into Zambia*. Salisbury [Harare]: Welston Press.

Bachelard, Gaston, 1971. *The Poetics of Reverie: Childhood, Language, and the Cosmos*, trans. Daniel Russell. Boston: Beacon Press.

Baden-Powell, R. S. S., 1897. *The Matabele Campaign 1896*. London: Methuen.

Bakhtin, Mikhail, 1987. 'Discourse in the Novel' in *The Dialogic Imagination*: Holquist. M. (ed.) Austin: U. of Texas Press.

—— 1999. *Problems of Dostoevsky's Poetics*. Minneapolis: U. of Minnesota Press.

Baker, Alan R. H. and Gideon Biger, (eds), 1992. *Ideology and Landscape in Historical Perspective*. Cambridge: Cambridge U.Press.

Barber, Karin, 2002. 'Social Histories of Reading in Africa'. Seminar paper, Roskilde: International Development Studies.

—— and Paulo Farias, 2002. 'Media and Religious Competition between Yorùbá Christians and Muslims'. Seminar, Roskilde: International Development Studies.

Barnes, Trevor J. and James S. Duncan (eds), 1992. *Writing Worlds: discourse, text and metaphor in the representation of landscape*. London: Routledge.

Barthes, Roland, 1982. *Image, Music, Text: Essays selected and translated by Stephen Heath*. New York: Hill and Wang.

Bate, Jonathan, 2001. *The Song of the Earth*. London: Picador.

Beach, Dennis Norman, 1994. *The Shona and their Neighbours*. Oxford: Blackwell.

Bennett, Tony, 1994. 'Popular Culture and the turn to "Gramsci"' in Storey. J. (ed.), *Cultural Theory and Popular Culture: A Reader*. London: Pearson Education.

Berkley, Bill, 1986. *Zimbabwe: Wages of War: A Report on Human Rights*. New York: Lawyers Committee for Human Rights.

Bethlehem, Louise Shabat, 1997. 'Under the Protea Tree, at Daggaboersnek: Stephen Gray, Literary Historiography and the Limit Trope of the Local'. *English in Africa* 24 (2): 27-50.

Bhabha, Homi K. (ed.), 1990. *Nation and Narration*. Routledge: London.

—— 1994. *The Location of Culture*. London: Routledge.

Bhebe, Ngwabi, 1979. *Christianity and Traditional Religion in Western Zimbabwe, 1859-1923*. London: Longman.

—— 1999. *ZAPU and ZANU Guerrilla Warfare and the Evangelical Lutheran Church in Zimbabwe*. Gweru: Mambo Press.

—— and Terence Ranger (eds), 2001. *The Historical Dimensions of Democracy and Human Rights in Zimbabwe. Pre-colonial and Colonial Legacies*. Harare: U. of Zimbabwe Publications.

Blake, William, 1996. *Complete Writings*: Keynes, G. (ed.). Oxford: Oxford U. Press.

—— 2001. 'All Religions Are One' in Wu, D. (ed.) *Romanticism: An Anthology*. Oxford: Blackwell.

Boehmer, Elleke, 2003. 'Tropes of Yearning and Dissent: The Troping of Desire in Yvonne Vera and Tsitsi Dangarembga'. *Journal of Commonwealth Literature* 38 (1): 135-48.

Bond, Patrick and Masimba Manyanya, 2002, *Zimbabwe's Plunge: Exhausted Nationalism, Neoliberalism and the Search for Social Justice*. Pietermaritzburg: University of Natal Press and (2003) Harare: Weaver Press.

Bourdillon, Michael, 1987. *The Shona Peoples: An Ethnography of the Contemporary Shona, with Special Reference to their Religion*. Gweru: Mambo Press.

Brettell, N. H., 1981. *Side-gate and Stile.* Bulawayo: Books of Zimbabwe.

—— 1994. *Selected Poems.* Cape Town: Snailpress.

Brittain, Victoria and Abdul, S. Minty, (eds), 1988. *Children of Resistance: On Children, Repression and the Law in Apartheid South Africa.* London: Kliptown Books.

Brown, Bill, 2003. 'The Secret Life of Things: Virginia Woolf and the Matter of Modernism' in Matthews, P. and D. McWhirter (eds), *Aesthetic Subjects.* Minneapolis and London: U. of Minnesota Press.

Brown, Penny, 13 January 2003. 'Refugees Recall a Different Zimbabwe'. *The Australian.*

Brutus, Dennis, 1968. *Letters to Martha and other poems from a South African prison.* London: Heinemann.

Bryce, Jane, 2000. Interview with Yvonne Vera, Bulawayo, 1 August.

—— 2002. Interview with Yvonne Vera, 1 August 2000, Bulawayo, Zimbabwe: 'Survival is in the Mouth' in Muponde, R. and M. Taruvinga op.cit.

Burke, Tim. 1996. *Lifebuoy Men, Lux Women: Commodification, Consumption and Cleanliness in Modern Zimbabwe.* Durham and London: Duke U. Press.

Cabral, Almicar, 1973. *Return to the Source.* London: Heinemann.

Cairns, Ed, 1996. *Children and Political Violence.* Oxford: Blackwell.

Campbell, Horace, 2003. *Reclaiming Zimbabwe: The Exhaustion of the Patriarchal Model of Liberation.* Cape Town: David Phillip and Trenton, NJ: Africa World Press.

Carney, Daniel, 1980. *Under a Raging Sky.* Salisbury [Harare]: Graham Publishing.

Catholic Commission of Justice and Peace and The Legal Resources Foundation, 1997. *Breaking the Silence, Building True Peace: Disturbances in Matabeleland and the Midlands.* Harare: CCJP/LRF.

Caute, David, 1991. 'Marechera in Black and White' in Kaarsholm, P. (ed.) *Cultural Struggle and Development in Southern Africa.* Harare: Baobab Books.

Chakaipa, Patrick, 1958. *Karikoga Gumiremiseve.* Salisbury: Longman.

—— 1967. *Dzasukwa Mwana Asina Hembe.* Salisbury: Longman.

Chakamba, Herbert, 1991. *Nziramasanga.* Harare: Longman.

Chan, Stephen, 2003. *Robert Mugabe: A Life of Power and Violence.* Ann Arbor: The U. of Michigan Press.

Chennells, Anthony John, 1982. 'Settler Myths and the Rhodesian Novel'. Ph.D. thesis.

—— 1993. 'Marxist and Pan-Africanist Literary Theories and a Sociology of Zimbabwean Literature'. *Zambezia* 20 (2): 109-29.

—— 1995. 'Rhodesian Discourse, Rhodesian Novels and the Zimbabwe Liberation War' in Bhebhe, N. and T. Ranger (eds), *Society in Zimbabwe's Liberation War.* Harare: U. of Zimbabwe Publications.

Cherer-Smith, R, n.d. (c.1980) . *Avondale to Zimbabwe*. Borrowdale [Harare]: Cherer-Smith.

Chidzero, Bernard, 1957. *Nzvengamutswairo*. Salisbury [Harare]: Longman.

Chigwedere, Aeneas, 1998. *Roots of the Bantu*. Marondera: Munhumutapa Publishing House.

—— 2001. *British Betrayal of the Africans. Land, Cattle and Human Rights. Case for Zimbabwe*. Marondera: Munhumutapa Publishing House.

Chikowo, Matthew, 1981. *Shanje Ndimauraise*. Harare: Longman.

Chikowore, Godfrey, 2002. 'Defending our Heritage. Armed Struggle Should Serve as Guiding Spirit'. *The Herald*. 16 February.

Chimhete, Caiphas and Henry Makiwa, 2003. 'Moyo Axes Mopani Junction off Air'. The *Standard*, 29 July, <http:www.zwnews.com/issuefull.cfm?ArticleID=7279>

Chimhundu, Herbert, 1991. *Chakwesha*. Harare: College Press.

Chinodya, Shimmer, 1989. *Harvest of Thorns*. Harare: Baobab Books.

Chinweizu, Onwuchekwa Jemie and Ihechukwu Madubuike, *Towards the Decolonization of African Literature: African Fiction and Poetry and Their Critics*. London: KPI.

Chipamaunga, Edmund, 1983. *A Fighter for Freedom*. Gweru: Mambo Press.

Chipembere, Ennie, 2002. 'Colonial Policy and Africans in Urban Areas – with special focus on housing, Salisbury, 1939-1964'. M.Phil. thesis: U. of Zimbabwe.

Chirasha, Ben, 1985. *Child of War*. Harare: College Press.

Chirere, Memory, 2004. 'Pursuing Garabha' in Chirere, M. and M. Vambe (eds), *History and the Ideology of Narrative in Charles Mungoshi's Fiction*. Pretoria: Unisa Press (forthcoming).

Chiunduramoyo, Aaron, 1977. *Ziva Kwawakabva*. Salisbury [Harare]: Longman.

Chivaura, Vimbai G., 1998. 'Conditioned Human Factor in Africa and its Implications for Development: The Example of Zimbabwean Writers in English from their Sensibility, Confessions, and Selected Works'. *Review of Human Factor Studies* 4 (1): 50-68.

—— and Claude G. Mararike (eds), 1998. *The Human Factor Approach to Development in Africa*. Harare: U. of Zimbabwe Publications.

Chiwome, Emmanuel M., 1996. *A Social History of the Shona Novel*. Kadoma: Juta.

—— 1998. 'The Interface of Orality and Literacy in the Zimbabwean Novel'. *Research in African Literatures* 29 (2): 1-22.

Christian, Barbara, 1996. 'The Race for Theory' in Mongia, P. (ed.), *Contemporary Post-Colonial Theory: A Reader*. London: Arnold.

Christian, Ed, 2001. 'Introducing the Post-Colonial Detective: Putting Marginality to Work' in Christian, E. (ed.), *The Post-Colonial Detective*. Houndmills: Palgrave.

Cobbing, Julian, 1976. 'The Ndebele Under the Khumalos'. Ph.D. thesis: U. of Lancaster.

—— 1983. *The Ndebele State* in Peires, J.B. (ed.), *Before and After Shaka*. Grahamstown: Institute of Social Economic Research.

Clifford, James, 1988. *The Predicament of Culture: Twentieth-Century Ethnography, Literature, and Art*. Cambridge, MA and London: Harvard U. Press.

Coetzee, J. M., 1980. *White Writing: On the Culture of Letters in South Africa*. New Haven: Yale U. Press and (1988) New York: Verso.

—— 1992. *Doubling the Point: essays and interviews*: Attwell, D. (ed.). Cambridge, MA: Harvard U. Press.

Collins, Wilkie, 1999. *The Moonstone*. Ware: Wordsworth Editions.

Crehan, Stuart, 1998. 'Rewriting the Land; or, How (Not) to Own It'. *English in Africa* 25(1): 1-26.

Dangarembga, Tsitsi, 1988. *Nervous Conditions*. Harare: Zimbabwe Publishing House.

Daniels, Stephen, 1993. *Fields of Vision: Landscape Imagery and National Identity in England and the United States*. Cambridge: Polity Press.

Darian-Smith, Kate, Liz Gunner and Sarah Nuttall, (eds), 1996. *Text, theory, space: land, literature and history in South Africa and Australia*. London: Routledge.

de Certeau, Michel. 1984. 'Walking in the City' in *The Practice of Everyday Life*. Berkeley and London: U. of California Press.

Deleuze, Gilles and Felix Guattari. 1987. *A Thousand Plateaus: Capitalism and Schizophrenia*, trans. Brian Massumi. Minneapolis and London: U. of Minnesota Press.

De Waal, Victor, 1990. *The Politics of Reconciliation: Zimbabwe's First Decade*. Trenton, NJ: Africa World Press, Cape Town: David Philip and London: Hurst and Co.

Derrida, Jacques, 1991. 'Che cos'è la poesia?' in Kamuf, P. (ed.), *A Derrida Reader: Between the Blinds*. London and New York: Harvester Wheatsheaf.

Donald, Bridget, 2000. 'Circling Back on the Road to Independence: Models of History and National Identity in Irish Children's Literature' in Webb, J. (ed.), *Text, Culture and National Identity in Children's Literature*: Helsinki: NORDINFO.

Dorman, Sara Rich, 2003. 'NGOs and the Constitutional Debate in Zimbabwe: From Inclusion to Exclusion'. *Journal of Southern African Studies* 29 (4): 845-63.

Driver, Dorothy, 1995. 'Lady Anne Barnard's *Cape Journals* and the Concept of Self-Othering'. *Pretexts* 5 (1-2): 46-65.

Eppel, John. 1994. *The Giraffe Man*. Cape Town: Quellerie Publishers.

Fairbridge, Kingsley, 1974 [1927]. *Kingsley Fairbridge: His Life and Verse*. Two vols. Bulawayo: Books of Rhodesia.

Fanon, Frantz, 2001. *The Wretched of the Earth*, trans. Constance Farrington. London: Penguin Books.

Ferguson, James, 1999. *Expectations of Modernity: Myths and Meanings of Urban Life on the Zambian Copperbelt*. Berkeley: U. of California Press.

Flockemann, Miki, 1992. '"Not-Quite Insiders and Not-Quite Outsiders": the "Process of Womanhood" in *Beka Lamb*, *Nervous Conditions* and *Daughters of the Twilight*'. *Journal of Commonwealth Literature* 26 (1): 37-47.

Fontein, Joost, 2003. 'The Silence of Great Zimbabwe: Contested Landscapes and the Power of Heritage'. Ph.D. thesis: U. of Edinburgh.

Fortune, George, 1973. *Ngano,* Vol. 1. Harare: Dept of African Languages, U. of Zimbabwe.

Fowles, John, 1980. Afterword. In A. Conan Doyle, *The Hound of the Baskervilles*. London: Longman.

Freeman, Paul, 1998. *Rumours of Ophir*. Harare: College Press.

Fuentes, Carlos, 1989. 'Words Apart'. *The Guardian* (Manchester), 24 February.

Fulford, Tim and Peter J. Kitson,1998. *Romanticism and Colonialism: Writing and Empire, 1780- 1830*. Cambridge: Cambridge U.Press.

Fuller, Alexandra, 2002. *Don't Let's Go to the Dogs Tonight: An African Childhood*. London: Picador.

Garbarino, James, Nancy Dubrow, Kathleen Kostelny and Carole Prado, 1992. *Children in Danger: Coping with the Consequences of Community Violence.* San Francisco: Jossey-Bass.

Gans, Eric, 1993. *Originary Thinking: Elements of Generative Anthropology*. Stanford: Stanford U. Press.

Gikandi, Simon, 2000. 'African Literature and the Social Science Paradigm'. U. of Michigan, Seminar paper.

Godwin, Peter, 1996. *Mukiwa: A White Boy in Africa*. London: Picador.

Glotfelty, Cheryll and Harold Fromm, (eds), 1995. *The Ecocriticism Reader*. Athens: U. of Georgia Press.

Glover, David and Cora Kaplan, 1992. 'Guns in the House of Culture? Crime Fiction and the Politics of the Popular' in Grossberg, L., C. Nelson and P. A. Treichler (eds), *Cultural Studies*. Newport and London: Routledge.

Gowe, O., 1987. 'Two Parties Merge as ZANU(PF)'. *The Herald*, 23 December.

Gramsci, Antonio, 1994. 'Hegemony, Intellectuals and the State' in Storey, J. (ed.) *Cultural Studies and the Study of Popular Culture: Theories and Methods*. Edinburgh: Edinburgh U. Press.

Gumbo, Mafuranhunzi, 1995. *Guerilla Snuff*. Harare: Baobab Books.

Gusdorf, George, 1980. 'Conditions and Limits of Autobiography' in Olney, James (ed.) *Autobiography: Essays Theoretical and Critical*. Princeton: Princeton U. Press.

Habermas, Jürgen, 1962. *Strukturwandel der Öffentlichkeit: Untersuchungen zu einer Kategorie der bürgerlichen Gesellschaft*, Frankfurt am Main. English translation (1989), *The Structural Transformation of the Public Sphere*. Cambridge, MA: The MIT Press.

Hammar, Amanda, 2002. 'The Articulation of Modes of Belonging: Competing Land Claims in Zimbabwe's Northwest' in Juul, K. and C. Lund (eds), *Negotiating Property in Africa*. Portsmouth: Heinemann.

—— Brian Raftopoulos and Stig Jensen (eds), 2003. *Zimbabwe's Unfinished Business: Rethinking Land, State and Nation in the Context of Crisis*. Harare: Weaver Press.

Hallward, Peter, 2001. *Absolutely Postcolonial: Writing Between the Singular and the Specific*. Angelaki Humanities series. Manchester and New York: Manchester U. Press.

Hartnack, Michael, ZW News Online, 4 December 2003: 'Succession lottery roll-over'.

Henry, Matthew A. 1997. 'Problematized Narratives: History as Fiction in E. L. Doctorow's *Billy Bathgate*'. *Critique*, 39 (1): 32-40.

Helen Suzman Foundation, 2000. *Zimbabwe: The Hard Road to Democracy*. Harare and Johannesburg, August.

Hodza, Aaron C. and George Fortune, 1979. *Shona Praise Poetry*. Oxford: Oxford U. Press.

Hofmeyr, Isabel, 1978. 'The Mining Novel in South African Literature: 1870-1920'. *English in Africa* 5 (2): 1-16.

—— 2002. Popular Literature and its Publics – NRF Research Proposal. Johannesburg: U. of the Witwatersrand.

Hourihan, Margery, 1997. *Deconstructing the Hero: Literary Theory and Children's Literature*. London and New York: Routledge.

Hove, Chenjerai, 1982. *Up in Arms*. Harare: Zimbabwe Publishing House.

—— 1985. *Red Hills of Home*. Gweru: Mambo Press.

—— 1988. *Bones*. Harare: Baobab Books.

—— 1991. *Shadows*. Harare: Baobab Books.

—— 1996. *Ancestors*. Harare: College Press.

—— 1998. *Rainbows in the Dust*. Harare: Baobab Books.

—— 2002. *Palaver Finish*. Harare: Weaver Press.

—— 2003. *Blind Moon*. Harare: Weaver Press.

Irele, Abiola, 1971. *Perspectives on African Literature*. London: Heinemann.

James, Allison and Alan Prout, 1990. 'A New Paradigm for the Sociology of Childhood? Provenance, Promise and Problems' in James, A. and A. Prout (eds), *Constructing and Reconstructing Childhood: Contemporary Issues in the Sociological Study of Childhood*. Basingstoke: The Falmer Press.

Jameson, Fredric, 1981. *The Political Unconscious: Narrative as Socially Symbolic Act*. London: Methuen and Ithaca, NY: Cornell U. Press.

—— 1986. 'Third World Literature in the Era of Multi-National Capitalism'. *Social Text*, 15, 65-88.

Jeyifo, Biodun, 1996. 'The Nature of Things: Arrested Decolonization and Critical Theory' in Mongia, P. (ed.), *Contemporary Post-Colonial Theory: A Reader*. London: Arnold.

Johwa, Wilson, 2003. 'Government Stifles Critical Voices in the Media'. *Independent Press Service*, Harare, 30 August. <http://www.zwnews.com/issuefull.cfm?ArticleID=7452>

Kaarsholm, Preben, 1989. 'Quiet After the Storm: Continuity and Change in the Cultural and Political Development of Zimbabwe'. *African Languages and Cultures* 2 (2): 175-202.

——1989a. 'Kampen om verdens mening. Krigslitteratur i Rhodesia og Zimbabwe'. *Den ny verden* 22 (1): 22-43.

—— 1991. 'From Decadence to Authenticity and Beyond: Fantasies and Mythologies of War in Rhodesia and Zimbabwe, 1965-1985' in Kaarsholm, P. (ed.), *Cultural Struggle and Development in Southern Africa*. Harare: Baobab Books.

—— 1994. 'Mental Colonisation or Catharsis? Theatre, Democracy and Cultural Struggle from Rhodesia to Zimbabwe' in Gunner, L. (ed.), *Politics and Performance: Theatre, Poetry and Song in Southern Africa*. Johannesburg: Witwatersrand U. Press.

—— 1999. '*Si ye pambile* – Which way forward? Urban development, culture and politics in Bulawayo' in Raftopoulos, B. and T. Yoshikuni (eds), *Sites of Struggle: Essays in Zimbabwe's Urban History*. Harare: Weaver Press.

—— and Deborah James, 2000. 'Popular Culture and Democracy in Some Southern Contexts: An Introduction'. *Journal of Southern African Studies*, 26(2) :189-208.

Kadhani, Mudereri and Musaemura Zimunya (eds), 1981. *And Now the Poets Speak*. Gwelo: Mambo Press.

Kahari, George, 1980. *The Search for Zimbabwean Identity: An Introduction to the Black Zimbabwean Novel*. Gwelo: Mambo Press.

—— 1986. *Aspects of the Shona Novel*. Gweru: Mambo Press.

—— 1990. *The Rise of the Shona Novel*. Gweru: Mambo Press.

—— 1997. *The Moral Vision of Patrick Chakaipa*. Gweru: Mambo Press.

Kanengoni, Alexander, 1983. *Vicious Circle*, Harare: College Press.

—— 1987. *When the Rainbird Cries*. Harare: Longman Zimbabwe.

—— 1997. *Echoing Silences*. Harare: Baobab Books.

—— 2003. One-Hundred Days with Robert Mugabe. *Daily News*. Harare, 12 April.

Katiyo, Wilson, 1976. *A Son of the Soil*. Harlow: Longman.

Kawadza, Terence, 2001. 'Deconstructing Critical Strategies in Zimbabwean Literary Historiography'. Paper delivered at symposium 'Scanning our Future, Reading our Past', University of Zimbabwe, 10-12 January.

Khumalo, Phelios, 1970. *Umuzi Kawakhiwa Kanye*. Salisbury [Harare]: Longman.

Killam, Douglas and Ruth Rowe (eds), 2000. *The Companion to African Literatures*, Oxford: James Currey and Bloomington: Indiana U. Press.

Klopper, Dirk, 1999. 'The Outsider Within: Marginality as Symptom in Marechera's "Throne of Bayonets"' in Veit-Wild, F. and A. Chennells op.cit. pp. 121-35.

Kopytoff, I. 1986. 'The Cultural Biography of Things: Commoditization as a Process' in Appadurai, A. (ed.) op.cit.

Kriger, Norma, 2003. *Guerrilla Veterans in Post-War Zimbabwe. Symbolic and Violent Politics, 1980-1987*. Cambridge: Cambridge U. Press.

Kronos: Special Issue on Visual History, Journal of Cape History, 2001, no 27.

Lan, David, 1985. *Guns and Rain: Guerrillas and Spirit Mediums in Zimbabwe*. London: James Currey, Harare: Zimbabwe Publishing House and Berkeley: U. of California Press.

Landau, Paul and Deborah Kaspin (eds), 2002. *Images and Empires: Visuality in Colonial and Postcolonial Africa*. Berkeley and London: U. of California Press.

Latham, Brian, 2003. 'I am a big brother, Mugabe tells MDC'. *The Star*. 25 September 2003. <www.zwnews.com>

Lazarus, Neil, 1990. *Resistance in Postcolonial African Fiction*. New Haven and London: Yale U. Press.

Leonard, Arthur G., 1896. *How We Made Rhodesia*. Rhodesiana Reprint Library Vol. 32. Bulawayo: Books of Rhodesia, 1973.

Lessing, Doris, 1994. *Under My Skin: Volume One of My Autobiography, to 1949*. London: HarperCollins.

Lindgern, Björn, 2002. *The Politics of Ndebele Ethnicity: Origins, Nationality, and Gender in Southern Zimbabwe*. Uppsala: Uppsala Univesitet.

Livingstone, David, 1857. *Missionary Travels and Research in South Africa*. London: John Murray.

Machel, Graca, 2001. *The Impact of War on Children*. London: C. Hurst/UNICEF.

Machingauta, Rodwell M., 1994. *Detective Ridgemore Riva*. Harare: Zimbabwe Publishing House.

Mahoso, Tafataona, 2000. 'Unwinding the African Dream on African Ground' in Givanni, June (ed.), *Symbolic Narratives/African Cinema: Audiences, Theory and the Moving Image*. London: British Film Institute.

Mail and Guardian, 25 March 2003 'US Slams Mugabe's "Black Hitler" Speech'.

Marechera, Dambudzo 1978, *The House of Hunger*. London: Heinemann.

—— 1980. *Black Sunlight*. London: Heinemann.

—— 1984. *Mindblast, or The Definitive Buddy*. Harare: College Press.

—— 1984a. Dambudzo Marechera: Zimbabwe's Prodigal Son (Interview). *New African* 2000: 64- 5.

—— 1990. *The Black Insider*. Harare: Baobab Books.

—— 1992. *Cemetery of Mind*. Comp. and ed. by F. Veit-Wild. Harare: Baobab Books.

—— 1994. *Scrapiron Blues*. Comp. and ed. by F. Veit-Wild. Harare: Baobab Books.

Magosvongwe, Ruby, 2004. 'In Pusuit of VaNhanga in *Kunyarara Hakusi Kutaura*?' in Chirere, M. and M. Vambe (eds), *History and the Ideology of Narrative in Charles Mungoshi's Fiction*. Pretoria: Unisa Press (forthcoming).

Makhalima, Eggie, 1987. *Ukhethwe yimi*. Gweru: Mambo Press.

Makhalisa, Barbara, 1974. *Qilindili*. Salisbury [Harare]: Longman.

Matenga, Edward, 1998. *The Soapstone Birds of Great Zimbabwe: Symbols of a Nation*. Harare: African Publishing Group.

Matsikiti, Claudius, 1980. *Shungu Dzomwoyo*. Harare: Longman.

Maughan-Brown, David, 1985. *Land, Freedom and Fiction: History and Ideology in Kenya*. London: Zed Books.

Maxted, Julia, 2003. 'Children and Armed Conflict in Africa'. *Social Identities*, 9 (1): 52-72.

Mazarire, Gerald, 2003. 'Changing Landscape and Oral Memory in South-Central Zimbabwe: Towards a Historical Geography of Chishanga, c. 1850-1990'. *Journal of Southern African Studies*. 29 (3): 701-715.

Mazorodze, I. V., 1989. *Silent Journey from the East*. Harare: Zimbabwe Publishing House.

McArthur, Tom (ed.), 1992. *The Oxford Companion to the English Language*. Oxford: Oxford U. Press.

McCallister, John, 2001. 'Knowing Native, Going Native: *African Laughter*, Colonial Epistemology, and Post-Colonial Homecoming'. *Doris Lessing Studies* 21 (2): 12-15.

Macaulay, David (ed.), 1996. *Minding Nature: The Philosophers of Ecology*. New York: Guilford Press.

McCartney, Irene and Chiedza Musengezi (eds), 2000. *Women of Resilience*. Harare: Zimbabwe Women Writers.

McClure, James, 1993. *The Steam Pig*. London: Faber and Faber.

McCracken, Scott, 1998. *Pulp: Reading Popular Fiction*. Manchester: Manchester U. Press.

McGann, James. 2001. *Green Land, Brown Land, Black Land*. Oxford: James Currey.

McGregor, JoAnn, 1995. 'Conservation, Control and Ecological Change: The Politics and Ecology of Colonial Conservation in Shurugwi, Zimbabwe'. *Environment and History* 1: 257-79.

McLoughlin, Tim, 1985. *Karima*. Gweru: Mambo Press.

Media Monitoring Project Zimbabwe, 8 September 2002. 'Mugabe's Speech Dominates Earth Summit Reporting.' <http://www.mmpz.org.zw/week2002/week32/2002.html>

Meinig, D. W. (ed.), 1979. *The Interpretation of Ordinary Landscapes: Geographical Essays*. New York and Oxford: Oxford U. Press.

Meintjies, Helen, 2001. '"Washing machines make lazy women": domestic appliances and the negotiation of women's propriety in Soweto'. *Journal of Material Culture* 6 (3): 345-63.

Meldrum, Andrew, 2004. *Where We Have Hope: A Memoir of Zimbabwe*. London: John Murray.

Meredith, Martin, 2002. 'Our Votes, Our Guns. Robert Mugabe and The Tragedy of Zimbabwe'. New York: *PublicAffairs*.

Mhando, Martin, 2000. 'Southern African cinema: towards a regional narration of the nation'. Paper to the Refiguring Postcoloniality Conference, 18 February 2000, Murdoch U., W. Australia. Available online at the 'Film and film-making in Africa' website: < http://www.szs.net.martin- mhando/southern-african-cinema.html >

—— 2003 'Documentary and History: a Discourse of Authority'. Online paper: <www.szs.net/martin-mhando/southern-african-cinema.html >

Mhiripiri, Nhamo, 1999. 'Danger! Stay Away from Meaningless Poems!' in Veit-Wild, F. and A. Chennells op.cit. pp. 151-60.

Mhizha, Memory, 2002. 'Unity Day special to all', *The Herald*, 17 December.

Middleton, Peter, 1992. *The Inward Gaze: Masculinity and Subjectivity in Modern Culture*. London and New York: Routledge.

Miller, Alice, 1990. *The Untouched Key: Tracing Childhood Trauma in Creativity and Destructiveness*. London: Virago Press.

Mhlanga, Cont, 1995. *Stitsha*. Bulawayo: Amakhosi Theatre Productions.

—— 2003. *Sinjalo*. Bulawayo: Amakhosi Theatre Productions.

Moffat, Robert, 1945. *The Matabeleland Journals of Robert Moffat 1829-1860*. Wallis, J. P. R. (ed.), Oppenheimer Series No.1. London: Chatto and Windus.

Moore, David, 1995: 'Democracy, Violence, and Identity in the Zimbabwean War of National Liberation: Reflections from the Realms of Dissent'. *Canadian Journal of African Studies* 29 (3): 375-402.

Moore, Donald S., 1998. 'Clear Waters and Muddied Histories: Environmental History and the Politics of Community in Zimbabwe's Eastern Highlands'. *Journal of Southern African Studies* 24 (2): 377-403.

—— 1998a. 'Subaltern Struggles and the Politics of Place: Remapping Resistance in Zimbabwe's Eastern Highlands'. *Cultural Anthropology* 13(3): 344-81.

Morrison, Toni, 1987. *Beloved*. London: Picador.

Moyo, Jonathan N., 1992. *Voting for Democracy: A Study of Electoral Politics in Zimbabwe*. Harare: U. of Zimbabwe Publications.

Mudenge, S. I. G., 1988. *A Political History of Munhumutapa, c. 1400-1902*. Harare: Zimbabwe Publishing House.

Mufuka, Ken, 2002. 'Zanu PF's paranoia against whites explained'. The *Standard*. Harare, 8 September.

Mugabe, Robert Gabriel, 2001. *Inside the Third Chimurenga: Our Land is Our Prosperity*. Harare: Department of Information and Publicity.

—— 5 September 2002. 'Speech'. *The Bulawayo Chronicle* and *The Herald*.

Mugabe, Robert, 2002a. Speech delivered at the Heroes Burial of Dr. B. T. G. Chidzero. August 12, National Heroes Acre, Harare. <www.zanupf pub.co.zw>

—— 2002b. Speech delivered at the Earth Summit in Johannesburg, South Africa. September 2, Johannesburg. <www.zanupfpub.co.zw>

Mungoshi, Charles, 1975. *Waiting for the Rain*. London: Heinemann.

—— 1975a. *Ndiko Kupindana Kwamazuva*. Gweru: Mambo Press in association with The Literature Bureau.

Muponde, Robert and Mandi Taruvinga, 2002. *Sign and Taboo: Perspectives on the Poetic Fiction of Yvonne Vera*. Harare: Weaver Press and Oxford: James Currey.

—— 2004. 'Roots/Routes: Place, Bodies and Sexuality in Yvonne Vera's *Butterfly Burning*' in *Body, Sex and Gender*. Veit-Wild, Flora and Dirk Naguschewski (eds). Amsterdam: Rodopi (forthcoming).

Musiyiwa, Mickias, 2002. Interview with Claudius Matsikiti. Harare: November.

Mutasa, N. Didymus. 1989. 'The Signing of the Unity Accord' in *Turmoil and Tenacity*. Banana, C. (ed.) Harare: College Press.

Mutasa, Garikai, 1985. *The Contact*. Gweru: Mambo Press.

Mutswairo, Solomon, 1956. *Feso*. Harare: Longman in association with The Literature Bureau.

—— 1974. *Feso*. Washington D.C.: Three Continents Press.

—— 1983. *Chaminuka: Prophet of Zimbabwe*. Harare: Longman.

Mzamane, Mbulelo V., 1983. 'New Writing from Zimbabwe: Dambudzo Marechera's *The House of Hunger*'. *African Literature Today: Recent Trends in the Novel*, 13: 201-25.

Ndebele, James Phambano, 1974. *Akisimlandu Wami*. Gwelo: Mambo Press.

Ndlovu, Elkhana, 1959. *Inhlamvu ZaseNgodlweni*. Pietermaritzburg: Shuter and Shooter.

Ndlovu, Sabelo, 2003. 'The Dynamics of Democracy and Human Rights among the Ndebele of Zimbabwe, 1818-1934'. Ph.D. thesis: U. of Zimbabwe.

Ndoda, David, 1958. *Uvusezindala*. Pietermaritzburg: Shuter and Shooter.

Negt, Oskar and Alexander Kluge, 1976. *Öffentlichkeit und Erfahrung*. Frankfurt am Main. English translation (1994), *Public Sphere and Experience: Analysis of the Bourgeois and Proletarian Public Sphere*. Minneapolis: U. of Minnesota Press.

Ngara, Emmanuel, 1985. *Art and Ideology in the African Novel: A Study of the Influence of Marxism on African Writing*. London: Heinemann.

—— 1990, *Ideology and Form in African Poetry*. London: James Currey.

News 24, 2004. 'Camps "decolonise" Zim youth'. News 24 (South Africa), 6. March. <www.zwnews.com>

Nhongo-Simbanegavi, Josephine, 2000. *For Better or Worse? Women and ZANLA in Zimbabwe's Liberation Struggle*. Harare: Weaver Press.

Nhunduma, Regis, 1985. *Wazvaremhaka*. Gwelo: Mambo Press.

Nomdlalo Township Theatre News, 1998. 'Matabeleland Atrocities: A Political Satire?', 4 (1). Theme issue. Bulawayo, January-March.

Nortje, Arthur, 2000. *Anatomy of Dark: Collected Poems*. Pretoria: U. of South Africa Press.

Noyes, John K., 2002. 'History, and the Failure of Language: The Problem of the Human in Post-Apartheid South Africa' in: Goldberg, D. T. and A. Quayson (eds), *Relocating Postcolonialism*. Oxford: Blackwell.

Nkomo, Joshua, [1984] 2001. *Nkomo: The Story of My Life*. Harare: Sapes Books.

Nuttall, Sarah, 1998. 'Telling 'free' stories? Memory and democracy in South African autobiography since 1994'. in Nuttall, S. and C. Coetzee op.cit.

Nuttall, Sarah and Carli Coetzee, 1998a. Introduction. In *Negotiating the Past: The Making of Memory in South Africa*: Nuttall, S. and C. Coetzee (eds). Cape Town: Oxford U. Press.

Nyagumbo, Maurice, 1980. *With the People: An Autobiography from the Zimbabwean Struggle*. Salisbury [Harare]: Graham.

Nyamfukudza, Stanley, 1980. *The Non-Believer's Journey*. Harare: Zimbabwe Publishing House and London: Heinemann.

—— 1988. 'Zimbabwe's Political Culture Today'. *Moto*, 71, 18.

—— 2004. 'Some Observations on Zimbabwe's Intellectual Development'. Ms of keynote speech delivered at the *Looking to the Future: Social, Political and Cultural Space in Zimbabwe*. International conference held at The Nordic Africa Institute, Uppsala, 24-26 May.

Nyamubaya, Freedom T. V., 1986. *On the Road Again. Poems during and after the National Liberation of Zimbabwe*. Harare: Zimbabwe Publishing House.

—— and Irene Mahamba, 1993. *Ndangariro*. Harare: ZIMFEP.

Okara, Gabriel, 1983. *The Voice*. Glasgow: Fontana/Collins.

Okonkwo, Juliet, 1981. 'The House of Hunger' (Review). *Okike* 18: 87-91.

Okri, Ben, 1986. 'Laughter Beneath the Bridge' in *Incidents at the Shrine: Short Stories*. London: Heinemann. pp. 1-22.

Owen, Wilfred, 1968. *Collected Poems*. London: Chatto and Windus.

Palmer, Jerry, 1978. *Thrillers: Genesis and Structure of a Popular Genre*. London: Edward Arnold.

Palumbo-Piu, David, 1996. 'The Politics of Memory: Remembering History in Alice Walker and Joy Kogawa' in Singh, Amritja, Joseph T. Skerrett, Jr. and Robert E. Hogan (eds) *Memory and Cultural Politics: New Approaches to American Ethnic Literatures*. Boston: Northeastern U. Press.

Pepetela, 1988. *Ngunga's Adventures*. Harare: Zimbabwe Publishing House.

Pikirayi, Innocent, 1999. 'David Beach, Shona History and the Archaeology of Zimbabwe'. *Zambezia* 26 (2): 135-144.

—— 2001. *The Zimbabwe Culture. Origins and Decline in Southern Zambezian States*. Oxford: Altamira Press.

Pongweni, Alec (ed.), 1982. *Songs that Won the Liberation War*. College Press: Harare.

—— 1996. *Shona Praise Poetry as Role Negotiation*. Gweru: Mambo Press.

Postman, Neil, 1994. *The Disappearance of Childhood*. New York: Vintage Books.

Pound, Ezra, 1977. *Selected Poems*. London: Faber.

Pratt, Mary Louise, 1992. *Imperial Eyes: Travel Writing and Transculturation*. London: Routledge.

Primorac, Ranka, 2001. 'Crossing Into the Space-Time of Memory: Borderline Identities in Novels by Yvonne Vera'. *Journal of Commonwealth Literature* 36 (2): 77-93.

—— 2002. 'Iron Butterflies: Notes on Yvonne Vera's *Butterfly Burning*' in Muponde, R. and M. Taruvinga, op.cit.

—— 2003. 'The Novel in a House of Stone: Recategorising Zimbabwean Fiction'. *Journal of Southern African Studies* 29 (1): 49-62.

Pwiti, G. (ed.), 1997. *Caves, Monuments and Texts*. Uppsala: Studies in African Archaeology 14.

Raftopoulos, Brian, 2001. 'The State in Crisis: Authoritarian Nationalism, Selective Citizenship and Distortions of Democracy in Zimbabwe'. Paper presented to conference on 'Rethinking Land, State and Citizenship through the Zimbabwe Crisis', Copenhagen, 4-5 September: Centre for Development Research.

—— 2002. 'Briefing: Zimbabwe's 2002 Presidential Election'. *African Affairs* 101 (404): 413-26.

—— 2003. 'The State in Crisis: The Authoritarian Nationalism, Selective Citizenship and Distortions of Democracy in Zimbabwe' in Hammar. A. et al., op.cit.

Ranger, Terence, 1967. *Revolt in Southern Rhodesia, 1896-7. A Study in African Resistance*. London: Heinemann.

—— 1970. *The African Voice in Southern Rhodesia, 1898-1930*. London: Heinemann.

—— 1985. *Peasant Consciousness and Guerrilla War in Zimbabwe*. Harare: Zimbabwe Publishing House and London: James Currey.

—— 1989. 'Missionaries, Migrants and the Manyika: The Invention of Ethnicity in Zimbabwe' in Vail, L. (ed.) *The Creation of Tribalism in Southern Africa*. London: James Currey.

—— 1994. 'Landscape Gendering in Zimbabwe'. *Southern African Review of Books*. Vol 6, No. 2, Issue 30, March-April 1994, pp. 7-8. <http://www. ulm.de/ ~rturrell/antho4html/Ranger.html>

—— 1999. *Voices from the Rocks: Nature, Culture and History in the Matopos Hills of Zimbabwe*. Oxford: James Currey, Bloomington: Indiana U. Press and Harare: Baobab Books.

—— 2002. 'The Zimbabwe Elections: A Personal Experience'. <http://cas1.clis.rug.ac.be/avrug/pdf02/ranger01.pdf.>

—— 2002a.'The Zimbabwe Elections: A Personal Experience'. *Transformation*, July 2002, 159- 68.

—— 2002b. 'History has its ceiling: The pressures of the past in the *Stone Virgins*', in Muponde, R. and M. Taruvinga (eds) op.cit.

—— (ed.), 2003. *Nationalism, Democracy and Human Rights*. Harare: U. of Zimbabwe Publications.

—— Forthcoming. Extracts from *Bulawayo Burning* (ms).

Rasmussen, Kent, 1978. *Migrant Kingdom: Mzilikazi's Ndebele in South Africa*. London: Rex Collings.

Reynolds, Pamela, 1996. *Traditional Healers and Childhood in Zimbabwe*. Athens: Ohio U. Press.

Reath, Jan, 3 March 2002. 'Reaping Racism's Harvest'. *The Australian*.

Riddell, R. C., 1978. *The Land Problem in Rhodesia*. Gwelo: Mambo Press.

Rooney, Caroline, 2001. *African Literature, Animism and Politics*. London: Routledge.

Rosenblatt, Roger, 1983. *Children of War*. New York: Anchor Press/Doubleday.

Runyowa, Genius, 1982. *Akada Wokure*. Gweru: Mambo Press.

Ryan, James, 1997. *Picturing Empire: Photography and the Visualisation of the British Empire*, Chicago: U. of Chicago Press.

Said, Edward, 1978. *Orientalism*. New York: Vintage Books.

Samkange, Stanlake. 1966. *On Trial for My Country*. London: Heinemann.

Scarry, Elaine, 1985. *The Body in Pain: the making and unmaking of the world*. New York: Oxford U. Press.

Schama, Simon, 1995. *Landscape and Memory*. London: HarperCollins.

Schmidt, Heike, 1995. 'Penetrating Foreign Lands: Contestations over African Landscapes. A case study from eastern Zimbabwe'. *Environment and History* 1: 351-76.

Selous, Frederick Courteney, 1881. *A Hunter's Wanderings in Africa*. Rhodesiana Reprint Library Vol. 14. Bulawayo: Books of Rhodesia, 1970.

—— 1893. *Travel and Adventure in South-East Africa*. Rhodesiana Reprint Library Vol 25. Bulawayo: Books of Rhodesia, 1972.

—— 1896. *Sunshine and Storm in Rhodesia*. Rhodesiana Reprint Library Vol. 2. Bulawayo: Books of Rhodesia, 1968.

Shaw, Angus, 2003. 'Zimbabwe Newspaper Directors Charged'. *Associated Press*, 22 September, <http://www.zwnews.com/issuefull.cfm?ArticleI D=7603>

Shamuyarira, Nathan, 1965. *Crisis in Rhodesia*. London: André Deutsch.

Sibanda, Joseph, 1982. *Kusempilweni*. Harare: Longman.

Sigogo, N. S., 1986. *Ngenziwa Ngumumo Welizwe*. Gweru: Mambo Press.

Silverstone, R. and E. Hirsch (eds), 1992. *Consuming Technologies: Media and Information in Domestic Spaces*. London: Routledge.

Simone, AbdouMaliq, 2004. 'People as infrastructure: Intersecting Fragments in Johannesburg'. *Public Culture*, 16:3, September.

Social Change and Development, 1996. 'Sexual Violence and War: when will we tell our own story? "Sarah"'.

Sithole, Ndabaningi, 1956. *Umvukela wamaNdebele*. Harare: Longman.

—— 1959. *African Nationalism*. Cape Town and London: Oxford U. Press.

—— 1977. *Roots of a Revolution: Scenes from Zimbabwe's Struggle*. Oxford: Oxford U.Press.

Slonim, Maureen B., 1991. *Children, Culture and Ethnicity: Evaluating and Understanding the Impact*. New York and London: Garland Publishing.

Smith, Ian Douglas, 1997. *The Great Betrayal: The Memoirs of Ian Douglas Smith*. London: Blake.

Snelling, John (ed.), 1938. *Rhodesian Verse 1888-1938*. Oxford: Blackwell.

Solidarity Peace Trust, 2003. National Youth Service Training. 'Shaping Youths in a Truly Zimbabwean Manner'. An Overview of Youth Militia Training and Activities in Zimbabwe. Harare.

Staunton, Irene (ed.), 1990. *Mothers of the Revolution*. Harare: Baobab Books.

Stone, Albert E., 1982. *Autobiographical Occasions and Original Acts: Versions of American Identity from Henry Adams to Nate Shaw*. Philadelphia: U. of Pennsylvania Press.

Style, Colin and O-Lan (eds), 1986. *The Mambo Book of Zimbabwean Verse in English*. Gweru: Mambo Press.

Sylvester, Christine, 2003. 'Remembering and Forgetting "Zimbabwe": Towards a Third Transition' in Paul Gready (ed.), *Political Transition: Politics and Cultures*. London: Pluto Press.

Tallmadge, John and Henry Harrington, (eds), 2000. *Reading Under the Sign of Nature: New Essays in Ecocriticism*. Salt Lake City: U. of Utah Press.

Taylor, Jane, 1998. *Ubu and the Truth Commission*. Cape Town: UCT Press.

Thomas, Edward, 1997. *Edward Thomas*. Ed. William Cooke. London: J M Dent.

Thomas, Thomas Morgan, 1873. *Eleven Years in Central South Africa*. Rhodesiana Reprint Library Vol.10. Bulawayo: Books of Rhodesia, 1970.

Tomaselli, Keyan, 1996. *Appropriating Images: The Semiotics of Visual Representation*. Hojbjerg, Denmark: Intervention Press.

Traicos, Chloe, 2002. *Stranger in My Homeland*. (unpublished play).

Tshaya, Clemence, 2003. 'Book Reveals Imbalances Created by British Imperialism'. *Herald*. Harare, 28 June.

Tsodzo, Thompson, K., 1972. *Pafunge*. Salisbury [Harare]: Longman.

Turino, Thomas, 2000. *Nationalists, Cosmopolitans and Popular Music in Zimbabwe*. Chicago: U. of Chicago Press.

Uwakweh, Pauline Ada, 1998. 'Carving a Niche: Versions of Gendered Childhood in Buchi Emecheta's *The Bride Price* and Tsitsi Dangarembga's *Nervous Condition*'. *African Literature Today* 21: 9-35.

Vambe, Lawrence, 1972. *An Ill-Fated People: Zimbabwe before and after Rhodes*. London: Heinemann.

Vambe, Maurice T., 2001. 'Strategic Transformations: Spirit Possession in the Black Novel in English' in Vambe, M. T. (ed.), *Orality and Cultural Identities in Zimbabwe*, Gweru: Mambo Press

Varadharajan, Asha, 1995. *Exotic Parodies: Subjectivity in Adorno, Said and Spivak*. London and Minneapolis: U. of Minnesota Press.

Veit-Wild, Flora, 1992. *Survey of Zimbabwean Writers: Educational and Literary Careers*. Bayreuth: Bayreuth U. (African Studies Series 27).

—— (ed.), 1992a. *Dambudzo Marechera: A Source Book of His Life and Work*. Harare: U. of Zimbabwe Publications.

—— 1993. *Teachers, Preachers, Non-Believers: A Social History of Zimbabwean Literature*. Harare: Baobab Books.

—— and Anthony Chennells, 1999. *Emerging Perspectives on Dambudzo Marechera*. Trenton, NJ, and Asmara: Africa World Press.

—— 1999. 'Carnival and Hybridity in Marechera and Lesego Rampolokeng' in Veit-Wild, F. and A. Chennells op.cit. pp.93-104.

Vera, Yvonne, 1993. *Nehanda*. Harare: Baobab Books.

—— 1994. *Without a Name*. Harare: Baobab Books.

—— 1996. *Under the Tongue*. Harare: Baobab Books.

—— 1998. *Butterfly Burning*. Harare: Baobab Books.

—— 2002. *The Stone Virgins*. New York: Farrar, Straus and Giroux and Harare: Weaver Press.

wa Mirii, Ngugi, 2004. 'Land basis for economic growth'. *The Sunday Mail*, Harare, 22. February and <www.sundaymail.co.zw>.

Walcott, Derek, 1995. 'The Muse of History' in Ashcroft, B., G. Griffiths and H. Tiffin (eds) *The Post-colonial Studies Reader.* London and New York: Routledge.

Wallis, J. P. R. (ed.), 1945. *The Matabele Mission: A Selection from the Correspondence of John and Emily Moffat, David Livingstone and Others, 1858-1878*. Oppenheimer Series No.2. London: Chatto and Windus.

Werbner, Richard, 1991. *Tears of the Dead: The Social Biography of an African Family*. Edinburgh: Edinburgh U. Press for the International African Institute.

—— 1996. 'In Memory: A Heritage of War in South-western Zimbabwe' in Bhebe, N. and T. Ranger (eds) *Society in Zimbabwe's Liberation War*. James Currey: Oxford.

White, Hayden, 1987. *The Content of the Form: Discourse and Historical Representation*. Baltimore and London: Johns Hopkins U. Press.

White, Luise, 2003. *The Assassination of Herbert Chitepo: Texts and Politics in Zimbabwe*. Bloomington: Indiana U. Press.

Wild, Flora. 1988. *Patterns of Poetry in Zimbabwe*. Gweru: Mambo Press.

Willey, Ann Elizabeth and Jeanette Treiber (eds), 2002. *Emerging Perspectives on Tsitsi Dangarembga: Negotiating the Postcolonial*. Trenton, NJ and Asmara: Africa World Press.

Wilson-Tagoe, Nana, 2002. 'History, gender and the problem of representation in the novels of Yvonne Vera' in Muponde, R. and M. Taruvinga op.cit.

—— 2003. 'Representing Culture and Identity: African Women Writers and National Cultures'. *Feminist Africa* 2 and <http://www.feministafrica.org>

Wiredu, Kwasi, 1998. 'The Moral Foundations of an African Culture' in *The African Philosophy Reader*: Coetzee, P. H. and A. P. J. Roux (eds). London and New York: Routledge.

Wylie, Dan, 2002. *Dead Leaves: Two Years In the Rhodesian War*. Pietermaritzburg: U. of Natal Press.

Zhuwarara, Rino, 1987. 'Zimbabwean Fiction in English'. *Zambezia* 14 (2): 131-46.

—— 1994. 'Three Generations'. *Southern African Review of Books*, 22. July/August.

—— 2001. *Introduction to Zimbabwean Literature in English*. Harare: College Press.

Zimbabwe Project in association with Organisation of Collective Co-operatives in Zimbabwe, 1985. *Another Battle Begun: Images of Collective Cooperatives in Zimbabwe, with Words of Members*. Harare: Zimbabwe Project.

Zimfep,1992. *Children of History*. Harare: Baobab Books.

Zimunya, Musaemura, 1982. *Those Years of Drought and Hunger: The Birth of African Fiction in English in Zimbabwe*. Gweru: Mambo Press.

—— 1982a. *Kingfisher, Jikinya and Other Poems*. Harare: Longman.

—— 1982b. *Thought Tracks*. Harlow: Longman.

—— 1985. *Country Dawns and City Lights*. Harare: Longman.

—— 1993. *Perfect Poise and Other Poems*. Harare: College Press.